COLLISION COURSE

San Diego Christian College
Library
Santee, CA

320.973
M194c

★ ★ ★ ★ ★

"Bob Maginnis provides insights about our rich Christian heritage, how it was compromised by evil forces and calls for an urgent change of course to avoid colliding across the coming moral tipping point." – *Lt. General Jerry Boykin (U.S. Army Ret.), Family Research Council*

The Fight to Reclaim Our Moral Compass Before It's Too Late

COLLISION COURSE

LTC ROBERT L. MAGINNIS
Author of *Deeper State* and *Progressive Evil*

DEFENDER

CRANE, MO

Collision Course: The Fight to Reclaim Our Moral Compass Before It's Too Late

By Robert L. Maginnis

Copyright 2020 Defender Publishing / All Rights Reserved

Printed in the United States of America

Scripture taken from the King James Version unless otherwise noted.

Cover design by Jeffrey Mardis

ISBN: 9781948014335

DEDICATION

To the Christian founders who gave America the principles and values that made her a land of promise and hope. May similar Christian patriots rise again to call this nation back to the Lord.

ACKNOWLEDGMENTS

I gratefully acknowledge…

I'm grateful to many for their contributions. I'm especially thankful for my wife, Jan, who lives out her Christianity before me every day and is a beacon of inspiration and hope. My friend Don Mercer continues to provide wise counsel and great edits as this and five of my previous books emerged from concept to finished product.

I am indebted to many fine Christian brothers and sisters who granted interviews. Their sage wisdom is cited in the final chapters, the plan to begin renewing America to recapture its Christian influence by helping to turn this country off its present collision course, back from the moral tipping point.

Above all, I acknowledge my Heavenly Father, without whom this book could never be written.

Robert L. Maginnis
Woodbridge, Virginia

CONTENTS

SECTION IV: A NEW BEGINNING FOR AMERICA: THE REEMERGENCE OF
"CHRISTIAN NATIONALISM" AND MAKING AMERICA CHRISTIAN AGAIN

FOREWORD

THE UNITED STATES of America was a Christian nation, at least in principle and demonstrable values, until recent years. It owes past success to a large degree to that Christian foundation, but in recent decades, America's culture has accelerated on a collision course to a tipping point whereby moral and religious decay are fast pushing her over the proverbial cliff into a sewer of sin that could end in destruction and last-times irrelevance.

Collision Course explores in four sections the moral and religious decline that jeopardizes America's future. It begins by outlining the roots of America's past success, and then explores what I call the conspiracy of evil—the forces, people, and compromised institutions that have pushed America away from her Christian roots toward an evil place.

Fortunately, there is hope for the future even at this late date. America can reverse this evil outcome, but it must act now. Christians—you and I—must once again recognize our calling in Matthew 5 to be salt and light in our anti-Christian culture by heeding God's eternal call. America needs a spiritual reawakening, renewal before we reach the edge of the approaching tipping point; otherwise, this nation will inevitably and irreparably crash morally, ending up in the garbage bin of history.

Collision Course provides a plan for that renewal, which begins with a call to the Christian church to be obedient to the Spirit's leading—a critical fight to reclaim our moral compass before it is too late.

INTRODUCTION

AMERICA IS ON a collision course to moral decay because it abandoned Christian principles and values, the foundation of this once-great nation. Its present amoral course is evidenced by cultural and political chaos that incrementally over the past decades has eroded every significant Christian principle and value woven into America's fabric by our founders, and thanks to a host of evil forces. Time is short to save this country from its current cultural and spiritual implosion.

America can avoid falling into the slimy trash heap of history, but time is short, and that effort will require a renewed, strong Christian church to battle the pervasive evil so evident today. Specifically, we must MACA (Make America more Christian Again) much like she began, a country once populated with people who mostly embraced biblical principles in their daily lives and who baked those principles into our foundation—our national conscience and governing documents—and the broader culture. That doesn't mean she hasn't had moral flaws (like slavery), but there has been for much of her history an underlying good, moral foundation. Even today, there remains a sliver of hope to reverse decades of calamitous evil that sank its claws into this mostly Christian country, but it will be an uphill battle—and one worth fighting!

America arrived at this moral precipice thanks, in part, to Christian neglect of the essentials of our faith. Many Christians abandoned our culture and political system to the secular and pervasive evil forces now parading like strutting peacocks across this nation. Like a cancer, these evil forces crept into America's institutions (government, businesses/corporations, family, schools, and churches), and slowly at first encouraged compromise in the name of tolerance and diversity, then more recently accelerated their push for radical, anti-Christian outcomes.

What's the evidence of America becoming morally unhinged and almost irreconcilably lost to an anti-Christian doom? Over time, we've seen how our courts have been harnessed by leftists as their weapon of choice to then marginalize Christian principles that once were our firewall against evils like abortion on demand and so-called homosexual rights. More recently, many of those same radicals have weaponized our federal government to push their anti-Christian agenda by harnessing the deep state's evil cadre of radicals within the bureaucracy, such as the miscreants who ran roughshod over our freedom from inside the Internal Revenue Service using the power of government to target pro-life, pro-faith, and freedom-loving Americans. There is also the example of purveyors of evil within our law enforcement bureaucracy like the Federal Bureau of Investigation who used their official powers to launch a silent coup against President Donald Trump, such as their abuse of the United States Foreign Intelligence Surveillance Act (FISA) court, meant to oversee requests for surveillance against foreign spies rather than American citizens inside the United States.

Our government-run education establishment—public education from kindergarten to graduate school—long ago abandoned God and Christianity to embrace progressivism that promotes secular humanism and anti-Christian morals. Nefarious and morally challenged radicals use our taxpayer-funded education establishment to promote an anything-goes gender dysphoria and deliver a pabulum of academic material that slowed our national competitiveness against the rest of the world.

Perhaps the worst assault on this former Christian nation is the evil cabal known as the cultural elite, the Hollywood crowd, the mainstream media, and their nefarious evil taskmasters who have weaponized modern communication platforms to manipulate Americans through mass indoctrination using media outlets such as the Internet (Google, Apple), social media (Facebook, Twitter), cable and broadcast networks (CNN, MSNBC, ABC, CBS, NBC, etc.), and much more. These purveyors of evil are the most destructive of Christian principles and values because virtually the entire country is now electronically tethered to their mostly biased, anti-Christian-spewing, psychologically half-truth-indoctrinating electronic platforms.

Collectively and in hindsight, we now understand that these radical agents of evil have almost succeeded. Yes, we are quickly arriving at a post-Christian America. These anti-Christian agents have leveraged our courts, the federal government's deep state, the country's public education system, and the mainstream media via their surrogates to bring America to its present moral tipping point. We could very easily and soon stumble across that approaching precipice into a moral hell unless their anti-Christian gains are reversed.

Other people and nations across the span of world history have been at a similar crossroads, and most fared poorly against such immorality. Many of those previous historic tipping points were not reversed before those people and nations crashed headlong into tragedy, which is instructive for us today. Consider some of those examples of past failings, beginning with the Bible's book of Genesis.

Mankind's wrong way lessons began very early with the Garden of Eden. Life for the "first couple," Adam and Eve, was wonderful in the garden—that is, until they willfully stumbled over the tempting forbidden fruit tree…their proverbial tipping point.

Scripture explains:

The Lord God made all kinds of trees grow out of the ground—trees that were pleasing to the eye and good for food. In the middle of the garden were the tree of life and the tree of the knowledge of good and evil. (Genesis 2:9, NIV)

And the Lord God commanded the man, "You are free to eat from any tree in the garden; but you must not eat from the tree of the knowledge of good and evil, for when you eat from it you will certainly die." (Genesis 2:16–17, NIV)

Most readers know this Scripture well. The "tree of knowledge" refers to the "forbidden tree" set in the Garden of Eden for two purposes. It presented the first couple with a choice: Either love, obey, and serve God—or rebel against Him by eating the forbidden fruit. Of course, the tree's fruit was not the source of sin. Rather, Adam and Eve failing to obey God's command "don't eat fruit of this one tree" was the true source of their downfall. God gave a clear command in Genesis, and they chose disobedience. The consequence of that disobedience was exile from paradise (their tipping point), a real heaven on earth.

Mankind's disobedience was on full display in Noah's time (Genesis 6:9–9:17), another tipping point. Noah spent years building the ark on dry land, which represented a tangible warning to his fellow men and women about their sin and the coming Flood (judgment). However, the ark project and Noah's frequent warnings weren't enough of a nudge for the lost people in his time. Then came the day when God closed the massive boat's doors, the waters rose from openings in the ground and the heavens, and soon all but Noah and his family perished in the ensuing deluge. Humanity in Noah's day had turned away from God in spite of clear warnings, and mankind crossed yet another tipping point that resulted in their utter destruction.

The nation of Israel is special to God, a covenant people (Genesis 12–17), yet it, too, stumbled and was chastened by God throughout its history. Early in Israel's national story, it embraced an amoral course that led it to exile in Egypt for 430 years (Exodus 12:40–41), but God heard their cry and had mercy on His people. He rescued them from

Pharaoh's wicked hand and returned them to the Promised Land, albeit after another forty years of testing in the desert—a time of hard lessons in obedience. Much the same happened centuries later and after Israel's and Judah's long disobedience.

The Israelites' (ten northern tribes) turned to pagan gods soon after arriving in the Promised Land of Canaan. They knew that God condemned idolatry, and they knew His price for their continued disobedience (Leviticus 26:35). Yet they tested God's command by crossing the tipping point of disobedience. God ripped these stiff-necked people from Canaan in 722 BC and allowed the Assyrians to destroy all but a remnant (2 Chronicles 36:21).

The nation of Judah followed its own collision course more than a hundred years after Israel fell, and those people also paid a high price for disobedience: The holy city of Jerusalem was completely destroyed, many Jews were killed, that country was laid bare, and the best of the Jewish remnant was taken captive to Babylon (2 Kings 24). Then, seventy years later, after the humbling of that great people, God paved the way for them to return home in renewed obedience.

These lessons from biblical history are clear. Time and again, man's disobedience led him to follow an amoral course that resulted in tragedy, which eventually gave way to remorse and then reconciliation. A similar sequence is evident in secular history as well.

Empires and kingdoms have risen through the millennia and, unfortunately, many have crossed a tipping point to their destruction. The Roman Empire, which lasted more than a thousand years, crumbled for many reasons—the invasion of the barbarians, a troubled economy, the rise of Eastern enemies (i.e., Islam), overexpansion, the migration of the Huns, and a weakened military. Certainly, the spread of Christianity contributed to the empire's eventual fall, another factor that led to the demise of the Romans' once-great empire.[1]

In the early nineteenth century, the French emperor Napoleon Bonaparte was the dominant power in continental Europe, but he followed a corrupted course to his end (a tipping point) at the Battle of

Waterloo. Napoleon's campaign of European dominance was an incremental effort that linked many victories over more than a decade. However, even though Napoleon's power lust was the source of his initial success, it was also the cause of his ruin. He overextended his army on three fronts (his Waterloo tipping point): against Great Britain, Portugal, and Russia. That error in judgment left him weakened militarily, which accelerated his downfall at the hands of the Anglo-led allied army under the British Duke of Wellington, who was allied at the time with the Prussian army.

In the twentieth century, Adolf Hitler won national prominence because the German people were tired of empty promises and the humiliation of defeat that ended the First World War. Slowly over the 1930s, Chancellor Hitler regrew Germany's might and its self-confidence, and then, in 1939, the Führer ordered the invasion of Poland to expand the Third Reich's reach into Eastern Europe. However, in time, the despotic, ambitious charlatan stumbled—his course led to destruction—at the hands of the allies who turned Hitler's early successes into dust (a tipping point) beginning with the D-Day invasion on June 6, 1944, which altered the course of history away from a German socialist outcome that threatened to transform the world.

Today, America is racing toward its own tipping point that has elements similar to the scenarios seen in the Bible and experienced in Europe with Napoleon and Hitler. The good news is that America doesn't have to suffer outcomes like those in previous times, because it has the opportunity to reverse the current collision course pushing us to the precipice of our own national tipping point.

The answer to reversing America's amoral collision course to a moral tipping point is simple: Return to America's spiritual roots, the Christian principles and values that formed the foundation of this nation's past success—Make America Christian Again. We must begin to understand our present path for what it is: evidence of moral and religious decay that jeopardizes the nation's future. The conspiracy of evil pushing this nation away from its Christian roots must be reversed, and that begins with the simple recognition of our current state and the evil forces arrayed against us.

In four sections, *Collision Course* walks the reader through the Christian history of America to her current amoral state, then identifies the evil players responsible for that implosion and concludes with a hopeful plan: Renewing America, making her more Christian again, which requires a revitalized, spiritually awakened church that must then put its collective shoulders into this critical effort; otherwise, she will continue to rush toward irrelevance at the prophetic end times.

SECTION I

AMERICA'S CHRISTIAN HERITAGE

America became a great nation because of her rich Christian heritage. This section will trace that Christian heritage, starting with the formative years during the Protestant Reformation, which ultimately compelled many Christians to abandon their European homes to strike out for the New World to find religious freedom and prosperity.

Chapter 1 explores those Christian roots and the inspired thinking that led our founders to draft a Constitution that rejected the establishment of a church-state marriage. That document was based on Christian principles that our forefathers intended would protect this nation and her rich Christian heritage.

Chapter 2 explores those roots by examining the very Christian principles that gave birth to America's values, her character, and the institutions that made her a unique and exceptional Christian nation.

CHAPTER ONE

Christian America

AMERICA WAS FOUNDED by Christians not to become a theocracy—although some preferred that outcome. Rather, our early colonial forefathers experimented with European-style state-religion marriages that taught them many hard lessons that, in time, convinced the drafters of our Constitution to take a different course when creating the United States' federal government. Specifically, they chose a faith-blind federal republic model that left in place a Christian nation.

The idea that the United States had a Christian founding is a controversial political and scholarly debate issue today. The substance of that debate is essentially over whether our founders intended to establish a secular or a Christian United States.

I believe our founders knew that America was a Christian nation from the start, and today's "Christian America" debate only muddies that history. In fact, the historical evidence is clear: The vast majority of the colonial population at the time self-identified as Christian, and their Christian churches were figuratively and literally at the center of every civil, public, and private activity. That, by definition, made America a Christian nation.

So why did our founders create a secular federal government? That's simple. They wanted to avoid the many tortured issues associated with state-established religions, such as those in their former European home-lands and more recently in the American colonies. Thus, our founders produced a government without an established religion, but that decision in no way meant America ceased being a Christian nation. Rather, the Christian influence was evident even in our founding documents—albeit rather subtle in the Constitution, but quite evident in the statements by prominent citizens from the period.

This chapter will explore the contentious faith-based issues leading up to and through the ratification of our Constitution and demonstrate why I believe America was a Christian nation before and after its formal founding. We begin that journey by first considering the problems in countries like England, which was ruled by a monarch who combined civil and religious power and prompted many to immigrate to the New World seeking freedom of religion.

Second, even though the American colonialists sought religious freedom in the New World, they created colonial-style, church-state marriages not that different from what drove them across the Atlantic Ocean. There are lessons from those experiments that influenced our founders' decision to form a secular federal government.

Finally, we will consider the formulation of our faith-free Constitution, examine the obvious Christian influence in that document, and conclude that—in spite of their formation of a secular republic—our founders always intended to leave in place a Christian America.

England's Religious Exclusivism Brought to Colonial America

The early 1600s saw the start of a growing tide of emigration from Europe to North America, a trend that grew from a few hundred English colonists to millions over the next three centuries. The early English immigrants crossed the Atlantic Ocean to the New World in small, over-crowded ships. Those cramped passengers endured voyages that lasted between six and twelve weeks and were battered by frequent storms while living off of meager rations.[2] But most felt the hardship worth the new life in America.

Most of those sixteenth-century Europeans were escaping political oppression to find freedom to practice their religion. They were the forefathers of the eighteenth-century American founders, who created a radically different kind of government in America, one free of religious persecution.

The situation in sixteenth-century England, which many of those early emigrants called home, was desperate for religious minorities. They were ruled by a monarch who held combined civil and sectarian power, which created an intolerable situation for many—especially those from a faith group other than the state religion.

The advent of a state religion was especially prevalent following the sixteenth century's Protestant Reformation that spawned religious dissenters, both Catholic and Protestant. Initially, England at the time was ruled Catholic under Henry VIII until 1534, then Protestant under the same Henry VIII until his death in 1553.

England in the late sixteenth century experienced perhaps the worst of the paradigm of a political-religious establishment under the reigns of Catholic Queen Mary (1553–1558) and Protestant Queen Elizabeth (1558–1603). Both queens required all members of their realm to profess the same faith or suffer death or exile.

Queen Mary, who restored papal supremacy in England, acquired the popular title of "Bloody Mary" for ordering nearly three hundred executions in her short, four-year reign.[3] Conversely, Queen Elizabeth was a Protestant who restored the title Henry VIII instituted—supreme head of the Church of England. She wasn't much better than Queen Mary, however. Elizabeth executed a few, but relied more on branding, imprisonment, and torture for religious renegades.[4]

For the English at the time, life was characterized by a single faith—either Catholic or Anglican—that was at the helm of political power and used the state's coercive arm to enforce its belief. Although across the ensuing centuries, England became more tolerant of other faiths, it remains today mostly a single-faith country, at least at the helm: Anglican, which continues to enjoy special favors.

Emergence of the Puritans

The English Puritans arose during the reign of Henry VIII. They considered the Reformation incomplete because "the Church of England should be purged of its hierarchy and of the traditions and ceremonies inherited from [Catholic] Rome." Evidently, Henry VIII's actions to cleanse the Church at the time were insufficient in the eyes of the Puritans, who "understood God's direction was to discipline the world."[5]

Queen Elizabeth's successor, James I (1603–1625), tried to run the renegade Puritans out of England, an effort that continued with his son, Charles I (1625–1649). Charles didn't help suspicion of his motives regarding the Puritans when he married a foreign Catholic woman, Henrietta Maria of France.

The Puritans' issue with Charles I was more fundamental than his religious allegiances and his foreign marriage. Charles was also Arminian in his theology, which was counter to the Puritans, who believed in predestination. The Arminians believed "that men by their own will power could achieve faith and thus win salvation."[6]

The Puritans were Calvinists, followers of a system of theology named for John Calvin, a sixteenth-century French theologian during the Protestant Reformation. Calvin, by contrast with the Arminians, embraced a predestination view of mankind that he said was "God's unchangeable decree from before the creation of the world that he would freely save some people (the elect), foreordaining them to eternal life, while the others (the reprobate) would be 'barred from access to' salvation and sentenced to 'eternal death.'"[7]

The Puritans used their influence in the British House of Commons for that body to pass resolutions to reverse Charles' Arminianism mandate. Predictably, the king reacted to the censure by dissolving Parliament, his practice when he disagreed with the members. Meanwhile, many Puritans became disgusted with their lot in England and left for a new religiously free life in America.

In 1630, a group of four hundred Puritans under the leadership of John Winthrop sailed for America under the official charter of the Massachusetts Bay Company. Their intent was not just commercial, as some secularists contend, but to create what "would be instead the citadel of God's chosen people, a spearhead of world Protestantism."[8]

The Puritan settlers took advantage of the liberal terms of their charter to set up their own government, "effectively remov[ing] the colony from control by the Crown." They intended to establish self-governance that "could create in New England the kind of society that God demanded of all His servants but that none had yet given Him."[9]

By 1640, more than twenty thousand mostly Puritans were settled in Boston and small towns in the vicinity, and by all accounts it was a thriving success.[10] It was the practice in each new Puritan community to establish Congregational churches that subscribed to Reformed theology and imitated the model developed in Calvinist Geneva, Switzerland, whereby every congregation was founded upon a church covenant that stipulated decision-making and church discipline.[11]

The Puritans brought with them the faith-based exclusivism they had practiced in England. They excluded all religions but theirs in the Massachusetts Bay Colony.[12] Specifically, in May of 1631, the Puritan leaders officially recognized only fellow church members as freemen and therefore those men were entitled to vote and hold office. Further, Puritan ministers were granted the power to define orthodoxy, which was enforced by the colony's magistrates; dissenters were often banished.[13]

Roger Williams arrived in Boston in 1631, but refused to associate with the Anglican Puritans and promptly moved to the separatist Plymouth Colony to Boston's south. However, he was soon back in Salem (a Boston suburb), where he became the pastor for a church, but quickly ran afoul of Puritan authorities who exiled him for his beliefs. Specifically, Williams publicly expressed the view that the Church of England

(Anglican) wasn't a true church, but one that aligned with the Catholic Church of Rome. Further, he maintained that a true church must be separated from the false Church of England.[14] However, it was Williams' views about the state-church relationship that earned him banishment.

Williams believed the civil authorities' "power extended only to the 'Bodies and Goods,' and outward state of men." Translated, that meant the issues of faith fell outside the realm of civil government, a direct challenge to the order the Congregationalists instituted in the colony. He argued that such a state-church arrangement was a violation of the Ten Commandments (Exodus 20:2–17) because those laws contained separate instructions for civil and religious governance. Specifically, Williams argued that commandments one to four were for Christian believers: Have no other gods before Me; do not make yourself a carved image; do not take the name of the Lord your God in vain; and remember the Sabbath day. The other six, according to Williams, were for civil government: Honor your father and mother; do not murder; do not commit adultery; do not steal; do not bear false witness; and do not covet your neighbor's belongings.[15]

Meanwhile back in England, and before John Winthrop first led the Puritans to their new home in Massachusetts, a new religious group emerged. These new believers declared that every person can experience an inner light given by God, a movement known as the Religious Society of Friends, or Quakers.[16]

Quakers Not Welcomed by Puritans

George Fox, an itinerant preacher, started the Quakers in the mid 1600s as radically different than any other (Christian) faith known at the time in England. Specifically, Fox said the Christian faith called for silent meditation, no music, and total abandonment of the High Church's (read "Anglican" or "Catholic") rituals and creeds.

Those early Quakers, called Friends, rebelled against the British

Crown and the established Anglican-dominated order. They refused to pay tithes to the state Church, take oaths, and serve in combat during war. To their credit, they fought for the end of slavery and for humane treatment of those incarcerated.[17]

Fox's young movement quickly spread to every county in England, and London became a major Quaker center at the time. The Quakers' confrontational style of proselytizing was especially noteworthy, which evidently threatened the orthodox Anglican establishment. So, in short order, the Quakers' challenge to the Anglican establishment led to state-sponsored repression, and many Quakers "faced accusations of witch-craft, treason, and being secret agents of the [Catholic] pope." Soon the Quakers, much like the Puritans less than two decades earlier, began to immigrate to the American colonies to find freedom of religion.

The Quakers faced opposition upon their arrival in the Puritan Massachusetts Bay Colony. Shortly after that, the Puritans passed anti-Quaker laws that included steep fines for any Puritan who entertained, concealed, or transported a Quaker in the colony.[18] The punishment for the Quaker was even worse. Exile was their standard punishment, but when three Quakers returned to Boston after being exiled, the Puritans cropped their ears, and soon that government passed a stiffer law calling for the death penalty for any Quaker who returned once banished.[19]

Virginian Anglicans Carry on Church-State Arrangement

The English Crown expanded Anglicanism to America beginning in 1606. At that time, King James incorporated the Virginia Company to bring the "Christian religion to such people, as yet live in darkness and miserable ignorance of the true knowledge and worship of God."[20] The Virginia Colony expedition consisted of three ships—Susan Constant, Godspeed, and Discovery—arriving April 6, 1607, at what is now known as the Chesapeake Bay.[21]

The Virginia colonists chose Jamestown Island for their settlement because it was defensible from attacks by other European states, notably the Dutch Republic, France, and Spain. Besides security, the early Jamestown residents focused on physical survival and then on making a profit from cultivating tobacco.

By 1609, Thomas Gates, the colony's new governor, arrived to lead a religious revival, hoping that would restore order.[22] A year later, Lord De La Warr, the colony's military governor, "imposed martial law on Virginians and made [the Anglican] religion a strategic part of gaining and exercising social and political control." That move cemented together, as in England, the Anglican Church and the fledgling civil government in Virginia.[23]

Decades afterward, the Virginia General Assembly in Jamestown (1619–1699) passed laws regarding uniformity. The first such statute called for "uniformities throughout this colony both in substance and circumstance to the cannons & constitutions of the Church of England as neere as may bee and that every person yeild readie obedience unto them uppon penaltie of the paynes and fortfeitures in that case appoynted."[24] And just like in England, people of other faiths were expected to submit to Virginia's established Anglican Church.[25]

Virginia was soon joined by Georgia, Maryland, North Carolina, and South Carolina in terms of the English church-state model, whereby all Anglicans were the direct beneficiaries of a mandatory tithe, state-controlled Anglican worship, and land grants.[26] Meanwhile, other faith groups like Baptists, Congregationalists (Puritans), and Catholics who found themselves in those early Anglican colonies were subject to imprisonment, fine, and expulsion. It is noteworthy that between 1720 and 1750, the number of indictments for failing to join the Anglicans exceeded the total of all other criminal indictments.[27]

In time, some colonies recognized multiple faith groups rather than a sole Christian denomination. Embracing multiple faiths meant at the time that the government would tax the people, then each taxpayer would designate the faith recipient (church) for his tax proceeds. However, it wasn't until the 1830s that disestablishment of the state-religion franchise finally died across the young United States.

America's colonial period was marked by examples of a single faith at the helm of political power, and those faith groups used the state's coercive arm to enforce citizen belief and tax them to fill the church's coffers.

Mixing Faith and Civil Government

The various Christian faith groups that made up the communities across the American colonies helped pave the political landscape with reason that persuaded America's founders to embrace a federal government free from a state-sponsored religion.

The colonial practice of establishing a government-sponsored religion ended by 1833 across the United States. We have to thank the various colonial religious leaders and their theologies for that disestablishment movement, which removed the federal and state governments from favoring one religion over another. However, that by no means meant America was not a Christian nation.

Congregationalists and Presbyterians

The Calvinists—Congregationalists and Presbyterians—taught America's founders to prevent "a fusion of governmental and religious functions." They established a distinction between church and state in Massachusetts. Specifically, a distinction was made in the Massachusetts Bay Colony by establishing multiple establishments (religions), which effectively meant each town could choose a minister to receive the annual tax.[28] This meant that one's taxes would allegedly go to the minister of the individual's choosing. However, in actual practice, the revenue always went to Congregationalist ministers.[29]

A major distinction between the Church of England and the early Congregational (Puritan) church at the time was the absence of the ecclesiastical courts. The absence of a hierarchical structure in the

Massachusetts Congregational church meant there were no ecclesiastical courts to probate wills or engage in matters associated with marriage and divorce.[30] Rather, those issues were handled by the civil government in the Massachusetts Bay Colony.

Meanwhile, the Massachusetts Congregationalists quickly separated church leadership from elected civil officials as well. Their intent was to prevent church control of civil affairs, a harsh lesson learned from the ecclesiastical courts in Anglican England.

The Congregationalists also recognized from their study of the Scriptures that God created three distinct spheres of operation: social, political and religious.[31] The principle was captured in one leader's statement: "Power is too intoxicating and liable to abuse."[32] That principle resulted in a practice that no public official could lose his position due to religious-based excommunication.

The result of such thinking was to separate the workings of the church and state, something left behind in England where those spheres were combined under the monarchy. In theory, this effort was laudable; in practice, especially among the Puritans, the church and state remained mutually supportive.

Puritan church leader John Cotton (1585–1652) captured the essence of the church-state relationship in his musing. He said the church and state "may be close and compact, and coordinate to one another and yet not be confounded."[33]

There was a serious flaw in this arrangement, however. The church-state relationship did not allow freedom of conscience. Therefore, dissenters to Puritan doctrine and tradition were punished, such as Baptists who rejected the Congregationalist practice of infant baptism.

Baptists believed in believer baptism (adult), while Congregationalists viewed the act as a symbol of an enduring covenant with God. Thus, the Congregationalists set in law infant baptism—and, predictably, the Baptists refused to comply. The Baptists' punishment for failing to baptize their infants was harsh, including court warnings, fines, and even possible whippings and imprisonment.[34]

The Congregationalists practiced an intolerant sort of religious freedom. Dissenters were asked to leave and take their views with them. That is why most Baptists and Quakers avoided the Boston-based colony rather than, as in the case of Quakers, face death for their religious dissent.

Congregationalists made an important contribution to our founders' view of the relationship between church and state. They demonstrated why the future federal government ought to avoid establishing a state religion.

Presbyterians

Presbyterians who immigrated to the American colonies were a religious minority where they landed. They came from Scotland, where they were the officially established church, but in the New World, they contributed to the disestablishment principles that arose in states where the Anglican Church dominated.

William Tennent, a South Carolinian Presbyterian, dissented against the established Anglican Church by calling for tolerance. He was especially adamant about the colonial government's demand that non-Anglicans financially support the Anglican ministry.

Tennent called out the unjust requirement in the law:

The law, by incorporating the one Church, enables it to hold estates, and to sue for rights; the law does not enable the others to hold any religious property, not even the pittances which are bestowed by the hand of charity for their support. No dissenting Church can hold or sue for their own property at common law. They are obliged therefore to deposit it in the Hands of Trustees, to be held by them as their own private property, and to lie at their mercy. The consequence of this is, that too often their funds for the support of religious worship, get into bad hands, and become either alienated from their proper use, or must be recovered at the expense of a suit in chancery.[35]

Tennent called for spreading the revenue to a number of religions, albeit Protestant faiths.[36] He rightly said granting state taxes to one religion was intolerable. The same equitability issue was evident in Virginia as well.

When a Virginia state tax for the benefit of the Anglican Church was proposed, the Hanover Presbyterian clergy first supported it on the theory that it could be expanded to include them, a view not inconsistent with that of Tennent. In fact, Virginia's James Madison, who was adamantly opposed to any assessment, described the Presbyterians at that time "as ready to set up an establishmt [sic], which is to take them in as they were to pull down that which shut them out."[37]

The Virginia Presbyterians shared the view that government should not be able to decide "what sect of Christians are most orthodox."[38]

The early American Presbyterians endorsed the promotion of the Christian religion, but not one at the exclusion of others.

Thus, as we have seen, the colonial Calvinists—Congregationalists and Presbyterians—believed in the independent functions for church and state. The Presbyterians, unlike the Congregationalists, advocated for the state to be nonpreferential between (Protestant Christian) religions, especially when it came to the distribution of the tax receipts.

Baptists

Baptists called for the right to one's own conscience. That is, government may not prescribe what may be acceptable in politics and religion or force citizens to confess by word or act their faith.

This view was evident in the period's Baptist leaders, especially Reverend Isaac Backus and John Leland. Backus, born into a Congregationalist family in Connecticut, converted to the Baptist faith during the Great Awakening (1730–1750). He became a critic of the Congregationalists by calling for them to end their discriminatory religious practices.[39]

Leland believed that Baptist theology mandated the freedom to believe. He called for "the notion of a Christian commonwealth" to "be exploded forever."[40] These efforts won exemptions over time for the Baptists, but the Congregationalists seldom honored those exemptions, such as paying church taxes.[41]

At the time in New England, Baptists petitioned King George III and were granted an exception. But that order from the monarch never resulted in relief from the Massachusetts tax collector. That reality left the Baptists with two choices: comply and be silent or disobey. They chose civil disobedience.

Reverend Backus argued that Baptists should not obey because of the God-given twin principles of toleration and disestablishment. He warned that in religious affairs, "we are most solemnly warned not to be subject to ordinances after the doctrines and commandments of men."[42]

He argued that government-supported clergy produces corruption. This view compelled Baptist leaders to petition the Continental Congress to disestablish Massachusetts, the Massachusetts Provisional Congress, and the Massachusetts General Assembly. Each of those efforts failed.

Backus then argued for the freedom to choose one's own minister, much like the freedom one enjoys to select his or her own doctor or lawyer. Backus expressed this view in a pamphlet:

As God is the only worthy object of all religious worship, and nothing can be true religion but a voluntary obedience unto his revealed will, of which each rational soul has an equal right to judge for itself, every person has an unalienable right to act in all religious affairs according to the full persuasion of his own mind, where others are not injured thereby. And civil rulers are so far from having any right to empower any person or persons to judge for others in such affairs, and to enforce their judgements with the sword, that their power ought to be exerted to protect all persons and societies within their jurisdiction from being injured or interrupted in the free enjoyment of this right under any pretense whatsoever.[43]

Eventually, Massachusetts formally disestablished in 1833, which ended the state tax on all religions that exclusively benefited the Congregationalists. However, Backus' avocation for a right of conscience helped pave the way to the founders' necessity to disestablishment and that civil government may not dictate religious belief.

John Leland, also a Baptist pastor, was a strong proponent of freedom of conscience and the separation of church and state. It is noteworthy that he opposed the notion of America as a "Christian nation" in order to embrace equality for all faiths.[44]

Quakers

Quakers advanced the no-coercion principle that government may accommodate the free exercise of religion and must not coerce support or participation in religion.

George Fox, the founder of the Society of Friends, Quakers, developed a form of Christianity focused on the individual worshiper. Fox wrote that "God, who made the world, did not dwell in temples made with hands…. But in people's hearts…. His people were his temple and he dwelt in them."[45]

Fox seeded the Quaker view that rejected the need for clergy. Rather, he believed "that God, through the Holy Spirit, could move anyone to speak, that all Christians could and should be ministers."[46]

Fox's clergy-free perspective proclaimed:

All people had within them a certain measure of the light of Christ…. Pagans who had no knowledge of the historical Jesus

could still experience the inward light of Christ, and, if obedient to it, could be saved without ever having heard Christian
preaching or knowing the Bible.[47]

The "light of Christ" perspective granted Quakers their characteristic tolerance because they believed all people were potential Christians.[48]
They also believed "women as well as men might be chosen by the inner
light as ministers," an issue that significantly distinguished them from
the other faiths in the colonies.[49]

William Penn (1644–1718), an Oxford-educated aristocrat, converted to Quakerism. In 1681, King Charles II granted him a tract of
land in America to pay the debts owed to Penn's father, an admiral who
supported the king after the restoration.[50] The land grant included all of
the present-day states of Pennsylvania and Delaware.[51]

Penn was the sole proprietor of the colony that came to be named
Pennsylvania, and governed as he saw fit. Predictably, he set up the colony as a Quaker "Holy Experiment," by which:

> All persons living in this province, who confess and acknowledge
> the one Almighty and eternal God, to be the Creator, Upholder
> and Ruler of the world; and that hold themselves obliged in con-
> science to live peaceably and justly in civil society, shall, in no
> ways, be molested or prejudiced for their religious persuasion,
> or practice, in matters of faith and worship, nor shall they be
> compelled, at any time, to frequent or maintain any religious
> worship, place or ministry whatever.[52]

In time, Penn altered the "Holy Experiment" document to add a
"Charter of Privileges" that enumerated specific protections for the civil
liberties and "stressed that coercion of conscience destroyed authentic
religious experience and 'directly invade[d] the divine prerogative.'"[53]

For the Quaker, according to the "Charter of Privileges," no man
"hath power or authority to rule over men's consciences in religious

matters," nor shall any citizen be "in the least punished or hurt, either in person, estate, or priviledge, for the sake of his opinion, judgment, faith or worship towards God in matters of religion."

Penn's colony valued freedom of conscience and non-coercion regarding one's faith. It remained theocentric, with the goal of permitting individuals to choose their own religious beliefs.[54]

The Quakers' value of tolerance was evident in the establishment of the University of Pennsylvania as a nonsectarian institution, which traces its roots to 1749, when Benjamin Franklin founded the Publik Academy of Philadelphia.[55] At the time, a nonsectarian institution was unusual because, after all, the Massachusetts Congregationalists founded Harvard University as a Congregationalist school, as was Yale University, and Virginia's College of William and Mary in Williamsburg was Anglican.

Quaker tolerance also permitted other religious communities to operate independently within the colony. However, the Quakers departed from other colonies by making Christianity a prerequisite to serve in government.[56] They also used the Christian litmus on voting and labor on the Sabbath; passed tough laws regarding sexual offenses and rude language; and insisted that citizens share their Christian moral values.[57]

Thanks to the Quakers, our founders came to embrace the concept that government must never coerce its citizens to believe what they are unwilling to believe.[58]

Catholics

Catholic colonialists were a minority among the sea of Protestant faith groups. It was fortunate for English Catholics that Sir George Calvert, who served as secretary of state for King James I and later as a minister of Parliament during the reign of Charles I, petitioned King Charles for a colony north of Virginia, which he named Maryland, for the king's French Catholic wife, Henrietta Maria.

Calvert died five weeks before the new charter was sealed, which left the Maryland colony to his sons Cecil (1605–1675) and Leonard (1606–1647). Leonard Calvert served as the first colonial governor of the province of Maryland.

Cecil Calvert, like his father, saw Maryland as his opportunity to establish a commercial center in the mid-Atlantic region. That goal required religious tolerance to ensure his commercial success.[59] Understandably, because Maryland was surrounded by Protestants, the governor insisted that religion remain a private affair and have no role in shaping the colony's progress, a view that was eventually codified by the Maryland assembly.[60]

By the middle of the seventeenth century, the Maryland assembly passed the act concerning religion, an unashamedly Christian statute that read:

> That noe person or persons whatsoever within this Province, or the Islands, Ports, Harbors, Creekes, or havens thereunto belonging professing to beleive in Jesus Christ, shall from henceforth bee any waies troubled, Molested or discountenanced for or in respect of his or her religion nor in the free exercise thereof within this Province or the Islands thereunto belonging nor any way compelled to the beleife or exercise of any other Religion against his or her consent, soe as they be not unfaithfull to the Lord Proprietary, or molest or conspire against the civill Governemt. Established or to bee established in this Province under him or his heires.[61]

Maryland's laws protected all Christians, without regard to their denomination. Further, that religious liberty law would not infringe upon the civil government's enforcement of the laws.

Maryland's (Christian) pluralism had its limits, however, especially among some Catholics—particularly the Jesuits.[62] They sought the same privileges their Catholic peers enjoyed in Europe and lobbied Calvert for exemptions as well as taxation. Unfortunately for the Catholics, their dominance in Maryland crumbled after the Glorious Revolution of William and Mary in England (1688). Maryland became an Anglican colony in 1692 and the religious freedom Calvert created for Catholics was lost.

Maryland Catholics understandably became supporters of the American Revolution, which promised to sever them from the grip of Anglicanism. Noteworthy was Charles Carroll, the son of a prominent Catholic family in Annapolis, who argued for the cause of independence under the pseudonym "First Citizen."[63]

The various Christian faith groups that made up the communities across the American colonies prepared the young nation's Christian landscape to embrace a government free from religious establishment. By 1833, no state had an established church, which was a long way from where those former colonies began, and we can thank the colonial religious leaders for the disestablishment of the previous church-state relationships and ultimately the creation of a secular, albeit religion-supporting (read "exclusively Christian"), future government.

Forming a Government Without a State Religion

The American colonies' diverse Christian affiliations were a primary motivation for the founders' formulation of a secular Constitution. However, that outcome in no way denies that, from the time of our founding, the United States was and continues to be a Christian nation.

What we've learned from the material already covered in this chapter is that the thirteen original colonies belonged to the British Empire, whose king presided over an imperial church, and thus every subject lived under Christian rule. It was in this environment that the Second Continental Congress drafted and then adopted the Declaration of Independence on July 4, 1776. It is noteworthy that much of the writing of the document is credited to Thomas Jefferson, who at the time and even now is considered to be a theist—certainly not an evangelical Christian.

It isn't surprising that Jefferson would write a document that acknowledged God and embedded within it such a profound understanding of the Scriptures, however. After all, Jefferson believed in a benevolent Creator God and wrote early in his life that "the God who gave us life, gave us liberty at the same time." He often made reference to "our God" in conversation, labeling Him "our Creator," the "Infinite Power, which rules the destinies of the universe."[64]

Perhaps the editing of Jefferson's original draft by the likes of Roger Sherman (a Connecticut Congregationalist) and Robert Livingston (a member of the committee of Congress that drafted the document, also a New York lawyer) explains the evident strong Christian views as well.[65] What's not in doubt is that America's Declaration of Independence is a landmark document imbued with a biblical worldview that reflected the thinking of most of our founders who grew up in the Christian-dominated colonies.

An examination of the document for biblical and Christian references illustrates the thinking of the fifty-six courageous men who signed the Declaration of Independence. The Declaration was the culmination of several efforts by the Continental Congresses, an association of leaders from the thirteen British colonies that spoke for the colonies as a whole. They catalogued their many grievances against the British Crown and brought to mind as British subjects, albeit colonialists, the liberties and privileges granted them under the English constitution and common law. They called out specific complaints against the king and Parliament, as well as the constitutional violations and acts of oppression.

By the summer of 1776, the Continental Congress was set on independence from Great Britain, and any thoughts of appealing to the king regarding constitutional violations were set aside. Rather, the Continental Congress' leaders appealed instead to grander "opinions of mankind" and "the laws of nature and of nature's god."[66]

Those drafting our Declaration tapped into the role of God-given, natural law to justify independence by revolution. The document declares:

> We hold these truths to be self-evident: That all men are cre-
> ated equal; that they are endowed by their Creator with certain
> unalienable rights; that among these are life, liberty, and the
> pursuit of happiness; that, to secure these rights, governments
> are instituted among men, deriving their just powers from the
> consent of the governed; that whenever any form of government
> becomes destructive of these ends, it is the right of the people
> to alter or to abolish it, and to institute new government, laying
> its foundation on such principles, and organizing its powers in
> such form, as to them shall seem most likely to affect their safety
> and happiness.

The Declaration's use of the term "laws of nature" is equivalent to the common law term the "law of nature," which British Sir William Blackstone (1723–1780), a jurist, judge, and Tory politician, wrote in his *Commentaries on the Laws of England* is better understood as the will of God as revealed in nature. He wrote:

> But as He is also a Being of infinite wisdom, He has laid down
> only such laws as were founded in those relations of justice, that
> existed in the nature of things antecedent to any positive pre-
> cept. These are the eternal, immutable laws of good and evil,
> to which the Creator Himself in all his dispensations conforms;
> and which He has enabled human reason to discover, so far as
> they are necessary for the conduct of human actions.[67]

The Bible-literate men drafting the Declaration would also appreci-
ate that the terms "laws of nature and the law of God" were derived from Scripture, an expression of God's will for all of creation.

After all, the Declaration states "That all men are created equal, that they are endowed by their Creator with certain unalienable Rights that among these are Life, Liberty and the pursuit of Happiness."[68]

The Bible declares God the Creator numerous times (Isaiah 40:28; 1 Peter 4:19; Genesis 1:1 and 27). And God, the Creator, gave man the unalienable rights identified in the Declaration: life (Genesis 2:7), liberty (2 Corinthians 3:17), and pursuit of happiness (James 1:17).

The Declaration's authors used biblical terms not only to describe man's origin, but for God's protection: "and for the support of this Declaration, with a firm reliance on the protection of divine providence, we mutually pledge to each other our lives, our fortunes and our sacred honor."

They borrowed from Judges 11:27 when writing: "We, therefore, the Representatives of the United States of America, in General Congress, Assembled, appealing to the Supreme Judge of the world for the rectitude of our intentions."

The Declaration also incorporates four biblical principles familiar to the authors: Rights come from God; the purpose of civil government is to secure those rights; the power of civil government is given by the consent of the governed; and the right to govern is forfeited by a tyrant.[69]

Thomas Jefferson's early draft of the document used the word "derived," which Benjamin Franklin and John Adams replaced with "endowed by their Creator." That changed the meaning of the Declaration to mean that it rested on rights as given to them by God. Translation: Our founders chose to establish the new nation upon the laws of nature and of nature's God.

The use of the word "endowed" is associated with "unalienable," which means: "What God has given for the benefit of all mankind cannot be given away by the recipient or taken away by the donor," a concept straight out of the Scriptures (Numbers 23:19 and 2 Chronicles 19:7).

The Declaration recognized the Christian writings that granted men the right to resist civil government as well. The term used by the authors is an "interposition," which means "the resistance to tyranny through lower magistrates." This theory dated back to the thirteenth century and the Magna Carta, when church leaders and local civil authorities joined to resist King John, who severely oppressed the British people through heavy taxes and the application of justice as he saw fit. That compact ended the oppression of the church by the state. And then, by extension, in the Protestant Reformation, the concept supported Christian resistance against the lawlessness of civil rulers to the point of armed resistance.

John Calvin said as much in his *Institutes* that Romans 13 may have denied individual Christians the right to oppose a lawless ruler, but it did permit a "lower civil magistrate of the people" to do so. In fact, the French Huguenots used Calvin's exegetical defense to challenge the absolute rule by the royalists of France. (Huguenots were French Protestants who held a Reformed tradition in the sixteenth and seventeenth centuries. They suffered severe persecution at the hands of the Catholic majority. Many immigrated from France to the United States.)[70]

The Declaration's authors also believed in absolute truths, not moral relativism. "We hold these truths to be self-evident," states the Declaration, and the only absolute truths are those pronounced by God.

We see in Romans 1:20 the use of the term "self-evident" to modify truth, a word given from God Himself (Romans 1:18–19). That truth also scratched the conscience of nonbelievers who knew the truth in their hearts because God placed it there (Romans 2:14–15).

Blaise Pascal, a seventeenth-century French philosopher and theologian, explained the concept in his work *Pensees*:

> What else does this craving, and this helplessness, proclaim but that there was once in man a true happiness, of which all that now remains is the empty print and trace? This he tries in vain to fill with everything around him, seeking in things that are not there the help he cannot find in those that are, though none can help, since this infinite abyss can be filled only with an infinite and immutable object; in other words by God himself.[71]

Writing a Secular Constitution

It is curious that the men who grew up in the Christianized English colonies where church was at the center of virtually every part of life would then write a constitution that formed a secular government. But that shouldn't surprise us, given the aforementioned history.

Even though every founder respected our Christian heritage at the time, they worried that religion would corrupt the state, as evidenced time and again during the colonial era, and the state by association also corrupted religion. In fact, this warning was expressed in the Federalist Papers by founder James Madison, who said religion in politics would lead men to "cooperate for their common good" and surmised that it "divided mankind into parties, inflamed them with mutual animosity, and rendered them much more disposed to vex and oppress each other than to co-operate for their common good."[72]

Founder Thomas Jefferson, the principal author of the Declaration of Independence, and James Madison advocated for a complete separation of church and state in the new republic. Others, like John Adams and George Washington, acknowledged that religion was essential for a virtuous society, but they signed the Constitution endorsing the idea that there should be no religious test.

Even during the Constitutional Convention (May 14 to September 17, 1787, in Philadelphia, Pennsylvania), the founders evidently didn't offer public prayer, unlike when the Continental Congress prayed as they crafted the Declaration of Independence. However, a precedent was set by our First Congress that implemented opening prayers in their meetings.[73]

The absence of prayer at the Constitutional Convention was called out by Benjamin Franklin, a self-proclaimed deist, who motioned that prayer be instituted. Franklin proposed: "How has it happened that we have not, hitherto once thought of humbly applying to the Father of Lights to illuminate our Understandings?"

Only a few delegates supported the proposal, and the motion never came to a vote. Franklin hurriedly scribbled a note about the proposal at the bottom of his prayer speech: "The Convention except three or four Persons, thought Prayers unnecessary!"[74]

The delegates' refusal to embrace Franklin's prayer proposal may be hard to understand given that the Constitution was built upon a Christian worldview. This is not a surprising outcome for our founders, who grew up surrounded by a Christian world, even though the document for purposes outlined above does not establish a state religion.[75]

It is true that our Constitution doesn't explicitly refer to God or the Bible, and at the time, that absence drew criticism from people like Timothy Dwight, the orthodox Christian president of Yale University. Dwight wrote:

> The nation has offended Providence. We formed our constitution without any acknowledgment of God: without any recognition of His mercies to us as a people, of His government, or even of His existence…. the convention, by which it was formed, never asked, even once, His direction, or His blessings, upon their labors…thus, we commenced our national existence under the present system, without God.[76]

Our Constitution is not a godless document, as some would argue and in spite of Timothy Dwight's correct observations about the convention. A glance behind the veil of the Constitutional Convention provides insights into the influence both the Bible and Christian teaching had on the new nation.

During the Convention on July 4, 1787, there was a church service for the members, evidence of the significance of their effort. Further, the founders were never truly agnostic regarding religion's influence on government and the broader American society. In fact, John Adams, one of the signers of the document, wrote after the convention in a letter to the Third Division of the militia of Massachusetts: "Our Constitution was made only for a moral and religious people. It is wholly inadequate to the government of any other."[77]

Noah Webster Jr. (1758–1843) was an American lexicographer, textbook pioneer, and political writer who stated:

The moral principles and precepts contained in the scriptures ought to form the basis of all our civil constitutions and laws. All the miseries and evils which men suffer from vice, crime, ambition, injustice, oppression, slavery, and war, proceed from their despising or neglecting the precepts contained in the Bible.[78]

The Constitution has numerous underlying biblical principles, such as the rule of law defined in the Ten Commandments. Our founders understood the sinfulness of man (Genesis 3 and Jeremiah 17:9), which infected government authorities as well, and thus they designed a system of checks and balances and separation of powers to prevent abuses.

The three branches of government created by our Constitution have parallels in the Scriptures (Isaiah 33:22, NIV: "For the Lord is our judge [judiciary], the Lord is our lawgiver [legislative], the Lord is our king [executive].") In fact, the provision that recognized an exception for Sundays in the count of days for the president to sign a bill (Article VII, Section 2) suggests that Sunday was a day of rest (Exodus 31:15, KJV: "Six days may work be done; but in the seventh is the Sabbath of rest, holy to the Lord: whosoever doeth any work in the Sabbath day, he shall surely be put to death.")

The Constitution (Article 1, Section 8) follows the example in Leviticus 19:34 regarding treatment of immigrants, and Deuteronomy 17:15 warns the Israelites not to let a foreigner rule over them, a concept adopted in our Constitution's requirement that a president be a natural-born US citizen.

The major lesson learned by our founders, given the establishment of religion issue imported from England, isn't found in so many words in the Constitution, however. In fact, there are only two references to religion in the Constitution's 7,652 words, which includes all twenty-seven amendments. One is found in Article VI, Section 3: "No religious test shall ever be required as a qualification to any office or public trust under the United States." (The Pennsylvania Quakers had such a test at the time.) The second is found in the First Amendment, which states, "Congress shall make no law respecting an establishment of religion, or prohibiting the free exercise thereof."

This dearth of religious words and the absence of any reference to God as compared to the Declaration of Independence suggests to many that our founders correctly intended to create a secular government. However, as demonstrated above, our founders took for granted the importance of a biblical foundation for the new government and would not have imagined a government completely removed from Christianity's broader influence.

Quite the opposite was the truth. Yes, the founders sought to deliberately keep religion at arm's length in the Constitution. However, there are some interesting similarities between the Declaration with its ample evidence of the influence of Christianity and the Constitution.

The Declaration was based on natural law, which consists of universal principles of justice, especially for monotheists like Christians. Natural law comes from the Creator, according to the Declaration: "endowed by their Creator with certain unalienable rights." This view was promoted by John Locke, a seventeenth-century English philosopher, who characterized concepts such as all men having equal dignity before God; God granting people rights or powers, with some alienable and others not; government being erected to protect people's rights; government being a fiduciary enterprise—a trusted agent for the citizens; and the people being able to alter government when it fails to serve their interests.[79]

The Constitution by contrast is a statement of positive law that consists of rules enforceable by civil authority. The founders believed this positive law was much the same as the natural law found in the Declaration of Independence, however.

The Declaration argued for the colonists that the positive law of the British Empire had abandoned natural law, thus forfeited its legitimacy as a governing authority over the American colonies. Therefore, the colonies were justified to revolt against the British crown's tyranny and replace it with a legitimate authority.

On the other hand, the Constitution was adopted to move the young United States' positive law closer to the ideals using two principal ways: 1) substantive rules and 2) procedures designed to produce better results.[80]

Substantive rules are evidenced in Article I, Section 10, regarding the contracts clause whereby the founders intended to prevent the state governments from cheating their citizens. It states:

> No State shall, without the Consent of the Congress, lay any Imposts or Duties on Imports or Exports, except what may be absolutely necessary for executing it's inspection Laws: and the net Produce of all Duties and Imposts, laid by any State on Imports or Exports, shall be for the Use of the Treasury of the United States; and all such Laws shall be subject to the Revision and Control of the Congress.

Admittedly, America's Constitution wasn't perfect, even though the founders intended it to move the young nation closer to natural law principles. A major blemish at the time was the failure to address slavery, which was opposed to natural law. The founders didn't ban slavery in the document, because had they tried, at least nine of the thirteen states never would have signed the Constitution. That would have resulted in a fragmented country, a result that waited until 1861 and the War Between the States.[81]

Of course, a defining issue for the republic's Constitution was the prohibition against the establishment of a state religion, not a surprising outcome, given the issues outlined earlier in this chapter. However, it's noteworthy that policy—no state-established religion—was already becoming rather widespread across the colonies at the time of the document's writing. Specifically, by the time our federal Constitution was signed, several states, including Rhode Island and Pennsylvania, had already adopted strong disestablishment principles. Others soon followed their lead. Only the Puritan (Congregationalist) stronghold in New England held out for another decade.

It seems clear that by the time our Constitution was ratified, most Americans believed the principle of disestablishment in the federal document should apply everywhere in the new nation.

Even though all our founders were in some sense Christians, even Franklin and Jefferson (deists), they rejected the idea that any particular set of religious beliefs or affiliations were necessary to being an American. Perhaps George Washington explained it best when addressing the three hundred-member Jewish congregation of Newport, Rhode Island, in 1790:[82]

The citizens of the United States of America have a right to applaud themselves for having given to mankind examples of an enlarged and liberal policy—a policy worthy of imitation. All possess alike liberty of conscience and immunities of citizenship.

It is now no more that toleration is spoken of as if it were the indulgence of one class of people that another enjoyed the exercise of their inherent natural rights, for, happily, the Government of the United States, which gives to bigotry no sanction, to persecution no assistance, requires only that they who live under its protection should demean themselves as good citizens in giving it on all occasions their effectual support....

May the children of the stock of Abraham who dwell in this land continue to merit and enjoy the good will of the other inhabitants—while every one shall sit in safety under his own vine and fig tree and there shall be none to make him afraid.

May the father of all mercies scatter light, and not darkness, upon our paths, and make us all in our several vocations useful here, and in His own due time and way everlastingly happy.

Washington's view regarding the secular nature of civil government is important. However, he totally endorsed the criticality of religion's influence to produce good citizenship. In his farewell address to the nation, the first president reminded the republic that "reason and experience both forbid us to expect that national morality can prevail in exclusion of religious principle." So, the United States became a secular government although it remained a predominantly Christian nation in terms of culture and the overwhelming percentage of the population. That's the paradox our founders bequeathed us.[83]

Conclusion

America's history from the time of its colonial founding to the ratification of our Constitution was known for Christian diversity and a close association of the church with civil government. However, that widespread church-state entanglement was transformed by our founders to achieve disestablishment in the new federal government and most states by the turn of the eighteenth century.

It is clear most of the founders were Christian believers who strongly believed that faith was necessary for building moral virtue, and they assumed the new republic would remain culturally Christian.

CHAPTER TWO

Christian Principles, Values, and Institutions, and How They Defined America

THE PREVIOUS CHAPTER reviewed America's early history, which was dominated by a significant Christian influence and contributed to the formation of the new republic. This chapter builds on that material by examining Christianity's impact on important social structures (values and institutions), the makings of a Christian nation, and America's character.

A Christian nation is defined as a large group of people bonded together by their common identity, which came about thanks to embedded Christian principles that shaped societal values and institutions.

For my purposes here, the terms "nation" and "society" are essentially the same. Each represents a phenomenon wherein shared values, laws, and traditions within a group of people guide that population in living in organized communities for mutual benefit. These people apply principles—behavior guides—within their daily lives to create certain values and social institutions. These social institutions, according to Dr. Jonathan Turner, a professor of sociology at the University of California, are structures that organize "stable patterns of human activity with respect to fundamental problems in producing life-sustaining resources, in reproducing individuals, and in sustaining viable societal structures within a given environment."[84]

Thus, the very essence of a nation is evidenced by the elemental building blocks of principles, values, and institutions. To understand the true nature of a nation, one needs only to study the underlying principles that formulate the defining values and social institutions.

There is one more important ingredient when building a nation. The building blocks must be based on an objective standard of truth, which, for Christian people, is the Bible. The Bible offers ultimate, objective, and absolute truth, which was a general consensus among most of our early founders. That standard remained true in America until the late twentieth and early twenty-first centuries.

It follows that it's only natural that our founders turned to the Bible for guidance when forming a government for a mostly Christian population. After all, that was the standard used by the earliest European colonialists, the Pilgrims, whose Mayflower Compact of 1620 wasn't to find religious freedom, because they left that behind in Holland. Rather, it was twofold. First, it was to establish a temporary democratic government that would lead to their ultimate right to self-government in New England. It was also, and importantly, for the "Glory of God and advancement of the Christian Faith." They were on a mission for God.

In the following pages, I will develop three conclusions that make the case that America was a Christian nation at its founding and remains so in spite of diminishing evidence. First, I will identify Christian principles that were embedded in early America (exclusively the thirteen original British colonies)—and many of those principles continue to be evident today. Second, I will identify, thanks to those embedded Christian principles, the key Christian values that blossomed in America's early colonial culture to define us as a unique Christian society. Finally, I will examine five key social institutions upon which the predominantly Christian American population learned to conduct its national life: family, education, religion, government, and economy. These American institutions all have rich Christian histories, as you will see. However, as I will explain in the next section, these institutions are under severe attack today and, should they be divested of their Christianity, the nation will cease to be what its founders intended.

Before addressing these issues, permit me to dispel a misconception about my claim that America is a Christian nation. Many Americans from our early years as a nation have considered this country Christian, but not because all citizens (much less all our leaders) were or are Christians. Neither is the United States Christian because our laws require everyone inside our borders to bow to Christian theology. In fact, there is no such provision in our Constitution, nor is there such a mandate from our courts.

It is also true that at least fifty of the fifty-five framers of our Constitution were self-proclaimed Christians from a variety of denominational backgrounds, and every American president has referenced God in his inaugural address. Every state constitution calls on God, and our Supreme Court even studied the matter to conclude in *Church of the Holy Trinity v. United States, 143 U.S.457 (1892)*: "This is a Christian nation."

No, the United States is a Christian nation for a very simple reason, which was explained by former Supreme Court Justice David Brewer (1837–1910): "In what sense can [America] be called a Christian nation? Not in the sense that Christianity is the established religion or that the people are in any manner compelled to support it."

The justice acknowledged what I already established in the previous chapter: that our Constitution does not promote any faith. "Congress shall make no law respecting an establishment of religion, or prohibiting the free exercise thereof."[85]

It's true that America was at the time of her founding and today open to people of all faith groups, although early Americans were predominantly Christian, albeit representing many denominations, both Protestant and Catholic. But in spite of Christianity's dominance, our founders wisely avoided establishing a national religion, and our federal government never required evidence of the Christian faith as a precondition for public service. So why, then, is America a "Christian nation," according to Supreme Court Justice Brewer?

Justice Brewer explained that America was "of all the nations in the world...most justly called a Christian nation" because Christianity "has so largely shaped and molded it." That is a simple fact and the thesis of this chapter. American society's defining values and her social institutions were all shaped by dominant Christian principles, practices, and values from the start, which made these United States of America a Christian nation.

Applied Christian Principles in Early America

The dominance of Christian, biblical principles in early America came about because the overwhelming majority of early Americans was comprised of Christians who mostly lived those underlying Christian principles in their lives, both private and public. That does not mean, nor did the founders envision, the creation of an America-based theocracy, however.

Consider those underlying Christian principles and how they influenced America's First Principles, which are credited with making America a great and Christian nation.

Let's begin by understanding that America's founders were mostly dissenting Protestants who insisted that civil government should have no role in the church or in matters of faith and conscience. We saw many compelling reasons for this pervasive attitude in the previous chapter. Yet those founders also understood that Americans would have to be governed from within by virtuous values, and most agreed that Christianity provided the principles that would produce those virtuous values that would in turn produce a moral, stable, and future prosperous America.

Those underlying principles are found in the Bible. **The first Christian principle is *faith in God as the Creator* (Genesis 1:1), the author of**

morality. Faith in the God of the Bible was essential to good citizenship, because a sense of obligation to a higher authority (Creator) guarded sinful man from selfish, unrestrained lives.[86]

Founder James Madison, the chief architect of our Constitution, wrote: "Before any man can be considered as a member of civil society, he must be considered as a subject of the governor of the universe."[87]

He continued:

The belief in a God All Powerful wise and good, is so essential to the moral order of the world and to the happiness of man, that arguments which enforce it cannot be drawn from too many sources nor adapted with too much solicitude to the different characters and capacities impressed with it.[88]

Our first president agreed with Madison's observation. In fact, one of President George Washington's first acts as the chief executive of the new republic was to declare November 26, 1789, as a Day of Thanksgiving. He wrote:

Whereas it is the duty of all Nations to acknowledge the providence of Almighty God, to obey his will, to be grateful for his benefits, and humbly to implore his protection and favor, and whereas both Houses of Congress have by their joint Committee requested me to recommend to the People of the United States a day of public thanksgiving and prayer to be observed by acknowledging with grateful hearts the many signal favors of Almighty God especially by affording them an opportunity peaceably to establish a form of government for their safety and happiness.[89]

Washington's acknowledgment of God and the necessity to do so was a commonly shared perspective in early America, and those who didn't believe in the existence of God found some of their fellow citizens rather hostile to their atheism. For example, a judge in New York rejected the testimony of a witness who appeared before him who claimed to be an atheist. The judge explained that denying the existence of God "destroyed all the confidence of the court in what he was about to say." The judge said that case was the first time he had ever met a person who denied God's existence, evidently an uncommon occurrence at that time.[90]

Believing in the all-powerful God of the Bible **was the second founding American principle that helped produce a prosperous and stable nation.** In fact, the Bible's importance was on full display at the opening of every session of the First Continental Congress. Bible readings and prayer were the representatives' first order of business before knuckling down to consider their legislative duties.

The respect accorded the Bible at that time is evidenced by the fact that the first English Bible published in America, in 1782, came with Congress' endorsement:

> Resolved: That the United States in Congress assembled, highly approve the pious and laudable undertaking of Mr. Aitken, as subservient to the interest of religion as well as an instance of the progress of the arts in this country, and being satisfied from the above report, of his care and accuracy in the execution of the work they recommend this edition of the Bible to the inhabitants of the United States and hereby authorize him to publish this recommendation in the manner he shall think proper.[91]

The Bible's important place in the life of America was demonstrated by some of our early presidents as well. Andrew Jackson, America's seventh president, said: "That book [the Bible], sir, is the rock on which our republic rests." Theodore Roosevelt, our twenty-sixth president, echoed that view: "No other book of any kind ever written in English has ever so affected the whole life of a people."[92]

The third Christian principle is *recognition of the fallen condition of mankind.* Man is sinful. Our founders believed that humanity was created in the image and likeness of God (Genesis 1–3). But man sinned and fell from grace in the Garden of Eden. That fall left him damaged goods, capable of terrible deeds.

Our fallen nature has played out throughout the history of mankind through wars, crime, and all sorts of inhuman behavior. Benjamin Hart, a historian and author of *The Christian Roots of American Liberty*, wrote: "A central assumption of America's founders was original sin, meaning the corruption of man's character."[93] That view explains founder James Madison's observation about the role of government: "If men were angels no government would be necessary."[94]

Our founders understood the truth about man's depravity, an issue addressed by theologian John Calvin, who significantly impacted the theology of especially the Presbyterians and Congregationalists who helped draft our Constitution. That's in part why the founders built into our Constitution an elaborate system of checks and balances to keep individuals and groups from gaining "power" that, as Sir John Acton (1834–1902), an English historian and moralist, warned, "tends to corrupt." He continued, "Absolute power corrupts absolutely. Great men are almost always bad men."[95]

Acton's warning reflects what the Bible teaches: that sinful humans are vulnerable to corruption (Hosea 9:9; Isaiah 1:4; Galatians 6:8). That's why our founders relied on Christianity to provide the moral and intellectual foundation for our country, which led to the necessity to put in place checks on man's sinful nature, the tendency to become corrupt.

The fourth Christian principle is the *necessity of widespread Christian faith* to produce a stable and prosperous nation. President George Washington declared in his Farewell Address (1796): "Of all the dispositions and habits which lead to political prosperity, religion [Christianity] and morality are indispensable supports."[96]

Evidently, Thomas Jefferson, the author of our Constitution, agreed with Washington's admonition. Jefferson made Washington's Farewell Address required reading at the University of Virginia, which he founded in his hometown of Charlottesville.[97]

Note that in his Farewell Address, Washington used the word "indispensable," which meant religion was not optional in a society. Also, every founder, when using the word "religion," was without exception referring to Christianity.

That unambiguous understanding of Christianity in Washington's address may offend today's politically correct. However, even Jefferson, who was often considered a nominal Christian or deist, confirmed my observation: "Of all the systems of morality that have come under my observations, none appear to me as pure as that of Jesus [the founder of Christianity]."[98]

Our founders understood that America's future success hinged on the moral character of the nation's citizens, guided by biblical values. That's why founder John Adams wrote: "We have no government armed with power capable of contending with human passions unbridled by morality and religion.... Our Constitution was made only for a moral and religious [Christian] people. It is wholly inadequate to the government of any other."[99]

The fifth Christian principle is *civil government's purpose to restrain evil and reward good* **(Romans 13:1–7; 1 Peter 2:13–14).** Christians are to pray for and obey authorities (1 Timothy 2:1–4)—that is, unless government forbids what God requires, and then civil disobedience becomes inescapable (Acts 4:18–31). Also, in a democracy, Christians are obligated to participate in civil government, not avoid the uncomfortable confrontation that's becoming all too typical today (Matthew 22:21).

Unfortunately, this principle is often distorted by secularists who insist that our founders meant freedom *from* religion not freedom *of* religion. That is a distortion of the founders' intention with the First Amendment ("Congress shall make no law concerning the establishment of religion or hindering the free exercise thereof"). Secularists cite to support their "freedom from religion" view Thomas Jefferson's use of the phrase "wall of separation" in an 1802 letter to the Danbury (Connecticut) Baptist Association. Jefferson's intent was to assure the Baptists,

a minority Christian denomination in an overwhelmingly Congregationalist state, that "government could not interfere with an individual's
right of conscience or make a person support a church with which he
did not agree."[100]

For Jefferson, the First Amendment was a wall erected to keep government out of the affairs of the church, not the other way around. Our
founders said "never again" to a state-established religion, as detailed
in the previous chapter. After all, they didn't want America to become
like England with a state church, from which our founders' parents and
grandparents fled. The founders simply wanted to protect citizens from
being forced to act against their religious beliefs. Further, they would be
astonished to see how modern America has distorted the First Amendment to try and totally disenfranchise religious liberty. Rather, they
intended to make certain that Christianity would be protected from
government intrusion to do its work of embedding values in the nation's
citizens and her social institutions.

**Finally, the sixth Christian principle is the *promotion of servant
leadership*.** Jesus was the classic servant leader. He set the example for
His disciples and even humbled Himself to wash their feet (Matthew
26). The servant-leader concept emerged in America thanks to the
Bible's influence on the population and due to our early leaders like
George Washington, a humble man who focused on others, not himself.

Author Dinesh D'Souza explained the concept of a servant leader in
his book *What's So Great About Christianity*. He wrote:

> Christianity enhanced the notion of political and social account-
> ability by providing a new model: that of servant leadership.
> In ancient Greece and Rome no one would have dreamed of
> considering political leaders anyone's servants. The job of the
> leader was to lead. But Christ invented the notion that the way
> to lead is by serving the needs of others, especially those who
> are the neediest. Mark 10:43 quotes Christ: "Whoever wants
> to become great among you must be your servant...for even

the Son of Man did not come to be served but to serve." And in Luke 22:27 we hear Jesus say, "Who is greater, the one who is at the table or the one who serves? Is it not the one who is at the table? But I am among you as one who serves." In the new Christian framework, leaders are judged by how well they respond to the concerns and welfare of the people. Over time, people once known as "followers" or "subjects" become "customers" and "constituents."[101]

Christian Principles Influenced the Nation's First Principles

Our founders translated these Christian principles into First Principles, the basic, foundational, self-evident propositions about our new government. Five First Principles are examined below. All fifty-five delegates to the Constitutional Convention embraced these, which influenced their design of America's founding government.

The first founding principle is the *rule of law*, a conceptual descendant of Hebrew law and the Ten Commandants (Exodus 20), which required obedience by every Israelite. Our founders understood that concept, which meant that all members of society are considered equally subject to the law, no exceptions.

By contrast, John Adams described the rule of the sword, the code that much of the world understood before and at that time. Adams explained:

In the earliest ages of the world, absolute monarchy seems to have been the universal form of government. Kings, and a few of their great counselors and captains, exercised a cruel tyranny over the people, who held a rank in the scale of intelligence, in those days, but little higher than the camels and elephants that carried them and their engines to war.[102]

Those past rulers governed through fear, whereby their citizens were no more than subjects beholden to the monarch. Christianity persuaded our founders to embrace the concept of the rule of law to promote a free and just government whereby every citizen, no matter his or her position, was equally subject. Therefore, America's early leaders crafted such public law to govern *all* citizens, which protected all our liberty. That meant, according to founder Samuel Adams, "There shall be one rule of Justice for the rich and the poor; for the favorite in Court, and the Countryman at the Plough."[103]

The second founding principle is *unalienable rights*, which recognizes that everyone is endowed by God with certain rights. Recall from chapter 1 that the Declaration of Independence proclaims the self-evident truth that "all men are endowed, by their Creator, with certain unalienable rights; that among these are life, liberty, and the pursuit of happiness."

Thomas Jefferson explained this first principle when he wrote, "A free people claims their rights as derived from the laws of nature, and not as a gift from their chief magistrate."[104] Translated, that means certain rights derive from nature, of which government may not take or violate.

This principle was a radical departure from the practice of the rest of the world. Past governments run by kings and nobility were the origin of authority, and they granted rights and privileges to their subjects. Any liberties the citizenry held depended solely upon the whim of the ruler. The American model was to be radically different. It held that some rights were endowed in people from God, and they were unalienable.

Founder Alexander Hamilton observed:

The sacred rights of mankind are not to be rummaged for among old parchments or musty records. They are written, as with a sunbeam, in the whole volume of human nature, by the hand of divinity itself, and can never be erased or obscured by mortal power.[105]

Americans' unalienable rights didn't come from government, and those in authority could not revoke them.

The third founding principle is *equality,* which accepts that all persons are created equal. The principle is called out in our Declaration of Independence: "All men are created equal."

Our founders embraced the Christian principle that the Creator created all individuals and that each person arises from God's handiwork. Each person is equal to all others, regardless of physical, mental, and social differences among citizens. In our republic, this first principle means that each person possesses the same opportunity to maintain survival and pursue happiness.

The founders had to reject the inequitable behavior seen in other forms of government, such as hereditary nobility, racial segregation, and the favor of one ethic group over another. Of course, as indicated earlier, for a variety of reasons, the founders ignored the obvious moral thorn in their eye, slavery.

Founder Benjamin Franklin expressed this principle clearly:

> The ordaining of laws in favor of one part of the nation, to the prejudice and oppression of another, is certainly the most erroneous and mistaken policy. An equal dispensation of protection, rights, privileges, and advantages, is what every part is entitled to, and ought to enjoy.[106]

This principle requires each person to be treated equally under the law, as well as to require equal protection of the laws be afforded to all.

The fourth founding principle is that of the *social compact,* an idea promoted by John Locke, a French philosopher. This principle says that government is instituted by the people and derives its just powers from the consent of the governed, meaning that the people are "boss," or "king"—a concept developed in the final chapter of this book.

This principle is recognized in the Declaration of Independence, which states that "governments are instituted among men, deriving their just powers from the consent of the governed." The same concept is captured in the first three words of our Constitution: "We the people…".

There are two parts to the social compact. The first part is that legitimate governments are instituted among the people to secure the peace among sinful men. Alexander Hamilton said that government becomes necessary to restrain "the passions of men." The alternative to restraining people to preserve liberty is vigilantism.

Thomas Hobbes, an English philosopher and founder of modern political philosophy whom America's founders favored, argued that in a state of nature, people don't get along, because humans are out for themselves. He affirmed that view in *Leviathan*, stating "the life of man solitary, poor, nasty, brutish, and short.… The condition of man…is a condition of war of everyone against everyone."[107]

The second part of the social compact is that people must consent to give the government its authority. Robert Yates, an antifederalist delegate to the Constitutional Convention, said, "In every free government, the people must give their assent to the laws by which they are governed. This is the true criterion between a free government and an arbitrary one."[108]

This two-part compact means the people have the right to alter or abolish any form of government because they are the only authorizing force to ratify the Constitution.

The fifth and final founding principle is *limited government*, which "means the protection of unalienable rights is the legitimate purpose and limit of government requires government to be strong enough to fulfill this purpose yet limited to that purpose."[109]

This principle rejects governments that possess unlimited power. Rather, government ought to protect unalienable rights and limit their reach. Founding father Thomas Paine (1737–1809), the political pamphleteer author of *Common Sense*, addressed this principle: "Man did not enter into society to become *worse* than he was before, not to have fewer rights than he had before, but to have those rights better secured." That view was shared by Thomas Jefferson, who said: "Our rulers can have authority over such natural rights only as we have submitted to them."[110]

Evidently, our founders wanted limited government in the form of a representative republic, but distrusted a direct democracy, which they characterized as mob rule. Also, James Madison opposed any system of government that allowed special interests to gain leverage, a problem they experienced during colonial times.

John Locke explained the role of government in dealing with citizens who had to relinquish some of their rights to secure life, liberty, and property. Locke said government:

> ...can have no other end or measure when in the hands of the magistrates but to preserve the members of that society in their lives, liberties, and possessions; and so cannot be an absolute, arbitrary power over their lives and fortunes which are so much as possible to be preserved.[111]

To protect against government oppression, the founders dispersed power across three branches (executive, legislative, and judicial) and put in place formidable checks on authority of every other branch.

So far, we've established that Christian principles influenced the First Principles that defined America's government. Next, we will demonstrate how the collection of Christian and First Principles gave birth to the values that permeated America and helped identify her as a Christian nation.

Christian Principles Spawned Christian Values and America's National Character

We established early in this chapter that principles spawn values, the substance of the nation's character, and no one should be surprised as a result that America's enduring identity has biblical roots. Consider American values that reigned supreme in early America.

We begin with the definition of core values, which are a "standard, or quality to which we are committed, that lies at the heart of what we are and defines our identity."[112] Perhaps the best known Christian core values are worship only God, respect all people, be humble, be honest, and live a moral life.

These and other Christian values accompanied America's early settlers to the New World and became deeply rooted in what this country was to become, a Christian nation. For Christians at that time, these values guided their decisions and set priorities—and, of course, are found in the Bible.

Consider a few biblical values that influenced early Americans that became part of our national character.

Serve God, not money. This value comes from Matthew 6:24 (NIV):

No one can serve two masters. Either you will hate the one and love the other, or you will be devoted to the one and despise the other. You cannot serve both God and money.

Be truthful. This value comes from a number of Scripture passages, including the following from Proverbs:

Better the poor whose walk is blameless than a fool whose lips are perverse. (19:1, NIV)

The Lord detests lying lips, but he delights in people who are trustworthy. (12:22, NIV)

Be a good example. This value comes from Luke 6:31 (NIV):

Do to others as you would have them do to you.

Be generous. This value is rooted in Acts 20:35 (NIV):

In everything I did, I showed you that by this kind of hard work we must help the weak, remembering the words the Lord Jesus himself said: "It is more blessed to give than to receive."

Be content with what you have. This value is found in Hebrews 13:5 (NIV):

Keep your lives free from the love of money and be content with what you have, because God has said, "Never will I leave you; never will I forsake you."

Show mercy. This value is found in Luke 6:32–42 (NIV):

If you love those who love you, what credit is that to you? Even sinners love those who love them. And if you do good to those who are good to you, what credit is that to you? Even sinners do that. And if you lend to those from whom you expect repayment, what credit is that to you? Even sinners lend to sinners, expecting to be repaid in full. But love your enemies, do good to them, and lend to them without expecting to get anything back. Then your reward will be great, and you will be children of the Most High, because he is kind to the ungrateful and wicked. Be merciful, just as your Father is merciful.

Do not judge, and you will not be judged. Do not condemn, and you will not be condemned. Forgive, and you will be forgiven. Give, and it will be given to you. A good measure, pressed down, shaken together and running over, will be poured into your lap. For with the measure you use, it will be measured to you.

He also told them this parable: "Can the blind lead the blind? Will they not both fall into a pit? The student is not above the teacher, but everyone who is fully trained will be like their teacher.

Why do you look at the speck of sawdust in your brother's eye and pay no attention to the plank in your own eye? How can you say to your brother, "Brother, let me take the speck out of your eye," when you yourself fail to see the plank in your own eye? You hypocrite, first take the plank out of your eye, and then you will see clearly to remove the speck from your brother's eye.

Show faith through works. This value is found in James 2:14–24 (NIV):

What good is it, my brothers and sisters, if someone claims to have faith but has no deeds? Can such faith save them? Suppose a brother or a sister is without clothes and daily food. If one of you says to them, "Go in peace; keep warm and well fed," but does nothing about their physical needs, what good is it? In the same way, faith by itself, if it is not accompanied by action, is dead.

But someone will say, "You have faith; I have deeds." Show me your faith without deeds, and I will show you my faith by my deeds. You believe that there is one God. Good! Even the demons believe that—and shudder.

You foolish person, do you want evidence that faith without deeds is useless? Was not our father Abraham considered righteous for what he did when he offered his son Isaac on the altar? You see that his faith and his actions were working together, and his faith was made complete by what he did. And the scripture was fulfilled that says, "Abraham believed God, and it was credited to him as righteousness," and he was called God's friend. You see that a person is considered righteous by what they do and not by faith alone.

Work hard. This value is found in Luke 15:8 (NIV):

Or suppose a woman has ten silver coins and loses one. Doesn't she light a lamp, sweep the house and search carefully until she finds it?

Judge yourself as you would others. This value is found in Matthew 7:1–5 (NIV):

Do not judge, or you too will be judged. For in the same way you judge others, you will be judged, and with the measure you use, it will be measured to you.

Why do you look at the speck of sawdust in your brother's eye and pay no attention to the plank in your own eye? How can you say to your brother, "Let me take the speck out of your eye," when all the time there is a plank in your own eye? You hypocrite, first take the plank out of your own eye, and then you will see clearly to remove the speck from your brother's eye.

Be forgiving. This value is found in Mark 11:25 (NIV):

And when you stand praying, if you hold anything against anyone, forgive them, so that your Father in heaven may forgive you your sins.

Be honorable in your dealings. This is found in Hebrews 13:18 (NIV):

Pray for us. We are sure that we have a clear conscience and desire to live honorably in every way.

Avoid corruption. This is found in Galatians 6:7–8 (NIV):

Do not be deceived: God cannot be mocked. A man reaps what he sows. Whoever sows to please their flesh, from the flesh will reap destruction; whoever sows to please the Spirit, from the Spirit will reap eternal life.

Be loving. This is found in 1 John 4:19 (NIV):

We love because he first loved us.

Provide for your family. This is found in 1 Timothy 5:8 (NIV):

Anyone who does not provide for their relatives, and especially for their own household, has denied the faith and is worse than an unbeliever.

Give to the less fortunate. This is found in Matthew 5:42 (NIV):

Give to the one who asks you, and do not turn away from the one who wants to borrow from you.

These biblical values and literally hundreds of others became central to America's identity, as evidenced by their use in our Declaration of Independence and the Constitution. Of course, they were secularized across the culture in the form of national values such as equality, liberty, justice, democracy, the right to private property, individual responsibility, and more.

These scriptural standards became central to the formation of a host of American characteristics, the very personification of those values lived out by her citizens and readily observable within the broader culture. Those characteristics describe what others came to identify as the Americans' ethos: optimism; confidence; commitment to progress; individual initiative (individualism); high moral character; respectability; practicality; respect for education and skill; self-reliance; religion; physical and spiritual courage; tolerance but moral decency patriotism; and activism in most everything in life.

Each characteristic has a story behind its development. Consider the formation of the characteristic of "American individualism." Perhaps no group of early Americans typifies this trait more than the new England Puritans, who placed value on self-reliance, privacy, and mutual respect—all components of individualism.[113]

Those views emerged from the Puritans' desire for religious reform in the New World to avoid the European authority tradition (monarchies) and their desire to develop a strong self-awareness. This idea is rooted in the Puritans' "justification-by-faith" concept that rebelled against the Catholic pope's religious authority that Catholics believed must bridge the gap between God and man. Rather, the Puritan view was that no intermediary (priest) was necessary between man and God. They believed that every Christian can communicate directly with God through prayer and faith in Him. For the Puritan, one's soul became free and independent apart from some religious hierarchy like that in Catholic Rome.

Another American characteristic with biblical roots is hard work, which has a Puritan theological foundation as well. The Puritans believed hard work was the way to please God, and through one's hard work and thrift—translated doing "good"—in this life, they were chosen for eternal life, their predestination doctrine.

Benjamin Franklin, who grew up in a Puritan, Calvinist home but later in life became what some label a moralized Christian, vigorously promoted the character trait of hard work and being thrifty. He encouraged in his public statements and writings the pursuit of wealth to conquer the wild American continent, as well as the importance of hard work. Franklin famously said, "Plough deep while sluggards sleep," and, "Doing your best means never stop trying."[114]

Another American characteristic with biblical roots is the Puritans' devotion to public education. Of course, they expected schools to instruct all people about their sinful nature, and the Bible was their textbook. They required that everyone must learn to read, and that meant reading the Bible for themselves. That view was promoted by the father of the Protestant Reformation, Martin Luther, who said:

Above all, the foremost reading for everybody, both in the universities and in the schools, should be Holy Scripture.... I would advise no one to send his child where the Holy Scriptures are not supreme.[115]

It's little wonder that soon after establishing themselves in the New World, the Puritans established colleges and opened public schools. The first such school, the Roxbury Latin School, was formed in 1635, and four years later, in 1639, the Puritans established the first American college—Harvard College, a seminary, a Puritan/Congregationalist institution that trained ministers for many years. In 1816, Harvard founded the Divinity School, which became the first nondenominational divinity school in the United States.[116]

This chapter began by identifying the Christian principles that are embedded in early America and how they led to the development of a system of values and characteristics that created this country's unique culture.

The final section of this chapter is an examination of five social institutions upon which the predominantly Christian American population learned to conduct its national life: family, education, religion, government, and economy.

Key American Institutions Helped Define Christian America

A nation is held together by key institutions that provide the structure upon which people chart and conduct their lives together. Destroy any one, and society begins to implode; destroy all five, and you no longer have a country.

America's prosperity and character were undeniably influenced by her Christian roots, especially the impact on the key defining institutions: government, education, family, religion (church), and economy.

We begin with the Christian influence on the institution of government, which was previously presented. As we introduced earlier, a definition for the institution of government is a community of people who agree to a purpose, a set of organizational policies, a mechanism for forming new policies, and a means of enforcement. Government identifies those ingredients in its constitution, which includes a statement of governing principles and a philosophy that balances those ingredients with individual freedoms.

The purpose of the United States government is found in our Constitution's Preamble, which states to "establish justice, insure domestic tranquility, provide for the common defense, promote the general welfare, and secure the blessings of liberty to ourselves and our posterity." Therefore, government's primary duty is to secure our freedom.

Indeed, the US Constitution establishes a federal democratic republic form of government, an indivisible union of sovereign states. It is democratic because people govern themselves by electing representatives. The founders also established three principles on which to govern: inherent rights, self-government, and separation of powers.

Our founders distrusted strong central governments because they tend to turn oppressive, like those experienced in Europe. Therefore, the founders designed a set of checks and balances with enough power for government to govern, while containing its urge to trample on the rights of the citizens.

French historian Alexis de Tocqueville explained this approach to government in his book, *Democracy in America*. He wrote:

I think that in no country in the civilized world is less attention paid to philosophy than in the United States.... Nevertheless it is easy to perceive that almost all the inhabitants of the United States conduct their understanding in the same manner, and govern it by the same rules; that is to say, that without ever having taken the trouble to define the rules of a philosophical method, they are in possession of one, common to the whole people. To evade the bondage of system and habit, of family maxims, class opinions, and, in some degree, of national prejudices; to accept tradition only as a means of information, and existing facts only as a lesson used in doing otherwise, and doing better; to seek the reason of things for one's self, and in one's self alone; to tend to results without being bound to means, and to aim at the substance through the form; —such are the principal characteristics of what I shall call the philosophical method of the Americans…[in] most of the operations of the mind, each American appeals to the individual exercise of his own understanding alone.[117]

This framework and philosophy of governing is where the American government started in the late eighteenth century, albeit influenced by Christian principles as developed in this and the first chapter.

Our founders provided wise counsel for later generations to remain close to the Constitution. Thomas Jefferson warned George Washington that "to take a single step beyond the boundaries [of the Constitution]…is to take possession of a boundless field of power."[118] James Madison also cautioned that government must "keep close to our chartered authorities."[119]

Both Jefferson and Madison were strict constructionists who believed our Constitution is a contract between the citizens and their government. Any authority assumed by government beyond the enumerated powers is a usurpation of power, unless properly amended.

Those exhortations are consistent with the Christian principles outlined earlier. However, one might then rightly ask: If America is indeed a Christian nation, then why did our founders avoid mentioning God or Christianity, much less religion in general, except in the First Amendment?

The founders, as explained earlier, created a federal government for limited purposes, notably enumerated in Article I, Section 8, of the Constitution. They agreed that any legislative action on religious or moral matters belonged to state and local governments. The First Amendment merely reinforces this view.

Further, our form of government is based on the Christian principles outlined earlier: faith in a creator; belief in the God of the Bible; acknowledgment that humans are sinful; widespread Christian faith; restrained civil government; and servant leadership. Those principles were embedded in our Constitution through the founding principles examined earlier: rule of law, unalienable rights, equality, social contract, and limited government.

America's founders also believed it permissible for the federal and state governments to encourage Christianity. Even though our Constitution doesn't explicitly mandate a secular polity, we must reject the secularist view that government is obligated to strip religion, especially Christianity, from the public square. After all, the founders' personal histories and colonial culture at our founding intended to encourage religion (read "Christianity") across every aspect of American society, as was the common colonial practice.

Then how should we understand the First Amendment? Keep in mind that the ratification of the Constitution didn't change the colonies' relationship with their established churches. However, it did guarantee that the new federal government would not establish an official national church or pass any laws that interfered with a person's religious choice. The new states were left free to continue their established church relationships, which we indicated earlier were eventually discontinued.

So, the passage of the First Amendment did not alter the religious conditions of early America. Consider the First Amendment's two distinct clauses.

The first is the establishment clause, which states that Congress "shall make no law respecting an establishment of religion," which practically meant that Congress may not establish a national church, collect taxes, or provide money to support any specific religion. The second clause is the free exercise clause, which specifies that Congress may not pass laws "prohibiting the free exercise" of religion, which means Congress may not interfere in any person's choice of faith.[120]

What's clear from colonial history is that our mostly Christian founders built into in our founding documents Christian principles and values. Our forefathers created a government based on principles that are traceable to the Christian Bible.

Early-American Christian Education

The American colonialists understood the divine mandate to educate their children upon a biblical foundation, which resulted in a remarkably high literacy level. Their mission to educate the next generation began at home, but in time branched to Christian grammar schools and later colleges.

Founder Samuel Adams explained the purpose behind the colonialists' education mandate:

> Let divines and philosophers, statesmen and patriots, unite their endeavors to renovate the age, by…educating their little boys and girls…and instructing them in the art of self-government, without which they never can act a wise part in the government of societies, great or small; in short of leading them in the study and practice of the exalted virtues of the Christian system. [121]

We already established that many of the early colonialists were religious exiles from Europe who were known as "people of the book [Bible]," a label that fit the most faithful like the Calvinists, which included the Pilgrims, Puritans, and Presbyterians. They relied on the Bible to teach the next generation how to reason from God's Word and function in a civil society, an idea Reformation-era's John Calvin matured in Geneva, Switzerland, and a practice Calvinists brought to America. [122]

As an aside, there is a curiosity about the English Pilgrims—"Separatists"—who first immigrated in the early 1600s to the Netherlands when they would no longer bow to the religious persecution under Queen Elizabeth I. Subsequently, in 1620, those same Pilgrims left their temporary home in Holland aboard the ship Mayflower for America and founded Plymouth colony. The Pilgrims, much like the Puritans who made up the Massachusetts Bay Colony, brought with them to America John Calvin's Geneva Bible, which contained marginal notes about civil government that so frightened King James I that the British monarch banned it and then commissioned his own translation, declaring, "There will be no marginal notes in my Bible!"[123]

King James was most afraid of Calvin's position on church-state matters outlined in his book, *Institutes of the Christian Religion.* Calvin's purpose in writing *Institutes* was to "aid those who desire to be instructed in the doctrine of salvation."[124] However, the part of the book that most offended the British monarch was the warning about mingling the kingdom of God and the kingdom of earth, the very model King James oversaw. Calvin wrote, "We must keep in mind that distinction which we have previously laid down so that we do not (as commonly happens) unwisely mingle these two, which have a completely different nature."[125]

The Geneva Bible preceded the King James Version by fifty-one years and was the primary Bible of sixteenth-century English Protestants and a treasure to the Pilgrims and Puritans. It was not only significant because it was mechanically printed, but also because it came with a variety of scriptural study guides and aids, to include citations that allowed the reader to cross-reference verses.

The Pilgrims took Calvin's instruction to heart when they crafted in the Mayflower Compact a Christian government based on biblical law that cautioned against comingling civil and church affairs. The Compact also mandated a Christian education for their children, and this led to the formulation of the first American education law, albeit in Massachusetts.

The first American education law originated with the Puritans in the Massachusetts Bay Colony legislature in 1642, which reflected the colonists' concerns for their children:

> Forasmuch as the good education of children is of singular behoof and benefit to any commonwealth and whereas many

parents and masters are too indulgent and negligent of their duty in this kind.[126]

The first American education law states:

It is therefore ordered by this Court and the authority thereof, That the selectmen of every town, in the several precincts and quarters where they dwell, shall have a vigilant eye over their brethren and neighbors, to see, first that none of them shall suffer so much barbarism in any of their families, as not to endeavor to teach, by themselves or others, their children and apprentices as much learning as may enable them perfectly to read the English tongue, and knowledge of the capital laws, upon penalty of twenty shillings for each neglect therein.[127]

That injunction was followed by the first school-focused law in the Massachusetts Bay Colony. The law reads:

It is therefore ordered by this Court and authority thereof, That every township within this jurisdiction, after the Lord hath increased them to the number of fifty householders, shall then forthwith appoint one within their town to teach all such children as shall resort to him, to write and read, whose wages shall be paid, either by the parents or masters of such children or by the inhabitants in general, by way of supply.... [And it is further ordered], That where any town shall increase to the number of one hundred families or householders, they shall set up a grammar school, the masters thereof being able to instruct youths so far as they may be fitted for the university.[128]

The Puritans quickly established a grammar school to comply with the law. That school, the Boston Latin School, was founded in 1635 and modeled after the European Latin School model, and of course it put an emphasis on Christianity, Latin, and classical literature. Latin was important, because speaking more than one language was the sign of an educated citizen. Not surprisingly, Latin proficiency became a requirement for admission to Harvard Seminary as well.[129]

The Puritans used the Bible and the *New England Primer*, the first reading primer designed for the American colonies to educate their children. That primer was used to catechize their children in Calvinist precepts as well as teach them the alphabet using familiar biblical illustrations such as "a," "in Adam's fall we sinned all" and "b" for "heaven to find, the Bible mind."[130]

It is little wonder that, with few exceptions, our founders were Christian men who were first educated at home by godly parents, then often in Christian-based grammar schools, through college where the Bible and Christian texts were used unapologetically.

Even George Washington, like most other children of his era, was homeschooled in Northern Virginia by his father, who died when George was eleven, and then his mother, Mary Ball, picked up that responsibility. Boys like George at the time learned arithmetic, geography, and handwriting by writing into a copy book from *110 Rules of Civility and Decent Behavior,* written by French Jesuits in 1595. (Jesuits are a member of the Society of Jesus, a Roman Catholic order of priests founded by St. Ignatius Loyola, St. Francis Xavier, and others in 1534, primarily to evangelize the world.) The "110 rules" focus on other people rather than on one's narrow self-interests—an important Christian virtue that influenced George's future.

George Washington's only formal education was in the science and practice of surveying. Yet, he was considered an educated Christian man who became known as the "Father of His Country" and the "Moses of America." He wrote more than forty volumes of personal correspondence, and his Farewell Address to the nation remains a lesson on the importance of religion and morality in politics. It is still considered one of the most important of our historical documents.[131]

As the country grew, so did our Bible-based education system. The grammar school (also known as the common school), which began in Boston, became part of every community's landscape. They were typically one-room affairs with a lone teacher. The students' parents initially paid tuition and provided housing for the teacher, but in time, those costs were paid by local taxes. Like the schools that began in New England, these popped up in communities small and large and followed the Puritan model of institutionalizing religion into the curriculum in order to instill good morals and obedience, besides instructing young minds in reading, writing, and ciphering (arithmetic).

What's clear about the early American educational institution is that it used the Bible as a textbook and the instruction, whether at home or in a more formal setting, was focused on Christian living and all that implies.

Early-American Family

Early American family life was especially challenging, a partnership for survival and the center of education and religious training for the next generations. Of course, the family was the original order of creation, the union of one man and one woman blessed with children.

Colonialists understood the concept of family, which comes from the book of Genesis. That book states that God first created first Adam (a man) to exercise dominion over all of creation, and then He made Eve (a woman) as the man's "suitable helper" (Genesis 2:18, 20, ESV). The Scripture commands: "Therefore a man shall leave his father and his mother and hold fast to his wife, and they shall become one flesh" (Genesis 2:24, ESV). This is God's formula for the natural family, whereby the phrase "become one flesh" refers both to the establishment of one new family and to the sexual union that leads to procreation of offspring, which fulfills God's command to "be fruitful and multiply and fill the earth and subdue it and have dominion" over all creatures (Genesis 1:28, ESV).

The colonial family was modeled on the first family (Adam and Eve) and, like in other nations, was the New World's critical social unit, a building block of that early society. Most important, family is God's creation to supply mankind's basic needs (survival)—food, water, shelter, and much more.

The colonial family took God's mandate seriously. One man and one woman came together in a covenant, a sacred bond instituted by and publicly entered before God. They understood vital, God-given principles about that relationship.

Christian marriage was permanent, because it was established by God (Matthew 19:6; Mark 10:9). For the colonialist, it represented a serious commitment that shouldn't be made lightly, and it involved a solemn promise before God.

For the Christian, colonial marriage was uniting a man and a woman in a "one-flesh" union (Genesis 2:23–25). Marriage involves leaving one's family and "being united" to one's spouse, thus forming a new family unit.

Marriage was also an exclusive relationship. For the colonist, that meant no other human relationship must impede the marriage commitment.

It was inside the covenant-marriage relationship that God blessed colonists with children, whom they taught morals, manners, and discipline. Naturally, the parents focused on surviving. In colonial America, there was no room for slackers and, as John Smith (1580–1631), the early colonial governor of Jamestown, decreed in the Virginia colony, "He who does not work, will not eat."[132] Everyone understood they had to work to survive—no exceptions.[133]

Surviving in the colonies was hard, and family life as a result was relatively unstable. As Smith said, the general premise was that everyone, male and female, young and old, had to work. Work sustained the family in the bleak environments of the early colonies.

Survival also meant a communal approach to society, whereby the community had the right to exercise control over individuals to promote the common interest. That also meant neighbors who were most certainly fellow church members helped one another on big chores like building barns—and, of course, everyone watched out for all the children.

The church played an important role for colonial families, and not just on Sundays. For example, in Congregationalist New England, "selectmen" oversaw perhaps a dozen families and would remove children from "unfit" parents as well as ensure that fathers properly managed (cared for) their families.[134]

Tough colonial life took its toll on most families, who too often ended up being blended. Specifically, colonial family composition varied widely because three children in ten died before reaching adulthood; because of the loss of at least one parent, stepfamilies were quite common.[135]

Colonial America was very much a patriarchal society, a Bible precept tracking back to Genesis. The father was invested with patriarchal authority, which meant he was the primary disciplinarian and set the standard for the family members by leading daily prayer and devotions, which too often ended up being delegated to the mother because of outside-of-home work demands.[136]

Colonial fathers also trained male children to acquire the family business or trade, and daughters relied on their fathers to play a role in finding appropriate suitors and their consent to marriage.[137]

Although the father was the family head, especially in New England, religious instruction often fell to the mother. Her daily duty was to bring the children up to be good Christians, and she often taught them to read so they could study the Bible for themselves.[138]

Understandably, the wife was an essential component of the nuclear colonial family, and without a strong woman, a family might not survive. It was rather common that when a husband died, suitors would appear with almost haste to bid for the services of the new widow through marriage.[139]

Colonial families were mostly Christian and traditional—married men and women with children. They performed the necessary roles outlined in the Bible and did their best to survive with the help of their local church and broader community, which were often the same people.

Early-American Christian Church

America's relationship with Christianity is both inspiring and formative, which tracks to the larger history of the Western world. The Crusades of the Middle Ages (eleventh to thirteenth centuries) contributed in part to the forces that led to the Protestant Reformation, which then nurtured the thinking that drove many Christian people to the New World.

The historic context is necessary to understand just how the Protestant Reformation came to the home of many of the former American colonists. We begin with the event that launched the movement.

The Protestant Reformation or the European Reformation, which began with Martin Luther (1483–1546), a German professor of theology, composer, priest, and monk, was the single most important European event for the colonies in modern times. Luther drafted the Ninety-Five Theses or Disputation on the Power of Indulgences, which were propositions for debate about the question of indulgences and publicly posted on the door of the Castle Church in Wittenberg, Germany, on October 31, 1517. That act led to a shattering conflict between the Roman Catholic Church and various Protestant groups that was played out on numerous European battlefields.[140]

The initial Reformation movement in Germany quickly spread to Switzerland, where other reformers arose, such as John Calvin in Geneva. Meanwhile, Western Christianity adopted different confessions to include the formation of the Church of England, the Anglican Communion.

That transformation began with the decision of England's King Henry VIII (1491–1547) to rebuke Martin Luther for issuing the list of grievances against the Catholic Church. For that public rebuke, Catholic Pope Leo X rewarded Henry the title of *fidei defensor*, or Defender of the Faith.[141]

A few years later, Henry wanted to end his first marriage because his wife, Catherine of Aragon, failed to provide him a male heir. Meanwhile, one of Catherine's ladies-in-waiting, Anne Boleyn, became the king's mistress. Henry asked Catholic Pope Clement VII to grant a divorce, but the pope refused the divorce because Henry's wife (Catherine) was the niece to King Charles V of Spain, the Holy Roman Emperor.[142]

Henry, who was evidently eager to marry Anne, decided to break with the Roman Catholic Church over the pope's divorce denial. He quickly appointed a Protestant advisor, Thomas Cranmer, as the Archbishop of Canterbury, who then granted Henry the divorce. Soon thereafter, the heavily pregnant Anne was crowned queen of England.[143]

The British Parliament then passed the Act of Supremacy in 1534, which officially made the break with the Catholic Church and named Henry the Supreme Head of the Church of England, thus establishing the church-state relationship. At the same time, the new Protestant Queen Anne helped England adopt "some of the lessons of the continental Reformation," including a translation of the Bible into English. England also used the opportunity to seize the Catholic Church's vast property, what was called at the time "the greatest redistribution of property in England since the Norman Conquest in 1066."[144]

Queen Anne failed to give Henry the desired son, although she gave birth to a daughter, the future Queen Elizabeth I. Meanwhile, as before, Henry fell for another lady-in-waiting, Jane Seymour, who conspired with Henry to engineer charges against Anne, who was then executed.

In 1537, Jane gave birth to Henry's first male heir, who became King Edward VI. The balance of Henry's life was marked by infighting among his advisors for influence, who were able to introduce a radical reformation of Protestant ideas in the previously all-Catholic England. However, the break led most English Protestants back to the Bible as the basis of their faith.

King Henry's break with the Roman Catholic Church was well received by the British people. They came to understand that the Catholic pope used them primarily as a source of money. Believers had to pay the church to marry, to have a child baptized, to bury a loved one, and more. These church fees made the Catholic Church wealthy, while most British citizens were poor.[145]

King Edward VI assumed the throne upon his father's death, and was replaced upon his death six years later by his Catholic half-sister, Queen Mary (Tudor) I ("Bloody Mary"), a staunch Catholic who persecuted Protestants and reversed both Henry's and Edward's many Protestant reforms. But it would be up to Anne Boleyn's daughter, Queen Elizabeth I, who followed Mary and ruled for a half century to complete the English Reformation King Henry VIII began.

The British crown's many Protestant reforms directly impacted the colonization of America, most notably the English Puritans and Pilgrims who escaped intolerable conditions thanks to the British monarch's church-state tyranny against those with contrary beliefs.

It was the immigration of mostly the Puritans to the New World that set the stage for many of the new American republic's traditions and ideals. Their congregational religion contributed to the colonies' early political structure, vis-à-vis their "New England town meeting," which remains a form of direct democracy even today.

The New England town meeting concept, whose origins were almost wholly religious in nature, had a similar parallel in the southern colonies, where the British Anglican church was dominant and part of the civic government's structure, as it was in England. It was under Anglican authority, especially at first in Virginia, where the county, or parish, was both the structure of church and political rule. That's the origin of county government that continues to be the norm in much of the south even today.

Other Christian groups brought to the New World their Christian attitudes, though doctrines differed. Catholics who settled Maryland passed laws of religious toleration. By contrast, the Virginia Anglicans brought with them the British idea of a state-church marriage that required Virginians to pay parish taxes.

One thing most of the Christian-based, New World refugees agreed upon was to leave religious-based conflicts in Europe. They knew first-hand the tragic consequences provoked by the Protestant Reformation, such as the Thirty Years War, the English Civil War, and numerous fights between Catholics and Protestants in France. Most of them also wanted to leave behind the state-church relationship common among European nations.

Some colonists called attention to the problem of civil-church relations, however. For example, Roger Williams, a dissenter from the New England Puritans, accused them of planting in the colony an unhealthy civil-church relationship that resulted in the failure to tolerate people of different faiths. Williams argued that the state had no right to dictate religious practice to its citizens. Of course, it would be many years before Puritan descendants disestablished the Congregational church from its tight relationship with civil government.

Gradually over many years, a sense of religious harmony emerged in the colonies, and by the time of the American Revolution (1775–1783), most colonists agreed they wanted a country free of religious strife and a clean break between civil and church government. Meanwhile, Christianity in the New World got a wake-up call: the Great Awakening.

The Great Awakening was a seminal event for colonial America. That event, which took place in the early to mid 1700s, was an era of spiritual revival—an ascension in religious fervor whereby itinerant preachers urged colonialists to return to faith in God. During this era, figures on church attendance and formation rose precipitously. Specifically, between 1700 and 1740, an estimated 80 percent of colonists attended Christian services. It was toward the midcentury that the Great Awakening finally swept from New England to the southern colonies.[146]

The Awakening included evangelicalism, the belief that true knowledge of God comes about through the "new birth," which happened thanks to the preaching of the Word of God. The Awakening pitted the

Baptists and Methodists—the evangelicals—against the opponents of the Awakening, the more High-Church Christians such as the Anglicans and Catholics. For the High-Church Christians, conversion was the public association with the Church as opposed to a "new birth" by the believer.

The Great Awakening came to be called a general outpouring of the spirit that bathed the colonies. Revivals sprang up featuring preachers like George Whitefield, who led many to a "new birth." Through the middle 1740s, the Great Awakening split the Congregationalists and the Presbyterians into supporters called "New Lights" and "New Sides" versus "Old Lights" and "Old Sides."[147]

Many of the New England "New Lights" became Baptists and the "New Sides" became Presbyterians, who then carried the Great Awakening into the southern colonies, which led to revivals that lasted well into the nineteenth century.[148]

Whitefield (1714–1770) had been ordained in the Church of England (Anglican), which he constantly opposed for a variety of mostly theological reasons. He became a preaching sensation in England, drawing large crowds. Then, in 1738, he traveled to the American colonies, where he quickly gained popularity preaching during the height of the Great Awakening. One such revival meeting in Boston drew a reported thirty thousand souls.[149]

Whitefield explained the "new birth," as prescribed by Christ for Nicodemus (John 3:1–8), as the necessary conversion experience leading to the Christian life. Whitefield admitted, "How this glorious change is wrought in the soul cannot easily be explained."[150]

Jonathan Edwards (1703–1758) was an early American preacher during the Great Awakening. He started his Congregationalist ministry in Northampton, Massachusetts, and then traveled widely, becoming not just an effective evangelical preacher but also the principal intellectual interpreter of the American Awakening.[151] It was during the Great Awakening that Edwards delivered the most famous sermon in American history, "Sinners in the Hands of an Angry God."[152]

The religious fervor associated with this movement provided impetus to our founders just prior to the American Revolution. As they plotted the colonies' freedom from the British Crown, they grasped the fixed view that the new nation must avoid the divisive role religion played in sixteenth- and seventeenth-century Europe.

George Mason made that issue clear in drafting the Virginia Bill of Rights, which stated that "all men are equally entitled to the free exercise of religion, according to the dictates of conscience."[153] However, Mason's desire wasn't as universal as some wanted, except in colonies such as Pennsylvania, which already at the time celebrated religious diversity.

Mason's concern became more pressing, thanks to British actions in the 1760s and 1770s. At that time, the British increased their efforts to dominate the American colonies, and that included employing the oppressive arm of the Crown's state Church, the Anglican Church.

Years later, in 1815, founder John Adams reflected on that situation in a letter to Dr. Jedidiah Morse. Adams explained the oppressive threat presented by the Crown's Church proxy, which fanned the colonial calls for revolution. Adams called out the "passive obedience and non-resistance, in the most unqualified and unlimited sense, were [the church's] avowed principles in government, and the power of the church to decree rites and ceremonies, and the authority of the church in controversies of faith, were explicitly avowed."[154]

The British Crown's overreach using the Anglican Church cemented for colonial leaders like Adams, Madison, and Jefferson the necessity for the new republic to avoid the use of the civil government's employment of religion for political purposes.

Meanwhile, Europe's Enlightenment Era (1715–1789), also known as the Age of Reason, infected colonial American thinking as well. It was a period when philosophers tried to find a path to the perfection of human society, which impacted all of mankind. The Germans called the period *Aufklärung*, a "clearing up," which is what man tried to achieve.

American political leaders such as Thomas Jefferson, Benjamin Franklin, James Otis, and John Adams were significantly influenced by

Enlightenment thinking, the *Aufklärung*. Specifically, it provided the philosophical basis for the American Revolution, beginning with the writings of philosopher John Locke, who argued that revolution in some circumstances is necessary.

The American Revolution became more than a protest against British tyranny; it also became a blueprint for a modern enlightened concept for democratic society. For example, the views expressed in our Declaration of Independence and Constitution are a direct result of the enlightened thinking at the time and created a legacy that avoids mixing Christianity with government.

The Christian church was ever powerful throughout the colonial period and up to and through the formulation of the new republic, the United States. It influenced every aspect of the young American republic's life to include the economic.

Early-American Economy

Early America's economic success is directly attributable to Christianity, specifically, the Protestant work ethic and capitalism. However, let's begin this section with a definition of terms and then consider an overview of early American economic history.

What is an economy? The term comes from the Greek οἶκος ("household") and νέμομαι ("manage") and is the result of the production, distribution or trade, and consumption of goods and services by different agents that come together within the context of culture, values, education, technology, history, social and political structures, legal systems, geography, and the availability of natural resources. Economic agents can be individuals, businesses, organizations, or governments with which we have "economic transactions" by agreeing to the value or price of goods or services, usually in terms of currency.

American colonialists operated within an economic capitalist system whereby the means of production were privately owned and success was gauged by competition on the free market. A capitalist economy is driven by the accumulation of capital—wealth in the form of money or other assets owned by a person or organization.

Early Americans became capitalists by virtue of the fact that, when they arrived, their first order of business was survival. They reached the New World with little more than the shirts on their backs and the determination to make a new life out of America's resources and opportunities. Thus, these settlers became, out of necessity, this nation's first entrepreneurs—true risk takers who blossomed in an unconstrained, fresh, capitalist setting.

Their survival instincts helped them find the necessities of life. Their initial hard work at the individual family level produced light sources (candles) and soaps, preserved food for the winters, and made their own clothing. Although 90 percent of early colonists' efforts were agriculturally focused, many quickly diversified their work to produce goods for export.

The New World gave the colonists many natural riches for exploitation, which led to a variety of trades. Those early Americans quickly determined that the Eastern Seaboard lands were not uniformly productive for agriculture. That resulted in the colonies' evolution into producing a variety of products.

In New England, the colonists dealt with rocky soil and often harsh winter weather, which made large-scale farming less viable. That's why the New England colonists turned to what they had—plentiful forests to harvest lumber for shipbuilding. In turn, their proximity to the Atlantic Ocean gave them access for their vessels to fishing, whaling, and commerce.

Soon, the New England colonists were able to profit from the combination of shipbuilding and ready access to the Atlantic Ocean using triangular trade, the movement of merchandise between New England, the West Indies, and England. The colonists shipped fish, grain, and lumber to the West Indies, where those commodities were exchanged for sugar and molasses, then shipped to Britain. There, those products were used to purchase manufactured goods, which were then taken back to America for sale.

That triangular trade arrangement eventually had an immoral twist, however. Often, colonial ships delivered rum to West Africa in trade for slaves, who were then shipped to the West Indies and in time to the colonies, especially the big plantations in the South.[155]

The middle colonies enjoyed a more favorable climate and fertile ground for agriculture. That region came to be called the "bread colonies" because of their ability to produce surplus grain (wheat, corn, and oats), which was then exported to England.

The southern colonies produced pitch and tar from their plentiful forests, vital ingredients for shipbuilding in New England. Those colonies also enjoyed favorable conditions for agriculture; indigo, rice, and tobacco were produced for export to England in exchange for manufactured goods. Also, partly because tobacco production tended to quickly exhaust the soil in Virginia and the Carolinas, acquiring new and larger lots of land became necessary, giving rise to large plantations and creating the demand that encouraged the slave trade.[156]

By the late eighteenth century, the colonies were tired of the economic exploitation at the hands of the British government. They were quite ready economically and politically for self-government.

What made the British colonies economically successful? The answer may surprise some readers: The Catholic Church and the Protestant Reformation.

Capitalism blossomed in colonial America, but its origin dates back to the Middle Ages. The Roman Catholic Church created the capitalist economic system. Historian Randall Collins said, "The Middle Ages experienced the key institutional revolution, that the basis of capitalism was laid then rather than later, and that at its heart was the organization of the Catholic Church itself."[157]

What was that groundwork? In the Middle Ages, the Catholic Church owned a third of all the land in Europe. To govern that land, it established law that provided administrative bureaucracies of arbitrators, jurists, negotiators, and judges to oversee those holdings, known as "canon law Latin."[158] That law provided the predictable economic activity that made capitalism work.

The English colonies were the perfect petri dish for a capitalist economy to blossom. Historian Carl Degler said, "The capitalists arrived in the first ships." They brought the entrepreneurial spirit, and soon British investors poured money into chartered companies in the colonies to gain a healthy return. Capitalism flourished in America.

The colonists welcomed the investments first for survival reasons, then to improve the quality of their lives. The ingredients for success in America included endless natural resources, natural harbors, broad rivers, productive land, and the colonists' Protestant work ethic.

The Protestant work ethic is attributed to the Calvinist work ethic, which came to America with the Puritans, Pilgrims, and Presbyterians, who emphasized hard work, discipline, and frugality in line with the values espoused by their faith.

Let's backtrack to better understand the origin of the Protestant work ethic. It traces back the Protestant Reformation and the Catholic Church's assurance of salvation to individuals who accepted the sacraments and submitted to clerical authority. Those assurances were discounted by the Protestant reformers, which left Protestant Christians with difficulty adopting to the new view of salvation.

Switzerland's John Calvin helped fill that salvation vacuum with his doctrine of predestination, which taught that, from the beginning, God chose some, not all, for salvation and eternity in Heaven. The individual's inability to chart his or her own salvation presented a difficulty for the reformers, however. The lack of self-confidence in one's salvation was the issue.

Calvin suggested that worldly success could provide assurance of salvation, and hard work and prosperity were the key, thus the Protestant work ethic was born. Working hard and being frugal became the motivation for Christian groups like the Puritans and Presbyterians, which blossomed in a capitalist economic system where the entrepreneur was king.

Early-twentieth-century German sociologist Max Weber studied the Protestant work ethic and wrote about it in *The Protestant Ethic and The Spirit of Capitalism*. He explained that the Calvinist response to the Protestants' yearning for assurance of salvation was hard work, writing:

> But in the course of its development Calvinism added something positive to this, the idea of the necessity of proving one's faith in worldly activity. Therein it gave broader groups of religiously inclined people a positive incentive to asceticism. By founding its ethic in the doctrine of predestination, it substituted for the spiritual aristocracy of monks outside of and above the world the spiritual aristocracy of the predestined saints of God within the world.[159]

Evidently, Weber also believed the Protestant work ethic included the concept of a job as a "calling," a concept that eventually became ingrained in America's character. He wrote:

> One's duty in a calling, is what is most characteristic of the social ethic of capitalistic culture, and is in a sense the fundamental basis of it. It is an obligation which the individual is supposed to feel and does feel towards the content of his professional activity, no matter in what it consists, in particular no matter whether it appears on the surface as a utilization of his personal powers. Or only of his material possessions (as capital).[160]

Others came along to confirm Weber's view of the Protestant work ethic. A paper by a Dutch economist states:

> Test[s] the relation between Protestantism and work attitudes using a novel method, operationalizing work ethic as the effect of unemployment on individuals' subjective well-being. Analyzing a sample of 150,000 individuals from 82 societies, we find

strong support for a Protestant work ethic: unemployment hurts Protestants more and hurts more in Protestant societies. Whilst the results shed new light on the Protestant work ethic debate, the method has wider applicability in the analysis of attitudinal differences.[161]

The Protestant work ethic motivated many Christian colonists to seek success in their secular capitalist world to please God. They came to view that not working was the same as failing to glorify God. Also, that ethic forbade wasteful use of hard-earned money on luxuries, a sin for them.

The Protestant work ethic came to America due to Calvinist views of predestination, which in time became embedded in much of our culture. Thanks to the combination of that work ethic with the Catholic-inspired capitalistic economic model, the new America republic became the economic envy of the world.

Conclusion

This chapter explores the particulars of America's Christian building blocks: principles, values, and institutions. We established that Christian principles are the very heart of our founding principles, which gave rise to Christian values that formed America's unique character and her government (Constitution). Finally, we tracked through five key American institutions to demonstrate how they became undeniably Christianized to establish a prosperous America.

The next section will examine how the aforementioned principles, values, and institutions have come under assault from a variety of sources and, if successful, they could well destroy this Christian nation.

Section II

EVIDENCE OF MORAL DECAY AND ANTI-CHRISTIAN ATTACKS

America is on a collision course rapidly approaching a moral tipping point, abandoning the baked-in Christian principles and values that made this a Christian nation.

We established in the previous section that our founders from the earliest colonial times embraced principles that established America's Christian foundation. That Christian foundation influenced the broader society and especially the key institutions: government, education, family, churches, and economy. However, over the past two and a half centuries, that Christian foundation has begun to erode—and, unless dramatic changes happen soon, America will continue down a course that leads to moral collapse much like other empires in history.

Today we are rapidly approaching that moral tipping point due to a real schism between two sides that disagree over the most basic moral issues facing mankind. Each side seeks to define every aspect of life in diametrically different ways.

The anti-Christian, evil forces (addressed in section III of this book) are taking America down a rancid path to the moral cliff, not unlike the circumstances that led this nation to civil war in 1861. At that time, one side defended the evil institution of slavery, which fueled their political and economic power. Quoting the Bible (Mark 3:25 and Luke 11:14 and following), President Abraham Lincoln addressed that division:

A house divided against itself, cannot stand. I believe this government cannot endure, permanently, half slave and half free. I do not expect the Union to be dissolved—I do not expect the house to fall—but I do expect it will cease to be divided.[162]

America did reunite after the Civil War (1861–1865) but not before hundreds of thousands of mostly soldiers died in battle and untold wealth was expended on a four-year-long war that tore this nation apart. The question before America today is: Will the current moral crisis dividing this country lead to another war? We cannot continue to have one side celebrating pure evil while the other tenaciously clings to the remnants of our diminished Christian heritage. Something must give!

The anti-Christian evil revisionists celebrate what God in His Word condemns: abortion, homosexuality, breakdown of the family, out-of-control government, evil-spewing education, and bankrupt religious communities. Meanwhile, much of Christian America remained silent as evil altered, perhaps forever, the founding fathers' intention for this nation.

The coming American "civil war" isn't the fault of any particular politician or political party. No, this tipping point perhaps about to push this former Christian America over the moral cliff embraces so many radical things today: beliefs that a man is a woman; right is wrong; borders are open doors; terrorists are civil rights groups; abortion is sacred; big government is a replacement for God; education is about reprogramming our children to serve big social change; the economy is to grow big government dependence; freedom of speech is reserved for the few; and others.

In this section of five chapters, I will explore just how far we are off course and close to the moral tipping point, crossing into a permanent, post-Christian America. I will answer the following question in each chapter: How far have we fallen, and what are the consequences for America's key institutions? Below is a brief overview of each chapter.

Chapter 3 demonstrates how the institution of government abandoned our founders' minimalist approach and has grown to become overbearing, spewing anti-Christian policies. It seeks to control every aspect of our lives and make us all dependent upon government's every whim.

Chapter 4 addresses the American educational institution—kindergarten to college—which has mostly abandoned its original calling to build citizens of character who embrace time-tested biblical values. The consequences of a bankrupted educational system are a twisted focus on teaching "social justice," environmentalism, and dysfunctional ideas of sex rather than useful subjects to help American youth become productive adults in a highly competitive world.

Chapter 5 shows just how evil forces have redefined the bedrock of America, the family. Edward Gibbon, the eighteenth-century author of the *History of the Decline and Fall of the Roman Empire*, said Rome fell because of the breakdown of the family. Today, American families are in crisis as well. Half of American children are born to an unmarried mother, and almost half live without a father in the home. The consequences of being born and raised by a single parent is a predictor of serious outcomes: incarceration, murder, rape, dropping out of school, suicide, and running away.

Chapter 6 shows the state of the Christian church in America, once the source of stability that dominated all private and public lives. Today less than half of Millennials (ages eighteen to thirty-five) consider themselves Christian, compared with 84 percent in the mid '70s. America is becoming less Christian and less religiously observant than at any point since the Pilgrims arrived in the New World four hundred-plus years ago.[163]

Chapter 7 considers how the institution of the American economy was taken captive by evil forces that are incredibly anti-Christian and anti-capitalist. They are pushing our culture down a collision course that, unless quickly changed, will cross over the moral tipping point.

These chapters provide significant evidence of America's approach to the moral tipping point, which was explained by the Old Testament prophet Micah. In Micah chapter 7, the prophet identified markers, signs that a country was in moral decline. Those markers are self-evident today in America and the issues addressed in this section: man abandons God; violence increases; corruption is evident among government and business leaders; trust is broken within society; and the institution of the family fails.

Micah's words ring loudly today. Moral implosion is almost here, and our present collision course is leading America to a moral tipping point.

CHAPTER THREE

Government Abandoned Founders' Prescription and Became Anti-Christian

THE PURPOSE OF the United States government is found in the Preamble of its Constitution: To "establish justice, ensure domestic tranquility, provide for the common defense, promote the general welfare, and secure the blessings of liberty to ourselves and our posterity." Unfortunately, some in the recent past and even today believe that government's purpose includes the promotion of anti-Christian policies and messages.

Founder James Madison warned that "men are not angels"; rather, they live in "a state of nature, where the weaker individual is not secured against the violence of the stronger." Thus, our government seeks to regulate men's behavior to fulfill the purpose outlined in the Preamble, which for our founders never included the recent flurry of anti-Christian actions hosted by government agents.[164]

An indicator of our founders' concern that some might use government's power to abuse citizens is evidence that they distrusted a strong central government, a concern voiced especially among the anti-federalists. That's why our Constitution includes a set of checks and balances to protect the rights of citizens—including the right of conscience and faith.

This framework and philosophy of governing is where the American government started in the late eighteenth century, but it changed over the coming years. Our forefathers without exception embraced Thomas Jefferson's warning to George Washington, as cited in the last chapter, that "to take a single step beyond the boundaries [of the Constitution]...is to take possession of a boundless field of power."[165] James Madison also cautioned that government must "keep close to our chartered authorities."[166]

Further, one of the tenets of our foundation was that government would maintain a healthy respect for religion and not interfere with its practice. Unfortunately, over the last couple of decades, especially during the Obama administration, some officials exercising federal government powers—all three branches—have increasingly demonstrated animosity, even hostility toward Christians.

The evidence that government hostility strayed beyond the authority and boundaries established by our founders is clearly realized in the form of well-documented, anti-Christian actions and words. Our federal government, as well as some state and local governments, has demonstrated profoundly anti-Christian views and actions, a perspective shared by the nation's distinguished attorney general, William Barr.

On October 11, 2019, Attorney General Barr spoke to the law school and de Nicola Center for Ethics and Culture at the University of Notre Dame in South Bend, Indiana. In that address, Barr acknowledged what most alert American Christians already know: Anti-Christian secularists are the enemy of American democracy, and they are using the levers of government to target Christians at every turn.[167]

General Barr said "secularists" are engaged in an "unremitting assault on religion and traditional values." For the attorney general, there is an equivalence between morality and religion, and between religion and Christianity. He clearly meant that "secularists" are targeting Christians.[168]

General Barr even went as far as to explain what I stated in chapter 1 about the founders' intent regarding the establishment of religion. He indicated that there is a plausible reading of the "nonestablishment" clause of the First Amendment to the Constitution, which he suggested wasn't an anti-religion provision, but the founders deferred such issues for states to legislate upon, since several states still had established religions at the founding. Then Barr explained that our founders intended America to always be a religious (Christian) nation by citing founder John Adams, who said: "Our constitution was made only for a moral and religious people; it is wholly inadequate for the government of any other."[169]

Mr. Barr concluded his speech with a promise to the Christian audience:

> As long as I am attorney general, the Department of Justice will be at the forefront of [the] fight for the most cherished of our liberties: the freedom to live according to our faith.[170]

That's a comforting promise from the nation's chief law enforcement officer. Unfortunately, those who came before him were abusive of Christians, and likely, unless things radically change, those who follow Mr. Barr will once again be anti-Christian and won't shy away from using the levers of the federal government, as well as of state and local governments, to target Christians.

Consider the federal government's record of anti-Christian actions, as evidenced by recent activities by the three branches: legislative, judicial, and executive.

Anti-Christian Legislative Branch

Some in Congress, both chambers, are using their positions to target Christians. Senate confirmations are a favorite venue for leftist, progressive, anti-Christian senators to take aim at Christian nominees seeking judicial and administration appointments.

In June 2017, socialist Senator Bernie Sanders from Vermont clashed with Russell Vought, President Trump's nominee to serve as deputy director of the Office of Management and Budget. Evidently, Vought, a Christian, wrote a blog regarding Islam that multiple Muslim groups considered Islamophobic. Specifically, Mr. Vought wrote in defense of Wheaton College's statement of faith about the centrality of Jesus Christ for salvation: "Muslims do not simply have a deficient theology. They do not know God because they have rejected Jesus Christ his Son, and they stand condemned."[171]

Evidently, the American Civil Liberties Union found Vought's reference to Muslims and shared it with Senator Sanders, who then grilled Vought at his nomination hearing. "In my view, the statement made by Mr. Vought is indefensible, it is hateful, it is Islamophobic, and it is an insult to over a billion Muslims throughout the world," said Sanders. The senator then concluded: "This country, since its inception, has struggled, sometimes with great pain, to overcome discrimination of all forms...we must not go backwards."[172]

Senator Sanders said after his exchange with Mr. Vought: "I would simply say, Mr. Chairman, that this nominee is really not someone who is what this country is supposed to be about."[173]

At the same nomination hearing, Maryland's Senator Christopher Van Hollen Jr. (a Democrat) read an excerpt from an article written by Mr. Vought, and then said:

> I think it is irrefutable that these kinds of comments suggest to a whole lot of Americans that, number one...you are condemning people of all faiths. I'm a Christian, but part of being a Christian in my view is recognizing that there are lots of ways that people can pursue their God.... It's your comments that suggest a violation of the public trust in what will be a very important position.[174]

Russell Moore, the Ethics and Religious Liberty Commission president, said of Senator Sanders' statements about Vought:

[His] comments are breathtakingly audacious and shockingly ignorant—both of the Constitution and of basic Christian doctrine. Even if one were to excuse Senator Sanders for not realizing that all Christians of every age have insisted that faith in Jesus Christ is the only pathway to salvation, it is inconceivable that Senator Sanders would cite religious beliefs as disqualifying an individual for public office in defiance of the United States Constitution. No religious test shall ever be required of those seeking public office. While no one expects Senator Sanders to be a theologian, we should expect far more from an elected official who has taken an oath to support and defend the Constitution.[175]

Unfortunately, many congressional Democrats believe there is a "religious test" for service in the federal government and, for the most part, anyone professing orthodox Christian views isn't qualified.

Every reader should recall the anti-Christian attacks on a Trump nominee in October 2018, when Judge Brett Kavanaugh was slandered by the Democrat senators on the Senate Judiciary Committee. He was viciously accused of numerous serious improprieties (more than thirty years prior), and his nomination was almost derailed. There was also the case of Notre Dame law professor Amy Coney Barrett, who was attacked by California Democrat Senator Diane Feinstein, who declared that the Christian "dogma lives loudly within you, and that's a concern." Both Kavanaugh and Barrett were eventually confirmed for their judicial positions in spite of the rancid attacks on their Christian faith.[176]

Other judges were attacked for their association with Christian organizations. Trump judicial nominee Judge Brian C. Buescher was attacked by Democrat senators Kamala Harris (California) and Mazie Hirono (Hawaii) for his membership in the 136-year old Catholic service organization, the Knights of Columbus, which disapproves of abortion on demand and favors biblical marriage.[177]

Matthew Continetti wrote for the *Washington Free Beacon* about other examples of anti-Christian views expressed in hearings by US senators:

> My concern is the anti-Catholic sentiment manifest in the Democratic Party. Last March, Feinstein demanded to know if Michael Scudder, now confirmed to the Seventh Circuit, worked with his parish "to establish a residential crisis pregnancy center." Last May, Senator Sheldon Whitehouse of Rhode Island asked Peter J. Phipps, now confirmed as a district court judge, about the Knights [of Columbus]. Last October, Feinstein, Harris, and three other Democrats wanted to know about the relationship between Fourth Circuit nominee Allison Jones Rushing and the Alliance Defending Freedom, a Christian nonprofit that supports religious liberty. Last November, Feinstein asked Third Circuit nominee Paul Matey, "If confirmed, will you recuse yourself from all cases in which the Knights of Columbus have taken a position?"[178]

Senate Democrats even opposed Trump nominees for administration positions who happen to self-identify as Christians. For example, Mike Pompeo's nomination to become the secretary of state was mostly along party lines (57–42) and in part because of his Christian faith. Mr. Pompeo, a Presbyterian, was "brought to Jesus Christ" during the time as a cadet at the United States Military Academy. Later, he served as a member of Eastminster Presbyterian Church in Wichita, Kansas, where he served as a deacon and taught Sunday School. He believes what the Bible says about life, sex, and marriage.[179]

High-profile administration officials like Secretary Pompeo are targeted by the left when they express their Christian beliefs even when at a Christian counseling conference in Nashville, Tennessee. At that October 2019 event, Pompeo spoke about being a Christian leader and said he drew on the "wisdom of God" to help him "be a force for good in the life of human beings."[180]

Predictably, Pompeo was criticized for "advancement of Christian leadership" because his Nashville speech, like all other speeches, was posted on the State Department's homepage. The American Humanist Association spokesperson Sarah Henry said in a statement:

> While today may be a great day to be a Christian nationalist, it's a terrible day to be a person who cares deeply about the United States of America, religious plurality and diversity, or true religious freedom.[181]

The left's congressional membership's hatred extends to God in general. Michigan's Congresswoman Rashida Tlaib "is representative of the Democratic Party's gradual march beyond the embrace of candidates and officials who criticize Israeli policy or its current government to a much uglier place in politics." Ms. Tlaib supports a "one-state solution" to the Israeli-Palestinian conflict, as well as the "boycott, divestment, sanctions" (BDS) movement against Israel, which is based on the premise that Israel is a racist apartheid state. But, of course, the real agenda of BDS is the demise of Israel.[182]

Princeton Professor Robert P. George warns that most congressional Democrats will turn on Israel. Why? Because Israel's existence is evidence that the God of the Bible is real, and most of these progressives hate God and—by association—Christians.[183]

The problem for anti-Christian Democrats is that Christians point people to the truth. The truth stings, such as what a church in California declared about a homosexual celebrity: "Bruce Jenner is still a man. Homosexuality is still a sin. The culture may change, the Bible does not."[184]

There are numerous examples of members of Congress using their perch on high-profile committees to target Christian nominees solely because of their Christian faith. Although most of those nominees were eventually confirmed, what's clear is that there may soon come a time when being Christian will become a disqualifier for service in our courts and the federal government. The Christian litmus test will disqualify many for future government service. That runs contrary to our founders' intent and will be a sad day for America.

Anti-Christian Judicial Branch

The political left has a long history of using the courts to legislate and attack its ideological opponents. This is especially true regarding their attacks on Christians and confirms why it matters whom a president nominates to our judicial branch.

The placement of strict constitutionalists on the Supreme Court is critical to Christian America. Specifically, consider that from the 1960s to recently, liberal and mostly anti-Christian individuals argued before the high court that the tyranny of the majority (Christians at that time) must not define the lives of secular citizens. The result of such arguments were court decisions that favored the rights of the non-Christian minority. The result of those decisions has been to define the public place of all religions in this country.

Fortunately, and because of President Trump's efforts to fill our judicial branch with stricter constructionist jurists, the Christians' lot is changing, though perhaps only momentarily. Pro-Christian attorneys are arguing in federal courts demanding minority protection under the Constitution, a twist from past majority-related approaches, and the judges and justices are favoring their arguments.

Three cases that recently made their way to the Supreme Court illustrate the new distortion in the church-versus-secularists' arguments regarding the alleged infringement of the First Amendment, the freedom of religion provision in the Constitution. In each case, the high court overruled the lower courts' decisions regarding the secularists' claims.

The first case involved the state of Missouri refusing to fund the resurfacing of a daycare center's playground solely because the center was run by a religious institution (a Lutheran church), even though the center served an impoverished community and met the state's objective criteria. Liberal justices Ruth Ginsburg and Sonia Sotomayor agreed with the lower court's ruling that government must avoid intermingling with religious organizations.[185]

Fortunately, the high court's majority disagreed with the dissent. They reasoned that Thomas Jefferson's "wall of separation" never meant that all government programs must remain exclusively secular. The majority based their judgment on the second provision of the First Amendment, the Free Exercise Clause, which protects religious practice.

The high court's majority found that treating a church daycare differently than a secular daycare facility was unconstitutional discrimination. Even liberal Justice Stephen Breyer favored the majority opinion, stating that we must consider "the basic purposes that the Religion Clauses were meant to serve: assuring religious liberty and tolerance for all, avoiding religiously based social conflict, and maintaining that separation of church and state that allows each to flourish in its separate sphere."[186]

The second case involved a homosexual couple that asked a bakery for a custom cake for their wedding. The owner of Masterpiece Cakeshop in Lakewood, Colorado, declined to make a cake for a homosexual wedding because it violated his religious convictions.[187]

The bakery owner said: "We would close down the bakery before we compromised our beliefs."[188]

The Colorado Civil Rights Commission sanctioned the baker for violating the state's anti-discrimination laws. That decision on appeal was reversed by the high court as a "clear and impermissible hostility" toward the baker's religious beliefs.[189]

At issue here was not the rights of the homosexual couple, but the baker's religious rights. Justice Anthony Kennedy said "hostility" was the key word in the ruling. Colorado's "hostility was inconsistent with the First Amendment's guarantee that our laws be applied in a manner that is neutral toward religion."[190]

The third case involved a dispute about a Christian cross on public property. The Bladensburg Peace Cross was set in a highway median outside of Washington, DC. The American Humanist Association claimed the presence of the cross in a public space violated the First Amendment. However, the Supreme Court disagreed with a lower court's findings. Justice Samuel Alito wrote for the majority that government hostility toward religion was impermissible: "A government that roams the land, tearing down monuments with religious symbolism and scrubbing away any reference to the divine will strike many as aggressively hostile to religion."[191]

Two lessons can be drawn from these cases. First, Christians are no longer the dominant religious majority, and, in such situations, they should argue that they are a persecuted minority with rights. The demographics are sobering. The number of Americans with no religious affiliation has risen dramatically, now accounting for a quarter of the nation's population. That means the once-Christian majority is now a minority, because we are now a more secular country with active churchgoers only representing a third of all Americans.

Second, those sitting on the federal bench really matter to the Christian community. Most of the anti-Christian federal court decisions are coming from cherry-picked judges appointed by past liberal or anti-Christian presidents, especially President Obama. It's obvious that voters must consider the presidential candidates' judicial philosophy when deciding who to elect, because as President Obama famously said, "Elections have consequences."[192]

Anti-Christian Executive Branch

President Barack Obama's administration was the most anti-Christian administration of all times and is a warning of just what might be on the horizon. That administration's weaponization of the federal government was extensive, and Christians were often the targets.

The Reverend Franklin Graham, the leading official for Samaritan's Purse and the Billy Graham Evangelistic Association, addressed the ways the Obama administration demonstrated its anti-Christian bias:

There is an anti-Christian bias that is now in our [Obama administration] government, has permeated our government, that's also permeated Washington but [also] at the state and local level. It's the progressives, whatever you want to call them, that are trying—and the president is into this and the attorney general [Eric Holder] is into this 100 percent—and that is, forcing on the American people a new morality.[193]

Why was Obama and his administration so anti-Christian? Graham explained:

One of the problems we have, the president [Obama], his father was a Muslim and his stepfather was a Muslim—[he] lived in Indonesia and went to Muslim schools. His mother must have been a Muslim. We don't know that, but she married two Muslim men, so there must have been something there. The framework that our president has [had] growing up, his influences on his life were that of Islam. My influences, growing up in this country as many in this country, were under the Christian influence and the biblical influence. But our president did not have that; it was Islam. Many feel that he's protecting Islam. I don't know that, but it certainly seems that way.[194]

It's noteworthy that the Samaritan's Purse and the Billy Graham Evangelistic Association were targeted by Obama's Internal Revenue Service, perhaps because of Graham's public criticism of Obama. Franklin Graham said that the IRS notified both organizations that they were conducting a "review" of their activities for the tax year 2010. Graham said, "While these audits not only wasted taxpayer money, they wasted money contributed by donors for ministry purposes as we had to spend precious resources servicing the IRS agents in our offices."[195]

Graham continued, "I believe that someone in the administration was targeting and attempting to intimidate us. This is morally wrong and unethical—indeed some would call it 'un-American.'"[196]

Reverend Graham said "in light" of the IRS admission that it targeted Tea Party groups for "added scrutiny...I do not believe that the IRS audit of our two organizations last year is a coincidence—or justifiable."[197]

The Obama administration's anti-Christian bias was both deep and wide. The impact of that clear bias was studied and exposed by a number of organizations, which includes one by the Washington, DC-based Family Research Council.

FRC found a 76 percent increase in religious freedom violations during the Obama administration, according to the group's report, "Hostility to Religion: The Growing Threat to Religious Liberty in America."[198]

Tony Perkins, FRC's president, said: "The recent spike in government driven religious hostility is sad, but not surprising especially considering the Obama administration's antagonism toward biblical Christianity."[199]

FRC's sixty-six-page report chronicles some pretty outlandish hostility that starts at the top of the federal government and permeates down to local public schools. For example, it cites the 2011 case of the class president at Hampton High School in Tennessee who wanted to deliver a prayer at graduation. The principal issued an edict that any student who attempted to pray would be stopped, escorted from the building by police and arrested.[200]

Other government-related anti-Christian cases cited in the FRC report include:[201]

- "An 11-year-old student in Hattiesburg, Mississippi was penalized for mentioning Jesus in a Christmas poetry assignment."
- "Principal Frank Lay and Athletic Director Robert Freedom were charged with criminal contempt because they prayed over a

meal. The pair was later found not guilty of violating an injunction banning the promotion of religious events at school."

- "A Christian acapella group at James Madison University was told they could not perform 'Mary Did You Know' because it was religious. They were directed to only sing secular songs."
- "An Ohio library banned a Christian group from meeting to discuss natural marriage unless the group also included supports of same-sex marriage."
- "San Diego firefighters were threatened with disciplinary action if they refused to participate in a gay pride parade. The firefighters were subjected to verbal abuse and sexual gestures during the parade."
- "An Oklahoma bank was forced to remove religious Christmas decorations under orders from the Federal Reserve."

Wallbuilders is an "organization dedicated to presenting America's forgotten history and heroes, with an emphasis on the moral, religious, and constitutional foundation on which America was built."[202] It published a report on the Obama administration's hostility to Christians, "America's Most Biblically-Hostile U. S. President," which highlights more than one hundred examples of either antibiblical actions or acts that granted preferential treatment for Islam. Some of the examples of antibiblical acts are highlighted below.[203]

The Obama administration's acts of hostility toward people of biblical faith:

- "December 2009–Present—The annual White House Christmas cards, rather than focusing on Christmas or faith, instead highlight things such as the family dogs. And the White House Christmas tree ornaments include figures such as Mao Tse-Tung and a drag queen."
- "May 2016—President Obama appoints a transgender to the Advisory Council on Faith-Based Neighborhood Partnerships—

an act of overt disdain and hostility toward traditional faith religions."

- "June 2013—The Obama Department of Justice defunds a Young Marines chapter in Louisiana because their oath mentioned God, and another youth program because it permits a voluntary student-led prayer."
- "February 2013—The Obama administration announces that the rights of religious conscience for individuals will not be protected under the Affordable Care Act."
- "December 2011—The Obama administration denigrates other countries' religious beliefs as an obstacle to radical homosexual rights."
- "November 2011—Unlike previous presidents, Obama studiously avoids any religious references in his Thanksgiving speech."
- "April 2009—When speaking at Georgetown University, Obama orders that a monogram symbolizing Jesus' name be covered when he is making his speech."
- "April 2008—Obama speaks disrespectfully of Christians, saying they 'cling to guns or religion' and have an 'antipathy' to people who aren't like them."

Acts of hostility from the Obama-led Pentagon toward people of biblical faith:

- "October 2016—Obama threatens to veto a defense bill over religious protections contained in it."
- "June 2016—A military prayer breakfast whose speaker was highly decorated Delta Force and [Army] Lt. General Jerry Boykin (Retired) was cancelled because Boykin was a traditional value Christian who has voiced his support for natural marriage and his opposition to Islamic extremism. (The atheist critic behind the cancellation had complained that Boykin

as a 'homophobic, Islamophobic, fundamentalist Christian extremist.')"

- "April 2016—At the orders of a commander, a 33-year Air Force veteran was forcibly and physically removed by four other airmen because he attempted to use the word 'God' in a retirement speech."
- "February 2016—After a complaint was received, a Bible was removed from a display inside a Veterans Clinic."
- "March 2015—A highly decorated Navy SEAL chaplain was relieved of duty for providing counseling that contained religious views on things such as faith, marriage, and sexuality."
- "March 2014—Maxwell Air Force Base suddenly bans Gideons from handing out Bibles to willing recruits, a practice that had been occurring for years previously."
- "December 2013—A naval facility required that two nativity scenes—scenes depicting the event that caused Christmas to be declared a national federal holiday—be removed from the base dining hall and be confined to the base chapel, thus disallowing the open public acknowledgment of this national federal holiday."
- "October 2013—A counter-intelligence briefing at Fort Hood tells soldiers that evangelical Christians are a threat to Americans and that for a soldier to donate to such a group 'was punishable under military regulations.'"
- "October 2013—The Air Force Academy, in response to a complaint from Mikey Weinstein's Military Religious Freedom Foundation, makes 'so help me God' optional in cadets' honor oath."
- "August 2013—A Department of Defense military training manual teaches soldiers that people who talk about 'individual liberties, states' rights, and how to make the world a better place' are 'extremists.' It also lists the Founding Fathers—those 'colonists who sought to free themselves from British rule'—as examples of those involved in 'extremist ideologies and movements.'"

- "August 2013—A Senior Master Sergeant was removed from his position and reassigned because he told his openly lesbian squadron commander that she should not punish a staff sergeant who expressed his views in favor of traditional marriage."
- "August 2013—The Air Force, in the midst of having launched a series of attacks against those expressing traditional religious or moral views, invited a drag queen group to perform at a base."
- "July 2013—When an Air Force sergeant with years of military service questioned a same-sex marriage ceremony performed at the Air Force Academy's chapel, he received a letter of reprimand telling him that if he disagreed, he needed to get out of the military. His current six-year reenlistment was then reduced to only one-year, with the notification that he 'be prepared to retire at the end of this year.'"
- "June 2012—Bibles for the American military have been printed in every conflict since the American Revolution, but the Obama Administration revokes the long-standing U. S. policy of allowing military service emblems to be placed on those military Bibles."
- "September 2011—The Army issues guidelines for Walter Reed Medical Center stipulating that "'No religious items (i.e. Bibles, reading materials and/or facts) are allowed to be given away or used during a visit.'"

Obama administration acts of hostility toward biblical values:

- "October 2015—The administration attempts to pick opponents for court cases dealing with Obamacare contraception mandate."
- "March 2014—The Obama administration seeks funding for every type of sex-education—except that which reflects traditional moral values."

- "August 2013—USAID, a federal government agency, shut down a conference in South Korea the night before it was scheduled to take place because some of the presentations were not pro-abortion but instead presented information on abortion complications, including the problems of 'preterm births, mental health issues, and maternal mortality' among women giving birth who had previous abortions."
- "June 2013—The Obama Administration finalizes requirements that under the Obamacare insurance program, employers must make available abortion-causing drugs, regardless of the religious conscience objections of many employers and even despite the directive of several federal courts to protect the religious conscience of employers."
- "April 2013—The United States Agency for Internal Development (USAID), an official foreign policy agency of the U.S. government, begins a program to train homosexual activists in various countries around the world to overturn traditional marriage and anti-sodomy laws, targeting first those countries with strong Catholic influences, including Ecuador, Honduras, and Guatemala."
- "December 2012—Despite having campaigned to recognize Jerusalem as Israel's capital, President Obama once again suspends the provisions of the Jerusalem Embassy Act of 1995 which requires the United States to recognize Jerusalem as the capital of Israel and to move the American Embassy there."
- "July 2012—The Pentagon, for the first time, allows service members to wear their uniforms while marching in a parade—specifically, a gay pride parade in San Diego."
- "October 2011—The Obama administration eliminates federal grants to the U.S. Conference of Catholic Bishops for their extensive programs that aid victims of human trafficking because the Catholic Church is anti-abortion."

- "September 2011—The Pentagon directs that military chaplains may perform same-sex marriages at military facilities in violation of the federal Defense of Marriage Act."
- "July 2011—Obama allows homosexuals to serve openly in the military, reversing a policy originally instituted by George Washington in March 1778."
- "March 2011—The Obama administration refuses to investigate videos showing Planned Parenthood helping alleged sex traffickers get abortions for victimized underage girls."
- "February 2011—Obama directs the Justice Department to stop defending the federal Defense of Marriage Act."
- "September 2010—The Obama administration tells researchers to ignore a judge's decision striking down federal funding for embryonic stem cell research."
- "August 2010—The Obama administration cuts funding for 176 abstinence education programs."
- "July 2010—The Obama administration uses federal funds in violation of federal law to get Kenya to change its constitution to include abortion."
- "September 16, 2009—The Obama administration appoints as EEOC Commissioner Chai Feldblum, who asserts that society should 'not tolerate' any 'private beliefs,' including religious beliefs, if they may negatively affect homosexual 'equality.'"
- "July 2009—The Obama administration illegally extends federal benefits to same-sex partners of Foreign Service and Executive Branch employees, in direction violation of the federal Defense of Marriage Act."
- "May 2009—The White House budget eliminates all funding for abstinence-only education and replaces it with 'comprehensive' sexual education, repeatedly proven to increase teen pregnancies and abortions. Obama continues the deletion in subsequent budgets."

- "May 2009—Obama officials assemble a terrorism dictionary calling pro-life advocates violent and charging that they use racism in their 'criminal' activities."
- "March 2009—The Obama administration shut out pro-life groups from attending a White House-sponsored health care summit."
- "March 2009—Obama orders taxpayer funding of embryonic stem cell research."
- "March 2009—Obama gave $50 million for the UNFPA, the UN population agency that promotes abortion and works closely with Chinese population control officials who use forced abortions and involuntary sterilizations."
- "January 2009—Obama lifts restrictions on U.S. government funding for groups that provide abortion services or counseling abroad, forcing taxpayers to fund pro-abortion groups that either promote or perform abortions in other nations."
- "January 2009—President Obama's nominee for deputy secretary of state asserts that American taxpayers are required to pay for abortions and that limits on abortion funding are unconstitutional."

Conclusion

Christians often are not treated with respect by our governments (federal, state, and local). So, what ought Christians to do when faced with obeying God or the government?

The Apostle Paul writes that there are no authorities except what God has established. Jesus said as much when confronting the Roman governor, Pontius Pilate: "You would have no authority over me at all unless it had been given you from above" (John 19:11, ESV).

Christians must be mindful that governments are not infallible; they often make mistakes. Only God is infallible. When there is a conflict between God, His Word, and government, we must make a choice as to which to obey (Acts 5:27–29, ESV)—"We must obey God rather than men." We also must be prepared to pay the consequences for any civil disobedience.

Expect that there may come a time in the not-too-distant future when Christians must side with God's commandments rather than with an anti-Christian government.

CHAPTER FOUR

America's Education Institution Is Anti-Christian

CHRISTIAN PARENTS ARE commanded to educate their children to become responsible Christian adults. Most of our early forefathers did that, but modern state schools do not. Instead, contemporary public schools teach our children a secular, humanistic worldview that is anti-Christian, which compels many children raised in Christian homes to abandon the church upon adulthood.

Our secular contemporary government sees the purpose of public education as preparing children for careers or occupations and to function in society. Further, society tells us to pursue an education for economic reasons, because a college degree or a trade-school diploma leads to a well-paying job, and that leads to affluence and comfort. Attaining material success to support one's family may be important, but that is not the biblical purpose of education.

The purpose of education from a Christian perspective, according to the Westminster Shorter Catechism, is "to glorify God, and enjoy Him forever." That command shows us how we ought to live and why.[204]

It is noteworthy that Harvard College's original mission statement defined the purpose of an education in a very similar manner as the Westminster Catechism. It states:

Let every student be plainly instructed, and earnestly pressed to consider well, the main end of his life and studies is to know God and Jesus Christ which is eternal life (John 17:3), and therefore to lay Christ in the bottom, as the only foundation of all sound knowledge and learning.[205]

This purpose was representative of early American thinking, which is consistent with the Scriptures (Luke 12:15 and Mark 8:36). Even Western philosophers at the time believed much the same. English poet and intellectual John Milton (1608–1674) said, "The end then of learning is to repair the ruins of our first parents [Adam and Eve] by regaining to know God aright, and out of that knowledge to love Him, to imitate Him, to be like Him."[206]

The Bible goes even further to provide a very prescriptive purpose for education. Specifically, Proverbs 22:6 (NKJV) reads: "Train a child in the way he should go, and when he is old, he will not turn from it." Translation: Education is a God-directed mechanism to nurture children in the truth by giving them meaning to life.

Therefore, Bible-believing parents should seek to raise their children to become people guided by Scripture, and education lays the foundation for that character-development process. A proper Christian education prepares our children to live in an alien culture that advances a contrary anti-Christian worldview. So, what does that education look like?

Early Americans followed the scriptural mandate to oversee the education of their children. They emphasized instruction that focused on the scriptural command to teach their children how to reason from God's Word in civil society, an idea Reformation-era Protestant John Calvin matured in Geneva, Switzerland, and a practice early colonists like the Puritans brought to America.[207]

The Calvinist tradition understandably influenced the education of early American children first at home where parents taught them to read, write, and cipher (do arithmetic), all with a careful eye on the cultivation of a virtuous character and a Christian conscience. Eventually, the colonists branched out to establish community-based grammar schools. The earliest such school was founded by the Puritans in 1635, the Boston Latin School, which was modeled after the European Latin School model, which emphasized religion, Latin, and classical literature.[208]

Over the subsequent two-plus centuries, American education radically changed, giving over to secular government most of the responsibility for educating the next generation, which resulted in poor academic results and regrettably abandoned most aspects of Christian influence.

Government Schools Failing

Yes, American public schools are failing at what they claim to do best—prepare our children to compete in the world by equipping them with the necessary skills; meanwhile, they're also failing Christian families and abandoning our Christian heritage.

A 2019 report from the Program for International Student Assessment evaluated fifteen-year-olds' academic performance in reading, math, and science. That assessment found American students lagging far behind European and East Asian students. On average, the US students ranked eighth of seventy-nine countries overall in reading, eleventh in science, and below average (thirtieth) in math.[209] That's appalling, in part because America's federal and state governments spend an estimated $620 billion annually on K–12 education, or $12,296 for every student in public school. Something is very wrong with this picture.[210]

Alarm over our education system isn't a new issue. Similarly, poor academic results prompted then-President Ronald Reagan to commission a study about the decline in American education. That 1983 study found that "we are a nation at risk." The report concluded: "If an unfriendly foreign power had attempted to impose on America the mediocre educational performance that exists today, we might well have viewed it as an act of war. As it stands, we have allowed this to happen to ourselves."[211] Where is the outrage?

Why are our public schools delivering such poor results? The answer is unfortunately very simple. Our schools were long ago taken captive by progressive educators who ignore the basics—reading, writing, and arithmetic. Rather, progressive-led public schools focus on brainwashing the next generation on "social justice," environmentalism, and sex. Even our universities are worse, having become secular seminaries for leftist ideologies. No wonder we are losing our competitive edge against the rest of the world. But our failing government school problem is even worse for Christians.

A Barna study found that most (64 percent) young adults who grew up in Christian homes have disengaged from the church.[212] Most (90 percent) of those surveyed had attended the public school system.[213] Arguably, the anti-Christian and ideological messaging fostered by the government schools plays a destructive role on our children. Yet, and unfortunately, most (70 to 80 percent) evangelical Christian parents still have their children in public schools.[214]

These facts demonstrate that our government not only spends vast sums on a failing education system, but it is also failing Christian families. This begs an important question: Why do most Christian parents keep sending their children to government schools that are failing in their academic mission—and worse, that are undermining Christian core values?

Government Schools: Anti-Christian—Philosophically and Publicly

Philosophically, government schools promote an anti-Christian worldview, a compelling reason for Christian parents to find an alternative educational venue for their children. Remember, Jesus warned us to understand the world in which we live. He said in Matthew 10:16 (NIV): "I am sending you out like sheep among wolves. Therefore, be as shrewd as snakes and as innocent as doves."

Similarly, C. S. Lewis, a noted British Christian author, reminded us to see the secular world for what it is—filled with "snakes":

To be ignorant and simple now—not to be able to meet enemies on their own ground—would be to throw down our weapons, and to betray our uneducated brethren who have, under God, no defense but us against the intellectual attacks of the heathen. Good philosophy must exist, if for no other reason, because bad philosophy needs to be answered.[215]

Yes, Christians are at war, whether or not they understand the nature of the enemy. However, few of our children in government schools are "armed" for the battle to defend themselves against heathen attacks. After all, public schools are a major battlefield vying for the literal hearts and souls of our children, and too few Christian parents really understand the enemy's ideology and the hostile environment into which they daily send their young, ill-equipped children.

It is beyond dispute, at least among informed Christians, that contemporary public schools are bastions of secular humanism that promote an anti-Christian agenda. Although secular school officials may claim to be neutral, most promote a worldview that advances a false god, and they attack Christianity on virtually every important issue, such as the origin of life and creation. For example, public school teachers use "science-based" evolution as evidence to contradict Scripture about a world created by God.

Some scholars admit their secular, anti-Christian biases regarding the role of public education. Henry Steels Commager (1902–1998), a liberal scholar from Colombia University known as the "dean" of American historians, said secular education is the first "American religion," a religion to which we must declare "our devotion."[216] Another influential educator, John Dewey, the father of modern progressivism, said: "If we have any ground to be religious about anything, we may take education religiously." He also saw a "Great Community" with government schools as the established church, and his philosophy of education is loudly declared in the Humanist Manifesto, which he helped to draft, that includes "religious humanists regard the universe as self-existing and not created."[217]

Thus, the character of modern American government education is religious—ideological—which is used to mold and shape young minds and souls like clay in a potter's hands. That view is supported by Professor Richard A. Baer Jr. of Cornell University, who revealingly said, "It is sheer mythology to think there is such a thing as value-neutral or religion-neutral education."[218] For many government education intellectuals, children are theirs for molding into whatever they want—generally a secularist, anti-Christian like them.

This view is long in the tooth. President Theodore Roosevelt's favorite social scientist, Edward Alsworth Ross, summarized the purpose of the public school. He explained that its role is "to collect little plastic lumps of human dough from private households and shape them on the social kneading board."[219]

Yes, public schools brainwash children, a concept defined as "a forcible indoctrination to induce someone to give up basic political, social, or religious beliefs and attitudes and to accept contrasting regimented ideas."[220] They do that by indoctrinating students through the daily repetition of information that, in time, leads to their acceptance of a secular worldview, which is very contrary to the Christian worldview.

A worldview shapes a person's thinking and outlook on life. The term comes from the German term *weltanschauung*, which means "a comprehensive conception or apprehension of the world especially from a specific standpoint."[221] German romanticists explained that cultures create a pattern or common outlook on life expressed in various fora—art, literature, social institutions. In fact, to understand the culture of a country, one must explore the underlying worldview.

A Christian worldview is diametrically opposed to the secular one outlined above. It addresses such important issues as who God is, the world He made, and our relationship with Him. It explains our role in this world in terms of metaphysics, epistemology, and values. It touches every aspect of our life; all areas of this physical domain have a distinctive Christian perspective, which defines our Christian worldview.

Education is a conduit for embedding a worldview in young minds.

Consider that a secular paradigm must distinguish between truth and falsehood, as does a Christian one. For the Christian, God is truth, and His truth doesn't change, no matter what others say. There aren't two kinds of truth—scientific and religious—as some secularists may argue. There is only one truth—Jesus Christ: "The Word became flesh and made his dwelling among us. We have seen His glory, the glory of the one and only Son, who came from the Father, full of grace and truth" (John 1:14, NIV).

Modern secularists who advance a so-called progressive worldview embrace two defining concepts, relativism and humanism. These are the "isms" secularists use in public schools to brainwash our children, a front for godless atheism. Consider both "isms."

Relativism is a prevailing philosophy in our culture that states that truth is relative. It declares that all values—even biblical ones—are tied to a respective culture. Relativism claims that no set of values is better than any other. Not surprisingly, for the relativist, all religions are basically the same, and no religion, such as Christianity, should claim exclusivity—i.e., Jesus Christ is the only way to eternal life. Also, for the relativist, morality is a personal preference; good and evil are just labels. Relativists reject Christian views that hold to moral positions on such issues as abortion and homosexuality.

Humanism is the progressives' religion, which puts emphasis on the inner man and seeks to improve mankind to the point of perfection. The humanist believes the key to reaching perfection is education—which, if done properly, will cure all social ills. For the humanist, behavior changes with learning, and the stimulus-response theory of man works to help man progress; right learning helps man progress to his ultimate end—perfection. However, that theory shows no accountability to absolutes—there is no infinite god, only one's self. Thus, the humanist, not God, decides on the best course of life and what is ultimately right and wrong (morals).

A secular worldview based on humanism and relativism is the very antithesis of Christianity. No wonder children educated in public schools for six hours a day, 180 days a year for twelve or thirteen formative years are confused, and many abandon Christianity.

Not surprisingly, many of our public schools are also aggressively and openly anti-Christian as well as guilty of advancing an anti-Christian, secularist worldview. There is nothing subtle about some government schools' opposition to Christianity, and it is getting worse.

Public Schools Aggressively Anti-Christian

Earlier in this chapter, I briefly introduced President Reagan's 1983 National Commission on Excellence in Education, which exposed many flaws within our government school system. The commission's report, "A Nation at Risk," concluded that America's mediocre educational performance is as threatening as an act of war. There is some truth to that view, but in a perverted way.

Is there any doubt among alert Christians that our children attending public schools are at war with the secularists' ideology? If it is true that government schools are an ideological battleground, then we ought to ask: Do we really need to send young Christian children into situations where they are vulnerable to lifelong effects from being bullied or teased for their faith, much less brainwashed about a secularist worldview?

The culture war inside the walls of our state schools is pretty bad and getting worse. Our children are exposed to lesbian, gay, bisexual, transgender (LGBT) teachings, the myth of evolution, and revisionist American history, and those same taxpayer institutions ignore the basic, rudimentary education that is the schools' alleged charter and what taxpayers should demand.

Matt Walsh, a commentator, called for a Christian mass exodus from public education in an article entitled "Christian Parents, Your Kids Aren't Equipped to Be Public School Missionaries." Walsh argues that because of state schools' off-the rails radicalism and anti-Christian agenda, then Christians must *en masse* abandon public education for the good of their children.[222]

Mr. Walsh dismisses the tired excuse often heard that our Christian children are public-school missionaries. As indicated earlier in this chapter, those kids are more likely to abandon their faith once out of the home because of attending public schools rather than share the Gospel of Christ with lost classmates. What Christian parent wants that outcome?

Even the spiritually strongest Christian children are exposed to aggressive, radical views that are hard to resist. Walsh comments:

> If we have not yet reached a point where a mass exodus from the public schools is warranted, when will that point arrive? Are we waiting until they start bringing in nude hermaphrodites to teach sex ed? I suppose even that wouldn't be enough incentive for some of us. "I can't shield my kid from what's going on out there!" "Be in the world, not of the world!" "Naked she-males are a part of life! I can't keep him in a bubble forever! He's 9 years old, for God's sake!"[223]

Government school-sponsored, anti-Christian behavior is beyond belief. Consider some recent examples.

Evidently, celebrating religious holidays in government schools can no longer include Christian nativity scenes, according to New York officials. A report from the Thomas More Law Center states: "Pursuant to the policy, city schools display the Jewish menorah and the Islamic star and crescent during Hanukkah and Ramadan, but not the nativity scene during Christmas." In fact, "One public school principal issued a memo encouraging teachers to bring to school 'religious symbols' that represent the Islamic and Jewish religions. No mention of Christianity was made in the memo."[224]

Author Ann Coulter wrote about a fourth grader reprimanded for praying before lunch:

In a public school in St. Louis, a teacher spotted the suspect, fourth grader Raymond Barnes, bowing his head in prayer before lunch. The teacher stormed Raymond's table, ordering him to stop immediately and sent him to the principal's office. The principal informed the young malefactor that praying was not allowed in school.[225]

A kindergarten student in Saratoga Springs, New York, was similarly accosted by a government school official for daring to pray with two classmates. She was reprimanded and reported to school officials. The principal sent the girl's parents a note stating that she was not permitted to pray in school under any circumstances.[226]

There are numerous other anti-Christian school-based assaults by government officials. For example, two Texas sisters had the audacity to carry Bibles to school, but were turned around by a vigilant teacher who marched them to the principal's office. Then there were three students who put Ten Commandment covers on their school books, which were ripped off the books and then thrown into the trash by an alert school official who labeled the material "hate speech."[227]

More and more public-school officials are brazenly anti-Christian in both political and religious behaviour as well as ideologically extreme. Those brainwashing institutions are also undermining the teachings of the Bible in the name of "tolerance," faux science, and multiculturalism.

Scriptural Mandate to Provide Christian Education

Yes, public schools are the petri dish in which Christian influence has vanished, replaced by a godless ideology, and now those same institutions have become aggressively anti-Christian. They foster an anti-Christian, secular humanistic worldview that regrettably persuades many of our Christian children to abandon the church. That is why it is past time

that Christian parents take seriously their biblical responsibility to protect and nurture their children through Christian education.

Christian education is not neutral either, and that's good. The Bible
is very clear that the education of children is a family, parental responsibility, not the government's job. Christian education exists to glorify
God, and it relies on the Bible as a textbook, the source of all wisdom.
Whether they homeschool their children or send them to Christian
school, it is the parents' responsibility to take seriously their God-given
responsibility to rear their children in the fear of the Lord, training them
to Christian maturity so they will be best equipped to face an unwel-
coming, hostile world for the glory of God.

The simple principles of Christian education are found in Deuteronomy 6:4–7 (NIV):

Hear, O Israel: The Lord our God, the Lord is one. Love the
Lord your God with all your heart and with all your soul and
with all your strength. These commandments that I give you
today are to be on your hearts. Impress them on your children.
Talk about them when you sit at home and when you walk
along the road, when you lie down and when you get up.

These verses are called the *Shema*, the Hebrew word for "hear." They
outline that education must be God-centered and carried out under
the watchful eye of parents. The passage also directs that God's Word
is relevant in every aspect of life, which includes the children's education. That's a view shared by the Apostle Paul, who wrote in his letter to
Timothy:

But as for you, continue in what you have learned and have
become convinced of, because you know those from whom
you have learned it, and how from infancy you have known the
holy Scriptures, which are able to make you wise for salvation
through faith in Christ Jesus. All Scripture is God-breathed and

is useful for teaching, rebuking, correcting and training in righteousness, so that the man of God may be thoroughly equipped for every good work. (2 Timothy 3:14–17, NIV)

So, what should Christian parents do about their children's education, in light of these Scriptures? They need to prayerfully consider whether government schools are best for their children given the family's circumstances. After all, we've already established that public schools are a hostile environment for Christians, and they're getting worse. But public schools have always been a danger for Christian children, and many children have survived to prosper spiritually.

Five centuries ago, theologian Martin Luther (1483–1546) weighed in on the issue:

I am very much afraid that schools will prove to be the great gates of hell unless they diligently labor in explaining the Holy Scriptures, engraving them in the hearts of youth. I advise no one to place his child where the Scriptures do not reign paramount.[228]

Even more recent theologians expressed outrage at the prospect of putting Christian children under secularist educators. Charles Spurgeon (1834–1892), an English Particular Baptist preacher known as the "Prince of Preachers," said: "To leave our youthful population in the hands of secular teachers, will be to sell them to the Ishmaelites."[229]

A similar view reminds me of the Barna survey about Christian youth who attended state schools and, once adults, abandoned the faith. Voddie Baucham Jr. (1969), an African-American pastor at Grace Family Baptist Church in Spring, Texas, wrote to exhort parents: "We cannot continue to send our children to Caesar for their education and be surprised when they come home as Romans."[230]

Christian parents wrestle with the issue of where to educate their children. Some single parents have little money, which means government schools are their only choice. For others, Christian schools can be prohibitively expensive—and besides, some Christian schools are Christian in name only, and are just as polluted as the average public school.

Christian parents must come to agree that government schools are no longer an option if they have choices—i.e., home school or Christian school. After all, as we've seen above, government schools are inherently hostile to our Christian values, and our children should not be considered disposable to such a rancid environment that tears them down psychologically while failing to equip them academically.

I know there will be readers who will make excuses and empty claims to justify sending their children to government schools. I'd encourage them to consider the following discussion about those common excuses.[231]

One view is that the public-school system needs Christian children. That may be true, as it was for the lions in the ancient Roman colosseum. No, I don't need to sacrifice my children to the secular, anti-Christian government education system. Nothing in God's Word says Christians must maintain government education at any cost. That attitude puts the secular system above our children's best interests.

Putting your children in "the system" may not be a sacrifice for "you," but your children are paying a high price. The burden of being "salt and light" in public schooling isn't something your children should necessarily shoulder, and you should resist making such a choice based on the fact that it's the easiest and most cost-effective option.

There is also the argument that children will eventually be exposed to bad things in life, so, the logic goes, let them experience those challenges at the public school. It is true they will eventually face bad things in life, but as parents we should protect our children until they are ready to battle life's pressing moral challenges. We need to prepare them and not just shove them into a government school where secularists are going to make value decisions for our ill-equipped children. That could do life-lasting harm to unprepared children.

Finally, how do you prepare your children to survive in the often hostile, amoral world of the government school? You can't be at their side for large parts of their waking hours while at school each week and for nine months a year. You must decide when your child is ready for such a hostile environment. Is five years old too soon, or is he/she ready for such a setting by age ten...or never?

No, the fact is that few children are ready to be a "missionary" for Christ in a hostile public school environment. Their faith needs maturity before they are sent to evangelize lost souls in hostile schools. Ask yourself: How many adult Christians act out their faith in the workplace and resist the evil assaults? What kind of "missionary" for Christ are you in the secular workplace? Do you really expect your young child to do any better?

Parents must remember that we're all engaged in a war for the souls of the next generation. Government schools are in many cases warriors for our spiritual enemy, and so far, those spiritual proxies are winning, because most Christian parents turn over their most precious possessions, their children, to be brainwashed by the state educational establishment. That is patently unbiblical and morally wrong in today's rancid culture that preys on the innocent, our children.

Conclusion

I'll conclude with a bit of personal testimony. Both my wife, Jan, and I attended public schools through college. That was in a different era, when Bible reading and prayer were embraced by public school officials. We were educated academically in a way that complimented our biblical values. I even met the Lord thanks to an evangelist who shared the claims of Christ in my school assembly. However, when it came time for us to decide how to educate our two children, we chose Christian schools and remained faithful to that choice all the way through their college education at Liberty University.

I tell you these things because I don't want you to believe that I'm saying one thing and doing another. I believe it is the parents' duty to God to protect and educate their children, and in today's world, the only choice for Christian parents is a Christian education for their children.

CHAPTER 5

Colonial Biblical View of Marriage and Family Replaced by Modern Perversions

AMERICA WAS FOUNDED by those who embraced mostly the biblical view of marriage and family, but over the past two plus centuries, that formula morphed and is no longer our sturdy foundation. Instead, we have eviscerated both institutions morally to the extent that the tipping point is dangerously close. Very little additional amoral influence is needed in order to accelerate the downward spiral from which we will never recover.

This chapter will define both biblical marriage and family and explain their foundational place in colonial society. Subsequently, we will consider how radically both have changed morally to this day, the resulting consequences, and what those radically altered institutions might become in the future.

Societal Foundation: Marriage and Family

Societal implosion can be blamed on a host of factors. For the ancient Romans, there were a number of contributing factors, but according to one eighteenth-century historian, Rome fell because so did the family.

The Roman Empire collapsed for a variety of reasons. Perhaps the most important was the decline in morals and values. It wasn't just that prostitution and wasteful spending on lavish parties and the gladiatorial displays in the Colosseum contributed to Rome's moral collapse. No, according to Edward Gibbon's eighteenth-century book, *The History of the Decline and Fall of the Roman Empire*, the most important contributor to that implosion was the breakdown of the family. In league with the failure of the family unit were heavy taxation, an insatiable craving for pleasure (wine and women), a massive arms buildup, and the decay of religion.

The institutions of family and marriage have long been the cornerstones of healthy societies. That was true for Rome and it was especially true for the young American republic. After all, America was colonized primarily by Christian immigrants who came here for religious freedom, and they brought with them their Bibles, their biblical doctrine, their families, their traditions, and an intense desire to follow God's prescription for life, which at the center was to glorify Him.

Glorifying God meant following His plan for mankind, which is spelled out in the first book of the Bible, Genesis. There, God defines "family" as "the union of one man and one woman in matrimony, which is normally blessed with one or several natural or adopted children."[232]

In the beginning, God created first a man (Adam) to exercise dominion over His creation, then He made woman (Eve) as man's "helper" (Genesis 2:18, 20). God then directs: "Therefore a man shall leave his father and his mother and hold fast to his wife, and they shall become one flesh" (Genesis 2:24, ESV). This is God's prescription for the natural family. "Become one flesh" refers to the establishment of one new family, but it also creates a sexual union that leads to the procreation of offspring: "Be fruitful and multiply" (Genesis 1:28, KJV).

Thus, the original prescription of creation was marriage, the irreplaceable role of male-female relations that reproduce the human race. This prescription is at the heart of civil law in every society that regulates marriage civilly. Although this marriage formula applies to all cultures and religions, the Christian has perhaps the best understanding because it comes from God's Word (the Bible), and the church through the ages has educated Christians and the broader culture about God's intentions for marriage and, by association, family.

The church has long taught that marriage and the family are God's ideas. We are not free to renegotiate or redefine what God ordained, however. Jesus warned against such attempts: "What therefore God has joined together let not man separate" (Matthew 19:6, NIV), because these institutions are part of a divine covenant.

A covenant is a contract between two parties and, in the case of marriage, God is the key witness, thus making marriage a permanent arrangement that God promises to safeguard. Remember that in a Christian wedding ceremony, the marriage partners pledge to each other to abide together "until death do us part." Those words mean, as God is the witness, they will conduct their relationship (marriage) based on God's design and plan.

Biblical marriage is based on at least five principles. First, it is a permanent relationship established by God (Matthew 19:6), which must not be entered lightly. Divorce is not permitted except under limited conditions (Matthew 5:32; 19:9).

Second, marriage is sacred, a commitment between two consenting adults before God. The Lord God defined marriage as between a man and woman and condemns relationships such as homosexual coupling, which He would never endorse for a marital bond (1 Corinthians 6:18; Jude 7).

Third, marriage is the most intimate of all human relationships— a man and woman become "one flesh" (Genesis 2:23–25). It requires "leaving" and "uniting" to establish a new family unit. The "one flesh" relationship is not just about sexual intercourse, but about forming a new, God-directed bond between two previously unrelated people—a new family is thus created.

Fourth, marriage is about unselfish support of the partner. The marriage partners are committed to one another without reservation, which means forgiving and steadfast love. These marriage roles are well defined in Scripture: Wives submit and husbands love, bearing responsibility before God (Ephesians 5:22–24).

Finally, marriage is an exclusive relationship, which means that no other relationship is to interfere. Extramarital relationships are illegitimate, a violation of the covenant (Exodus 20:14; Proverbs 6:32; Mark 10:11–12).

Children are given two responsibilities in a Christian family: obey their parents and honor them (Ephesians 6:1–3). They are to obey their parents until they reach adulthood, and then they are to honor their parents for a lifetime. In turn, God promises to bless those who honor their parents.

The result of biblical marriage and family is that all members fulfill their God-appointed roles and, as a result, there is peace and harmony in the home. Absent this prescription, the relationships and home suffer.

Early-American Christian Family

At the time of America's founding, the vast majority of American families followed the biblical prescription: They were married in a Christian church, followed the roles described in Ephesians, and raised their children as outlined above. With few exceptions, those couples stayed married until death. Divorce was rare in early America and, where permitted, a special government act was often required to dissolve the marriage.

The mostly British heritage colonists brought to America an understanding of the biblical and civil marriage roles. Specifically, women lost their legal identity once married, essentially becoming the property of their husbands. William Blackstone, an eighteenth-century British jurist, explained the English common law that prescribed the marriage of a man and women as a contract that created "one person in law: that is, the very being or legal existence of the woman [wa]s suspended during the marriage, or at least [wa]s incorporated and consolidated into that of the husband."[233]

Colonial women were wholly dependent upon and subordinate to men, and their role as a wife in the marriage relationship was to serve her husband at home. Women at the time could not own property, enter contracts, or sue another.

The husband was the provider for his family and had a duty to meet his wife's needs. Further, in "exchange" for the man's providing, the husband had the right to expect the wife's "services," which included sex, whether or not she consented. That view was supported by American courts such as the Louisiana Supreme Court, which explained the husband's right to sex: "The husband of a woman cannot himself be guilty of an actual rape upon his wife, on account of the matrimonial consent which she has given, and which she cannot retract" (*State v. Haines, 25 So. 372, 372* (La. 1899).[234]

The marriage tradition made the husband responsible for his wife's behavior, and as a result, he had the responsibility to correct her for disobedience—albeit, without inflicting permanent injury on her. Further, if his wife had an affair, the husband could sue that man for damages because he had taken the husband's "property."

Early American law and culture mostly kept sex within marriage. State laws criminalized sex outside of marriage (fornication), living together outside marriage (cohabitation), and having children outside of marriage (bastardy). Children born outside of marriage were treated harshly and were considered the child of no one (*filius nullius*). However, the mother of the nonmarital offspring was required to support the child, but there was no such expectation of the sperm donor (the biological father).[235]

Consider the realities of daily life for the early American family before considering the modern family and how it prospered economically but abandoned its biblical roots.

I was struck by criticism of claims that eighteenth-century American families were better off than families today. That may be true in terms of creature comforts, medicine, and longevity. However, the eighteenth-century family stuck together (admittedly in part out of necessity to survive) and produced children who integrated well into society and maintained a morally sound society.

Life for eighteenth-century marriages and families was tough, however. They depended upon one another far more than do spouses and families today. Consider for a moment a description of eighteenth-century American family life offered by author Matt Ridley in his book, *The Rational Optimist: How Prosperity Evolves*. It's a sobering account of early American life and demonstrates, from my perspective, just how important family was to our founders.[236]

Mr. Ridley's account of eighteenth-century American life is a far cry from the upbeat accounts portrayed in some contemporary movies and books about that era. Ridley soberly wrote:

> The family is gathering around the hearth in the simple timber-framed house. Father reads aloud from the Bible while mother prepares to dish out a stew of beef and onions. The baby boy is being comforted by one of his sisters and the eldest lad is pouring water from a pitcher into the earthenware mugs on the table. His elder sister is feeding the horse in the stable. Outside there is no noise of traffic, there are no drug dealers and neither dioxins nor radioactive fall-out have been found in the cow's milk. All is tranquil; a bird sings outside the window.
>
> Oh please! Though this is one of the better-off families in the village, father's Scripture reading is interrupted by a bronchitic cough that presages the pneumonia that will kill him at 53—not helped by the wood smoke of the fire. (He is lucky: life expectancy even in England was less than 40 in 1800.) The baby will die of the smallpox that is now causing him to cry; his sister will soon be the chattel of a drunken husband. The water the son is pouring tastes of the cows that drink from the brook. Toothache tortures the mother. The neighbour's lodger is get-

ting the other girl pregnant in the hayshed even now and her child will be sent to an orphanage. The stew is grey and gristly yet meat is a rare change from gruel; there is no fruit or salad at this season. It is eaten with a wooden spoon from a wooden bowl. Candles cost too much, so firelight is all there is to see by. Nobody in the family has ever seen a play, painted a picture or heard a piano. School is a few years of dull Latin taught by a bigoted martinet at the vicarage. Father visited the city once, but the travel cost him a week's wages and the others have never travelled more than fifteen miles from home. Each daughter owns two wool dresses, two linen shirts and one pair of shoes. Father's jacket cost him a month's wages but is now infested with lice. The children sleep two to a bed on straw mattresses on the floor. As for the bird outside the window, tomorrow it will be trapped and eaten by the boy.

It is miraculous that so many early American marriages and families survived such rigors, much less prospered. But in fact, they did both, and I believe it is because of their Christian faith and God's prescription for both marriage and family.

Modern American Family Abandoned Its Origins

Founder John Adams wrote, "The foundations of national morality must be laid in private families."[237] Unfortunately, for the most part, America's modern families have their feet firmly planted in quicksand, a moral quagmire much like ancient Rome just before it fell. Unless America's current course is soon and dramatically redirected, that outcome will be repeated here as well.

The moral landscape in America for marriage and the family dramatically changed from the time of our founding. We abandoned the morality of Moses and Jesus Christ and embraced that of Charles

Darwin, John Dewey, and contemporary progressives who promote an anti-Christian worldview governed by humanism and relativism.

Indeed, marriage and family life have radically transformed to arrangements that today are temporary and fragile. Noted scholars confirm that view. "The scale of marital breakdown in the West since 1960 has no historical precedent and seems unique," explained historian Lawrence Stone.[238] James Q. Wilson, a social scientist, said we are witnessing a "profound, worldwide, long-term change in the family that is likely to continue for a long time."[239]

These scholars identify a trend toward a "post-marriage" culture marked by shallow commitments and a collapse of our moral landscape. Consider the contemporary moral landscape for both American marriage and family.

America's marriage rate is at an all-time low, with 6.8 marriages per one thousand people.[240] Today, according to the Pew Research Center, only 51 percent of American adults are married, compared with 1960, when 72 percent of all adults were married.[241]

Divorce was extremely rare in colonial America, because it violates God's intent for marriage, and God makes it clear that He hates it (Malachi 2:16). However, today the marriage rate has radically declined, and divorce rates in America are the highest in the world. Specifically, in 1974, divorce replaced death as the principal cause of the failure of marriages in America. This avalanche of divorce led to "no fault" divorce laws beginning with California in 1969, which contributed to more national acceptance of divorce.

Divorce often leads to another moral problem, polygamy, a violation of God's plan for marital monogamy. Yes, there are examples of polygamy in the Bible, and in each case, there were serious consequences. Abraham, Esau, Jacob, Gideon, Elkanah, David, and Solomon were all polygamists. However, polygamous marriage is not God's design in these cases, and they resulted in well-documented problems to include the decline into idolatry.

Adultery is the breaking of one's marriage vows, a problem not unknown in early America. However, colonists caught in the act were severely punished, so the incidents of adultery tended to be limited. No doubt colonial preachers often reminded their congregations of the commandment, "You shall not commit adultery" (Exodus 20:14), and they would perhaps use the illustration of David's infidelity with Bathsheba (2 Samuel 11) to remind the congregants about their marriage vows.

Today, sex outside of marriage (adultery and fornication) is very common. The evidence and consequences are pretty breathtaking. Sex before marriage is very common, according to the federal government's National Survey of Family Growth, which found that by age forty-four, virtually all Americans (99 percent) had had sex, and 95 percent had done so before marriage.[242]

The consequences of extramarital sex are tragic, both for the individuals involved and for society. For example, approximately one-third of the entire US population has a sexually transmitted disease (STD), according to the Centers for Disease Control and Prevention (CDC).[243] That is the highest STD rate in the entire industrialized world, and the CDC estimates that fifteen to twenty-four-year-olds account for half of the twenty million new STD infections each year.[244] We also lead the world in teen pregnancy, and one of every four teen girls has at least one STD.[245]

Out-of-wedlock births occurred during colonial America, but they were relatively rare. However, by 1994, Americans reached the unenviable goal of half of all firstborn children being born were born out of wedlock.[246] Worse, perhaps, more than three in four of all out-of-wedlock births were to teenagers.[247]

Single parenthood was rare in colonial America as well, in part because of the stigma of having an out-of-wedlock birth and also because remarriage was practically essential for women and children to survive. Today, single-parent families are common, with more than one-third of American children living apart from their biological fathers.[248]

The problem of single-parenthood is growing. Half a century ago (1960), only 5 percent of all births were outside of marriage. A decade later (1970), that figure doubled, and by the year 2000, fully one-third of all births were to unmarried woman. Today, that figure has stabilized at four in ten.[249]

Cohabitation was rare in colonial America, in part because the church-dominated communities knew most everything about everyone and they would never permit open sin (adultery and fornication). Today, more than half of all eventual marriages are preceded by a period of cohabitation, and for many today, living together is replacing marriage. Predictably, according to sociologist Pamela J. Smock, "only about one-sixth of cohabitations last at least three years and only one-tenth last five years or more." Further, for those who cohabit before marriage, the chance of divorce almost doubles as compared with couples who marry prior to living together.[250]

The scourge of pornography may be a modern phenomenon, but the essence is ancient. Pornography is defined as "printed or visual material containing the explicit description or display of sexual organs or activity, intended to stimulate erotic rather than aesthetic or emotional feelings."[251] Today, 30 percent of all Internet traffic goes to adult (pornographic) websites and, perhaps surprising for some, 70 percent of all men age eighteen to twenty-four visit at least one adult website each month, with the average high school boy spending two hours on adult websites every single week.[252]

Pornography wasn't a problem among our colonial ancestors. However, it arose from the ashes of other social problems outlined above and the Bible speaks of issues related to pornography such as adultery, sexual immorality, and temptation (1 Corinthians 6:9; 1 Peter 2:11; Colossians 3:5). Scripture provides advice about preserving the sacred essence of the marriage and the partner, the true victims of pornography.

Homosexuality was known in colonial times and harshly addressed even by General George Washington, who drummed out of the Continental Army a lieutenant for "attempting to commit sodomy."[253] Scripture doesn't mince words about homosexuality, beginning with Genesis 2:24: "A man [masculine] shall leave his father and his mother and hold fast to his *wife* [feminine], and the two shall become one flesh" (emphasis added). Heterosexual marriage is God's only provision, and He expects the married couple to remain faithful. Homosexual behavior involves same-sex intercourse that can't lead to procreation; it is labeled unnatural and can't involve God-prescribed marriage.

Noah Webster, the father of American scholarship, defined the homosexual act, sodomy, in his dictionary as "a crime against nature." Sodomy was a felony offense in all US states until 1962 and was considered a mental disorder by the American Psychological Association until 1973, when a protest erupted at one of their conferences compelling the association to change its political stance regarding homosexuals. Unfortunately, the US Supreme Court legalized homosexual "marriage" (*Obergefell v. Hodges,* 576 U.S. (2015)), and the culture has normalized it to the point it is now considered a right.

America's marriage landscape is terrible, and so is the moral picture regarding the family, especially the impact for children growing up in the amoral adult world just described.

Sociologist Charles Murray wrote in his 2012 book, *Coming Apart,* that only one segment of society succeeding today knows the secret of family prosperity, the well-to-do, and their secret is traditional (Christian) values and intact families. Another sociologist and former US senator, Daniel Patrick Moynihan, agreed with Murray. Moynihan said: "The biggest change, in my judgment, is that the family structure has come apart all over the North Atlantic world."[254]

The American family suffers as a consequence of the failing marriage relationship, and our children pay a high price. The symptoms of the problem of the breakdown of the family are legion: more abortions, more sex outside of marriage, more juvenile delinquency, more poor academic performance, and others.

The cultural shift in marriage roles negatively impacts children as well. Consider three examples.

There are fewer stable households. Colonialist families were very predictable, with Mom at home, Dad being the breadwinner, and children being educated either at home or a local grammar school. Today's family is quite different, according to the Pew Research Center, which found that two-parent households are on decline due to high rates of divorce, remarriage, and cohabitation.

Compare the family structure in 1960 with that of today. In that year, the height of the post-World War II Baby Boomers, 73 percent of all children lived in a family with two married parents in their first marriage. That number contracted to 61 percent by 1980, and today, the number of traditional families accounts for less than half (46 percent) of all families. Living arrangements for children are becoming chaotic as a result. For example, according to Pew, "Over a three-year period, about three-in-ten (31%) children younger than 6 had experienced a major change in their family or household structure, in the form of parental divorce, separation, marriage, cohabitation or death."[255]

One of the worst contemporary family structure issues is fatherlessness, which creates serious consequences, according to the studies cited on fathers.com. Children from homes without fathers tend to be poor, become involved in drug and alcohol abuse, drop out of school, and suffer health and emotional problems. Boys from such households are more likely to become involved in crime, and girls are more likely to become pregnant as teenagers.[256]

More modern moms are working outside the home, another family-structure change that impacts children. Specifically, over the past century, more and more mothers joined the workforce. Less than half (47 percent) of mothers were in the workforce in 1975, the first year such data was collected. By 2000, that figure grew to 73 percent, and today it remains at 70 percent among all mothers of children younger than eighteen. It is noteworthy that two-thirds (64 percent) of moms with preschool-aged children work full time outside the home.[257]

What are the consequences for children thanks to these and other modern family structural changes? Now, of course, all youth problems are not directly attributable to dysfunctional families, but certainly there is some correlation. Consider:

- "Ten percent of all abortions in this country are performed on teenagers" (Randall K. O'Bannon, "What New CDC Numbers Tell Us about Abortion in America," NRL News Today, December 3, 2019).
- More than 1.4 million gang members are involved in thirty-three thousand criminal gangs. Most of these members joined the gang as teenagers (Penny Starr, "FBI: 33,000 Criminal Gangs, 1.4 Million Members Active in U.S.," Breitbart, June 15, 2017).
- The average American less than twenty-one years of age spends ten thousand hours playing video games (Shannan Younger, "Kids and Video Games: What Games Are Safe, and How Much Should They Play?," Between Us Parents, February 27, 2013).
- There are more than 3.6 million child-abuse referrals every year ("Child Abuse Statistics & Facts," ChildHelp, accessed April 25, 2020).

These numbers are but the tip of the iceberg of problems facing American children today. One figure that might also explain in part the growing problem is the fact that religious affiliation is declining across the population. In fact, in 1972 only 7 percent of adults had no religious affiliation. Today that figure stands at 25 percent and growing.[258]

The current situation with the American family is dire. Parents are less committed to marriage, and families, as a result, are far more unstable. Children evidence that lack of stability with behaviors that produce unhealthy adults and, consequently, push this country closer to the tipping point.

Future American Family

Where does the American family go from here? At this point, there doesn't seem to be any widespread interest in returning to the past—the 1950s-era, classic nuclear family.

The trends outlined above are rather discouraging, especially for Christians and traditionalists. My attention was drawn to one view about the future American family at the midpoint of this century (2050). I suspect if we keep going as we have recently, then the following is the future.

Future families will be more diverse than even today. That outcome is partly due to the lower birth rate, but also because of immigration. The prediction is that the American family by midcentury will be more ethnically and racially diverse than today. In fact, the US Census Bureau estimates that eighty-six million Americans will be foreign-born by 2050—that's nearly 20 percent of the expected total population.[259]

The midcentury family will be represented by more single-parent households. That shouldn't surprise us, because more adults today (58 percent) believe that having children outside of marriage is not nearly the stigma it was only a few years ago, and is likely to grow as morality becomes more relativistic. Technology also fans the movement to single parenting, as seen in medical breakthroughs such as in vitro fertilization (IVF), which makes it possible for most anyone to become a parent without a marriage partner.

By midcentury, children are also expected to have more than two parents, thanks to divorce and remarriage rates, IVF, surrogacy, adoption, and same-sex parents. It's already a phenomenon in, you guessed it, California, where children can legally have up to four parents named on their birth certificates.[260] Expect government to incentivize such outcomes as well just to sustain a viable workforce.

More children will have working moms by midcentury than today, and many will have stay-at-home dads. Today more than two-thirds (70 percent) of mothers with children age eighteen or younger are in the labor force. The phenomenon of men staying at home raising the children is growing as well. That's a growing trend especially among Millennial (ages eighteen to thirty-five) fathers, and is expected to keep growing. Further, government and industry-provided childcare (a giant industry), surrogate parenting, and government educational institutions all seek to socially program the future generation.

The size of the average family will also shrink even more than the current 1.9 children per married couple. That's below the replacement rate, so there will be a variety of incentives to have children, but not too many. Keep in mind that many Millennials are already foregoing having children, which in part explains why America is not replacing itself. One estimate indicates that by the middle of the century, there will be virtually no American families with four or more children. Today (2019), the average number of people in the American family is 3.14.[261]

I fully expect the children from these future, fractured families will be at least as dysfunctional as the current crop of children with their assortment of pathologies. Likely, and unfortunately, things will continue to get worse.

Conclusion

American opinion surveys find that our nation is worse today than ever in the past—our morals are the worst ever. We are experiencing the same type of cultural and moral rot that took ancient Rome under, and to a large degree, it is due to the moral collapse of marriage and the family.[262]

America's current culture has a host of dysfunctional, moral-based indicators that suggest the coming implosion. There is a dwindling sense of moral depravity, thanks to a complicit media and condoning government policy. No wonder people's misguided moral compass is turning our political system into a corrupt, deep-state cesspool.

Modern marriage and family are radically different from what they were in the late eighteenth century. Our continued moral decline will most certainly contribute to pushing this nation past the moral tipping point into a much worse future. And remember, Jesus said the world would be just like the days of Noah—lawlessness, immorality, self-indulgent—when He returns. We are there and He is coming.

CHAPTER SIX

American Church and Anti-Christian Agenda

THROUGH THE HISTORY of the United States, the "church" has waxed and waned in terms of tolerance for outsiders, nonbelievers. Today the Christian "church" is facing an intolerant, anti-Christian backlash across our culture, and that could ultimately threaten the future of this democratic republic.

For my purposes here, I define "church" as it is used in the Bible. The Greek term is *ecclesia* (Ephesians 1:22, 5–25, 32; Matthew 16:18), which can mean the collection of individuals through the ages who have trusted in Jesus Christ as their Savior. Thus, the immigrating Christian "church" brought to America biblical principles and values that it infused into most aspects of life. However, that influence is quickly waning today, thanks to anti-Christian actions and a lackluster response from the "church."

Yes, attacks on especially orthodox, committed Christians are increasing, which leads one to ask whether we are facing a true post-Christian future. The fact is, if America is becoming post-Christian, then the anti-Christian assaults now pervasive within the culture are to be expected—and in time, Christian life will become very difficult, if not impossible, for the "church."

This chapter begins with a short review of where Christian immigrants—the "church"—began and just how vibrant was their religiosity. Then by contrast, we explore the demographics of the contemporary "church," where they are spiritually today, their Christian worldview, and how many are truly committed believers, the real targets of the growing anti-Christian movement.

We conclude the chapter with an explanation of the growth in anti-Christian actions now lighting up the culture, which is a precursor to section III of this book, where we will detail the forces of evil now opposing the American "church."

Religious Tolerance: In the Eyes of the Beholder

Christianity came to North American thanks to Europeans beginning in the sixteenth and seventeenth centuries. The Spanish and French settled in the southern portion of the continent and introduced Roman Catholicism, their dominant strand of Christianity. The northern Europeans brought a diversity of Protestant beliefs to New England down the Atlantic Coast to the Carolinas—Anglicans, Methodists, Baptists, Congregationalists, Presbyterians, Lutherans, Quakers, Mennonites, and Moravians.

The Spanish were the first to establish settlements in the New World, beginning at St. Augustine, Florida, in 1565. Soon they built Roman Catholic missions to spread Roman Catholicism—thanks to the conquistadors, first in Florida, then in Georgia and the Carolinas. Eventually, Spanish explorers and Catholic priests established missions in the territories that are now Texas, New Mexico, Arizona, and California.

The French did much the same by setting up Catholic missions with their American colonies in places from New Orleans to what is now North and South Dakota, and all the way up the winding Mississippi River basin.

The British colonies hugged the New World's Eastern Seaboard, and were predominantly Protestant except for Maryland, as described in the first section of this book. What's clear is that all the European colonies were Christian, one strand or the other. However, by the late eighteenth century, the North American continent would become dominated by Britain's thirteen colonies, which were largely Protestant.

The colonists spread out through the wilderness areas and, because of the nature of their survivalist lifestyle, they seldom had direct contact with a priest or minister, much less ever attended an actual church facility. However, in spite of their isolation from others with some notable exceptions, they would still self-identify as Christian, which for many tended to be a cultural phenomenon, not a declaration of their personal spiritual relationship with Jesus Christ.

The most orthodox Christians at that time were the Pilgrims and the Puritans. The Pilgrims came from the Netherlands with a primary mission spelled out in the Mayflower Compact:

> Having undertaken for the Glory of God, and Advancement of the Christian Faith, and the Honour of our King and Country, a Voyage to plant the first Colony in the northern Parts of Virginia; Do by these Presents, solemnly and mutually, in the Presence of God and one another, covenant and combine ourselves together into a civil Body Politick, for our better Ordering and Preservation, and Furtherance of the Ends aforesaid.[263]

The Puritans (Congregationalists) of New England were orthodox Christians as well and perhaps the best known because they kept extensive records of virtually every aspect of their private and public lives. Their religiosity (a strong feeling and practice of belief) is the subject of considerable study by scholars.

One study of the colonists' religiosity considered the Revolutionary War-era Germantown, Pennsylvania, Christian community, which provides us some indication of early church attendance, a marker of religiosity. That study estimated that half of the residents attended church.

Stephanie Wolf, the author of the study, said Christian service participation was in part due to the community's as much as the citizens' religious vigor. A broader study found that the percentage of church-attending colonists relative to the population is more than four times greater today than it was at the birth of our nation.[264]

Church attendance did grow with the young nation, especially during the Great Awakening. One minister in the early nineteenth century wrote: "There are American families in this part of the country who never saw a Bible, nor heard of Jesus Christ...the whole country, from Lake Erie to the Gulf of Mexico, is as the valley of the shadow of death."[265]

These early Americans were not "Bible thumpers," as some contemporary Christians might portend. Rather, they (especially those in the mostly rural wilderness) blended their Christian understanding with nativist views.

Yes, if asked, those colonists would likely identify as vaguely Christian, and their values were most certainly based on Christian principles, a concept developed in the first section of this volume. Their general inclination and values made them especially open to the evangelical movements in the late eighteenth and early nineteenth centuries—the Great Awakenings—as gospel preachers brought the message of Christ to the scattered and unorganized communities.

It wasn't until the late nineteenth century that significant numbers of churches—congregations with a physical facility—were formed and churchgoing (regular meetings to worship) became an American norm. In fact, America's Christian peak was reached in the 1950s when church-building and attendance boomed. That coincided with the Baby Boom, the immediate aftermath of the Second World War.

What can we conclude about Christianity's influence from the early times? Beginning in the colonial era, there was always a core of vibrant, highly religious Christians, but most colonists, especially those in remote areas, were mostly cultural Christians, thanks to their heritage—but certainly not because of their orthodoxy.

Modern American Christian Demographics

America's Christian landscape remains large and influential although it is changing. The Pew Research Center surveyed Americans in 2018 and 2019 to find that 65 percent of American adults self-identify as Christian, a drop of 12 percentage points over the past decade. Currently, according to Pew, 43 percent of Americans are Protestant, down from 51 percent in 2009 and one in five adults (20 percent) is Catholic, down from 23 percent in 2009.[266]

Those who drifted away from Christianity tend to describe their religious preference as "nothing in particular." Meanwhile, non-Christian religions in America have grown modestly, while self-described atheists grew from 2 to 4 percent; agnostics make up 5 percent.[267]

Pew also measured the frequency of church attendance, a factor of religiosity. It found that the share of Americans who attend services at least once or twice a month dropped 7 percentage points over the past decade.[268]

Pew concludes that the US is "steadily becoming less Christian and less religiously observant as the share of adults who are not religious grows." Of course, the anti-Christian crowd jumped on this report to celebrate the demise of Christianity in America. However, those cheers are way off base.[269]

A Harvard study throws cold water on arguments that Christianity is shrinking. Glenn Stanton, the director of Family Formation Studies at Focus on the Family, a Colorado Springs, Colorado, nonprofit organization, took issue with the raft of articles claiming that Christian affiliation is declining and boasting that soon "religious faith in America is going the way of the yellow pages and travel maps."[270]

Mr. Stanton cites the research from scholars at Harvard University and Indiana University Bloomington, who crush that myth. That research questioned the "secularization thesis," which finds "the U.S. is following most advanced industrial nations in the death of their once vibrant faith culture." The researchers found just the opposite. That is,

American religion continues to enjoy "persistent and exceptional intensity," and they admit that this country "remains an exceptional outlier and potential counter example to the secularization thesis."[271]

The study considered the nature of the faith, intensity, and seriousness factors that Americans hold and practice that faith. The researchers, as we've already seen, found that mainline American churches are tanking, and those members are simply going to churches elsewhere. The research found that the inventory of the truly faithful—those who attend church more than once a week, pray daily, and accept the Bible as wholly reliable and deeply instructive—remains constant and has for the last fifty years or more.

What is the size of that cohort? Stanton says one in three Americans fits the above description (truly faithful), which is many times greater than in other countries. They attend services more than once a week, twice the rate of those in other industrial countries. And, not surprisingly, one-third of Americans hold to the belief that the Bible is God's Word as well.

These indicators of Christian belief, says Stanton, make the US "exceptional," and that exceptionalism hasn't declined over time. In fact, the researchers argue that the number of Americans who fit this description is actually increasing.[272]

Stanton says the numbers of those with strong faith are actually growing. He compares a 1989 study that found 39 percent of the religious actually held strong beliefs and practices to today's number, which is now 47 percent.[273]

Stanton characterizes the growing Christian gulf as between the "faithful" and the "dabblers." He explains that the distinction is obvious. Congregations of the "faithful" teach the Bible "with seriousness, [call] its people to real discipleship, and [encourage] daily intimacy with God."

Perhaps the southern novelist Flannery O'Connor said it best. Stanton writes, "If your church isn't going to believe and practice actual Christianity, then 'to hell with it,' this is what people are saying with their choices."[274]

J. Warner Wallace, a senior fellow at the Colson Center for Christian Worldview and an adjunct professor of apologetics at Biola University, agrees with Stanton and offers a useful explanation of the Christian demographics registered by Pew's surveys.[275]

Wallace illustrates the current situation with American Christianity using three objects. His illustration requires an empty shoe box, a kitchen pot that is about three-quarters the size of the box, and a teacup—or better, a tiny espresso cup.

The shoebox, according to Wallace, represents everyone in America—believers and unbelievers. There are Americans who populate the box—Christians, Muslims, and Jews, atheists, agnostics, and other religions.

The pot inside the shoebox represents all Americans who identify themselves as Christian. Recent surveys indicate the number of those who self-identify as Christian is shrinking about 1 percent each year and is now standing, according to Pew, at 65 percent of the entire US population.

The espresso cup resting inside the large Christian pot is what the Barna Group, according to surveys, identifies as the 17 percent of American Christians "who consider their faith important and attend church regularly actually have a biblical worldview." They are the genuine article, what Wallace says are "those who claim to be Christians and actually know what Christianity teaches."[276]

These "espresso cup" Christians are strongly affiliated with their faith, attend church regularly, read and believe the Bible, and allow their faith to shape the way they view the world. Wallace asks: "How large is the cup?" He concludes that these "espresso cup" Christians are only a small fraction of the larger "pot" of those who self-identify with the faith.

Wallace draws a number of conclusions from his useful illustration about the size of the serious American Christian population. What is clear, says Wallace, is that today there are fewer people who claim a Christian affiliation than ever before—they jumped out of the pot into the larger shoebox to join the atheists, agnostics, and other religious groups.

On an encouraging note, however, the remnant that is in the "espresso cup" isn't shrinking. They continue to pursue their faith with both vigor and purpose in spite of cultural pressures and America's move to secularization.

Wallace also concludes that engaged Christians are more likely to be in the cup. Certainly, as liberal Christian churches fold, other churches, especially those "committed to teaching classic Christian principles are far more likely to grow." Wallace writes, "Theology and rationality matter," a conclusion that Stanton would agree with.

Wallace explains with optimism that those who jumped out of the pot don't immediately embrace atheism, either. They're still open to hearing "a reasoned, accurate and articulate description of the Christian worldview." They can be re-attracted to Christianity, and the "espresso cup" Christians must engage them and show them why Christianity matters.

Further, it should not surprise America's committed Christians that the "espresso cup" Christians in our culture are almost exclusively in conservative churches, according to a study by a Canadian professor of religion.[277]

Professor Millard Haskell at Wilfrid Laurier University, Ontario, Canada, identified using statistical analysis the factors most associated with church growth. Not surprising, conservative Protestant theology, taking the Bible literally, is a key predictor of church growth. Meanwhile, many mainline Protestant churches are hemorrhaging membership to the tune of more than one million a year, which results in hundreds of churches closing annually.[278]

The American churches that are growing hold to traditional Christian beliefs, such as that Jesus Christ rose physically from the grave. Also, the pastors of those growing churches tend to be the most theologically conservative and the declining churches the least conservative.

Another predictor of church growth or decline was whether the Bible was taken literally or metaphorically. The conclusion is that theology and church growth are linked.

Professor Haskell cites another study that found similar results, "The Faith Communities Today Study," which found that "growing churches had clergy and congregants who were theological conservatives." That matches both Wallace's and Stanton's views, cited earlier.

There is also a liberal myth that theology doesn't matter, which Haskell's study debunks. What matters, according to critics of Haskell's research, is that the congregants believed strongly and could articulate those beliefs. Not true, finds Haskell.

The growing, conservative church clergy held to the conviction that it is "very important to encourage non-Christians to become Christians." Those pastors rightly believe that Jesus is the only way to salvation and that the Body of Christ must "go and make disciples everywhere."

The shrinking theologically liberal church crowd embraces a polar opposite view to that of the conservatives regarding salvation. The liberals hold to the belief that conversion of non-Christians is not a priority and, in fact, there are many paths to salvation.

Haskell states that from a purely social scientific perspective, and putting aside theological rightness of one doctrinal position over another, conservative Protestant doctrine is a clear winner.

So, what have we found about modern American Christianity? There remains a vibrant core of committed American Christians—"espresso cup" Christians—who overwhelmingly find their homes inside mostly evangelical, fundamentalist Protestant churches.

Avalanche of Anti-Christian Attacks on the Modern Church

So far in this chapter, we've established that Christianity was embedded in the American culture from the earliest European founding in the sixteenth and seventeenth centuries. However, true Christian orthodoxy wasn't widespread until the nineteenth century, with a few exceptions, such as among the Pilgrims and Puritans. But with time, America saw the emergence of a cohort of committed, "espresso cup" Christians, which remains true today. Along with that phenomenon came three issues that helped to shape the contemporary American church: vacillating religious tolerance, mixing worldviews, and growing anti-Christian actions.

First, religious tolerance was a flagship issue for America from her founding. To America's credit, beginning with the first European settlers, this land was known as a destination for those seeking religious freedom. That expectation brought many of our early colonists to this country, but over the intervening years to the present, America has demonstrated a spotty history regarding true religious tolerance, which is once again raising its ugly head today.

Some of the early colonialists abandoned true religious tolerance, however. Instead, they sided with their established "church," such as the Puritans (Congregationalists). They vigorously attacked nonconformists such as Baptists as religious interlopers and even put some to death.

The serious influence of colonial Christian denominational affiliation really tested the principal of religious tolerance leading up to the founding of the United States. An early spark that advanced true religious freedom (tolerance) came thanks to eighteenth-century evangelical Christians and their ensuing sacrifice at the hands of government-sponsored churches.

The Reverend John Waller, a Baptist preacher, visited Caroline county, Virginia, in 1771. While preaching there, he was viciously attacked by an Anglican minister who walked up to the pulpit where Waller was preaching and unceremoniously jammed the butt end of a horse whip into Waller's mouth. Then the Anglican minister, with the support of state officials, dragged Waller outside the church, where the local sheriff beat the Baptist preacher into a bloody pulp before throwing him in jail for 113 days for the crime of being a Baptist preacher in an Anglican state. Evidently, there were at least 150 similar attacks against Baptists in Virginia between 1760 and 1778, many carried out by Anglican Church officials.[279]

Similar antireligious freedom activities took place even after the birth of the new republic. For example, in the early nineteenth-century New York City, Samuel Morse, the inventor of the Morse code and the telegraph, assailed Catholic immigrants to America. His anti-Catholic beliefs and actions were echoed elsewhere, whereby Protestant mobs burned convents, sacked Catholic churches, and continued those types of attacks well into the twentieth century.

Unfortunately, similar egregious behavior was part of America's history even in the twentieth century. In the 1920s, Congress restricted Jewish immigration, as did President Franklin Roosevelt's State Department during World War II. Those anti-Semitic decisions likely condemned an unknown number of Jews to Nazi death camps.

The second issue that helped shape the contemporary American church, even the "espresso cup" Christians, is a compromised worldview. Today, according to pollster George Barna, even those who claim to embrace a biblical worldview are influenced by dangerous alternative worldviews.[280]

Barna partnered with Summit Ministries to investigate among adherent American Christians how much other worldviews infiltrated their thinking. Specifically, they considered new spirituality, secularism, postmodernism, and Marxism and found some of those worldviews infiltrating the views of Christians.

Nearly four in ten practicing Christians evidenced sympathy with some Muslim teachings, 61 percent favored some new spirituality ideas, and 54 percent found some common interest with postmodernist views, 36 percent even found support for ideas associated with Marxism and 29 percent embrace ideas based on secularism.[281]

The pollution of Christian worldviews with other perspectives is revealing and especially evident among Millennials (born 1981 to 1996) and Gen-Xers (born 1965 to 1980), up to eight times as likely as the Baby Boomers (born 1946 to 1964). The ideas the young believers embrace is shocking.

New spirituality emphasizes the supernatural as well as dissatisfaction with institutions like formal churches. Nearly a third (28 percent) of practicing Christians agree with the worldview that "all people pray to the same god or spirit, no matter what name they use for that spiritual being." A third of practicing Christians also strongly agree that "if you do good, you will receive good, and if you do bad, you will receive bad." More than half (52 percent) of practicing Christians also embrace this karmic statement that the Bible teaches that "God helps those who help themselves." That's not in the Bible, but founder Benjamin Franklin helped to popularize the motto in his *Poor Richard's Almanac.*[282]

Many practicing Christians embrace secularism's materialism, the view that the material world is all there is—nothing beyond this life. Thus the "meaning and purpose comes from working hard to earn as much as possible so you can make the most of life," a view embraced by 20 percent of practicing Christians. A third of millennials and Gen-Xers favor this materialistic view as well.[283]

Barna found that one-fifth (19 percent) of practicing Christians embrace the postmodernist view that "no one can know for certain what meaning and purpose there is to life." Nearly a quarter of all practicing Christians (23 percent) also strongly endorse the view that "what is morally right or wrong depends on what an individual believes."[284]

Some practicing Christians even embrace select Marxist views about economic and property issues. Specifically, one in nine (11 percent) practicing Christians agrees that "private property encourages greed and envy," a view embraced by one in five Millennials and Gen-Xers. It is frightening that 14 percent of practicing Christians strongly agree that "the government, rather than individuals, should control as much of the resources as necessary to ensure that everyone gets their fair share."[285]

Finally, contemporary Christians are being shaped by the current groundswell of anti-Christian attacks. The primary target of those attacks tends to be the most outspoken Christians, the "espresso cup" Christians, the core of America's faithful.

In 2019, Vice President Mike Pence warned Liberty University graduates that they should be prepared to be "shunned or ridiculed" for their Christian faith.[286]

Mr. Pence was the speaker at Liberty's 46th Commencement, where he offered advice to the new graduates about people of faith facing increased attacks for their beliefs. "Some of the loudest voices for tolerance today have little tolerance for traditional Christian beliefs," Pence said. "So, as you go about your daily life, just be ready, because you are going to be asked not just to tolerate things that violate your faith, you're going to be asked to censor them, to bow down to the idols of popular culture."[287]

The vice president and his family know firsthand the sting of anti-Christian attacks from the political left. Early in 2019, liberals expressed outrage that Karen Pence accepted a teaching position at Immanuel Christian School in Springfield, Virginia, which requires students, parents, and employees to pledge that they accept traditional Christian beliefs.

The vice president was attacked by South Bend, Indiana, Mayor Pete Buttigieg, a then-candidate for the 2020 Democratic presidential nomination and an openly gay man, who implied that Pence's Christian-based views about homosexual "marriage," is a "quarrel" with God. Pence believes in the biblical understanding of marriage as a union between a man and a woman.

Anti-Christian attacks are evident within the higher education establishment. Dr. Jerry Falwell Jr., president of Liberty University, said anti-Christian vitriol is commonplace, especially on our nation's college campuses. He explained that Christian groups are too often banned or harassed, and courses are held to combat things like "Christian privilege" and teach students how to "queer the Bible."[288]

The mainstream media fans the anti-Christian attacks. Dr. Falwell called out the *New York Times*, which solicited online examples of "how traumatizing those bastions of bigotry are" by attacking Christian schools.

Other media outlets identified Pence's commencement address at Liberty as an example of "bigotry dressed up as Christianity." Another outlet portrayed Mr. Pence's "anti-abortion stance" as a way to paint pro-life views as a form of intolerance.

The anti-Christian bigotry tossed at Vice President Pence exposes the growing trend of vitriolic attacks by progressives and their complicit liberal media allies.

Sociologist George Yancey is familiar with the growing anti-Christian actions against especially the "espresso cup" Christians. He studied thirty-plus years of data tracking approval ratings for evangelical and fundamentalist Christians in America. Yancey concludes that the number of those who dislike conservative Christians hasn't changed, but their profile has transformed. Specifically, according to the American National Election Studies questionnaires, those who rate evangelical and fundamentalist Christians most negatively are politically liberal, highly educated, and less religious. Recently, this cohort of haters added an important factor to their profile; they are now richer than in the past.[289]

The new wealth of these critics means their anti-Christian hostility comes at a higher price. Yancey references a study in the *Review of Religion Research,* which states "but if those with anti-Christian hostility have gained economic power, then Christian activists may be correct in that they now pay a stiffer price for that animosity."[290]

Evidence of that anti-Christian economic power was obvious when several states considered Religious Freedom Restoration Act legislation. Those anti-Christian deep pockets pushed major companies like Disney, Angie's List, and Walmart to complain that such laws would be discriminatory.

As just noted, the growing avalanche of anti-Christian hostility is especially focused on evangelicals and fundamentalist Christians, according to the Pew Research Center. Evidently, Pew writes, Americans had a more positive view of evangelicals if they had evangelical friends, but such relationships tend to be rare among leaders in academia, entertainment, and other social spheres of influence.

Yancey also studied and wrote about "christianophobia" (the fear or hatred of Christians) at secular universities. He indicates that Christianity's cultural dominance is fading, and as that happens, conservative Christians sense a growing animosity toward them and their faith.[291]

Evidently, the sense of anti-Christian hostility has empirical backing. The previously cited American National Election Studies, which includes questions about animosity toward various social groups, found that a third of respondents rated conservative Christians much lower than all other religious and racial groups except for atheists. Predictably, the most consistent negative ratings came from white, highly educated, politically progressive, and well-heeled respondents.[292]

Another Pew study documents the growing hostility to Christians as well. Pew found that about half of all Americans believe that evangelicals face discrimination. What's clear is that we are living in a post-Christian society where our faith is no longer automatically respected and "christianophobia" is a real phenomenon.

Earlier, we established that, according to Pew and Barna surveys, many Americans have an unfavorable view of conservative Christians, and we profiled those who are more likely to demonstrate anti-Christian attitudes. But just how bad is the problem?

Yancey's research tried to measure the intensity of the anti-Christian attitudes. He found that progressive activists evidenced true "christianophobia." He posed questions to elicit the degree of their animosity using a range that began with mild disgust up to irrational hatred that can lead to discrimination. The results are truly frightening. For example, one respondent said: "Kill them all, let their god sort them out." Another wrote: "A torturous death would be too good for them."

Yes, there is unreasonable hatred and anti-Christian discrimination targeted at the "espresso cup" Christians. Such views have tangible consequences and appear to be getting worse and more frequent. And perhaps not surprising, Yancey found that one consequence was that half of his academia respondents were less willing to hire a fundamentalist Christian.

Conclusion

America is experiencing significant and growing anti-Christian discrimination. Moving forward, the anti-Christian rabble rousers intend to remove all vestiges of Christianity from our culture, pushing this country over the moral tipping point.

Pope Benedict XVI called our attention to this startling threat. He explained that a society that rejects Christ does not simply move forward, but necessarily becomes anti-Christian—and the end of that process is serious.[293]

There is no middle ground between being once Christian based and becoming secular—America's likely end state, barring radical renewal. America needs the tenets of Christianity to survive as a democracy, a view shared by Catholic Cardinal Joseph Ratzinger, the former prefect of the Congregation of the Doctrine of the Faith, who said:

> Meanwhile, the fact remains that this democracy [modern] is a product of the fusion of the Greek and the Christian heritage and therefore can survive only in this foundational connection. If we do not recognize this again and accordingly learn to live democracy with a view to Christianity and Christianity with a view to the free democratic state, we will surely gamble away democracy.[294]

CHAPTER SEVEN

Anti-Christian American Business

AMERICAN BUSINESS IS a reflection of the nation's moral foundation. For much of this nation's early history, that moral foundation was Christian-based—but how times have changed, making the contemporary business sector anti-Christian much as our governments and public schools.

This chapter will describe early American business and how it was built on an ethical Christian foundation, and it will explain why our nation's prosperity is due in a large part to that foundation. However, especially in recent years, a number of anti-Christian factors are quickly eroding that foundation, making American businesses more anti-Christian.

Christianity's Influence on Early-American Business

The nineteenth-century French aristocrat and cultural observer Alexis de Tocqueville said in his book, *Democracy of America*: "There is no country in the world where the Christian religion retains a greater influence over the souls of men than America."[295]

The moral principles that guided most human action in early America were rooted in Christianity, as de Tocqueville pointed out. Although all our founders weren't in agreement about every Christian principle, most drew their moral and ethical guidelines from the Ten Commandments and the teachings of Jesus Christ.

Those founders firmly believed that liberty and justice, especially in economic issues, depended on the moral and ethical demands of Christian teachings. Founder Benjamin Franklin is considered a deist by some historians; nevertheless, he emphasized in a letter to Ezra Stiles in 1790 that "as to Jesus of Nazareth, my opinion of whom you particularly desire, I think the system of morals and His religion, as he left them to us, the best the world ever saw or is likely to see."[296]

Founder John Adams agreed with Franklin. Adams wrote in an 1810 letter to Benjamin Rush: "Religion and virtue are the only foundations, not only of republicanism and of all free government but of social felicity under all governments and in all the combinations of human society."[297]

Yes, the colonialists came to the New World for a variety of reasons. Many, as outlined earlier in this book, came to escape religious persecution, while others, such as those who came to Virginia, came primarily for business purposes—profit. No matter their primary reason for coming to the New World, they shared something in common with what both Franklin and Adams asserted in their letters: The Christian religion played a critical role in all aspects of colonial life, as evidenced in the previous chapters in this section.

Those who came to establish the Virginia colony had a charter from the British Crown and were funded by a group of stockholders who clearly expected personal gain. Their charter was issued by the British monarch, who expected the colonialists to reflect the Crown's authority in the New World, as well as to embrace the Anglican Church, and in fact Virginia formally established Anglicanism as the colony's state religion.

The establishment of a formal Christian religion was expected, whether the colonialists were English, Spanish, or French. What was not disputed at the time was that religion, politics, and economics were integrally interwoven within every aspect of colonial life, especially prior to the Revolutionary War.

The morality of the British Crown's economic policies became a significant contentious issue for the English colonies just before the Revolutionary War, however. By 1770, disputes arose in the English colonies, especially over Britain's taxation policy. The colonialists hoped to persuade the Crown to modify English taxes and regulations governing commerce because they significantly disadvantaged the colonies. However, matters between the Crown and the American colonies got out of hand and soon all-out war erupted.[298]

The American Revolution (1775–1783) was as much about economics as it was about politics and freedom from the monarchy. The deafening cry for political and economic independence from the colonial middle class was especially loud. In fact, many colonialists embraced the rallying cry of British philosopher John Locke, who famously advocated for the disadvantaged: "unalienable rights to life, liberty and property," popular Christian values then and now.

Locke also said the oppressed had the right to revolt against the Crown. He said:

Whenever the Legislators endeavor to take away, and destroy the Property of the People, or to reduce them to Slavery under Arbitrary Power, they put themselves into a state of War with the People, who are thereupon absolved from any farther Obedience, and are left to the common Refuge, which God hath provided for all Men, against Force and Violence. Whensoever therefore the Legislative shall transgress this fundamental Rule of Society; and either by Ambition, Fear, Folly or Corruption, endeavor to grasp themselves, or put into the hands of any other an Absolute Power over the Lives, Liberties, and Estates of the People; By this breach of Trust they forfeit the Power, the People had put into their hands, for quite contrary ends, and it devolves to the People, who have a Right to resume their original Liberty.[299]

Locke's cry rang true for the colonialists, which is why the founders embedded the Crown's injustices in our Declaration of Independence and the important rights in our Constitution (the Bill of Rights). That founding document paid very special attention to apply those rights to economic matters, which contributed to American prosperity from the very outset.

Specifically, America's Constitution includes an economic charter of sorts that was both informed by Christianity as well as a general reaction to the lessons learned from being under the oppressive rule of the tax-drunk British Crown. That "economic charter" spawned a "common market" of sorts for the new states by regulating interstate commerce and prohibiting tariffs among the member states. It also established a bankruptcy law, a currency and fixed standards of weights and measures; stood up a postal system; established federal roads to help interstate commerce; and fixed rules governing "intellectual property"—patents and copyrights.

America's economic model was ideally designed to leverage what Christianity had already established within the colonies—a robust capitalist economy. I explained in chapter 2 of this book the significant role the Roman Catholic Church played in the emergence of capitalism, as well as John Calvin's theological contribution that compelled Europeans to embrace a new understanding of the importance of hard work, the Protestant ethic, a winning motivator when combined with capitalism.

Economic historian David Landes came to the same conclusion. He said capitalism and the Protestant ethic delivered to the Western world true economic success. In fact, by the time of the Revolutionary War, the average income of the colonialists exceeded that of their counterparts in England, making the British colonies the envy of the world.

The colonies' economic success, according to Landes, included five factors that led to economic prosperity and are derived from the capitalist model combined with the Protestant ethic: the joy that each person is made in the image of God; the religious value of hard and good work; "the theological separation of the creator from the creature, such that nature is subordinated to man, not surrounded by taboos;" the Judeo-Christian sense of linear time (progress); and respect for the marketplace.[300]

This dynamite formula was necessarily joined by *caritas* to create America's economic exceptionalism. *Caritas* is Latin for "charity," a Christian term. Durante di Alighiero degli Alighieri, commonly known as Dante, described *caritas* in his epic poem, "The Divine Comedy," as "the love that moves the sun and all the stars." It is the nonmaterial element that holds things together: families, associations, nations, and economies.[301]

Understand that capitalism isn't just about materialism and profit, as some modern capitalists espouse. No, *caritas* is the necessary Christian ingredient that makes capitalism work. Successful economies are fueled by hard work and opportunity, but also by *caritas*, God's spiritual gifts—charity, honesty, trust, teamwork, respect for the law, and more.[302]

Numerous leading academics endorse Christianity's significant influence for America's early economic life. For example, Dr. Christopher Clark, a Harvard professor of eighteenth- and nineteenth-century North American and US social and cultural history, summarized a number of scholarly papers that address the notion of "putting the morality back in" the studies of the early American economy, and "putting the economics back in" the studies of religion, morality, and ethics in the colonial and early national periods.[303]

Dr. Clark and other historians' observations about America's economic history help us appreciate Christianity's early impact for the American economy. Specifically, Clark calls out the work of Katherine Carti-Engel, a professor of religious studies at Texas A & M and an affiliate fellow of the Center for the Study of Religion at Princeton University. Dr. Carte-Engel claims there was congruence between religion and economic development in early America. She said the concept was "that commerce, rather than morality [Christian doctrine], actually promoted moral regeneration, that is, the process of establishing the connections of trust essential for successful trade [which] reinforced moral character and rewarded ethical behavior."

Another aspect of Christianity's relationship with economic development was explained by Dr. Thomas Haskell, a twentieth-century American historian who served as a professor at Rice University. He argued that international trade promoted humanitarianism, a Christian virtue, by advancing human empathy "and by demonstrating causes and effects not just within face-to-face communities, but at great distances and between strangers."[304]

Mark Valeri, a professor of history at Washington University St. Louis, wrote: "The late seventeenth and early eighteenth centuries brought important Puritan leaders towards an acceptance of money as a commodity, and of interest payments as justifiable, that would have been rare only a few decades previously."

This view demonstrates an active role by the clergy and, by association, Christianity's influence in early American economics.

Jack D. Marietta, a professor at the University of Arizona, wrote that "Quaker doctrines appear to have fostered intolerance for excessive indebtedness in theory, and often enough in practice, as a trail of disownments of prominent Friends."[305] Benjamin Franklin, a representative to the Constitutional Convention from Pennsylvania, was heavily influenced by Quaker theology and put forth the same view about indebtedness and frugality in his many statements.

He famously said:

The way to wealth is as plain as the way to market. It depends chiefly on two words, industry and frugality: that is, waste neither time nor money, but make the best use of both. Without industry and frugality nothing will do, and with them everything.[306]

A nation's economic policies are linked to its moral foundation, a view evidenced above and also by Professor Clark. The Harvard professor asserts:

Debt, as scholars well recognize, was not merely a material or technical arrangement; indebtedness entailed a skein of social connections and obligations. Theologians, pastors, and spiritual leaders had to consider not merely the economic aspect of indebtedness but the social entanglements it entailed.

Clark continued that thought, saying:

Meanwhile, Lutheran and Catholic traditions in the eighteenth century continued to reject usury [borrowing, lending money at high rates of interest], and these churches continued officially to restate this position well into the nineteenth century.

Such church-endorsed views about economic issues influenced early American lawmakers to govern responsibility.

Accordingly, there is also evidence, suggested in all the papers summarized by Professor Clark, that religious groups tended over time to lead (or be pushed) towards acceptance of the practices of an expanding market economy—a capitalist model. There were several reasons for this.

As Professor Jose Torre with the College at Brockport, a state university of New York, explained, the "spheres of action accorded to God were during the seventeenth century became increasingly constrained by the natural laws of physics. That's when the concept of 'Providence' was 'increasingly invoked as a way of interpreting God's will while ensuring that God remained inert, and conforming to the rules that He had manifestly laid down.'" Translation: The early theologians came to recognize that capitalism was okay for a Christian people.

Lori Merish, a professor of English at Georgetown University, wrote in her book *Sentimental Materialism* to suggest that, by the 1820s or so, "this [the invoking of God] had led to the acceptance in many evangelical churches of the notion that comfort and acquisitiveness were not evils to be eschewed but indications of divine favor." Thus, becoming wealthy was not against Christian teaching.

The above demonstrates that economics, much like politics, is indeed a reflection of the moral and ethical principles of society. Early American society was very Christian, and as a result, so was its economic system—but over the ensuing two-plus centuries, much of that Christian foundation was secularized or abandoned.

America Abandoned Economic Moral Foundation

Christianity has lost much of its original influence over the United States. As one pastor said, "There is no country in the world where the Christian religion has lost more of its moral influence over the souls of men than in America."[307]

The pastor's correct observation reminded me of the warning the prophet Micah delivered more than two millennia ago. In Micah 7:3–4 (NIV), the prophet wrote:

> Concerning evil, both hands do it well. The prince asks, also the judge, for a bribe, and a great man speaks the desire of his soul; so, they weave it together. The best of them is like a briar, the most upright like a thorn hedge. The day when you post your watchmen, your punishment will come. Then their confusion will occur.

What does that say about today's economy? Our founders would agree that morality springs from religious faith, and people with no Christian theology will have an impaired moral philosophy for all efforts—including business. No wonder contemporary America faces economic crises today. It is rapidly abandoning Christian principles and values that previously established our economy's foundation.

Yes, corruption, the issue warned of by the prophet Micah, has become a serious problem for American businesses. Most every day, business is called out for its corruption thanks to rampant greed, and that is a reality for almost half of all Americans, according to recent opinion surveys.

A 2018 Gallup poll found that almost half (47 percent) of adults believe corporate greed is the cause of America's moral decline. In fact, four in five adults (79 percent) believe the morals and values of America are declining across all areas of life.[308]

Who are the most corrupt in our society? To gauge corruption, Gallup asked about people's views regarding the degree of honesty and ethical behavior among the leading professions and occupations. Most (58 percent) of the respondents ranked our political class, specifically our Congress, as low or very low in ethics and honesty. Only 8 percent of respondents held a high or very high impression of members of Congress concerning honesty and ethics.[309]

The "business sector" wasn't much better than Congress. Only 17 percent ranked business executives high or very high in honesty and ethics. Others in the business community fared little better in terms of honesty and ethics: building contractors ranked at 29 percent, bankers earned 27 percent, stockbrokers were low with 14 percent, and advertising professionals got a paltry 13 percent.

Why is our business sector corrupt? Why is the business sector also becoming especially anti-Christian? There are a number of culprits contributing to the corruption perception as well as the business sector's growing anti-Christian trend. Consider these issues separately, first business corruption and then the growing anti-Christian bias.

The business sector is evidencing more corruption today because it is abandoning its original Christian foundation.

First, politicians work with the business sector to address poverty and societal inequality, which lead to corruption. Contemporary policies aim to have both liberty and equality, but those concepts can't truly coexist in a capitalist economy. Achieve one and the other ceases to exist. However, progressives in modern government tell citizens they are entitled to be equal with everyone in terms of material wealth. What does that do? It inevitably pulls down those on the top of the economic scale and fuels greed and envy at the bottom. That's commonly considered socialism—whereby government takes from the rich and gives to the poor, ruining motivation to work at both ends.

Second, some within our culture seek to remake America by encouraging more diversity, which includes welcoming immigrants who hold onto the ways of the nations left behind. The US Census Bureau predicts that America may soon cease to embrace our founding and a long commonly held moral philosophy because immigrants bring with them philosophies and cultures inimical to our Christian roots; they refuse to thoroughly integrate in our culture. The outcome of that phenomenon is the destruction of what made this country exceptional: the combination of capitalism, the Protestant work ethic, and the foundational Christian principles, as well as the spiritual gifts of *caritas*.

Leonard Read, the founder of the Foundation for Economic Education, said: "Economics is a branch of moral philosophy." That means if we separate our economic realm from our Christian foundation, we are doomed to failure and certainly to more corruption.[310] That's what is happening today.

Finally, the ethical principles of a free market are rapidly disappearing in America's economy due to the desire by some to paint "profit" as a dirty word, a concept embraced by our founding Christian model.

Dr. Richard Ebeling, a professor of economics at the Citadel, the military college of South Carolina, wrote that we are abandoning free markets that rely on Christian principles. He states:

> The hallmark of a truly free market is that all associations and relationships are based on voluntary agreement and mutual consent. Another way of saying this is that in the free market society, people are morally and legally viewed as sovereign individuals possessing rights to their life, liberty, and honestly acquired property, who may not be coerced into any transaction that they do not consider being to their personal betterment and advantage.[311]

What is the basis of these free-market principles? They are familiar to students of the Christian Scriptures. Professor Ebeling wrote:

> You don't kill, you don't steal, and you don't cheat through fraud or misrepresentation. You can only improve your own position by improving the circumstances of others. Your talents, abilities, and efforts must all be focused on one thing: what will others take in trade from you for the revenues you want to earn as the source of your own income and profits?[312]

Unfortunately, a growing number of influential people today, especially on the political left, believe "profit" is a dirty word and the pursuit of it is at the root of man's troubles. That view is representative of progressive thought that would put the nation's material and production resources into the hands of big government to equally redistribute the wealth based on need. Of course, that's the definition of socialism, which scuttles liberty and is contrary to the principles of capitalism and the Protestant work ethic, the driving forces of American economic success.

Our economic model works because it harnesses that time-tested model, and especially because of the American entrepreneur's desire to stay in business by satisfying his customers. That is just the opposite of how big government operates when it oversees an economic enterprise. Are government-run US Postal Service and public schools cost-effective? Not really. There are far more cost-effective alternatives—and besides, public "services" depend on political coercion to operate, and they use threats of punishing consequences for noncompliance as well as legally pick our pockets—through taxation—to fund these "services." The truth is these government enterprises could care less whether the "customer" (the taxpayer) is pleased with their service, and they seldom pay for their poor performance.

Yes, big, government-run services like the post office provide a glimpse into what we give up to embrace socialism as opposed to a free-market economy. Unfortunately, our growing progressive political class seeks to make socialism our future economic model. Progressive politicians have a simple message for all Americans: You don't have to work hard. Just vote for me and I'll meet your needs out of other citizens' pockets. That message is inimical to our founding, Christian-based economic model.

That cancerous way of thinking is catching fire across America, however. Today, more than four in ten (43 percent) Americans believe socialism would be good for America. Socialism is especially welcomed by many leading self-identified Democrats and in fact, since 2010, a majority of Democrats (57 percent) have said they have a positive view of socialism.[313]

The surge in misguided economic policy (the corruption of our Christian economic model) and especially the rise in the appeal of socialism are accompanied by a surge in anti-Christian actions by the business sector. That's not a coincidence, and this is why our economic system is in trouble. Consider:

First, American atheists are using the business sector to target Christians. In the past, atheism was simply the belief that there is no god. That changed in these modern times to mean an ideological movement that is rank anti-Christian. Contemporary atheists are the leading cohorts who use cultural Marxism in the business world to push an anti-Christian agenda.

Cultural Marxism is a "revolutionary leftist idea that traditional culture is the source of oppression." It attacks the foundations of modern culture—the traditional family, marriage, patriotism, Christian-based morality, law, and order—as well as seeks to establish economic Marxism, a tyrannical version of socialism.[314]

These modern anti-Christian atheists use cultural Marxism in the business sector for their political purposes. They are especially focused on Christianity as evil, and religion in general as an oppressive scourge on society.

Modern American atheists tend to be more affluent than the ideological godless in the past. As a result, they use their newfound deep pockets to leverage the business sector to set conditions that discriminate against Christians and their belief system. Specifically, they force the business sector to attack America's Christian foundations and specifically advance anti-Christian issues such as homosexual marriage, abortion on demand, and even more subtle matters like forcing businesses to work on Sundays when the owners' faith is conflicted.

Second, the ideology of humanism is pervasive across our culture, creating a hostile environment for Christians even in the business world.

Humanists, who most often self-identify as progressives, have produced a thoroughly anti-Christian cultural revolution. They typically don't believe in God (at least the God of the Bible), but they do believe in using social justice approaches to better man's lot in life.

They espouse reason, ethics, and the search for human fulfillment while rejecting God and any religion-based morality. In fact, humanists believe that man alone is capable of being ethical and moral. They focus on understanding of free thought, speech, and the intrinsic potential of mankind. They promote tolerance of all types of diversity.

This is the sort of nonsense that is pervasive in today's public schools and within our government. It is becoming, in part by association, an aspect of the business sector as well.

Russian author and Christian ethicist Alexander Solzhenitsyn observed that humanism offers no solution to man's condition:

> If humanism were right in declaring that man is born to be happy, he would not be born to die. Since his body is doomed to die, his task on Earth evidently must be of a more spiritual nature.

Solzhenitsyn's statement about the dead matches the truth in the Scriptures about our spiritual nature: We should seek God (Acts 17:26–27) and embrace Christ as our Redeemer (Hebrews 6:9); Christ will then open the door to salvation (Revelation 3:20).[315]

Humanists, like atheists, tend to use their economic means to advance their revolution against Christians. Those efforts include the intimidation of businesses to marginalize and discriminate against Christians and their religion by forcing government to target them for disadvantage.

In summary, a number of factors are eroding our Christian economic foundation: big-government policy; foreign anti-capitalist business philosophies brought here by immigrants who fail to integrate into our culture; the growing popularity of socialism; and the ideological, insidious, atheistic-fueled, anti-Christian movement and its humanist partners who use business levers to advance anti-Christian political agendas.

Anti-Christian Movement Employs the Business World

It is instructive to examine how other nations deal with similar problems before considering how the above changes to our economic model play out in a growing anti-Christian America. Specifically, Europe often experiences societal movements before they come to full bloom in the United States, and that may be true in the case of the anti-Christian movement now attacking European countries.

In 2019, anti-Christian hostility peaked in Europe. The motivation for those anti-Christian attacks varies. For example, radical feminists and secularists attacked church facilities because they perceived Christian churches as symbols of patriarchal power and authority. Others attacked Christians because of their rejection of homosexuality, and a growing Islamic minority in Europe demonstrates deep-seated, faith-based hostility toward Christians.[316]

The French Catholic bishop of Frejus-Toulon, Dominque Rey, said the attacks against Christian churches in Europe are taking place within the "context of a European society marked by secularism, nihilism, hedonism, cultural and moral relativism, consumerism, and the widespread loss of the sense of the sacred."[317]

These anti-Christian attacks are quite revealing regarding the radical cultural transformation across Europe. The bishop explained:

> In the past, even those who said they were non-Christian lived in a cultural context marked by Christianity....roots that have been abandoned by our culture and by our societies. Once the Christian roots, which were the common denominator, were removed, people turned to communitarianism, which led to a social fragmentation that is leading to a break. To find a common base of values and points of reference, Europe must restore centrality to its Christian roots....
>
> There is an evolution of acts of profanation against monuments, but also against the Catholic faith itself. In the past, even if one was not a Christian, the expression of the sacred was respected. We are facing a serious threat to the expression of religious freedom. Secularism must not be a rejection of the religious, but a principle of neutrality that gives everyone the freedom to express his faith.
>
> We are witnessing the convergence of laicism—conceived as secularism, which relegates the faithful only to the private sphere and where every religious denomination is banal or stigmatized—with the overwhelming emergence of Islam, which attacks the infidels and those who reject the Koran. On one hand, we are mocked by the media...and on the other, there is the strengthening of Islamic fundamentalism. These are two joint realities.[318]

Jerome Fouquet, a French political analyst, writes that de-Christianization of France is occurring in part due to mass migration from the Muslim world. He explains in his book, *French Archipelago: Birth of a Multiple and Divided Nation*, that France's detachment from Christianity is far-reaching, effectively making the country "post-Christian." He elaborates:

There is a growing de-Christianization, which is leading to the "terminal phase" of the Catholic religion.… For hundreds of years the Catholic religion profoundly structured the collective conscience of French society. Today this society is the shadow of what it once was. A great civilizational change is underway.[319]

A similar multipronged, anti-Christian bigotry campaign is assaulting America on all fronts as well. Certainly, the topic of this chapter, the business sphere, is a sector where anti-Christian bigotry is raising its ugly head at all levels.

The background for the current avalanche of anti-Christian bigotry in America is outlined in the previous section of this chapter: government (progressive agenda); immigrants bringing contrary philosophies; and a major effort by those ideologically opposed to our Christian foundation and especially those who target the core of American Christians for special ridicule and intimidation, what I labeled in the previous chapter the "espresso cup" Christians.

Set aside for now our antagonists' anti-Christian motivations and consider the growing number of businesses across America, small and giant, that are either targets themselves of anti-Christian attacks or embrace anti-Christian agendas.

Fortunately, there are groups that monitor such anti-Christian attacks. One is the American Family Association (AFA), which calls out individuals and organizations that advance anti-Christian bigotry. The AFA identifies these factions as atheists, humanists, homosexual rights associations, and others.

A favorite target for anti-Christian attacks are Christian businesses. "Families and businesses that express a Christian worldview on social issues often face vicious retaliation from anti-Christian zealots, and it's time to call them out for their intolerance," said AFA President Tim Wildmon.[320]

"Because of anti-Christian bigotry," Mr. Wildmon said, "private business owners have been sued and forced to close their businesses."[321]

Some anti-Christian groups even publish lists of so-called hate groups, which identify Christian organizations and individuals for special targeting. The Southern Poverty Law Center (SPLC) produces one such list, which identified the Washington-based Family Research Council as a hate group. That list, according to federal court records, influenced an armed man to enter FRC's offices and shoot and wound a security staff member, but the attacker was stopped before he could wound or perhaps kill more of the staff. That gunman, Floyd Corkins II, was sentenced to twenty-five years in prison for attempted mass murder.[322]

Many anti-Christian individuals and groups leverage businesses to embrace their cause and are making significant headway. Also, there are big-money organizations and not a few corporations that use their resources to persuade governments at all levels to support law changes that infringe upon Christian beliefs. This is especially important if a business chooses to take a stand that satisfies the left's "politically correct" anti-Christian agenda.

In the first case, there are literally hundreds of cases of anti-Christian discrimination over the past few years targeting Christian family businesses that were or are being shut down because their ideological opponents characterize them as homophobes and label the Christian claims of "religious liberty" as "bigotry." Other Christian opponents say such "religious liberty" claims are evidence of white privilege, even though there is no such thing as "white Christian" beliefs.

Consider a few cases of Christian-owned businesses that were attacked because of the owners' Christian faith.

The owners of Christian bakeries are often targeted by pro-homosexual radicals to compel the bakery owners to violate their convictions to bake a wedding cake for a homosexual "wedding." One such case in Oregon involved the Sweet Cakes by Melissa, a bakery, which, according to the Oregon Bureau of Labor and Industries, discriminated against a lesbian couple when the bakery's owners refused to make a cake for the couple, citing their Christian beliefs.

The homosexual community and the state viciously attacked the Oregon Christian baker as a result. Soon the state charged the baker with violating the Oregon Equality Act of 2007 and threatened to impose hundreds of thousands of dollars in fines. Meanwhile, homosexual activists launched protests and pickets appeared outside the family's bakery. They even threatened wedding vendors who did business with the bakery, and it also got very personal. The family's children received death threats.[323]

Bakeries are a favorite target of the anti-Christian left, but so are photographers. Elaine and Jonathan Huguenin, a Christian couple with a photography business, were forced by a New Mexico state court to pay $6,600 in fines after they declined based on their faith to photograph a lesbian "commitment ceremony."[324]

The Wildflower Inn in Vermont was sued for turning down a request to host a lesbian couple's wedding reception. The Christian owners said they would hold the same-sex reception but asked the homosexual couple to acknowledge the owners' personal opposition to such events. This small request was unacceptable to the couple, and the state court went ahead, fining the inn's owners ten thousand dollars. Now the inn no longer hosts weddings or receptions.[325]

Perhaps the most noteworthy attack on a presumed Christian business happened in 2019. The fast food chain, Chick-fil-A, acknowledged that its past donations to some faith-based organizations that held anti-homosexual values were harmful to their brand and would no longer be supported.[326]

The fast food chain's philanthropic staff announced it would end cash donations to such Christian organizations as the Salvation Army and the Fellowship of Christian Athletes beginning in 2020 after being criticized by lesbian, gay, bisexual, and transgender (LGBT) and human-rights groups.

That criticism was especially important to the Atlanta-based corporation because it seeks to expand its international footprint. As a result, the criticism and unwelcomed media attention impeded the company's growth, according to a Chick-fil-A spokesman. One such incident took place in early 2019.

In March 2019, Chick-fil-A's giving record made news in Texas when the San Antonio city council rejected its application to set up a concession at the local airport. The city leaders cited the company's financial support for anti-LGBT groups. However, in the past, the chain stood by its intention to stick with its Christian principles.[327]

The food chain's founder, S. Truett Cathy, a devout Baptist, has long kept to the company's decision to close on Sundays, because "he and his employees could set aside one day to rest and worship if they choose." Truett's son, Dan, now the company's CEO, told a Baptist website in 2012 that the chain is "guilty as charged" in its support of traditional marriage. But the Truetts' Christian convictions have now surrendered to their ambition to expand the food chain.[328]

Now, Chick-fil-A says its philanthropic efforts will focus on education, homelessness, and hunger. A corporate statement read: "Moving forward you will see that the Chick-fil-A foundation will avoid donating to faith-based charities that espouse anti-LGBT views."[329]

The list of cases such as those above that involve Christian business owners citing religious freedom to avoid radical anti-Christian agendas is long, troubling, and growing. Some, like Hobby Lobby, an arts-and-crafts franchised retailer, stood firm while others like Chick-fil-A surrendered to anti-Christian pressure. In that case, the Obama administration pressed to force Hobby Lobby's cofounders, David and Barbara Green, to provide employees life-terminating abortion drugs and devices against the owners' religious convictions. Fortunately, the Supreme Court granted a landmark victory by ruling that individuals do not lose their religious freedom when they open a family business and then stand by their religious liberty.[330]

"This is a landmark decision for religious freedom," said Lori Windham, senior counsel for the Becket Fund for Religious Liberty and counsel for Hobby Lobby. "This ruling will protect people of all faiths. The Court's reasoning was clear, and it should have been clear to the government. You can't argue there are no alternative means when your agency is busy creating alternative means for other people."

A second category of business-related anti-Christian actions is all too common as well. These anti-Christian actions occur when businesses embrace issues such as the promotion of abortion on demand, homosexual marriage, explicit sex, and gender dysphoria, and even provide a platform to attack Christianity and Christians.

Big commercial corporations and even small firms are beginning to hold anti-Christian agendas. That's why we hear more calls today from Christian groups recruiting believers to join boycotts of offending businesses and corporations.

Some Christians rally to oppose such stark business-fueled anti-Christian efforts, and boycotts can be launched because the Christian community isn't without means. Faith-based consumers claim that Christian consumers in America are a strong cohort, numbering perhaps as many as forty-one million, and they generate $2 trillion in annual spending. That's potentially a lot of potential leverage if used against retailers.[331]

Faith Driven Consumers is an organization that engages and activates Christians to proactively live out their faith, which includes where they shop, what they buy, and their entertainment choices. That firm alerts Christians to offending merchants and then helps rally support to oppose blatant discrimination.

Unfortunately, there is no shortage of anti-Christian businesses. Faith Driven Consumers indicates that literally hundreds of merchants adopt anti-Christian policies. One example is Target, the giant department-store chain that announced it would allow men in women's bathrooms and changing rooms. That anti-Christian policy set off a call for a boycott. Even the coffee-chain giant Starbucks created another firestorm of protest with its presentation of Christmas as "a blank canvas" on its drink cups.[332]

These are the sort of offensive, anti-Christian actions by a growing swath of merchants that the founder of Faith Driven Consumer, Chris

Stone, said indicate an increasingly influential progressive movement that champions diversity but excludes and offends Christians from the mainstream culture.

"As the diversity-inclusion movement grows, and more and more companies become diversity-centric, what you really begin to see is a glaring gap that exists," Mr. Stone told the *Washington Times*. "As a Christian, you begin to see that you're being excluded from the culture, excluded from the conversation."[333]

"We're seeing language that changes 'free exercise,' which is the Constitution, to 'freedom of religion,' which means you can do what you want within the four walls of your church, but you can't bring it out," Mr. Stone explained.[334]

To underscore this point, Faith Driven Consumer publishes a Faith Equality Index, which rates how welcoming specific businesses are to religious people. AT&T, for instance, scores a perfect 100 with the pro-homosexual Human Rights Campaign's Corporate Equality Index, but received only an 18 out of 100 from Faith Driven Consumer.

"While each company states that they do not discriminate—even on the basis of religion—in practice that is exactly what they are doing," Mr. Stone said.

Anti-Christian attacks on Christian-owned businesses and the advancement of anti-Christian policies by many American businesses is a serious threat, and it will only get worse. In fact, this reminds me of Revelation 13:16–18, which says in the end times Christians will no longer be able to buy or sell anything, but are banned because of their faith from all trading and commerce.

Conclusion

Little wonder American Christians tell pollsters they are facing more discrimination today than in the past, and it's getting worse. That view is supported by LifeWay Research, a Christian organization focused on equipping church leaders with insights, found that majorities of Christians agree that religious-based tolerance is declining as is religious liberty.[335]

Much of America's business community is guilty of abandoning our Christian foundation and embracing a humanist approach that is becoming radically anti-Christian. It will get worse if we don't soon change course. Failing to stop these assaults will contribute to pushing America over the moral tipping point.

ANTI-CHRISTIAN CABAL PUTS AMERICA ON A COLLISION COURSE TO A MORAL TIPPING POINT

Who are the anti-Christian conspirators pushing America beyond the point of equilibrium where the slide downward cannot be easily halted? That cabal is exposed in this section of *Collision Course*.

America was founded in part by Europeans seeking religious freedom. They were either tired of kowtowing to state-established churches headed by tyrants or they had genuine differences with their country's official religious teachings and were prohibited from practicing their faith. So, they left for the New World, full of hope to find genuine religious freedom.

Fortunately, in the intervening years, our founders wisely embraced the First Amendment to our Constitution that protects religious freedom, and since that time, the federal courts have stalwartly stood by the founders' original intent with few exceptions. However, as we've seen in the previous section of this book, there is a true groundswell of anti-Christian sentiment across America, and it is getting worse. Our religious freedom is seriously challenged within the key societal institutions, and if something isn't done and soon, it could drag the United States into situations that are all too common elsewhere in the world.

Just how real is the persecution of Christians in other lands? Might American Christians begin to experience the same sort of persecution now so commonplace in other places across this globe?

Christian persecution is a very serious and a growing global problem. One report indicates that almost three hundred million Christians—nearly one in every seven Christians across the world's 196 countries—suffer some form of anti-Christian persecution. Those human-rights violations come in the form of arbitrary arrest, violence, economic discrimination, and even murder.[336]

Open Doors, a Christian ministry that tracks such anti-Christian activities, found the number of Christians murdered for their faith in 2018 exceeded four thousand, and other reports indicate that at least eleven Christians are killed every day in the worst-offending countries. Meanwhile, Pew Research Center reports that the number of countries where Christians are subject to a degree of government-enforced restrictions and communal hostility has grown from 108 countries in 2014 to 143 countries in 2017.[337]

Consider a sampling of some of the worst treatment, mostly Islamic-inspired anti-Christian persecution in 2019. Clearly, as pointed out in the previous section, there are significant groups, not just Islamists, who perpetrate anti-Christian persecution on many other fronts as well.

- Some 150 Christians died in Islamist-inspired suicide bomb attacks on churches in Sri Lanka on Easter morning 2019.[338]
- In the first half of 2018, Nigeria's Fulani (Muslim) militants killed thousands of Christians and drove another fifty thousand from their homes.[339]
- World Watch Monitor reports that assailants in Burkina Faso (an African country) asked the Christians to convert to Islam, but the pastor and the others refused. So "they called them, one after the other, behind the church building where they shot them dead."
- Mission Network News reported that in Indonesia, "a new form of persecution is on the rise—Christian girls are being targeted by Muslim men…. Influential leaders are literally training young men to target Christian girls to impregnate them…. [T]hey're

forced into marrying that daughter into a Muslim family.... Once girls are married into the Muslim families, they're often cut off from or abandoned by their families and they face even more difficult circumstances. In some cases, girls are the second or third wife of their persecutor and they have few freedoms."

- The British Pakistani Christian Association reported: "The mob began shouting outside our home asking for our family to exit our home and receive divine retribution for our sin. It did not seem very divine—we just saw raging evil violent people ready to kill us."

- In Egypt, a Muslim employee murdered his Christian supervisor "because of his Christian faith," notes a report. Surveillance footage from a nearby building captured the incident. While passing each other, the two men speak briefly before the Muslim man returned with a knife and butchered the Christian, who left behind a wife and two boys aged fifteen and nine. "The Islamic holy month of Ramadan began nearly two weeks ago," the report adds. "It is common for Christians to suffer increased violence and harassment during this time. Persecution is a constant theme of life for Egyptian Christians, as they are already viewed as second class citizens in this Islamic nation."

- Syrian Islamic militants bombed a Christian village; five children and a thirty-five-year-old woman were killed. "The kids went out to play after some days of calm" near a monastery, said a local priest, when a rocket struck near them, "instantly killing five and wounding others...the woman was killed in a nearby street by a separate rocket."

- A Pakistani Muslim man kidnapped and tortured his Christian employee to death after he tried to quit his job. Javid Masih, forty-five, worked as a livestock farmhand for Abbas Jutt. According to a source acquainted with the case, "Masih wanted to quit because he was often subjected to discrimination and religious hatred." The deceased's widow confirms: "We had been experiencing religious hatred from [Jutt] and his colleagues; however, we had no courage to register this with police. We are poor and belong to a downtrodden segment of society. Therefore, we are never heard. Jutt has damaged our lives and we have nothing to live for now."

- Iranian authorities directly under the control of the Supreme Leader raided an Assyrian Presbyterian Church on May 9. They tore down the church's cross, changed the church's locks, and made it clear that worship was no longer be permitted at the church. Apparently, the church's crime was that it used the Persian language alongside its own Assyrian language; because the overwhelming majority of Iran's Muslim population speaks only Persian, conducting church services in that language is seen by the Islamist regime as a seductive threat to the Muslims' faith.

Fortunately, the persecution of Christians seen elsewhere across the world hasn't yet come to the United States. However, I can see the possibility that such persecution could soon come to America, given the shift in our culture described in section II. Yes, the erosion of our religious freedom could lead to scenes described above happening in this country.

That brings us to this section of *Collision Course*. It is here we examine what I will identify as the power behind the attacks on Christians. Understand that the use of the prefix "anti" means "to be against," or "opposed to." So, the anti-Christian actions taking place across the world and now in America are nothing new. The Apostle John wrote in 2 John 4:3 that the spirit of the anti-Christ lives within humans and it manifests itself through action within the host culture. The attacks are aimed at Jesus Christ, His message, His person and His character. We Christians may feel the brunt of the assaults but the target is our Savior, Jesus Christ.

This section profiles America's anti-Christian cabal in four chapters. The eighth chapter sets the stage to understand the others. The key figure in the anti-Christian campaign is the ring leader, Satan, the original fallen angel and his supporting army of demons. Don't believe in the unseen realm? You must if you are to understand what's happening today! Much of the anti-Christian war raging across this world is literally invisible but very real.

The ninth chapter identifies the loudest mouthpiece of the visible anti-Christian movement, America's mainstream media. Many so-called objective journalists put on full display their anti-Christian bias every day on talk shows, in television sitcoms, in music lyrics, and on the widescreen. The examples of anti-Christian bias are in your face, quite flagrant, and getting worse.

The tenth chapter profiles the true ground troops in the anti-Christian camp who are represented by various advocacy groups, associations as well as competing religious entities, especially the vast army of the Islamic faith.

The eleventh chapter identifies some of the leading anti-Christian individuals assaulting believers. They use their deep pockets and access to government, media, and the international community to advance their radical and perverted ideologically driven hatred for Christians.

It is the Christian's responsibility to identify the enemy and his proxies. Knowing one's enemy allows the Christian to intelligently pray about the threats and prepare himself for the future.

CHAPTER EIGHT

The Anti-Christian War in the Unseen Realm

If you know the enemy and know yourself, you need not fear
the result of a hundred battles. If you know yourself but not the
enemy, for every victory gained you will also suffer a defeat. If
you know neither the enemy nor yourself, you will succumb in
every battle.[340]

—Sun Tzu, *The Art of War*

You cannot understand the anti-Christian movement today
without first knowing about the enemy and the particulars of his strategy. The problem for many is that although the anti-Christian war may
manifest itself in the visible domain, most of the real fight against Christians is waged in the invisible realm, which makes this such a hard fight
to understand.

Yes, the battle Christians face today is a spiritual one, where fallen
angels rule. Jesus wants us to understand that this fight is not one of
just the physical realm, but of the spiritual, which requires faith. And,
of course, as a result, one must be spiritually discerning to even "see" the
overwhelming evidence of the ongoing battles.

The Apostle Paul identifies the nature of the present fight in his letter to the Ephesians:

For we wrestle not against flesh and blood, but against princi-
palities, against powers, against the rulers of the darkness of this
world, against spiritual wickedness in high places. (Ephesians
6:12, KJV)

We become warriors for Christ in this war when we accept Him as
Savior. The battles we join are not really against flesh and blood, as the
apostle describes above, but against spiritual wickedness in high places.
That's why Jesus spent three years training His disciples for spiritual warfare, a litmus test for those early warriors and a model for Christian
warriors today.

Christ wanted His disciples and future Christians to understand the
spiritual power they have in His name. He set an example and constantly taught His disciples and then put them to the test. He sent them
as missionary—spiritual—warriors on a training mission outlined in
Luke 10:1–5 (NKJV). The purpose of that mission was to prepare them
for the coming war. The Scripture states:

1. After these things the Lord appointed seventy others also, and
   sent them two by two before His face into every city and place
   where He Himself was about to go.
2. Then He said to them, "The harvest truly is great, but the
   laborers are few; therefore, pray the Lord of the harvest to
   send out laborers into His harvest.
3. "Go your way; behold, I send you out as lambs among wolves.
4. "Carry neither money bag, knapsack, nor sandals; and greet
   no one along the road.
5. "But whatever house you enter, first say, 'Peace to this house.'"

Warriors learn by doing and practicing their "mission," as evidenced
in the above illustration. Christ knew the disciples needed to learn for
themselves by doing and discovering the true source of power (the Holy
Spirit) as well as their enemy. That's the purpose of this chapter as well,

a necessary introduction before we examine the human proxies that our unseen enemy employs to advance his evil agenda.

We must begin with an understanding of the players, those associated with our adversary's camp. Most readers are familiar with the prophetic end-times scenario that is ushered in with the appearance of the Antichrist. He is profiled in the Scriptures as blaspheming the true God; claiming to be god and being worshiped; displaying miraculous powers; rising from the dead; ruling in full authority; controlling the world's economy; desecrating God's temple; and attempting to destroy Israel. However, if you read Revelation 19 and 20, you know the end of the story.

In Revelation, we learn that Jesus Christ returns to destroy the Antichrist and his armies and casts them into the Lake of Fire (Revelation 19:11–21). Christ then binds Satan in the abyss for a thousand years; meanwhile, Christ rules on earth for a thousand-year period (Revelation 20:1–6).

Those events are in the future, which could come at any time. However, by contrast, this chapter addresses the occurrences leading up to the Antichrist's entrance on the world stage. The spiritual war now raging is the warmup act for the coming of the real Antichrist, as explained by the Apostle John:

Dear children, this is the last hour; and as you have heard that the Antichrist is coming, even now many antichrists have come. This is how we know it is the last hour. (1 John 2:18, NIV)

So, according to the Apostle John, we are in the "last hour" because we are seeing "many antichrists" that will usher in the end time's arrival of the true Antichrist.

The next three chapters will introduce the visible proxies of the present spirit of the antichrist, or as the apostle wrote, the "many antichrists." The Apostle John identifies these lower-caste antichrists in 1 John 2:22 (NIV) beginning with a question: "Who is the liar? It is whoever denies that Jesus is the Christ. Such a person is the antichrist—denying the father and the son."

This chapter sets the scene for the current fight by taking a close look at the real contemporary enemy behind the veil of all the present human antichrists, Satan and his army of demons. We will examine the battlefield upon which we are fighting him, Satan's arsenal, and his goal, as well as Satan's weaknesses. You must grasp the dimensions of this real enemy and the battlefield, and only then can you appreciate the human proxies (the contemporary antichrists) that are fighting for Satan's cause seeking to destroy every vestige of Christianity and all Christ followers.

We begin with an introduction.

Who is Satan?

Satan means "the adversary" in Hebrew, and his *nom de guerre* is *devil*, a Greek word meaning "false accuser." He is a fallen angel thanks to his rebellion against God, and he is among us humans on earth (albeit in another dimension) to accuse the saved of their sins that are already forgiven and to encourage unsaved people to reject the salvation Christ offers to all of humanity.

Scripture provides some insight into Satan's character. Isaiah and Ezekiel refer to him as the "morning star," translated "Lucifer." He rules over all the fallen angels, the evil spirits known as demons in the Bible (Matthew 12:24–27). Numerous times in the Gospels, Jesus Christ is identified by demons who without exception cower from His authority as God.

Satan made his original appearance in the first book of the Bible, Genesis, by tempting Adam's wife, Eve, to sin. Later he spoke with Job, the righteous God-follower, and tried to turn him away from the Lord. He even tries to tempt Jesus (Matthew 4:1–11), and he tempted the Apostle Peter to deny the Christ (Luke 4:1–13).

Satan is not only deceiving, as seen above, but he is a prideful and bloodthirsty murderer. Ezekiel 28:17 (NIV) identifies Lucifer (Satan) as full of himself: "Your heart became proud on account of your beauty, and you corrupted your wisdom because of your splendor." He is evidently a narcissist who sought the honor and glory that belonged to God alone.

Jesus identifies Satan as a murderer as well. The Lord confronts the scribes and the Pharisees in the Jerusalem temple:

> You belong to your father, the devil, and you want to carry out your father's desires. He was a murderer from the beginning, not holding to the truth, for there is no truth in him. When he lies, he speaks his native language, for he is a liar and the father of lies. (John 8:44, NIV)

Satan came to destroy life and make our earthly existence eternally miserable. His greatest strength is that many people don't believe he even exists. Some dangerously and naively portray him as a caricature with horns and a spiked tail. However, Jesus took him seriously, and so He should, because Satan employs his army of demons to cause havoc across the world, often using human proxies to convince the lost to ignore their only path to eternal salvation through Christ.

Satan's Army

The ranks of Satan's army are demons, fallen angels, spirits that influence people and take over the bodies of some (possession), as seen in the Bible (Leviticus 17:7 and 2 Chronicles 11:15).

These invisible warriors were banished from Heaven because they rebelled against God:

> Then another sign appeared in heaven: an enormous red dragon with seven heads and ten horns and seven crowns on his heads. His tail swept a third of the stars out of the sky and flung them to the earth. (Revelation 12:3–4, NIV)

Jesus, in His public ministry, dealt with demons. They presented themselves in a variety of ways: making a person mute, deaf, and blind, causing convulsions, manifesting superhuman strength, and displaying self-destructive behavior. The disciple Matthew made the distinction between those with illnesses and those truly demon possessed. He wrote:

> News about him spread all over Syria, and people brought to him all who were ill with various diseases, those suffering severe pain, the demon-possessed, those having seizures, and the paralyzed, and he healed them. (Matthew 4:24, NIV)

Demons knew Jesus' true identity and obeyed His command. We saw this when He cast out unclean spirits from the men possessed by demons. Jesus cast the demons—"My name is Legion; for we are many"—into a herd of swine (pigs) that subsequently rushed over a steep bank into the Sea of Galilee and perished in the water (Mark 5:1–13, NKJV).

It is important to understand that demons are deceptive and often disguise themselves in many ways and venues to fool us humans. That is why God forbids humans from participating in divination, witchcraft, channeling, and wizardry (Deuteronomy 18:10–12), practices that invite demons into our lives.

Satan's army of demons is real, engaged across the world, and doing his bidding.

Who Does Satan's Demonic Army Attack?

Revelation 12 provides a picture of the archangel Michael and his angels fighting Satan and his demons. The dragon (Satan) and his cohort are cast to the earth just before Christ returns to bring "salvation, and strength, and the kingdom of our God, and the power of His Christ have come, for the accuser of our brethren, who accused them before our God day and night, has been cast down" (Revelation 12:10, NKJV).

Looking to that day, God's angels announce:

Therefore rejoice you heavens and you who dwell in them! But woe to the earth and the sea, because the devil has gone down to you! He is filled with fury, because he knows that his time is short. (Revelation 12:12, NIV)

Satan desperately turns his wrath on the people of God, the spiritual "Israel of God," the members of Christ's Body, the Church (Galatians 3:7, 29; 6:16). The victims of Satan's assaults include not just the natural physical offspring of Israel, but also "the dragon was enraged at the woman and went off to wage war against the rest of her offspring—those who keep God's commands and hold fast their testimony about Jesus" (Revelation 12:17, NIV).

The targeting of the followers of Christ is warned about in the gospels. Christ said, "Then they will deliver you up to tribulation and kill you, and you will be hated by all nations for My name's sake" (Matthew 24:9, NKJV).

Satan's Geographic Areas of Control

The Apostle John tells us that some physical places are controlled by demonic spirits (John 3:19). This issue is illustrated by the reaction of the people in the area of the Gadarenes called out in Matthew 8:28–34 and mentioned earlier in this chapter.

That Scripture finds Christ confronted by two men who were "demon-possessed." The men said to Christ (Matthew 8:29 NIV), "What do you want with us, son of God?" they shouted. "Have you come here to torture us before the appointed time?"

They begged Jesus, "If you drive us out, send us into the herd of pigs" (Matthew 8:31, NIV). Jesus responded, "Go!" And the demons came out of the men and went into the swine, and the whole herd rushed down into the sea and perished in the waters.

The most interesting part of this Scripture comes in verse 34, when the people "of the Gadarenes" (near the city of Gadara), no doubt Gentiles—non-Jews—came to Jesus to ask him to leave their region.

Gadara was part of the cities of the Decapolis, a federation of ten Hellenized (Greek) cities in Galilee, located along the eastern shore of the Sea of Galilee, the present-day Golan Heights.

Evidently, the people in that Gentile area wanted nothing to do with Jesus. That was an area of demonic activity; darkness reigned. Just by going to the region, Jesus demonstrated how to claim an area for the Lord, but He was unwelcomed and faced opposition.

The scriptural principle applies today as well. Demons have dominion over some geographical areas, which explains why certain cities and regions may vehemently oppose the gospel and especially those who bring the good news of Jesus Christ.[341]

Parenthetically, I'm compelled to address this issue based on personal experience. I perceive that Washington, DC, is like Gadara, a place claimed by Satan and his demons, and a place over which hangs a very dark cloud of evil. I have experienced confrontations with human proxies who evidence rank evil—demonic influence—in Washington over the past half century of working in the Washington area. Those vicious personal attacks validate the truth of my past observations: Satan and evil proxies lay claim to our nation's capital.

What Are Satan's Goals?

Satan seeks to destroy humanity even though he knows he is fighting from a losing position. His strategic goals are to prevent as many humans as possible from coming to salvation, as well as to marginalize those who are saved.

We read in 2 Corinthians 4:3 (NIV) that the gospel is "veiled to those who are perishing." Satan intends to keep it that way and employs all his powers to prevent the message of salvation from reaching the lost.[342]

His secondary goal is to keep the saved defeated—ineffective—because when in that state, they are marginalized; they are ineffective at advancing the kingdom of God. That frees Satan to focus on preventing the lost from being saved.

What Does Satan Attack?

Satan attacks the human mind. We know that psychological warfare is an important tool for the human warfighter, a tool designed to influence the mind of the enemy. The US Department of Defense defines psychological warfare as:

> The planned use of propaganda and other psychological actions having the primary purpose of influencing the opinions, emotions, attitudes, and behavior of hostile foreign groups in such a way as to support the achievement of national objectives.[343]

Satan uses a variety of psychological warfare tools to influence our opinions, emotions, attitudes, and behavior. He employs these tools to control our minds, a tool identified in 2 Corinthians 4:4 (NIV), which states, "The god of this age [Satan] has blinded the minds of unbelievers, so that they cannot see the light of the gospel that displays the glory of Christ, who is the image of God."

The word for "mind" here is *noēmata*, which means "thought" or "purpose."[344] In other words, what humans think is what Satan wants to control so as to blind them to the truth of the gospel.

The Apostle Paul warns Christians about Satan's attack on our thoughts (our minds). He cautions us to be of one mind and guard our thoughts against the ways of this world (Philippians 4:7).

Control people's minds and you control all human activity. Saved people have a different way of thinking, because God's Holy Spirit dwells with them, freeing them from Satan's absolute control of their mind.[345] However, Satan is not without the means to distract the believer as well.

What are Satan's weapons to control the mind of unbelievers and to keep Christians distracted? He has a significant arsenal of effective weapons to defend against the spread of the gospel and to keep Christians defeated.

He maintains control of the minds of the unbelievers through lust. The word for "lust" in the Greek is *epithumia*, which means "desire," "craving," and "longing, the desire for what is forbidden." The Apostle John explains this weapon in 1 John 2:16 (KJV): "For all that is in the world—the lust of the flesh, the lust of the eyes, and the pride of life—is not of the Father but is of the world [the devil]."

The physical and psychological manifestation of lust is detailed in Galatians 5:19–21 (NIV). These verses identify the tools Satan has at his disposal to keep the unbelieving human's mind captive.

> The acts of the flesh are obvious: sexual immorality, impurity and debauchery, idolatry and witchcraft; hatred, discord, jealousy, fits of rage, selfish ambition, dissensions, factions and envy; drunkenness, orgies, and the like. I warn you, as I did before, that those who live like this will not inherit the kingdom of God.

We now turn our attention to how Satan deals with Christians, true Spirit-filled believers. He employs three weapons to keep the believing Christian marginalized: lies, temptations, and manipulations. He uses these covertly to deceive and blind us to God's direction. For example, he presents us with false gods, pollutes our thinking with other worldviews, imbues in us selfish desires, and introduces despair, doubt, fear, anger, and more.

Remember, Satan is the father of lies: "When he lies, he speaks his native language, for he is a liar and the father of lies" (John 8:44, NIV). Also, recall that Satan's first appearance in the Bible is in Genesis 3:1

(NRSV), and there he said to Eve, "Did God say, 'You shall not eat from any tree in the garden'?" Then the father of lies quickly answered his question with a falsehood: "You will not die; for God knows that when you eat of it your eyes will be opened, and you will be like God, knowing good and evil" (Genesis 3:4–5, NRSV). Satan attempts to deceive us similarly today by twisting or changing God's Word and confusing us about sin.

Satan also tempts us in order to cause us to compromise, which renders us ineffective in our calling to be light for Christ. We read the account of Satan tempting Christ in the wilderness (Matthew 4:1–11) and the success Satan had at tempting Judas in the last hours of Jesus' earthly life (Luke 22:3–6). Paul warns Christians to be alert for such temptations: "I am afraid that as the serpent [Satan] deceived Eve by his cunning, your thoughts will be led astray from a sincere and pure devotion to Christ" (2 Corinthians 11:3, NRSV).

The Apostle Mark warned that Satan wants to choke our faith as well. He writes in Mark 4:15 (KJV): "And these are they by the way side, where the word is sown; but when they have heard, Satan cometh immediately, and taketh away the word that was sown in their hearts."

Later, Paul explained in 1 Thessalonians 3:5 (NIV): "For this reason, when I could stand it no longer, I sent to find out about your faith. I was afraid that in some way the tempter [Satan] had tempted you and that our labors might have been in vain."

Satan and his demons often masquerade as believers to gain entrance into a fellowship, then once inside, they teach what Paul calls "doctrines of devils" (1 Timothy 4:1, KJV). Jesus calls out this behavior: "Watch out for false prophets. They come to you in sheep's clothing, but inwardly they are ferocious wolves" (Matthew 7:15, NIV).

Satan manipulates us by masquerading as the truth to provoke us to sin, as indicated above. The Apostle Paul writes in 2 Corinthians 11:14–15 (NLT): "Even Satan disguises himself as an angel of light. So, it is not strange if his servants [demons] also disguise themselves as servants of righteousness."

Satan is a master of distraction using these three tools: lies, temptations, and manipulation. We saw this played out with Eve and the serpent in the Garden of Eden. It's a concept addressed by British author C. S. Lewis in his book, *The Screwtape Letters,* in which Screwtape, the senior demon, tells the young Wormwood how to distract Christians and lead them into sin:[346]

The real trouble about the set your patient is living in is that it is merely Christian. They all have individual interests, of course, but the bond remains mere Christianity. What we want, if men become Christians at all, is to keep them in the state of mind I call "Christianity And." You know—Christianity and the Crisis, Christianity and the New Psychology, Christianity and the New Order, Christianity and Faith Healing, Christianity and Psychical Research, Christianity and Vegetarianism, Christianity and Spelling Reform. If they must be Christians, let them at least be Christians with a difference. Substitute for the faith itself some Fashion with a Christian colouring. Work on their horror of the Same Old Thing.[347]

That is precisely what is happening today among many Christians. They are distracted thanks to Satan's lies, temptations, and manipulations to compromise their witness, which leads many astray and away from obedience to Christ's Great Commission. That is Satan's objective, and, sadly, it is rather effective here in America as well as elsewhere.

Satan Has Weaknesses

Satan is evil, wicked, cruel, and selfish, but he also has notable weaknesses. He can't read our minds, nor can he touch us without God's permission.

Satan and his demons have the same power given to angels. We read in Genesis 19 that angels struck men with blindness and in Daniel 6:22 that an angel shut the lions' mouths. But nowhere in the Scripture does it say that an angel or demon can read our minds. However, like a good psychologist, Satan is an observer of human behavior. He's been doing that for thousands of years and has a pretty good idea of what you and I are thinking under most circumstances and how we might respond to lies, temptations, and manipulations.

Another weakness is that he can't touch you or me without God's permission. This weakness is illustrated in the Book of Job.

In Job 1:10–13 (ESV), Satan asks God:

Have you not put a hedge around him and his house and all that he has, on every side? You have blessed the work of his hands, and his possessions have increased in the land.

But stretch out your hand and touch all that he has, and he will curse you to your face.

And the Lord said to Satan, "Behold, all that he has is in your hand. Only against him do not stretch out your hand." So Satan went out from the presence of the Lord.

Clearly Satan is limited to what God allows. We see much the same arrangement in the New Testament regarding Satan's desire to test Peter. Jesus told Peter at the Last Supper that Satan wanted to "sift him as wheat," but the Lord was confident that the test would strengthen Peter's faith, so permission was granted.

Luke wrote about that scene:

And the Lord said, "Simon, Simon, Satan has asked to sift all of you as wheat. But I have prayed for you, Simon, that your faith may not fail. And when you have turned back, strengthen your brothers." (Luke 22:31–32, NIV)

Yes, Satan has his limits. God placed a hedge of protection around His people. Satan can tempt us, but we have the power to resist. And we can trust, as it says in 1 Corinthians 10:13 (NIV), that:

> No temptation has overtaken you except what is common to mankind. And God is faithful; he will not let you be tempted beyond what you can bear. But when you are tempted, he will also provide a way out so that you can endure it.

Conclusion

We are engaged in a war for the souls of mankind. Much of the fight is in the invisible realm. This chapter profiles our enemy, Satan, and his army of demons, along with some details about his areas of control, goals, weapons, weaknesses, and who he targets as well as how.

The next three chapters in this section will apply your understanding of Satan and his army to three groupings of human proxies in the global anti-Christian spiritual war: the media (journalists), anti-Christian organizations, and key anti-Christian leaders.

CHAPTER NINE

Mainstream Media's
Anti-Christian Bigotry

US MAINSTREAM MEDIA tends to be anti-Christian, the mouthpiece for America's progressive secularists, and an example of the "antichrists" spoken of in 1 John 2:18. Many journalists among the mainstream media outlets shun true free expression by frequently displaying anti-Christian bigotry in the form of encouraging popular intolerance of amoral behavior on television, in movies, and across the social media. At this point, there is every reason to expect this problem to fester into something much worse.

This chapter profiles the growing and insidious, across-the-board, anti-Christian assaults by many journalists in the mainstream media. It also explores the reason for these assaults—the backstory. A plan for responding to such outrage and the growing avalanche of anti-Christian sentiment poisoning our culture is addressed in section IV of this book.

Evidence the Media Is Anti-Christian

A 2019 study commissioned by the British foreign secretary found that the vast majority (80 percent) of global religious persecution targets

Christians. The mainstream media plays a role in that groundswell of anti-Christian persecution primarily because many journalists fail to be objective in their reporting or just use their outlets to display their rank bias against Christians. Besides, they also ignore an avalanche of anti-Christian persecution, which leaves most Americans and citizens of other countries blind to what is happening to this vital faith. Some journalists' anti-Christian bias likely contributes to the current growing level of Christian persecution.[348]

The anti-Christian media problem is especially growing overseas, but is also festering inside the United States. There are at least three categories of anti-Christian behavior displayed by much of the mainstream media that warrant exposure. Consider examples of each category.

Failure to Report Anti-Christian Activities

Homer, the ancient Greek poet, wrote in his epic poem, "The Odyssey," the phrase "out of sight, out of mind."[349] That is evidently the philosophy of many in the mainstream media journalists when it comes to anti-Christian persecution.

It used to be that media editors selected stories because their readers wanted to know what was happening in the world. Apparently, the fact that Christians are being massacred for their faith in record numbers across a significant swath of this planet is not considered newsworthy, at least according to a growing segment of the mainstream media editors. The evidence of that neglect abounds.

The news editors who control what you and I see on television and read in the papers or online consider Christians to be one of the media's obstacles to "progress" in this country. So, they refuse to invest space or time reporting on the growing number of tragedies directly impacting Christians across the world.[350]

Ignoring atrocities against Christians explains why the vast majority of Americans do not know that 4,136 Christians were killed for faith-related reasons in 2018—about eleven per day.[351]

The fact is Christians in much of the world face a variety of significant types of persecution, from economic sanctions for their faith to arrest, imprisonment, and a growing number of murders. There are also numerous examples of Christians targeted by mob violence, and in an increasing number of countries, Christians suffer state-sanctioned terror.

Consider the case of America's paper of record, the *New York Times*, which ignores flagrant and significant anti-Christian attacks. In March 2019, the *Times*, which claims to print "All the news that's fit to print," completely ignored the story that Nigerian Fulani jihadists butchered more than 120 Christians in central Nigeria using machetes and gunfire. The anti-Christian rebels also destroyed over 140 Christian homes and spread terror.[352]

The *New York Times* wasn't alone in ignoring this significant news story. The massacre of African Christians evidently wasn't newsworthy to the *Washington Post, Chicago Tribune, Detroit Free Press*, the *Los Angeles Times*, and many other major papers in the United States.[353]

Earlier that year, in January, Muslim extremists bombed a Roman Catholic cathedral in the Philippines, killing twenty people and injuring many dozens as well. This mass casualty action, another anti-Christian event, was ignored by almost all of the mainstream media as well.[354]

The mainstream media's record of ignoring the wanton killing of Christians knows no bounds. They even demonstrate a proclivity for ignoring anti-Christian activities when widespread persecution involves perhaps millions of believers inside significant countries like the People's Republic of China (Communist China).

The Chinese President Xi Jinping warned against foreign infiltration through religion and promised to stop "extremists" spreading their ideology, which includes Christianity.[355] Xi's government is waging a campaign to destroy Christians, remove crosses from their churches, and destroy church buildings.[356]

What's curious about China's ongoing anti-Christian campaign is its effect. The campaign presents a significant irony in the history of Christianity, according to Vice President Mike Pence. Today's China is seeing the fastest growth in the Christian faith, "more than we've realized anywhere on earth in the last 2,000 years."[357]

History buffs will recall that seventy years ago under the tyrannical Chinese Communist dictator Mao Zedong (1893–1976), there were fewer than half a million Chinese Christians. Today, two generations later, there are more than 130 million Chinese Christians.[358]

It seems that as Christianity grows, so does the number of the Chinese government's anti-Christian attacks. Chinese authorities ban the sale of Bibles, yet there are more Christian Bibles in China than in any other country on earth. Chinese Communists ban Christian church construction, yet more Christian churches are built in that country every year than any other country on the planet.

Vice President Pence explained the mystery of the resiliency of the Chinese Christians. He said there is a time-worn truth about such issues: "The pathway through persecution lies in the faith and resilience of the persecuted."[359]

Anti-Christian persecution is worse in China's next-door neighbor, North Korea. For the last few years, we've read a lot about North Korea and the tyrant leader Kim Jong-un, the young dictator whom President Trump once labeled "Rocket Man" for his proclivity to test rockets.

North Korea's Chairman Kim is one of the world's leading persecutors of Christians, a fact seldom reported by Western mainstream media. Yet that country is called out as a major human-rights violator by the United Nations.

The United Nations Commission on Human Rights reported:

The violations of human rights in the DPRK [Democratic People's Republic of Korea—North Korea]…constitute crimes against humanity…the gravity, scale, and nature of which has no parallel in the contemporary world.[360]

Open Doors, a Christian ministry that monitors global, anti-Christian persecution, identified North Korea as the worst persecutor of Christians today. The regime formally demands that its government officials seek to "wipe out the seed of [Christian] reactionaries." And, as you might expect, possession of a Bible is a capital (punishable by death) offense, thanks to the North Korean dictator.[361]

Today, up to seventy thousand North Korean Christians are being held as political prisoners in prison camps, and others face unbelievable torture. Some have been hung on crosses over fires, crushed under a steamroller, herded off bridges, and trampled underfoot. Perhaps two hundred thousand North Korean Christians have been executed for their faith over the term of the dictatorship. That's newsworthy information, but seldom do such reports earn any space with our mainstream media outlets.[362]

The democratic Asian country of India hosts significant anti-Christian persecution as well, but word of those acts is seldom reported. For example, an elderly Christian woman in a village in India's Tamil Nadu state was beaten for the offense of walking on a road during a Hindu festival, as were a dozen Christians who came to her rescue. That incident is among one of more than a thousand attacks on Christians over a fifteen-month period leading to March 2019 in India alone.[363]

Local Indian governments stand accused of colluding with anti-Christian extremists to persecute Christianity because it is considered something left from the colonial era that must be removed. The current surge in anti-Christian sentiment is linked to the rise to power of Nardendra Modi, that country's prime minister, a member of the Rashtriya Swanyamsevak Sangh (RSS) Hindu nationalist organization.[364]

The American hemisphere doesn't earn much attention for anti-Christian persecution either. In Nicaragua, President Daniel Ortega and his vice president violently suppress dissent and condone thugs who repress and intimidate Catholic Church leaders for defending religious freedom.[365]

Nicaragua's next-door neighbor, Venezuela's dictator, Nicolas Maduro, pushed through "anti-hate" laws in order to prosecute Catholic clergy who protest against his tyrannical regime. Such hate-filled actions are seldom, if ever, reported by mainstream media.[366]

The Middle East is terribly oppressive of Christians. Most of the Christians fled Iraq over the last two decades and, of course, Syria under the Islamic State of Iraq. Syria tortured Christians and chased most of them outside that country as those barbarians established their caliphate, but thanks to President Trump, that radical group lost its grip on the region in 2018.

The persecution of Christians is especially significant across the entire Mideast. The Saudis label Christians as infidels and have absolutely no tolerance for them. Egypt, another American ally in the region, is known for high levels of Christian persecution.

In 2016 in Egypt's capital city, Cairo, more than twenty-nine Christians were killed and many dozens were injured by a suicide bomber who struck during a Sunday mass. The Egyptian Catholic bishop said, "There is a feeling among many who attend mass that under the seat there is a bomb." Then, four months later, on Palm Sunday, suicide bombers targeted two other churches, killing 44 and injuring more than 120.[367]

My 2015 book *Never Submit: Will the Extermination of Christians Get Worse Before It Gets Better?* addresses the genocide of Christians in the Middle East. The problem is old, bloody, and continues even today.

Perhaps the persecution of Christians overseas is just not newsworthy for American audiences, according to most mainstream media editors. That view might explain why such horrendous events are seldom covered. Yes, we've seen a number of church shootings in the United States; however, none of those tragic events comes close to the scope of the massacres in Nigeria and Sri Lanka. But even the growing number of domestic anti-Christian cases don't earn much attention from our mainstream media.

The only logical conclusion is that our culture is too far gone morally to care about such anti-Christian persecution. After all our "news" tends to be filled with morally bankrupt, salacious stories about the latest account of political infighting or the sexual exploits of some deranged Hollywood starlet or media moguls like Harvey Weinstein, who was sentenced to twenty-three years in jail for rape and criminal sex acts.[368] Violence against Christians, which is becoming commonplace worldwide and here at home, just doesn't earn much attention today.

Bias in Reporting Anti-Christian Activities

The mainstream media's anti-Christian bias is palpable when stories are even reported. A number of very memorable examples of the left's anti-Christian outrage are worth reviewing.

Remember the story of a Covington, Kentucky, Catholic youth who attended a pro-life march in Washington and was attacked by mainstream media outlets for alleged smirking when approached by an elderly Native American beating a drum? This is a classic case of anti-Christian media bias!

Both news media and Hollywood heavyweights (and a few high-profile political figures) rushed to judgment after the video clip of the event emerged that gave some critics an inaccurate impression of Nick Sandmann, the sixteen-year-old who allegedly "harassed" the Native America man, Nathan Phillips. A longer video revealed that Sandmann and his fellow Catholic student classmates were accosted and yelled at before Phillips and others approached them. Just prior to the taped encounter, the Black Hebrew Israelites, who contend they are descendants of the ancient Israelites, shouted abuse at the Catholic students for wearing "Make America Great Again" hats.

Mr. L. Lin Wood, Sandmann's attorney, promised to file "hundreds" of lawsuits against media outlets that pushed the false narrative that Sandmann bullied the Native American. Mr. Wood told *Fox News* host Sean Hannity that the attacks were indirectly against President Trump. Wood said:[369]

If Nicholas had not purchased that souvenir [MAGA] cap that day—if he was not wearing it—none of us would know who Nick Sandmann is. He would still be living his life privately, going to school without worrying about how his school and his classmates and the world feel about him.

Here is a 16-year-old kid, Sean. It is tough being 16. Think about what this young boy is having to deal with at age 16 when the entire world saw him the way that the media portrayed him as literally the face of evil.

It is inexcusable, reprehensible conduct by the media. And the *Washington Post* led the way.

Nick Sandmann won his case against CNN in federal court. "CNN brought down the full force of its corporate power, influence and wealth on Nicholas by falsely attacking, vilifying, and bullying him despite the fact that he was a minor child," the lawsuit read.[370] Other lawsuits are in the process.

On another front, many Americans will recall the criticism the nation's second family faced because of their affiliation with a Christian school. Vice President Mike Pence's wife, Karen, is a part-time art teacher at a Christian school in Springfield, Virginia. The complaint registered by the mainstream media was the Christian school where Mrs. Pence teaches requires students and teachers to subscribe to a biblical view of homosexuality.

Vice President Pence admitted that "we're used to the criticism." But, he continued, "to see major news organizations attacking Christian education is deeply offensive to us."[371]

"We have a rich tradition in America of Christian education, and frankly religious education broadly defined," Mr. Pence continued. "We'll let the other critics roll off our back, but this criticism of Christian education in America should stop."[372]

Even rapper Kanye West's performance at a Texas prison drew anti-Christian mainstream media condemnation. In November 2019, Kanye performed a Sunday church service for which the anti-Christian organization, Freedom from Religion Foundation, blasted Texas authorities. Evidently, Kanye's performance of "Jesus Walks" for inmates at the Harris County Jail in Houston was unacceptable by some anti-Christian groups and their media supporters.[373]

Media reports fumed over the rapper's temerity to take his Christian ministry to Texas prisons. However, Texas Governor Greg Abbott was appreciative of the rapper's services at both male and female detention facilities. The governor tweeted his compliments, saying, "If he [Kanye West] moves just one person closer to God the world will be a more peaceful place."[374]

It won't surprise some readers that Kanye revealed that some mainstream record contracts forbid artists from saying Jesus' name. On Super Bowl Sunday 2020 at Bayfront Park in Miami, Kanye told the worship service, "God using us to show off, to show God is better than the devil." He was referring to the successes of his latest albums, "Jesus is King" and "Jesus is Born." Then he surprised the audience.[375]

"The devil took all the producers, the musicians, the designers. He moved us all out to Hollywood, moved us all out to New York. Chasing gold statues. Literally signing a contract and selling our souls," Kanye said. Then he revealed that the artists that moved to Hollywood "got contracts out there that say, 'You can't say Jesus.' When we were working on this album, people were coming to the studio just to say 'Jesus' as loud as they wanted to. You can say Jesus in 'Ye studio,'" the Chicago native continued.[376]

Even professional football players who profess their Christian faith are viciously attacked by biased media outlets. Consider the case of New Orleans Saints quarterback Drew Brees, who appeared on a Focus on the Family video promoting "Bring Your Bible to School Day."[377]

Allyson Chiu, a *Washington Post* reporter, identified Brees' participation in the Focus film, and labeled that Christian ministry as an "anti-LGBT religious group." Evidently, according to Chiu, any association with Focus or anyone who holds other than an affirming view of homosexual issues is no longer socially acceptable. Predictably, Chiu cited the Human Rights Campaign (a homosexual group) as a source in the article, which described Focus as "one of the most well-funded anti-LGBTQ organizations in America."[378]

Christians are attacked even when they serve their country. MSNBC targeted a Trump administration appointee, Kerri Kuper, because she graduated from Liberty University Law School, a Christian institution in Lynchburg, Virginia.

Rachel Maddow, the ultraliberal MSNBC hostess, said on an NBC podcast:

> We've got a new Justice Department spokesperson who's from Liberty University, and Liberty University was founded by a televangelist so that your Christian child wouldn't be corrupted by actual higher education.[379]

It is noteworthy, and according to Shannon Bream, the hostess for *Fox News at Night*, a Liberty graduate herself and a lawyer, that Ms. Kuper graduated from Liberty's law school, which has a 96 percent first-time bar pass rate, which is about twenty points ahead of the national average. Those facts were not mentioned in the MSNBC attack.[380]

Liberty president, Jerry Falwell Jr., responded to Maddow's biased report. "She [Maddow] needs to study her history," Falwell said. "Harvard, Yale, Princeton, Brown—most of the Ivy League schools—were founded by preachers and evangelists, and that's a long tradition in this country, and she just shows her ignorance and religious bigotry by making comments like that."[381]

Another 2019 mainstream media attack demonstrates the palpable anti-Christian bias of many so-called journalists. On February 13, 2019 ABC's star of *The View*, Joy Behar, attacked Vice President Mike Pence's faith on the air, calling Christianity a "mental illness." Viewer reaction was swift, as thousands of emails and calls poured into the network demanding an apology. Yet for days, ABC maintained a stony silence amid considerable public outrage.[382]

It took all that viewer pressure and more than a week before ABC said Behar privately called the vice president to apologize, but even though Mr. Pence encouraged her to make an on-air public apology, that never happened.

ABC said they are doing absolutely nothing about the anti-Christian insult, however. The outrage should have subjected Behar's comments to a review by the network's editorial standards and practices department, and someone should be subjected to discipline.

Evidently, according to Fox News, ABC refused to say anything until Disney-ABC Inc. CEO Bob Inger was confronted at a shareholder meeting about the incident. Audio from that meeting revealed Mr. Iger, when confronted by Behar's insult, said she had apologized to the vice president but was obviously "irritated and dismissive of the shareholder, sharply cutting off the exchange."[383]

Media Research Center president Brent Bozell said Behar's apology is insufficient. Bozell said his group would continue to campaign against "anti-Christian bigotry" in the media. In this instance, Bozell's group ran a campaign urging viewers to contact *View* advertisers about Behar's "hateful, anti-Christian remarks." Those efforts resulted in thirty thousand calls placed to ABC news, and the show's advertisers received more than ten thousand angry calls.[384]

Anti-Christian bias is rampant in the mainstream media. It sours the culture against Christians and in a country where religious freedom is a flagship issue, that sort of behavior should not be tolerated.

PC Media Buries Stories or Hides the Truth

Years ago, when many of us relied on the pulp morning paper for our daily dose of news, we often took a quick glance at the headlines and only turned inside the paper if one of the headlines caught our attention. Today, the news is delivered very differently, which makes finding out about Christian-related persecution or perhaps something good about Christianity very hard to find.

The various media outlets from which we get our news tend to bury stories about Christianity or obfuscate those few accounts with political correctness. However, reports of Christians alleged to be involved in misconduct, like the Catholic priests' sexual scandals, are front and center, above the fold, hard to miss. That's evidence of a double standard and political correctness run amok.

Consider some pretty flagrant examples of such abuse. You might be forgiven if you don't recall the Sri Lanka Easter massacre in 2019 that claimed more than 290 lives and injured more than 500. The Sri Lankan government accused an Islamist group, the National Thowheed Jamaath, for the April 22 bombings, and most of the victims died in nearly simultaneous suicide bombings at three Roman Catholic churches in the region of Colombo.[385]

How did the American mainstream media cover the massacre? Not well. The *New York Times* found space on page A-8 and the mainstream broadcast media (ABC, CBS, CNN, MSNBC, and NBC) thought the genocide story was of little importance. Only Fox News covered the heartbreaking story.[386]

Then, in December 2019, the *Wall Street Journal* ran an opinion piece online by Bernard-Henri Levy, "The New War Against Africa's Christians." The balance of the media ignored the story that prompted Levy's heartbreaking piece, which began: "A slow-motion war is under way in Africa's most populous country. It's a massacre of Christians, massive in scale and horrific in brutality. And the world has hardly noticed."[387]

Levy met with Nigerian survivors of the horrendous anti-Christian attacks, who offered blood-curdling details: "The mutilated cadavers of women. A mute man commanded to deny his faith, then cut up with a machete until he screams. A girl strangled with the chain of her crucifix."[388]

The group behind these anti-Christian attacks isn't the now famous Nigerian Boko Haram; no, it's a much worse group, if that's possible. It is another Muslim group known as the Fulani, from northern Nigeria who moved south, as introduced earlier in this chapter. "They are Islamic extremists of a new stripe," said a Nigerian Pentecostal Christian who directs a nongovernmental organization working with Nigeria's Christians and Muslims.

That director said, "I beg you, come and see for yourself." Yes, the Fulani are far more deadly than Boko Haram and now account for the majority of the country's 2,040 documented terrorist fatalities in 2018. But the quickened flow of Christian blood in Nigerian streets earns scant attention from American media.

Here in the United States, the mainstream media's politically correct bias shines brightly when it comes to Christian bigotry. Consider the case of CNN's town hall on October 10, 2019. The event was cohosted with the pro-homosexual lobbying group Human Rights Campaign, and the participants were many of the 2020 Democrat presidential candidates who competed to outdo one another on the LGBT issues and at the same time demonstrate their politically correct anti-Christian bigotry.[389]

The leading Democrat presidential candidates used that CNN program to express their support for the Equality Act, a bill in the House of Representatives at the time that would enshrine new sexual orthodoxy into law by banning discrimination on sexual orientation and gender identity. Of course, and predictably, the Democrats and CNN know those issues violate Christian doctrine, but political correctness demands promoting such antibiblical views.

Another aspect of this category of anti-Christian media bias is the distortion of the facts, what most people call lying or hiding the truth (important facts) from the reader.

In 2019, there was a shooting incident in a Colorado school where the suspect was identified as a homosexual student. He was accused of wounding nine fellow students, but what the mainstream media reported wasn't the obvious and an important aspect of the story. That is, the shooter's Facebook page was filled with expressions of hatred for Christians and President Trump.[390]

The shooter wrote on his Facebook page, "You know what I hate? All these Christians who hate gays, yet in the Bible, it says in Deuteronomy 17:12–13, if someone doesn't do what their priest tells them to do, they are supposed to die. It has plenty of crazy stuff like that. But all they get out of it is 'ewwwwww gays.'"

Common sense says that sort of theological opinion readily available to anyone on social media (Facebook) is newsworthy and ought to be reported. However, there was nary a mention of the inflammatory posts in the news reports on the incident.

Our entertainment media is especially incendiary in its politically correct anti-Christian vitriol. Consider celebrities like singer Lady Gaga.

Gaga used her platform to attack Vice President Pence's Christian faith. "And to Mike Pence, who thinks it's acceptable that his wife work at a school that bans LGBTQ, you are wrong," she said at a concert, and continued:

> You say we should not discriminate against Christianity; you are the worst representation of what it means to be a Christian. I am a Christian woman and what I do know about Christianity is that we bear no prejudice and everybody is welcome. So, you can take all that disgrace Mr. Pence and you can look yourself in the mirror and you'll find it right there.[391]

The Reverend Franklin Graham responded to Gaga's attacks on the Pence family

> As Christians, following Christ means following the teachings of God's Word. The Bible makes it clear that homosexuality is a sin—among many others—and they all have a cost. We are to seek to live our lives in obedience to His Word. He set the rules, not us; He is the one who defined sin, and out of His love and

mercy, He provided a remedy for sin—all sin—through repentance and faith in His Son, Jesus Christ.[392]

Political correctness trumps truth and full-disclosure for today's mainstream media, especially when it comes to reporting on Christian-related stories.

Why Are Journalists Anti-Christian?

Many mainstream journalists are anti-Christian because they've been conditioned by the progressive education establishment, which makes writing politically correct, anti-Christian reports totally acceptable. Besides, they were coopted by perks to play the role that supports the societal elites who have the real power.

Who are today's journalists? A journalism student took a stab at answering that question in her college research, which was later captured in an article. Her thesis is that journalists affect public perceptions regarding Christians, mostly in a negative manner. That led the journalism student to investigate news coverage to determine how it might perpetuate anti-Christian stereotypes.[393]

Katherine Dempsey, a then-journalism student at Northwestern University's Medill School, published her findings in 2013. She selected the topic because "news coverage has perpetuated anti-Christian stereotypes that do not reflect the Christians I know or who I am as a follower of Jesus."[394]

Ms. Dempsey began her study with a Barna survey noting that a quarter of a national sample of Americans could not recall any positive contributions from Christians in recent years. That observation helped her conclude that journalists, the gatekeepers of public information, are influencing the public in a derogatory way about Christianity.

She also cited a study published in the *Journal of Media and Religion* that found a serious anti-Christian bias in how nightly television network news broadcasts were "consistent, mildly negative" in their reporting on "fundamentalist" Christian stories.

She failed to find data that indicated whether journalists as a class were involved in spiritual matters, nor did she discover any evidence that religious affiliation affected their reporting. That's not surprising, because as a group, journalists tend to be liberal Democrats, and many are progressive in their ideology.

A journalist's political affiliation and worldview (dominant ideology) do matter. That is why it's not surprising that only 7.1 percent of journalists self-identify with the Republican Party, according to a study cited in the *Politico*. Professors Lars Willnat and David Weaver with Indiana University found a radical change in journalists who identified as Republican, which dropped from 25.7 percent in 1971 to the current level. By way of comparison, today most (50.2 percent) journalists say they are politically independent, while 28.1 percent are Democrat.[395]

Another media reporter with *Politico* did a revealing study to find out why the mainstream media missed the 2016 Trump victory. Not surprisingly, the reporter discovered that the national media really does work in a bubble, which is growing extreme. The media bubble is concentrated "heavily along the coasts, the bubble is both geographic and political. If you're a working journalist, odds aren't just that you work in a pro-Clinton county—odds are that you reside in one of the nation's most pro-Clinton counties."[396] The journalists' location matters because it influences access, relationships, and even ideology.

At present, there is no evidence to suggest that journalists are going to pop their bubble and relocate to Kansas and Wyoming. So, it is likely they will maintain the status quo, and that includes their worldview, or their prevailing ideology: progressivism that is anti-Christian.

My search for insights into the thinking of progressive journalists led me to an article by James Ostrowski, "Why Progressives Make Bad Journalists." He makes a lot of sense that certainly parallels the conclusions in my 2019 book, *Progressive Evil*.[397]

Mr. Ostrowski, who writes for the opinion site Lewrockwell.com, provides an eight-part definition for progressivism that is necessary to review before I summarize why he believes progressives make bad journalists.

He defines progressivism with eight factors. Progressives demonstrate a fixed mindset about politics; have no rational basis; are utopian; favor using democratic government to solve human problems; want government force to produce results; have no theory of costs, thus deny the often extraordinary costs of their proposed solutions; embrace a form of therapy against existential fears; and have no limiting principle, which makes them prone to totalitarianism.

I agree with those factors, which are exhaustively addressed in *Progressive Evil*. Now, given these defining factors, Mr. Ostrowski asks: Can a progressive be a good journalist? He says there are two functions necessary for a good journalist: reporting and evaluating facts.

Mr. Ostrowski contends that most journalists are left of center ideologically, Democrats, and progressives. That matches my observations and most of the available survey data. Progressives also tend to favor journalism as a career because of their desire to make the world a better place through positive government action.

The problem for progressives becoming journalists is that they cannot completely set aside their political mindset (ideology) when reporting facts, nor do they recognize their political bias. Mr. Ostrowski argues, and I agree, that progressivism is also a "self-imposed mental disability that robotically prevents the progressive from noticing certain facts and impels the progressive to exaggerate the importance of other facts."[398]

He blames the progressives' public-school education for that indoctrination fix—implanting that mindset, worldview. That is certainly by design, if one accepts the intent John Dewey had for American public education: to remake our children into progressive robots. Dewey is frequently identified as the father of modern American progressivism.

The progressive's worldview biases his/her job, says Ostrowski. That translates into a set of preordained, fixed views about the way things must happen: government action cannot cause a problem; they always look for nongovernment scapegoats to blame for societal challenges; nongovernment solutions to problems are never an option; and only government solutions are considered.

Mr. Ostrowski argues that, because of these fixed views, true progressives can never be trusted to ferret out the relevant facts of a story. They will always bias the story to fit their fixed expectations (worldview).

Thus, he concludes that progressives generally make bad journalists. The problem today for the rest of us (consumers of journalists' work) is that because progressives dominate journalism, we should not be surprised that the vast majority of the news-consuming public remains ignorant about the true important issues of the day, which may in part explain why many Christian stories are never reported, are buried, or are displayed with a clear, politically correct, anti-Christian bias.[399]

The other factor that makes journalists anti-Christian is political correctness.

I turned to Stella Morabito, a senior contributor at the *Federalist*, to help me appreciate why journalists are anti-Christian. The simple answer is that they totally embrace political correctness, and being anti-Christian due to their progressive credentials is an aspect of being politically correct today.

Ms. Morabito illustrates her thesis with a quote from a foreign film that provides a glimpse into how power elites (both human and spiritual) seek to control the media and subvert objective journalism.[400]

They've decided you're to go into journalism. It's a great honor. We have to strengthen the press. It's full of bourgeoise elements and reactionaries. We don't send just anyone there.—In the screenplay "Angi Vera," newspaper editor and Communist Party hack Anna Trajan speaks to her young protégé, groomed to destroy anyone standing in the way of the party's narrative.[401]

The source of this quote is the 1978 Hungarian film, *Angi Vera*, which is a depiction of corruption set in Stalinist Hungary in 1948, just after the Soviets imposed communism. As a result, every aspect of that nation, including journalism, was forced to conform to the Communist Party line. Only the politically correct survived.

The movie shows the predatory nature of the one-party, politically correct communist system. The main character, Vera, climbs her way up the communist system's journalist ladder to a comfortable life, no matter the compromises. The personal qualities required to reach the lofty heights of journalism at that time included corruptibility, malleability, and conformity. Ms. Morabito explained that these are what the "power elites look for when recruiting journalists, and rewarding them."[402]

Objective journalism wasn't the goal in the communist system. As the quote from the movie suggests, "Those in power always hope to prevent any perceived critic from having a voice." There is no place for the fourth estate to govern power mongers/brokers (the elite). What those power brokers seek is to turn journalists into propagandists, explained Morabito.[403]

There is no such thing as an objective journalist, either—or, as Vera's mentor said in the quote, a "bourgeois and reactionary" thing. Freedom of speech is an obstacle to the elites' quest for power. That means, therefore, "the first order of business for a power-monger is to break down free expression, to control the language."[404]

American journalists aren't that much different from those who grew up in the former Soviet republics. They seldom deviate from politically correct agitprop (political propaganda). We've seen this especially in recent years in the US, thanks to the likes of the Clinton machine's alleged ways of manipulating the truth, whether regarding emails, buying off media personalities, slipping insider information about an adversary's campaign, fixing an FBI investigation, or money-laundering and pay-to-play schemes at the State Department.

Further, given America's recent unsavory "deep state" political history, many in the mainstream media enjoyed the support of leftist politicians, as demonstrated by a plethora of scandals—Russia hoax, Ukraine impeachment of President Trump, the IRS targeting conservative groups, and the Obama administration's Justice Department's Fast and Furious program. It is no wonder the American people are convinced that our mainstream media has no objectivity

Polling confirms that widespread view. A *USA Today* poll found that Americans believe by a wide margin (ten to one) that, in 2016, the media wanted Ms. Clinton to win.[405] Another poll asked Americans about the threat to election integrity. Almost half (45.5 percent) named the media as the primary threat to election integrity, followed (27 percent) by the political establishment.[406]

What's become obvious to many media observers is that political correctness is in the DNA of the journalists' culture. Stella Morabito points out what the communist operative stated to Vera in *Angi Vera*: "You're to go into journalism. It's a great honor." True, it was an "honor" for both the communist regime and for journalists. The journalist gained access to society's influencers, earned their trust, and affirmed the power-brokers' desired narrative. It's a rigged system "in which privilege is the only currency of value." Yes, it's about shameless pandering, but that's the system then and, regrettably, today.[407]

Don't believe that's true here in America? Political correctness is the job description of most American journalists. Just spend a few days in their pond (I've spent decades) to see the stark "PC" reality, especially in Washington. You pay to play the media game in Washington, just like Hillary Clinton told foreign agents seeking favors from her State Department.

What happens to the rare objective journalists who are driven to report the real (true) news? They don't survive. The political correctness bred into the journalists' DNA culture filters out the nonconformists.

So, the PC journalists support the power elites who want to control the flow of news because information is power. When the elite power-brokers control the journalists, all you get from the media is propaganda.

So, where does that leave us? We established that most journalists are progressive in their ideology, which means that facts don't get in their way of reporting. They bring their progressive views to the table—and that means their ideologically driven, anti-Christian bias as well. They especially don't like fundamentalist Christians who believe in Jesus Christ and the Bible, which points out their sin and the idea that every soul must make an eternal choice.

We also learned that these progressive journalists are driven by political correctness. Their job is to gain access, which means compromising their principles to cozy up to those who hold the power (information). Thus, what they produce is mostly propaganda.

Progressive, politically correct journalists don't report on Christian persecution either, and when they rarely do, it is biased to fit their anti-Christian, ideological views.

Let me juxtapose the mainstream media with my personal experience with *Fox News* personalities. The *Fox News* crew isn't perfect, but I find them, as advertised, relatively "fair and balanced." I've done many hundreds of interviews with numerous current and past program hosts and hostesses, and with few exceptions, they never fed me any politically correct line and allowed me to express my personal views. In fact, some, like Shannon Bream (a Liberty University graduate), are Christians.

Further, it is my view that many *Fox News* personalities embrace Christian perspectives and honestly try to be objective in their interviews and commentaries. By comparison, I've sat in the studios of most of the major media networks and experienced firsthand a leftist, anti-Christian bias that was unmistakable.

Conclusion

We began this chapter profiling the way the mainstream media treats Christians and the avalanche of anti-Christian activities across the world. They often ignore them, demonstrate bias, and/or bury reports while hiding the truth because of political correctness. I then explain why we have such an anti-Christian landscape, which is due to two factors: most journalists are progressives ideologically, and they survive in their culture by being politically correct with the power-brokers—seen and unseen.

Admittedly, that's an ugly picture. I believe many journalists are truly proxies of power-brokers who are directly or indirectly tethered to the unseen realm outlined in chapter 8.

CHAPTER TEN

Three Categories of
Anti-Christian Groups

THIS CHAPTER REVIEWS groups that are the enemies of Christianity—the representatives of the world as called out in the Bible. They represent different venues, but share in common a fundamental opposition to Christians because of their theologically based principles and values.

There are three categories of groups examined in this chapter, beginning with advocacy groups that demonstrate an anti-Christian bias carried out in the public arena via the courts, media, and other public means. Second, there are commercial groups such as corporations and businesses that reflect an anti-Christian bias and carry out their agenda in the public workplace and marketplace. Finally, there are religious groups that attack Christians for theological reasons and do so in a very public way, including through violence.

Each "world" category of groups will be addressed with at least one example to demonstrate why I consider them to be the Christian's enemies and Satan's proxy.

The Anti-Christian World

The word "world" in Greek is κόσμος, "cosmos," which, according to *Strong's Concordance*, can mean "worldly affairs"—an enemy of Christ, according to the Scriptures.[408] The term as used here is not about the physical ground we stand on, but indicates the interactions of societies, groupings of humans, that form around anti-Christian agendas and are often inspired, if not directed, by Satan and his army of demons. They are manipulated by lies—demonic deception—that corrupt the "cosmos."

The Apostle John writes about the manipulated "cosmos" in 1 John 2:15–17. He explains how Christians must recognize the world's social order (the manipulated groups) as an enemy, tools of Satan. The apostle wrote:

> I love not the world, neither the things that are in the world. If any man loves the world, the love of the father is not in him. For all that is in the world, the lust of the flesh, and the lust of the eyes, and the pride of life, is not of the father, but is of the world. And the world [κόσμος] passeth away, and the lust thereof: but he that doeth the will of God abideth forever. (KJV)

A similar warning is found in Revelation 12:9 (NIV), where the Apostle John says Satan "leads the whole world [οἰκουμένην, 'inhabited world'] astray." In other words, mankind is blinded to the truth, and mankind (at least the spiritually blinded) don't see the error of their thinking. This was explained in chapter 8, where I describe Satan's goal to control our minds (thoughts).

Satan and his army use these three categories of groups—advocacy, corporations/businesses, and other religions—to target Christians in the marketplace of ideas. They promote antibiblical government policies and use their cultural leverage and even economic means to manipulate popular thinking through the media and culture to hide the truth at

Christians' expense and keep the lost, lost. They also have the motivation in some instances to strike out violently against Christians.

Anti-Christian Advocacy Groups

Satan uses advocacy groups within the "cosmos" to target Christians and the message of Christ. There are more of such groups than you may realize.

The Christian Civil Rights Watch compiled a list of 162 groups across the United States that promote animus towards Christian people because believers hold to traditional values about life, biological sex differences, and the health hazards of homosexual lifestyles.[409]

These groups seek to advance an anti-Christian agenda via the courts, media, government, and public opinion. Consider some of the most noteworthy groups.

American Atheists (AA)

The American Atheists (AA) was founded in 1963 by Madelyn Murray O'Hair (1919–1995) and strives for "complete and absolute separation of church and state" as well as the eradication of religious influence in government.[410] The AA is best known for lawsuits against the displays of crosses and the Ten Commandments, as well as religious practices in schools and the military. It has also campaigned for an anti-Christian agenda by erecting billboards promoting anti-Christian messages, and employs a network of local atheist chapters to influence local officials to embrace anti-Christian policies. The AA also has its own television channel to propagandize the nation with its anti-faith views.[411]

In 2019, AA launched an attack on those who organize youth tour groups to the Ark Encounter and Creation Museum, both Christian educational destination sites. AA worked with Freedom from Religion Foundation (FFRF), also an anti-Christian group, to threaten public schools not to send classes to visit those Christian facilities. Specifically, both groups sent threatening letters to government parks and recreation departments "demanding that they cease promoting upcoming trips to the Answers in Genesis' Creation Museum and Ark Encounter."[412]

Government parks and recreation offices often sponsor school group tours to well-known attractions. However, the students, not the taxpayers, pay for admission. Evidently, the threats from the AA and FFRF persuaded some state officials to cancel some trips, but not all.[413]

Keep in mind that when state agencies kowtow to anti-Christian groups like AA and FFRF, they contribute to making Christians into second-class citizens. Of course, such actions are part of a much larger campaign against freedom of religion in America, such as AA's "Fairy Tales" campaign.

In 2014, AA launched an anti-religion "Fairy Tales" campaign in the Bible Belt—an informal region in the Southern US that tends to be socially conservative, evangelical Protestant—over the Christmas holidays to urge people to skip church and reject the faith of their parents.

One billboard advertisement sponsored by AA showed a little girl writing a letter to Father Christmas, and the caption read: "Dear Santa, All I want for Christmas is to skip church! I'm too old for fairy tales." Those billboards were along highways in three Bible Belt states—Tennessee, Arkansas, and Missouri.[414]

The AA president at the time, David Silverman, said regarding the anti-Christian billboard campaign: "Today's adults have no obligation to pretend to believe the lies their parents believed." He continued, "It's ok to admit your parents were wrong about God, and it's definitely ok to tell your children the truth."[415]

What you seldom hear is that atheism is a religion that promotes its ideology as an alternative to all others, and that includes Christianity. Atheists teach that all life is the result of natural processes—evolution. They don't believe there is a god who created anything, and that all people are accountable to no one except themselves. They also base their morality upon what they believe to be right and wrong (relativism), not on a religious teaching such as that found in the Bible.[416]

American Civil Liberties Union

The American Civil Liberties Union (ACLU) is the largest and most aggressive opponent of people of faith in America. The ACLU was founded in 1920 by a Soviet Union (communist) sympathizer, Roger Baldwin, who said:

> We are for socialism, disarmament, and ultimately for abolishing the state itself.... We seek the social ownership of property, the abolition of the propertied class, and the sole control of those who produce wealth. Communism is the goal.[417]

The ACLU is a giant organization with a full-time staff of one hundred personnel. It has a vast membership, which "is actually a carefully decentralized grassroots network of fifty-one separately incorporated affiliates, over four hundred local chapters, and approximately five thousand volunteer lawyers from coast to coast."[418] It uses our legal system to remove Christian influence across the culture.

Even though the ACLU provides token support to religious liberty, its record includes legal attacks on virtually every aspect of public Christianity: school prayer, Bible reading, religious clubs, Bible studies, prayer gatherings, Ten Commandment memorials, pro-life activities, veterans' memorials that include crosses, family businesses that operate based on their faith, and others.

The ACLU not only goes after pro-Christian activities and displays such as those mentioned above, but it supports policies that are clearly antibiblical. Specifically, it supports same-sex marriage, the legalization of prostitution, the rights of homosexuals to adopt children, and abortion on demand. It defends pornography, the decriminalization of all illegal drugs, opposition to parental choice in children's education, and the designation of various homosexual groups as a constitutionally protected class.

It also seeks to rewrite America's Christian history. The German socialist revolutionary Karl Marx described what the ACLU's agenda is evidently: "If I can steal their history I can steal their country."[419] That's a progressive strategy and precisely what the ACLU is doing to our Christian history: It tries to rewrite the history of our country by removing all aspects of Christianity's influence using the courts—harnessing judicial activism, a progressive tool.[420]

Consider examples of ACLU court cases that demonstrate a clear bias against Christians and our Christian heritage.

Anti-Christian education: The ACLU of Maine supported that state's policy of denying taxpayer money to religious education. The group filed an amicus (friend of the court) brief in the case of *Carson v. Makin*, which supports the state's opposition to a case demanding Maine's taxpayer-funded tuition program pay for children to receive religious instruction at Bangor Christian Schools in Bangor and Temple Academy in Waterville.[421]

The ACLU was joined by the Americans United for Separation of Church and the State in that case, which also took issue with the Christian schools' admission and employment policies that explicitly require all teachers to be born-again Christians "who know the Lord Jesus Christ as savior." One of the schools, Temple Academy, requires the teachers to sign an employment agreement stating that "God recognize[s] homosexuals and other deviants as perverted."[422]

Seldom mentioned in such cases is the fact that public schools are paid by local taxpayers. The Maine case would allow some of those taxes taken from Christian parents to be used to educate their children. Of course, that would erode the left's control of public education and the taxpayers' right to benefit from their contributions (taxes).

Anti-Christian foster care: The ACLU also showed its anti-Christian colors when it opposed Christian-only criteria for foster-care parenting. The backstory is that the Miracle Hill Ministries in Greenville, South Carolina, had a policy that only Christian parents need apply to their foster-care program.[423]

"Our existence and identity are tied to our faith in God and belief in Jesus Christ," explained Reid Lehman, Miracle Hill's president. He said, according to the *Washington Post*, "The ministry would drop out of the foster-care program rather than work with parents who aren't Christian." ACLU attorney Leslie Cooper said, "When they [the state] hire agencies to care for them [foster children]…they should not be using religious criteria to deny children access to families that they desperately need."[424]

The ACLU would require the ministry to hide their Christian motivation in order to serve the needs of the community. That was never the intent of our founders and the primary motivation of the ministry's volunteers and donors.

Miracle Hill Ministries dates back to the pre-World War II era to meet needs. Today, "Miracle Hill Ministries operates four rescue missions, two addiction recovery programs, two youth homes, transitional homes, a foster care program, a food ministry program, eight thrift stores, and an auto sales operation."[425]

The ministry's foster care program is desperately needed in South Carolina. "There are more than 4,600 children in foster care in our state, yet there are only around 2,800 South Carolina foster families. That means there are around 1,800 children in our state with no place to call home," according to the ministry's website.

Blame of the Christian community, not the terrorist: ACLU attorneys also blamed Christian political activism for the June 2016 Muslim extremist's killing of forty-nine people and wounding another fifty-three at an Orlando homosexual nightclub.[426]

"These ACLU lawyers have sunk to a new low," said Susan A. Carleson, chairman/CEO of the American Civil Rights Union, a conservative group that opposes the ACLU's radical agenda. "Caught between a rock and a hard place, they [the ACLU] are defending the indefensible by shifting the blame to an innocent community."[427]

Termed one of the worst shootings in US domestic history and the worst terrorist attack since September 11, 2001, the hour-long shooting spree and hostage standoff early Sunday morning beginning at 2 a.m.

ended after a police SWAT team killed the gunman, Omar Mateen. Mr. Mateen called 911 after the shooting began, pledged allegiance to the Islamic State, and cited the Tsarnaev brothers' Boston Marathon deadly bombing in 2013.

(The Islamic State at the time was also known as the Islamic State of Iraq and Syria [ISIS] and by its Arabic-language acronym Daesh. It continues to be a terrorist militant group that follows a fundamentalist, Salafi jihadist doctrine of Sunni Islam.)

In news reports of the shooting's aftermath, witnesses said that Mateen had frequented the Pulse gay club, where the shootings took place, and had used a gay dating app.[428]

Yet, as reported by Kevin Daley of the DailyCaller.com:

Chase Strangio, a staff attorney with the ACLU's LGBT and AIDS Project, claimed the social and political environment cultivated by Christian conservatives in recent months was to blame for the shooting.... The Tweet: The Christian Right has introduced 200 anti-LGBT bills in the last six months and people blaming Islam for this. No. #PulseNightclub — Chase Strangio (@chasestrangio) June 12, 2016.[429]

High school graduation not held in church: The ACLU of Connecticut demanded that school officials in Enfield stop holding high school graduation ceremonies at a Christian church. They insisted the school must find a secular alternative location.

The ACLU sent a letter to the attorney for the Enfield public schools stating that students, families, and other guests are unconstitutionally and "coercively subjected to religious messages as the price of attending high school commencement." They continued, "Students and family members of minority religions, as well as those who do not subscribe to any religion at all, are immersed in a religious environment of a faith not their own."[430]

The complaint against the Enfield Public Schools (located north of

Hartford, Connecticut) dates back to 2007, when the schools held their high-school graduations in the sanctuary of a Christian church, the First Cathedral, the fifteenth-oldest historically black church founded in the city of Hartford, which has a seating capacity of two thousand. Specifically, the ACLU and other anti-Christian groups objected to the white cross atop the Cathedral's roof, the stained-glass window with religious images, and banners that proclaimed "I am GOD" and "Jesus Christ is Lord."

The complaint alleged that holding graduation ceremonies in the church violates the Establishment Clause. In 2010, US District Court Judge Janet C. Hall said in her decision:

> Upon consideration of the evidence from the perspective of such a reasonable observer, the court concludes that plaintiffs have made a substantial showing that they are likely to succeed on the merits of their claim that holding 2010 graduations at First Cathedral constitutes an impermissible endorsement of religion because it conveys the message that certain religious views are embraced by Enfield Schools, and others are not.

That decision was upheld by the US Court of Appeals for the Second Circuit.[431]

In 2019, Enfield High School hosted its graduation outdoors at the school's football field. The inclement-weather, indoor site for the ceremony was the school's gymnasium with limited seating.[432]

Americans United for Separation of Church and State (AUSCS)

Americans United for Separation of Church and State attacks virtually any contact between religion and government. It uses a wide assortment of platforms as weapons—courts, media, legislation, and more. It strives to ban "God" from graduation speeches, shut down prison ministries, outlaw school vouchers for parents who seek to send their children to faith-based schools, and tear down war memorials—especially those with crosses.

The AUSCS went after Kentucky public schools when that state legislature passed a law that encourages high schools to teach the Bible. Other states are following Kentucky's lead. The AUSCS responded to the offending legislation by recruiting other like-minded, anti-religious groups to oppose the multistate movement known as Project Blitz.[433]

Rachel Laser, a reformed Jew and the president of Americans United, said, "It's part of an effort to establish this sort of narrow Christian agenda as the norm for our country, the government-sanctioned and—supported norm."

It wasn't all that long ago that public schools included Bible readings as part of their literature classes (especially the Book of Job) and, of course, hosted daily devotions.

Southern Poverty Law Center (SPLC)

In 2019, twenty-five Christian and conservative leaders signed a letter to the CEOs of Facebook, Twitter, Google, and Amazon to urge them to end their working relationships with the Southern Poverty Law Center (SPLC). The SPLC is known for listing Christian and conservative groups as hate groups. The twenty-five-leader letter states:

> It is now clear that the SPLC has proven to be a hate-filled, anti-Christian, anti-conservative organization and nothing more than a weapon of the radical Left, whose goal is to bully people into compliance with their ideology. Fail to comply with their demands, and you will be labeled as a hate group or an extremist.[434]

Consider the group's background. In 1971, SPLC was founded by Morris Dees, a civil rights attorney, who stood up the center to combat racism in the South and reportedly used that platform to enrich himself in the process. Once his campaign against racism diminished, he found a new cause "to frighten people into still donating."[435]

Real Clear Politics writer Carl Cannon quotes Dees as saying that "scaring the bejesus out of people requires new bogeymen, and lots of them." Cannon says the SPLC's new bogeyman became "mainstream conservative groups."[436]

Even the left targets the SPLC such as Stephen Bright, a Yale law professor and president of the Atlanta-based Southern Center for Human Rights, who described Dees as a "con man" and a "fraud."[437]

The SPLC targets Christian groups for special wrath because of their beliefs about sexuality and marriage. For example, the Family Research Council is listed as a hate group by the SPLC, and thanks to that listing, a deranged man believed the SPLC's "hate group" propaganda and, as court records demonstrate, charged into the Christian group's Washington headquarters intending to kill as many staff as possible, but was stopped by the guard, which he wounded in the process.

Fortunately, there are people in high positions who are taking notice of the SPLC's suspicious actions. Senator Tom Cotton (R-AR) called on the IRS to investigate the SPLC's nonprofit and review its tax-exempt status. He told *Fox News* that the SPLC has "become kind of a hate group themselves." He continued, "Serial repeated defamation against what you see as a political opponent is not a tax-exempt purpose."[438]

SPLC has very deep pockets, with an estimated $328 million stored in offshore banks.[439] Why? Senator Cotton said, "I don't know many charitable advisors who say it's best practice to send your endowment to overseas accounts in the Caribbean. That's why Charity Watch gives them [the SPLC] an 'F' rating."[440]

Many of the 162 anti-Christian organizations identified by Christian Civil Rights Watch are philosophically based on humanism. These groups more often than not trace their roots to the last century and, like progressives, their ideological cousin, seeded the current anti-Christian cultural revolution. Consider a couple of the most influential humanist, anti-Christian groups.

The American Humanist Association (AHA)

The American Humanist Association (AHA) attacks most faith groups with the objective of purging their influence on the country. The AHA is much like the groups already mentioned in that it sues in court to remove crosses and other religious imagery from public places, stop public prayer, and attack any public references to God.

The AHA states in its website that it strives "to bring about a progressive society where being good without a god is an accepted and respected way to live life. We are accomplishing this through our defense of civil liberties and secular governance, by our research to the growing number of people without traditional religious faith, and through a continued refinement and advancement of the humanist worldview."[441]

The AHA was founded in Illinois as a tax-exempt educational and religious group. Its bylaws "reflect that the association has a legal status as a 'religious organization."[442] The AHA, which was incorporated in 1941, derives its religious stature from the Unitarian faith. "Unitarianism is the belief that God exists in one person, not three. It denies the doctrine of the Trinity as well as the full divinity of Jesus. Therefore, it is not Christian."[443]

In the recent past, the AHA sponsored a national advertising campaign critical of religious-based Scriptures with a special focus on biblical morality. There were advertisements in major print media claiming Christianity had no right to claim the moral high ground. These advertisements juxtapose Scriptures with humanist statements. One such pairing was a quote from 1 Timothy 2:11–12 (NIV): "A woman should learn in quietness and full submission. I do not permit a woman to teach or to have authority over a man; she must be silent." The humanist statement says: "The rights of men and women should be equal and sacred—marriage should be a perfect partnership," a statement attributed to Robert G. Ingersoll, a noted nineteenth-century humanist.[444]

Humanists never try to understand the Scriptures in the context. The 1 Timothy verse is not about equality between men and women, but about spiritual roles in the church—but facts never stopped the left, antichrists, from attacking Christians.

Planned Parenthood

The Planned Parenthood Federation is a humanist organization that dates back to 1916, when Margaret Sanger founded the first birth-control center in the United States. In 1963, Planned Parenthood became associated with the World Population Emergency Campaign, a private organization set up to alert Americans to the danger of the "world population explosion" and to raise money for birth-control programs (read "abortion on demand").[445]

Planned Parenthood founder Sanger was named humanist of the year in 1957, thanks to her anti-Christian agenda regarding the promotion of premarital and extramarital promiscuity, abortion on demand, and condom distribution. She even claimed at the time the pseudoscience of eugenics is a Christian concept. The following quote comes from her book:

> Dean Inge believes Birth Control is an essential part of Eugenics and an essential part of Christian morality. On this point he asserts: "We do wish to remind our orthodox and conservative friends that the Sermon on the Mount contains some admirably clear and unmistakable eugenic precepts. 'Do men gather grapes of thorns, or figs of thistles? A corrupt tree cannot bring forth good fruit, neither can a good tree bring forth evil fruit. Every tree which bringeth not forth good fruit is hewn down, and cast into the fire.' We wish to apply these words not only to the actions of individuals, which spring from their characters, but to the character of individuals, which spring from their inherited qualities."[446]

Sanger is loose and fast with the Scriptures to advocate for a master race. She even recruited Christian ministers to advance her radical eugenics ideas.

In the 1930s, Sanger set up the "Negro Project," an effort to discourage black Americans from having children. Sanger outlined her objective for that project in a letter:

[We propose to] hire three or four colored ministers, preferably with social-service backgrounds, and with engaging personalities. The most successful educational approach to the Negro is through a religious appeal. And we do not want word to go out that we want to exterminate the Negro population, and the minister is the man who can straighten out that idea if it ever occurs to any of their more rebellious members.[447]

No wonder Planned Parenthood's abortion mills are located in poor, minority communities today.

The nation's largest provider of abortion services formed a clergy committee led by Tom Davis, a United Church of Christ minister, who in his book, *Sacred Work: Planned Parenthood and Its Clergy Alliances*, portrays Planned Parenthood as doing God's work.[448]

The foreword to Davis' book claims that Planned Parenthood is a "secular humanist" organization. Secular humanists don't acknowledge the existence of God, Heaven, or Hell, much less a divine purpose for mankind.

Planned Parenthood's anti-Christian credentials are widely evidenced in their publications as well. In the 1970s, they distributed a pro-abortion comic book, *Abortion Eve*. The comic's story portrays a young girl with cross earrings (allegedly a Christian person) who considers abortion but is afraid of what her pastor would say. Another character in the comic says to the first girl:[449]

"Is church making it hard for you to decide? Because if it makes it hard for you like I think it must, then I say SKIP that part of church! I use the church when it HELPS me, not when I have to fight it. I don't wanna fight God and I don't think God wants to fight me."

Another teen then adds: "Seems to me that those church rules don't take into account that women are people too!"

Planned Parenthood's anti-Christian agenda is totally unapologetic. For example, in the 1990s, the organization sent out a holiday card with the slogan "Choice on Earth." Predictably, Christians complained but Planned Parenthood reissued the card for years.

In conclusion, this section highlighted some of the nearly two hundred anti-Christian organizations in the United States, many which embrace humanism (progressivism) as their governing philosophy. These groups seek to implement their radical anti-Christian ideas through public policies that restructure all social, political, and cultural institutions. Those humanistic ideas promote values that are antithetical to Christianity.

Anti-Christian Corporations and Businesses

Satan uses corporations and businesses within the "cosmos" to target Christians and the message of Christ. These groups seek to advance an anti-Christian agenda using economic levers. Consider some of the most noteworthy corporate and business groups.

Bible Blender, a Christian nonprofit, identified 136 corporations and businesses that "have publicly supported policies, laws, or standards which most Christians deem inappropriate and immoral or have publicly or reportedly denounced religion and/or Christianity."[450]

Some of the anti-Christian offending corporations, businesses are profiled below along with some of their offending practices.

Aetna, the insurance giant, was fined $4.5 million by the state of Missouri for illegally funding abortions as well as paying for the abortifacient RU-486. This was the insurance company's second violation, and if it reoffends, it will lose its license to sell insurance in Missouri. Aetna's pro-abortion agenda is also evident when it denies employers using the insurance company's services the option to provide employees with contraceptive coverage. Meanwhile, the insurance company refuses to pay for diagnosis and treatment of such health issues as autism spectrum disorders.[451]

New York Life Insurance Company partners with the National Gay and Lesbian Chamber of Commerce (NGLCC), which promotes anti-Christian values about marriage and sexuality. New York Life's lawyers even filed an amicus brief in the Supreme Court case that endorses sweeping sexual-orientation and gender-identity protections. The insurance giant supports the Susan Komen Foundation, a funder of the abortion-provider Planned Parenthood.[452]

Prudential Financial, an insurance and investment firm, is very anti-Christian as well. It supports the leftist Center for American Progress, which supports the pro-abortion and homosexual agendas. Like New York Life, it supports the NGLCC and the Human Rights Campaign, a pro-homosexual organization. It also participates in gift matching for Planned Parenthood and supports other pro-abortion organizations such as United Way and Girls Inc.[453]

As the above paragraphs indicate, the corporate and business worlds are becoming incredibly anti-Christian, thanks to the aggressive pressure from the left. Perhaps the worst piece of federal legislation to ever be considered is the off-and-on-again, so-called Equality Act, which enjoys significant support within the corporate world.

The Equality Act is the future threat to Christians and other people of faith, should progressives come to dominate both chambers of Congress. Most every reader is quite aware of past court cases regarding Christian bakers and photographers who refused to provide services to homosexual couples based on their religious objections. The Equality Act would go much farther in normalizing and making homosexuality a mainstream protected class.

The Equality Act as pushed by Democrats in Congress in 2017, 2018, 2019, and 2020 is gaining steam and has plenty of corporate supporters. The act as proposed in 2019 failed to pass. It would ban all forms of "discrimination," no excuses—even religious. It would essentially criminalize orthodox Christianity by forcing virtually every institution in society to hire, service, and promote homosexuals and individuals confused about their gender.[454]

The act as proposed would enshrine "sexual orientation" and "gender identity" in a statute, which would embed these concepts into the Civil Rights Act of 1964; even pedophilia would be protected under the title "sexual orientation."[455]

That means it would enshrine actual and perceived "sexual orientation and gender identity" into federal statutes—creating a new protected class. That would put the federal government's stamp of approval on America's version of the biblical Sodom and Gomorrah.

The 2019 version of the bill, which progressives are expected to push each year until it passes, states that religious freedom may not be used as a defense. It would apply to all churches, religious schools, religious hospitals, religious employers, gathering places, sports, all government entities, and more.[456]

Churches would lose their tax-exempt status if they do not submit to such a radical law, and Christian schools would lose their accreditation as well.

Virtually every citizen would be affected by the proposed law. Men who claim they "identify" as women would be permitted to use women's restrooms, showers, and change areas, and this would apply even in church settings.[457]

Evidently, the homosexual lobby is making great strides in recruiting corporations and businesses to support the Equality Act. For example, the Human Rights Campaign (HRC) announced in 2019 that it recruited more than one hundred top businesses as cosponsors of the Equality Act. That means those companies are likely to remain supportive of the proposed legislation, even if the Democrats can't get it through in the next couple of years. It is a clear window into the future.[458]

Of course, the HRC is celebrating the groundswell of business support for the Equality Act. "The more than 100 businesses that have joined HRC's business coalition for the Equality Act are sending a loud and clear message that the time has come for full federal equality," said HRC president Chad Griffin.[459]

The HRC business coalition includes some of the nation's leading businesses: Amazon, Apple, American Express, Bank of America, Chevron, and many more.[460] It is obvious that more and more corporations and big American businesses are joining the anti-Christian bandwagon.

Anti-Christian Religious Groups

Satan uses other religions within the "cosmos" to target Christians and the message of Christ. The best-known offender is Islam, which uses violence and intimidation to target Christians and Christianity.

This section answers three questions. First, why is Islam considered an anti-Christian faith? Second, what do Islam's holy texts say about Christians? Finally, how widespread is anti-Christian persecution at the hands of Muslims?

1. Why is Islam considered an anti-Christian religion?

Islam is an antichrist religion as defined in the Bible. The term "antichrist" appears five times in the Bible, all in the epistles of John. Further, the term isn't about a person here, but about a theology or system of doctrine.[461] Consider what 1 John 4 says: "But every spirit that does not acknowledge Jesus is not from God. This is the spirit of the antichrist, which you have heard is coming and even now is already in the world" (1 John 4:3, NIV).

John makes it clear that the word "antichrist" is a spirit that denies that Jesus Christ came in the flesh. Earlier in the epistle, John acknowledged that the spirit of the antichrist is in the world. He states in 1 John 2:18 (NIV): "Dear children, this is the last hour; and as you have heard that the antichrist is coming, even now many antichrists have come. This is how we know it is the last hour."

The next use of the term "antichrist" is in 1 John 2:22 (NIV), which states: "Who is the liar? It is whoever denies that Jesus is the Christ. Such a person is the antichrist—denying the Father and the Son."

The conclusion from this verse is that those who deny that Jesus is the Christ (the Messiah), and deny the Father and the Son, are an antichrist. "I say this because many deceivers, who do not acknowledge Jesus Christ as coming in the flesh, have gone out into the world. Any such person is the deceiver and the antichrist" (2 John 1:7, NIV).

The consistent theme in John's epistles is the denial of the deity of Jesus Christ.

All religions that deny the deity of Christ, based on the above Scriptures, display the antichrist spirit. That's true of the Jehovah Witnesses, the Mormons, and Islam.

Islam as a religion satisfies all aspects of 1 John 2:22 to qualify as true antichrist, however. It denies the deity of Christ as well as the Father and the Son. In fact, Islam teaches that Allah, their god, is not a father, and he has no son.

2. What Do Islam's Holy Texts Say about Christians?

It is important to understand what Islamic texts say about non-Muslims and especially Christians to appreciate their motivation to persecute Christians.

We begin by contrasting the worldviews of Christianity and Islam. Bernard Lewis, the West's greatest historian and interpreter of Islam, wrote:

> Christianity means a religion, in the strict sense of that word, a system of belief and worship and some clerical or ecclesiastical organization to go with it. If we say Christendom, we mean the entire civilization that grew up under the aegis of that religion, but [it] also contains many elements that are not part of the religion, many elements that are even hostile to that religion.[462]

"Islam as a religion embraces 'far more than it does in the Christian' world," Lewis explained. Islam is the primary basis of both the Muslim's

identity and loyalty. Instead of thinking of a nation subdivided into religions like the mostly Christian United States, orthodox Muslim people think of their religion subdivided into nations. For Muslims, every
aspect of their lives—political, economic, sexual, war-making, worship,
and even dealings with non-Muslims—is dictated by Islam. No wonder
the Western mind has a difficult time understanding the Muslim world
and how it views and treats non-Muslims."

The Islamic religion is defined by a combination of the words
of Allah (Arabic for "god") found in the Koran and the words of the
prophet Muhammad, found in the Sunna. That text is based on two
other volumes, the Sira (Muhammad's life story) and the Hadith, a collection of stories about Muhammad.

The Hadith dictates directives for Muslims to follow, especially those
recorded in the Sahih al-Bukhari, the collection by the ninth-century
imam Muhammad al-Bukhari. That collection of pronouncements is
considered the most authentic.

The Koran divides humanity into two groups: those who believe
Muhammad is the prophet of Allah and the *kafir* (the unbeliever,
non-Muslim), who are depicted as evil and subhuman. It is useful to
understand that a very small part (3 percent) of the trilogy of Islamic
documents address Christian *kafirs*. However, the topic of the *kafir* is
allotted significant (81 percent) attention in the documents, which provides important guidance for the orthodox Muslim and a warning to
people of other faiths.

Muhammad hated the Jews and Christians, as seen in many hadiths
and the Koran. It is true that Muhammad labeled Jews and Christians
as special "people of the book," a reference to the Bible. However, these
people were still *kafirs*, unbelievers, which means they are subjected to,
at best, second-class treatment.

A review of Islamic teachings makes it clear that *kafirs* are to be hated
and can be enslaved, raped, beheaded, deceived, plotted against, terror-
ized, warred against, and humiliated. These teachings are quite clear
across the trilogy of Islamic texts and contribute to our understanding

of the motivation of contemporary orthodox Muslims as they respond to Christians.

The following material is taken from my 2015 book, *Never Submit*, which provides a detailed analysis of the Islamic faith especially as it relates to Christians, *kafirs*.

Kafirs (Christians and other non-Muslims) are to be hated:

They (*kafirs*) who dispute the signs (Koran verses) of Allah without authority having reached them are greatly hated by Allah and the believers. So, Allah seals up every arrogant, disdainful heart.[463]

Muslims can enslave the *kafir*: When some of the remaining Jews of Medina agreed to obey a verdict from Saed, Mohammed sent for him. He approached the Mosque riding a donkey and Mohammed said, "Stand up for your leader." Mohammed then said, "Saed, give these people your verdict." Saed replied, "Their soldiers should be beheaded and their women and children should become slaves."[464]

A Muslim may rape a *kafir*: On the occasion of Khaybar, Mohammed put forth new orders about forcing sex with captive women. If the woman was pregnant, she was not to be used for sex until after the birth of the child. Nor were any women to be used for sex who were unclean with regard to Muslim laws about menstruation.[465]

A Muslim may behead a *kafir*: When you encounter the Kafirs on the battlefield, cut off their heads until you have thoroughly defeated them and then take the prisoners and tie them up firmly.[466]

A Muslim may deceive a *kafir*: Some among them listen to you [Mohammed], but We have cast veils over their [*kafirs'*] hearts and a heaviness to their ears so that they cannot understand our signs [the Koran].[467]

A Muslim can plot against a *kafir*: They plot and scheme against you [Mohammed], and I plot and scheme against them. Therefore, deal calmly with the *kafirs* and leave them alone for a while.[468]

A Muslim may terrorize a *kafir*: Then your Lord spoke to His angels and said, "I will be with you. Give strength to the believers. I will send terror into the *kafirs'* hearts, cut off their heads and even the tips of their fingers!"[469]

A Muslim can make war on and humiliate a *kafir*: Make war on those who have received the Scriptures [Jews and Christians] but do not believe in Allah or in the Last Day. They do not forbid what Allah and His Messenger have forbidden. The Christians and Jews do not follow the religion of truth until they submit and pay the poll tax [*jizya*], and they are humiliated.[470]

A Muslim must never befriend a *kafir*: Believers should not take *kafirs* as friends in preference to other believers. Those who do this will have none of Allah's protection and will only have themselves as guards. Allah warns you to fear Him for all will return to Him.[471]

There is even a dehumanizing hadith suggesting that killing a *kafir* is not a capital crime:

[Abu] asked Ali, "Do you know of any sources of law that were revealed to Mohammed other than the Koran?" Ali responded, "None except for Allah's law, or the ability of reason given by Allah to a Muslim, or these written precepts I possess." I said, "What are these written rules?" Ali answered, "They concern the blood money paid by a killer to a victim's relatives, the method of ransoming a captive's release from the enemy, and the law that a Muslim must never be killed as punishment for killing a *kafir*.[472]

The Koran states that there is hope for the *kafir* who submits to Islam—and then the person will go to paradise. However, neither the "path of those who anger you [the Jews] nor the path of those who go astray [the Christians]" will gain paradise. In fact, Muhammad states the same idea another way: "According to Allah, any Jew or Christian that is aware of me, but dies before accepting my prophecy will be sent to Hell."[473]

Muhammad established a very special relationship for *kafirs*. Once a Muslim army conquered the Jews at Khaybar (Arabia), the jihadists (those engaged in holy war) seized the Jewish property as the spoils of war. Then the jihadists struck an agreement called a *dhimma* with the conquered Jews in Arabia. That agreement called for the Jews to stay and farm the land, but they must surrender half of their profits to the Muslims. That is apparently the origin of the term *dhimmis*, whereby a group of conquered or otherwise subject people come under the protection of Islam in exchange for the fruits of their labor.[474]

The *dhimmi* practice continues today and translates into a second-class citizenship whereby Muslims dominate and the *dhimmi* abides by Islamic rules. They pay a heavy poll tax called the *jizya*; they enjoy limited rights, and the only way out of that status is to convert to Islam or leave.[475] Muslims like the *dhimmi* system, which explains why they have imposed it on most of the non-Muslim people conquered over the past fourteen hundred years.

Umar II, aka Umar Ibn Abd al-Aziz, an Umayyad caliph who ruled AD 717 to 720, outlined the expectations of *dhimmitude* for the newly conquered Christians:

We shall not build, in our cities or in their neighborhood new monasteries, churches, convents, or monks' cells, nor shall we repair, by day or by night, such of them as fall in ruins or are situated in the quarters of the Muslims.

We shall keep our gates wide open for passersby and travelers. We shall give board and lodging to all Muslims who pass our way for three days.[476]

The *kafirs* who lived under *dhimmitude* were obliged to comply with all Islamic rules. They had to dress differently than Muslims and were to always defer to the Muslims in public. They couldn't display crosses or ring church bells or recite the gospels aloud, and they were forbidden to build new churches. There were off-limit areas to *kafirs* such as Mecca and Medina, and they were never to enter a mosque without permission.

3. How widespread is anti-Christian persecution at the hands of Muslims?

Not all Muslims believe, much less practice, the above teachings. However, enough do believe and act on those beliefs to explain the worldwide, anti-Christian persecution at the hands of Islamic believers.

Open Doors, a Christian ministry that tracks Christian persecution, publishes an annual world watch list profiling the fifty countries worldwide "where it's most difficult to be a Christian." Their findings clearly point to Islamic-based attacks on Christians as the most significant source of anti-Christian persecution.[477]

"In seven out of the top 10 world watch list countries, the primary cause of [Christian] persecution is Islamic oppression," states Open Doors. This means life for many millions of Christians in Muslim-majority countries is that of a second-class citizen. They are "discriminated against for jobs or even violently attacked."

There is no doubt that Islamic extremist groups seek to destroy Christians. Open Doors continues:

> In some areas of the world, there are radicalized extremist groups who wage war against anyone who doesn't adhere to their specific interpretation of religion. For instance, in places like the Middle East and Nigeria, Islamic extremist groups terrorize communities and churches, killing those they consider to be "infidels" (often in coordinated bombings), raping and kidnapping women and burning down homes and churches. Their vic-

tims can be fellow adherents of a religion—for instance, Boko Haram attacks Muslims in Nigeria—but they always target Christians out of hatred for other faiths.[478]

Consider statements by some of the leading Islamic terrorists. These statements conclusively demonstrate the role Islam plays in their motivation to violently persecute Christians.

Thereligionofpeace.com (TROP) is a pluralistic, nonpartisan website concerned with Islam's political and religious teachings according to its texts—Koran, Hadith, and Sira. The purpose of the site is to explain the threat Islam poses to human dignity and freedom, and to expose the violence and dysfunction that comes from the influence of the Islam's supremacist ideology.

TROP captured on its website a list of targeted acts of terrorism on Christian civilians and church workers by religious Muslims since the al-Qaeda attacks on America on September 11, 2001. The victims are innocent Christians who were singled out solely because of their faith in Christ by Muslims who characterized their motivation to their religion (Islam).[479]

A few representative statements are outlined below and provided by TROP. We begin with the mass murderer, Osama bin Laden, who clearly identifies his Islamic motivation.

Al Qaeda's leader who planned the 911 attack on America:

"I am one of the servants of Allah. We do our duty of fighting for the sake of the religion of Allah. It is also our duty to send a call to all the people of the world to enjoy this great light and to embrace Islam and experience the happiness in Islam.... Our primary mission is nothing but the furthering of this religion."
—*Osama bin Laden, May 1998*

Afghanistan: [The Taliban are] "simply [a] band of dedicated youths determined to establish the laws of Allah on earth....

The Taliban will fight until there is no blood in Afghanistan left to shed, and Islam becomes a way of life for our people." —*Mullah Omar, Taliban leader*

Egypt: "There is nothing more right in God's religion (Islam) than those who speak of the infidelity, reneging on Islam and abandonment of religion, and call for the necessity to fight." —Abu Mohammed al-Adnani, an al-Qaeda spokesperson

Egypt: "Allah is our objective, the Quran is our Constitution, the Prophet is our leader, Jihad is our way, and death for the sake of Allah is the highest of our aspirations." —*Credo of the Muslim Brotherhood, which has spawned attacks and numerous subsidiary terrorist organizations*

France: "This group of believers from the soldiers of the Caliphate (may Allah give them strength and victory) targeted the capital of prostitution and vice, the one that carries the banner of the cross in Europe, Paris. This group of believers advanced toward their enemy hoping to be killed for Allah's sake, doing so in support of His religion and His Prophet.... They were truthful with Allah and Allah granted victory upon their hands and cast terror into the hearts of the crusaders.... All praise, grace and favor belong to Allah." —*Statement released by the caliphate, taking credit for the November 13, 2015 Paris massacre*

Germany: "By the name of Allah, we have come to slaughter you.... Oh brothers, immigrate and wage jihad for the sake of Allah, support this religion. Everyone should do what he can. Every person should support the religion with whatever he can. Those who are able to immigrate should immigrate; those who can carry out local attacks should do so, and those who are in Europe should fight those pigs, crusaders." —*Anis Amri, the migrant who massacred a dozen people at a Berlin Christmas market*

Iran: "Those who know nothing of Islam pretend that Islam counsels against war. Those who say this are witless. Islam says:

'Kill all the unbelievers just as they would kill you all! Kill them, put them to the sword and scatter their armies' …. Islam says: 'Whatever good there is exists thanks to the sword and in the shadow of the sword! People cannot be made obedient except with the sword! The sword is the key to paradise, which can be opened only for holy warriors! There are hundreds of other [Koranic] psalms and hadiths urging Muslims to value war and to fight. Does all that mean that Islam is a religion that prevents men from waging war? I spit upon those foolish souls who make such a claim.'" —*The Ayatollah Khomeini, leader of the Islamic Republic of Iran*

Islamic State of Iraq and Syria: "We are fighting for no other reason than to extract people from the *kufr* [nonbelievers] and to usher them into the fold of Islam." —*ISIS Commander*

Libya: "All praise is due to Allah, the strong and mighty, and may blessings and peace be upon the one sent by the sword as a mercy for all the world…chopping off the heads that have been carrying the cross delusion for a long time…. They supplicate what they worship and die upon their paganism…. We will conquer Rome, by Allah's permission, the promise of our prophet." —*A statement by Islamists as they are beheading twenty-one Christian laborers on a beach in Libya*

Nigeria: "For peace to reign in the land, all Christians must convert to Islam. Allah has tasked all Muslims in Quran chapter 9 verse 29 to continue to attack Jews and Christians who refused to believe in him and his messenger, Prophet Mohammed." — *Abu Qaqa, explaining why his band massacred nearly one hundred worshipers, including children, in a series of attacks on churches in a single Sunday morning.*

Syria: "We are fighting to apply what Allah said to the Prophet Muhammad, peace be upon him. We are fighting so people don't look to other people but only to Allah. We don't believe in complete freedom: it is restricted by Allah's laws." —*A* *member of al-Nusra, an al-Qaeda affiliated group responsible for hundreds of terror attacks*

Turkey: "The Koran says: 'Fight them until evil disappears and all religion becomes Allah's [religion].' The suicide activists who blow themselves up are carrying out the Koran's commandment." —*Ali Osman Zor, Great East Islamic Raiders Front terrorist organization*

United Kingdom: "Our religion is Islam—obedience to the one true God, Allah, and following the footsteps of the final prophet and messenger Muhammad…. This is how our ethical stances are dictated." —*Mohammad Sidique Khan, London subway bomber, explaining his motives on a prerecorded videotape*

United States: "We call on every Muslim who believes in Allah and wishes to be rewarded to comply with Allah's order to kill the Americans and plunder their money wherever they find it." —*Statement released on the nineteenth anniversary of the 9/11 attacks*

United States: "In the name of Allah, the merciful (Arabic), Praise be to Allah, and prayers as well as peace upon the prophet of Allah. I let you know, I'm in Orlando and I did the shootings." —*Omar Mateen, while massacring forty-nine innocents at a gay night club in Florida*

Globally Islamic terrorists have carried out more than 36,224 deadly attacks since the September 11, 2001 (9/11), attacks on America. Specifically, to date, 2,977 Americans have died inside the United States thanks to Islamic terror just since 9/11. Also, since 9/11 another 158 Americans have been killed in fifty-three separate acts of deadly Islamic terror or Islam-related honor killings in this country. Fortunately, many other plots have been thwarted.

It is rather troubling that as the Muslim population increases in the US, the number of Islam-inspired attacks may well rise, in part because a significant number of American Muslims believe that violence in defense of their faith is justified—especially inside the Christian nation of America.[480]

We reviewed earlier in this section some of the antichrist teachings in the Islamic holy texts. What's clear is that Islam is not a peaceful faith. Consider the following verses not previously mentioned:

As to those who reject faith, I will punish them with terrible agony in this world and in the Hereafter, nor will they have anyone to help. (Quran 3:56)[481]

The punishment of those who wage war against Allah and His messenger and strive to make mischief in the land is only this, that they should be murdered or crucified or their hands and their feet should be cut off on opposite sides. (Quran 5:33)[482]

I will cast terror into the hearts of those who disbelieve. Therefore, strike off their heads and strike off every fingertip of them. (Quran 8:12)[483]

O ye who believe! When ye meet those who disbelieve in battle, turn not your backs to them. Whoso on that day turneth his back to them, unless maneuvering for battle or intent to join a company, he truly hath incurred wrath from Allah, and his habitation will be hell, a hapless journey's end. (Quran 8:15–16)[484]

Fight everyone in the way of Allah and kill those who disbelieve in Allah. (Ibn Ishaq 992)[485]

Christians are too often victimized by antichrist attacks prompted by Islamists that embrace the above mandates.

Each year across the world, thousands of Christian homes and churches are destroyed by Muslim mobs and thousands of Christian believers die at the hands of Islamic extremists. Their crime, according to the Islamists, is apostasy or evangelism, to purposed blasphemy of Islam.[486]

Christians tend to be very restrained when facing Islamic discrimination, kidnapping, rape, torture, and murder—especially in Muslim-majority countries. In fact, with good reason, Muslim clerics in the West don't fear for their safety as do their Christian counterparts across the world.

Yes, a significant part of global Christian persecution, which includes the United States, is directly attributable to Islamists.

My 2015 book, *Never Submit: Will the Extermination of Christians Get Worse Before It Gets Better?* includes a chapter on what to do about the Islamic threat to the United States. Below is a summary of my recommendations, which still apply today as well. I state in *Never Submit:*

> It is time for Christians, local churches and their communities to aid in the defeat of the Islamist threat against Christians abroad before it comes any further to our neighborhoods. Simultaneously we need to vaccinate American communities against Islamization, anticipating that Middle East style atrocities and genocide of Christians could eventually happen here as well.[487]
>
> The perception that Islamic terrorism is growing for America is widespread, according to national polling. Americans are more concerned today than at any time in the last few years about the Islamic extremist threat to our homeland and as a result are willing to support committing U.S. ground troops once again to fight the terrorist enemy in the Middle East before it gets worse and perhaps comes here.[488]

I identify six areas of concern and proscribe in *Never Submit* what Americans must do to resist Islamization and avoid the radical consequences. Those areas are:

Vaccinate citizens from misinformation and ignorance: Christian pastors must inform and call their congregations to action. Former Congressman Frank Wolf, a champion for the persecuted, said the American "church is apathetic" and "silent" about the situation in the Middle East.[489] Wolf cited Ecclesiastes 4:1 to emphasize his view of the American church:

> So, I returned, and considered all the oppressions that are done under the sun: and behold the tears of such as were oppressed, and they had no comforter; and on the side of their oppressors there was power; but they had no comforter.

"The church totally ignores the issue of Christian persecution," Retired Lieutenant General Jerry Boykin, now the executive vice president for the Family Research Council, said in agreement with Congressman Wolf.[490] David Curry, president of Open Doors, a ministry that supports persecuted Christians, was less blunt: "Many pastors have yet to fully realize the impact of persecution and the potential threat to the West."[491]

Vaccinate against a crippling Muslim *hijra*: More Muslims are immigrating into the US than even Congress knows about and with them come potentially significant challenges for local communities. We need to stop Muslim immigration as long as the war with Islam continues and simultaneously increase the immigration of persecuted Christians.

In April 2015 (then) Congressman Trey Gowdy (R-SC), chairman of the House Judiciary Subcommittee on Immigration and Border Security, sent a letter demanding the Department of State halt the resettlement of refugees in the city of Spartanburg in his district. Gowdy objected to the "lack of notice, information and consultation afforded to me and my constituents" and then posed questions such as "Do any of the refugees to be resettled in the Spartanburg area have criminal convictions?"[492]

The necessity for more oversight of the refugee process is an emergency that warrants the immediate attention of every community especially when considering Muslim immigration which is a form of jihad called *hijra* that dates back to the time of Mohammed.

> I charge you with five of what Allah has charged me with: to assemble, to listen, to obey, to immigrate and to wage Jihad for the sake of Allah —Quote from Hadith (five "charges" for Muslims)[493]

Hijra means "migration" and is an Islamic organizational strategy that has the goal of jihad by non-violent means—also known as *civilization jihad* or *Islamization*. Migration is a religious obligation, according to Sam Solomon and E. Al Maqdisi in their book *Modern Day Trojan Horse: The Islamic Doctrine of Immigration.*[494]

Vaccinate local Muslims from extremism: There are at least two possible ways to vaccinate local Muslims against extremism: Lead them to salvation through Jesus Christ or help them reform their faith to reject extremism.

Christians are morally obligated to reach out to Muslims in the name of Christ. McDonnell indicated that "befriending Muslims is the first step." Franklin Graham agrees that "God loves Muslims and Christ died for Muslims" and "Yes, we should reach out to Muslims."

Tom Doyle has considerable experience working with Muslims both in the Middle East and in America. He points out that 60 percent of self-identified Muslims don't practice Islam. "Muslims are open" to the gospel," Doyle said, but Satan has created a "log jam" to "keep Christians from reaching out to Muslims. The "log jam" is keeping "Christians in fear of and hating Muslims." But Doyle says that's an unbiblical view. In fact, the bible calls on Christians more than three hundred times not to fear. Rather, we are to love our enemies.[495]

Vaccinate public schools from Islamic proselytizing: The restrictions on separation between church and state evidently don't universally apply when it comes to Islamic proselytizing in American schools. In fact, across the US, many taxpayer-funded schools, while excluding any reference to Christianity, are waging a propaganda war that extols Islam under the guise of multiculturalism.

Vaccinate communities' Islamic extremist groups: Many Islamic groups operating in the US engage in political action but are identified as religious organizations. Communities need to monitor these groups to ensure they are engaged in legal actions that don't promote extremism.

The Clarion Project hosts a website (wwww.clarionproject.org) that features 108 Islamic groups found in twenty-nine states. The largest and best-known group is the Council on American Islamic Relations (CAIR). Consider some facts about CAIR that make it a concern.

CAIR is "America's largest Islamic civil liberties group," which grew out of the Islamic Association for Palestine, an organization associated with Hamas, a Palestinian terrorist group, according to the US State Department.[496]

Vaccinate communities from sharia (Islamic) law: Political Islam aims to replace American constitutional law, which would be catastrophic for non-Muslims, women, and the American way of life.

Islamic groups like CAIR and all Muslim Brotherhood associated entities intend to impose Shari (Islamic) law on American communities. That's a key aim of the Muslim Brotherhood dating back to founder Hassan al-Banna, who said: "It is in the nature of Islam to dominate, not to be dominated, to impose its law on all nations and to extend its power to the entire planet."[497]

Sharia law deals with a broad range of issues: crime, politics, economics, and personal matters to include sex and even social etiquette. For Muslims, sharia is considered the infallible law of god and is used as a significant source of legislation in most Muslim countries.

Vaccinate youth from Islamic terrorism: American communities must take action to vaccinate their youth from the influence of Islam. Otherwise, more young Americans will join ISIS and others will turn their anger on soft targets here at home.

There are an estimated 180 Americans fighting for ISIS in Iraq and

Syria, according to the Department of Homeland Security.[498] Many are just like Hasan Edmonds, who was stopped before boarding an airplane on March 25, 2015, on his way to join ISIS.

Vaccinate our prisons from Islamic extremism: There are three physical venues best suited for Islamic radicalization: radicalized mosques, education establishments, and prisons. A 2008 Rand Corporation report states, "Imprisonment may increase a prisoner's susceptibility to adopting new and radicalized ideas or beliefs."[499]

The Rand report indicates a prisoner's susceptibility to radicalized ideas is referred to as a "cognitive opening." The report suggests similarities between the "psychological experiences that make young Muslims susceptible to radicalization and the psychological impact of imprisonment on individuals in general." Thus, incarcerating young Muslims in prison may well compound their vulnerability to radicalization.[500]

Conclusion

This chapter identified three categories of groups that are anti-Christian. Although they occupy different societal spaces, they are in union when it comes to opposing fundamental Christian principles and values. They represent the world's antichrist spirit and are in league with Satan and his army of demons.

CHAPTER ELEVEN

Rogues' Gallery of
Antichrist Personalities

WHO ARE SATAN'S most effective human proxies? In other words, who are the most anti-Christian humans walking the face of the earth that do Satan's bidding by keeping the lost in spiritual darkness and Christians marginalized?

Over thousands of years of human history, we've seen the emergence of a rogue gallery of dysfunctional, evil personalities. Most of those people were just plain evil and not necessarily or exclusively anti-Christian. The harm they perpetrated was rather indiscriminate impacting people of all ethnicities, races, geographic areas, and most of the major religions.

A list of the best-known rogues includes Isoif (Joseph) Vissarionovich Stalin (1878–1953), the dictator of the former Soviet Union who ruled that nation with terror and violence claiming at least twenty million lives. Stalin sadistically said, "One death is a tragedy, a million deaths is simply a statistic."[501]

Mao Zedong (1893–1976) was another rogue, the dictator of Communist China who created the largest genocide in history. His actions led to the death of perhaps seventy million people through evil policies of forced labor, execution, and starvation.[502]

More contemporary rogues include the likes of Pol Pot (1925–1998), the leader of a Cambodian revolutionary group, the Khmer Rouge. He ordered the mass genocide of his own countrymen. This sadistic man kept the skulls of people he had killed and ordered babies to be torn limb by limb. [503]

In 2003, the United States military invaded Iraq to topple the rogue Iraqi dictator Saddam Hussein (1937–2006). Hussein idolized Joseph Stalin, a man notable for paranoia-induced execution sprees. The Iraqi dictator is credited with policies that resulted in the death of more than two million people. He was known for unimaginable evil: chemical attacks that killed both Iraqis and Iranians, eye-gouging, beatings, shock treatment, systematic rape, and much more.

These men were terrible, evil people who demonstrated a stark inhumanity, but religion was not necessarily their primary motivation— perhaps with the exception of Hussein's hatred for Shia Muslims and especially Iranian Shia. However, over the ages, religion has often been the primary motive that drove some leaders to mass persecution and war. For example, the French Wars of Religion (1562–1598) pitted Catholics against Protestant Huguenots. The Thirty Years' War was another conflict between Catholics and Protestants during the seventeenth century. However, Christians have more often than not been the victim of rogue anti-Christian leaders than the aggressor.

The first-century Christian church was persecuted by the pagan Roman government, specifically Emperor Nero. The emperor blamed the great fire in Rome (AD 64) on Christians. The annals of Tacitus record what happened and how it reached back to Jesus Christ Himself. The Roman historian wrote:

> Nero fastened the guilt and inflicted the most exquisite tortures on a class hated for their abominations, called chrestians [sic] by the populace. Christus, from whom the name had its origin, suffered the extreme penalty during the reign of Tiberius at the hands of one of our procurators, Pontius Pilatus, and a

most mischievous superstition, thus checked for the moment, again broke out not only in Judæa, the first source of the evil, but even in Rome, where all things hideous and shameful from every part of the world find their centre and become popular. (*Tacitus' Annals* 15.44)[504]

Many years later, the Christian crusades, a series of campaigns organized by the Roman Catholic Church and spanning the eleventh to the thirteenth centuries, sought to reconquer the Holy Land and other territories lost to Muslim invaders. You will recall that the seventh-century leader of the Muslim religion started the war against the Christian world. At that time, the Prophet Muhammad claimed to be the last prophet of the biblical God worshiped by Abraham, whom Muhammad called Allah (Arabic for "god" and, more specifically, "the ancient moon god," which explains the crescent moon on many Islamic flags).[505] Almost immediately, Muhammad created a violent and imperialistic movement that used the sword to consume most of Christendom's territories by AD 732, which included much of the underbelly of Europe. Centuries later, the Crusades recaptured that land in the name of Christ.

In the late nineteenth and early twentieth centuries, the Islamic Ottoman Empire oversaw the genocide of Christians. The sultan, Abdul Hamid, issued a policy of genocide against Armenian Christians in 1894 that resulted in mass arrest and murder of Christian leaders. Ultimately the sultan's genocide policy claimed an estimated 3.5 million Christian lives across the region.[506]

Christians were also victimized in World War II by one of history's worst rogues. Adolf Hitler (1889–1945) was the chancellor of Germany (1933–1945) and one of the most intelligent, creative and brutal dictators of all time; he was very anti-Christian and anti-Jewish.

Although Hitler's family was Catholic, he didn't participate in the rites of the Catholic Church as an adult. In fact, he frequently derided Christianity and appeared to be more attracted to Islam's militant expansionism than Christianity's "weakness." Albert Speer, Hitler's minister of

armaments and war production, wrote that Hitler said, "The Moham-
medan [Islamic] religion…would have been much more compatible to
us [Germans] than Christianity. Why did it have to be Christianity with
its meekness and flabbiness?"[507]

After World War II, intelligence reports revealed that Hitler had
preferred to purge Germany of Christianity before the Second World
War, but felt the church a necessary evil. So, he created a Nazi German
Christian group to control believers through manipulation to conform
to Hitler's political and ideological agenda. However, in time, Hitler's
patience wore thin and he turned on the Confessing (Christian) Church
and its clergy as well as on the Catholic Church. In fact, toward the end
of the Second War, besides murdering six million Jews in the Holocaust, he also dismantled the German Catholic Church, murdered most
priests, and imprisoned 2,720 clergy (to include many Protestant pastors) at Dachau, near modern-day Munich, Germany.[508]

What is clear from this brief history is that religion has often been
a motivation for war, and Christians were a common target. In many
instances, Christians were the explicit target of tyrants, rogues, and that
hasn't changed in modern times, as indicated by numerous examples
outlined in the previous chapter of this book.

Who Are Some of the Most Anti-Christian Leaders Today?

The previous chapters in this section of *Collision Course* identified three
enemies of contemporary Christians: Satan and his army of demons and
Satan's contemporary human proxies—many journalists in the mainstream media and anti-Christian groups (associations, corporations,
businesses and religions especially Islam).

Joining this phalanx of anti-Christian proxies are a host of significant contemporary personalities who are doing Satan's work. It is possible that some of these individuals are in fact under direct or indirect

demonic influence. The topic of demon-possession is an issue for an entire book. However, a short review of demon-possession and demons' influence on humans is appropriate here before we consider the anti-Christian record of some very evil people.

The Bible provides numerous examples of people possessed or influenced by demons (Matthew 9:32–33, 12:22, 17:18; Mark 5:1–20, 7:26–30; Luke 4:33–16; Acts 16:16–18). Demon-possession of some manifests itself as physical ailments. In others, it causes the individual to do evil, such as in the example of Judas. In the case of the slave girl, it caused her to demonstrate insights beyond her years, and yet other instances of demon-possession gives superhuman strength.[509]

Although many in the West dismiss satanic (demonic) involvement in people's lives, it is a phenomenon taken very seriously, particularly among missionaries in primitive cultures. Demonic possession can change personality, as seen by depression or aggression, immodesty, anti-social behavior, or even special insights. Spiritual attributes of someone under demonic influence may include a refusal to forgive (2 Corinthians 2:10–11) and the "belief in and spread of false doctrine, especially concerning Jesus Christ and his atoning work" (2 Corinthians 11:3–4, 13-15; 1 Timothy 4:1–5).[510]

How does one become possessed by a demon? John 12:6 tells us that Judas opened his heart to evil (greed). Possession may happen if one allows his or her heart to engage in habitual sin (as did Judas), an open invitation to demons. Missionaries indicate that demon possession is often associated with worship of idols or possession of occult materials. That's why Deuteronomy 18:10 warns against such evil practices.

Individuals don't have to be under the influence of a demon to be a proxy for Satan, however. All they need to do is be complicit in helping to accomplish Satan's goals.

We know from chapter 8 Satan's two primary goals. First, he uses proxies to prevent the message of salvation from reaching the lost. Second, he tries to marginalize Christians from doing their part to fulfill the Great Commission (Matthew 28:18–20).

Satan has an arsenal of weapons to equip his proxies to accomplish his two goals. Those weapons that help keep the lost eternally separated from God include the list identified in Galatians 5:19–21 (sexual immorality, idolatry, witchcraft, hatred, jealousy, selfish ambition, drunkenness, and more). Satan has other weapons to distract Spirit-filled, born-again Christians from fulfilling their gospel commission: lies, temptations, and manipulations.

That brings us to the question posed at the beginning of this chapter: Who are Satan's most effective human proxies? Before calling out contemporary candidates by the title, "One of Satan's most effective human proxies," we must consider some criteria to use in identifying these people.

Satan's most effective human proxies could be ordinary people. However, for illustration purposes, I will focus only on those with the most significant potential impact. There are two primary qualifications for this designation.

First, to qualify, the person must have significant means and influence (cultural, economic, psychological, and/or autocratic/political) to keep the unbelievers lost and forever in spiritual darkness (separated from God). These proxies use their influence to trigger the weapons identified in Galatians 5:19–21 to keep nonbelievers from seeking God's salvation through Jesus Christ.

Second, these "most effective human proxies" have the means and influence (cultural, economic, psychological, and/or autocratic/political) to marginalize believers through lies, temptations, and manipulations. Satan uses these proxies to help create false gods, pollute our thinking with other worldviews, imbue in our mind selfish desires, and introduce despair, doubt, fear, and anger. As C. S. Lewis said, as quoted earlier, "What we want, if men become Christians at all, is to keep them in the state of mind I call 'Christianity and.'"

Keeping the Lost in Spiritual Darkness and Marginalizing Believers

Satan's most effective human proxies demonstrate at least one of the above two criteria. There are some very obvious candidates for this designation. They are effective proxies helping to realize Satan's goals, and their impact is seen across a large swath of humanity.

North Korea's Kim Jong-un, Head of State

North Korean dictator Kim Jong-un richly deserves the title, "Satan's proxy." He satisfies both criteria in spades. He directly targets Christians for abuse and removal (death), which discourages (marginalizes) that country's Christian population from sharing their faith. Kim's efforts create a very oppressive environment that keeps many among the lost safely in Satan's corner (eternally in spiritual darkness).

The facts about North Korea's anti-Christian environment are alarming. Kim exercises absolute authority over the people of North Korea and earned the worst rating for creating "the most oppressive place in the world for Christians," according to the US State Department. In spite of Kim's absolute earthly power, an estimated 36 percent of North Korea's population practices their faith in Christ, albeit in secret.[511]

Kim uses his autocratic power to torture and imprison Christians, and have many put to death. An estimated seventy thousand Christians are imprisoned in concentration camps in North Korea today, and most will not survive the experience, according to the Database Center for North Korean Human Rights. The few North Korean defectors who reach the West indicate that Christians are often used as human guinea pigs to test biological weapons and suffer other unimaginable abuse.[512]

The regime also rewards citizens who turn in Christians to government authorities. There is a saying in North Korea: "The walls have eyes and the fields have ears." Indeed, they do. That's why Christians must be incredibly careful to hide their faith, even from nonbelieving friends and family members.[513]

Vernon Brewer, founder and president of World Help, a humanitarian organization, tells the story of a third-grader North Korean named Eun who was given a class assignment to go home and "look for a book." If it was the right book, she was to be honored in class. Eun found a Bible at home and reported her find to her teacher. "The next day she received a prize at her school. But when Eun returned home, her parents weren't there," Brewer said. "It's hard to imagine such cruelty that would unknowingly turn children on their own parents."[514]

The good news is that "despite efforts to eradicate Christians, we have found the church in North Korea is actually growing," Brewer explained. "They know only God is powerful enough to break through the darkness of the most oppressive regime on earth."[515]

Chinese President Xi Jinping, the Twenty-first Century's Mao

China's President, Xi Jinping, is perhaps worse than former Communist dictator Mao Zedong (1893–1976). Today Xi targets religious believers, especially Christians.

Fenggang Yang, director of the Center on Religion and Chinese Society at Purdue University and a leading expert on Christian religion in China, said that the current environment for religion in China is like the era of Mao and the Cultural Revolution, during which religion was brutally oppressed.[516]

"The personality cult of Xi is catching up with that of Mao. During the Cultural Revolution under Mao, all religions were banned," Yang said. Xi appears to be following the same path.

In 2016, President Xi demanded that all Communist Party members must be "unyielding atheists." Further, he directed that "religious groups…must adhere to the leadership of the Communist Party of

China (CPC)." Communists must "resolutely guard against overseas infiltrations via religious means," a clear reference to Christianity, which Xi considers a foreign invading ideology.[517]

Mr. Xi argues that China allows its citizens "freedom of belief," but he opposes extremist ideologies (read "Christianity"). "We should guide and educate the religious circle and their followers with the socialist core values," the Chinese president said.[518]

The watchdog group China Aid accused President Xi of targeting Christians in an ongoing church cross demolition campaign, which resulted in hundreds of rooftop crosses and churches demolished. In fact, according to China Aid, one government-sanctioned church demolition team attempted to bury alive a house church leader and his wife because the couple opposed the destruction of their facility. In fact, tragically, the wife did not survive the incident.[519]

China Aid president Bob Fu said the burying alive of a "peaceful and devout Christian woman, was a cruel, murderous act." He called for Chinese authorities to hold "those accountable and take concrete measures to protect the religious freedom of this house church's members."[520]

Mr. Fu acknowledged that the government's ongoing persecution of Christians is evidence of their concern about the growing number of believers. "The top leadership is increasingly worried about the rapid growth of Christian faith and their public presence, and their social influence," Fu said.[521]

"It is a political fear for the Communist Party, as the number of Christians in the country far outnumbers the members of the Party," Fu explained.[522]

It is true the number of Chinese Christians is exploding. The Pew Research Center said that in 2010 there were sixty-seven million Christians (combined Protestant and Catholic) in China. As recently as 2018, that number topped one hundred million, and it is noteworthy that China is the world's largest producer of Bibles.[523]

President Xi's Chinese Communist Party has taken a number of steps to address the growing Christian community. For example, it now demands that teachers psychologically manipulate children with anti-Christian propaganda by building on new government regulations regarding religious affairs that ban anyone under the age of eighteen from entering a church. [524]

An Italian publication, *Bitter Winter*, put out a report on Chinese persecution based on anonymous accounts of children coming home to chastise their parents for their faith. In government schools, children are taught that Christianity is a *xie jiao* ("cult") and children were told to warn their parents to abandon such practices. "If you believe in it, you will leave home and not take care of me. You might set yourself on fire, too," a little boy told his mother. [525]

That mother found her child's school textbook, *Morality and Society*, which explained how to resist *xie jiao*. As a result, the mother hid all Christian symbols in the house, but as children will, the little boy came across a Christian pamphlet at home and proceeded to destroy it out of fear for his parents. [526]

The Chinese government also forbids any religious activities outside of a church facility. That means church camps, home Bible studies, and church-run health clinics are all forbidden. [527]

These outcomes reflect President Xi's hardline, anti-Christian approach. "There's only one allowed religion in China, and that's secular socialism," Steven Mosher, president of the Population Research Institute, a Christian who studied in China. "And the Church is the community party, the acolytes, its members, and their pontiff, Chinese president Xi Jinping himself." [528]

It is pretty obvious that Chinese authorities want to eradicate all vestiges of Christianity. They understand that Christianity and, by association, human rights is a Western plot to subvert control of that country. Thus, President Xi oversees a campaign to "Sinicize" religion, meaning that all citizens must profess loyalty to the Communist Party, never to a religion, especially a foreign one like Christianity. [529]

Former President Barack Hussein Obama

Mr. Obama was the most anti-Christian president in the history of the United States. He qualifies as a proxy of Satan based on his administration's policies and his personal behavior during his tenure in office.

Wallbuilders compiled a long, well-documented list of Obama administration actions that suppressed Christians while advancing anti-Christian policies. Mr. Obama used the power of the Oval Office to advance Satan's agenda.[530]

Consider a snapshot of Obama's extensive anti-Christian agenda. For a more thorough appreciation of the extent of Obama's long and radical anti-Christian agenda, visit the Wallbuilders' homepage and study "America's Most Biblically Hostile U.S. President." (See https://wallbuilders.com/americas-biblically-hostile-u-s-president/.)

Obama oversaw acts of hostility to Christians, both direct and indirect, that ultimately contributed to Satan's two goals.

Some of his actions were subtle, such as changing the White House Christmas cards from being about the Christian faith to featuring the family dogs or decorating the White House Christmas tree with ornaments that included figures of Mao Zedong and a drag queen. More overt was Mr. Obama's appointment of a transgender person to the Advisory Council on Faith-based Neighborhood Partnerships and his order to have a monogram symbolizing Jesus' name covered while he was delivering a speech at Georgetown University.

Mr. Obama even hosted a dinner for the visiting Catholic pope that included guests he knew would be morally offensive to the pontiff.

The Obama Justice Department evidenced the president's anti-Christian agenda when it defunded a Young Marines' chapter in Louisiana because the group's oath mentioned God, and another group lost DOJ funding as well because it permitted voluntary, student-led prayer.

Obama's administration argued in court that the First Amendment provides no protection for churches in hiring pastors, and even attacked other countries' religious beliefs as an obstacle to advance so-called homosexual rights.

The president's radical, in-your-face, anti-Christian push of homosexuality knew no limits. Recall the night when Obama ordered the White House to be lit in the colors of the homosexual flag? On June 26, 2015, the White House was lit up in rainbow colors—red, orange, yellow, green, blue, indigo, and violet—to celebrate the Supreme Court's ruling on homosexual marriage. At the time, Obama issued a statement that the symbolic colors of "gay" pride "demonstrates our unwavering commitment to progress and equality, here in America and around the world." President Obama hailed the High Court's 5-4 decision as "a big step in our march toward equality."[531]

Mr. Obama also targeted the pro-life community for special denigration. Healthcare rules were changed to override religious conscience protections for medical workers in the areas of abortion and contraception. He even nominated three pro-abortion ambassadors to the Vatican, a slap to the pro-life Catholic Church.

President Obama demonstrated great hostility to Bible-believing military personnel. His Pentagon changed the military's policies to allow open homosexuality and pushed women into dangerous ground combat positions. Further, Obama officials threatened to veto a defense bill over religious protections, and even removed an Air Force veteran who attempted to use the word "God" in a retirement speech. They removed a Bible from a display inside a veterans' clinic and canceled a military prayer breakfast because an atheist complained that the speaker, retired Army Lieutenant General Jerry Boykin, was a "homophobic, Islamophobic, fundamentalist Christian extremist."

The Obama administration was openly hostile to biblical values, no matter the setting. It even cherry-picked opponents for court cases dealing with the Obamacare contraception mandate, and it funded every type of sex education, except that which reflects traditional biblical values. Obama's foreign-aid program shut down a conference in South Korea because it would not schedule pro-abortion presentations, and another program trained homosexual activists on how to overturn foreign countries' traditional marriage and anti-sodomy laws.

Mr. Obama was the most biblically hostile president in history, which makes him a proxy of Satan's efforts to marginalize Christianity and Christians while keeping nonbelievers lost.

Billionaire George Soros, Philanthropist

Mr. George Soros is perhaps the world's foremost philanthropist. He reportedly has given away more than $32 billion through his Open Society Foundation.[532] That wealth has gone to efforts that are quite anti-Christian.

His economic leverage helps keep the lost in the darkness and marginalizes some believers. Consider the impact of his largess across the world, and especially here in the United States.

Mr. Soros, a self-identified atheist, uses his shady, tax-exempt foundations to manipulate Christian views on issues like abortion and the New World Order, and he even tries to manipulate entire national churches.[533]

In 2016 a leaked memo by DCleaks.com from Soros' Open Society Foundation delineates a plot to coopt Catholic officials to push radical views within that church. Soros funded two "faith" groups to do his dirty work: PICO (People Improving Communities through Organizing) and FPL (Faith in Public Life).

Soros' strategy was to provide "essential resources" to secure the "buy-in of individual [Catholic] bishops to more publicly voice support of economic and racial justice messages." The strategy was intended to create a "critical mass of bishops" to advance Soros' interpretation of Pope Francis' perceived anti-free-market activism and "racial justice agenda." A number of leading Catholics indicated that Soros distorted the pope's message to advance an anti-Catholic agenda.

A similar effort took place in Central Asia. In 2016, Soros used his economic leverage to try to persuade the Republic of Georgia to join the European Union (EU) in order to advance his globalist, New World Order agenda. Soros' strategy was to gain the endorsement of Georgian Orthodox Church leaders whom he considered the lynchpin to persuading that nation's government leaders to seek EU membership.[534]

Why recruit church leaders? Soros correctly believed that the Georgian Orthodox Church was the most trusted institution in that country. So, Soros used his money to "train" pastors as to how to love the EU and promote it to their congregations. That was a back-door way of turning the Georgian government to favor the EU and its radical, anti-Christian agenda.[535]

The EU is particularly progressive and anti-Christian, which explains why Soros first tried to manipulate Christian leaders to push the Georgian government. The fact is the EU is rabidly opposed to traditional marriage, especially those who express biblical views about homosexuality as a sin. It promotes an assortment of social issues such as abortion on demand, open borders, and other positions that many Christians find especially antibiblical.

Soros, who is appropriately called "Dr. Evil," has also donated more than $10 billion to promote his extreme anti-Christian views in the United States. It won't surprise most readers that Soros financed Obama and Hillary Clinton's run for the presidency, he was the deep pockets behind the radical Black Lives Matter and Occupy Wall Street movements, and his money bought political election victories for progressive Democrats even in my home state of Virginia.[536]

Soros was especially successful with his investment in President Obama. Mr. Obama advanced Soros' radical progressive agenda on many fronts: the trafficking in human baby organs and other body parts, the abandonment of a biblical view of marriage, pushing the transgender agenda, and promoting open borders and "sanctuary" cities where drugs, disease, crime, and gangs prevail. Obama also forced foreign-refugee resettlement in American cities without citizen consent while his officials rejected admission by qualified and persecuted Christians.

Soros also recruited "progressive" American Christians to advance his radical political agenda. A coalition of influential Christian American leaders caught wind of that effort and responded by calling on those Christian recruits to "repent."

Kelly Monroe Kullberg and Dr. Alveda King, along with a coalition of 630 influential Christian leaders, asked via a letter that "progressive" Christians recruited by Soros "repent" of their support for helping the billionaire. The letter called out a number of prominent Christians for following the lead of Soros' Open Society Foundation. A leaked Soros document identified some of these recruits as Christian "mascots" serving as validators for Soros' radical causes.[537]

What individual Christians and Christian groups took Soros' money? The coalition of 630 Christian leaders named names.

At a time when many Christian ministries are struggling, a few of the Soros network "faith" and "interfaith" grantees are Jim Wallis of Sojourners, Richard Cizik's New Evangelical Partnership, Telos, J Street to malign Israel, Catholics in Alliance for the Common Good, Faithful America and Gamaliel. Faith in Public Life has worked to "counter" Christians and the Tea Party in the media and, with PICO, advocate for amnesty, mass Islamic migration even seeking to influence the visit and priorities of Pope Francis himself. Billions of additional dollars to "Christian VOLAGs" for large scale "refugee" and migrant resettlement comes from the Obama administration.[538]

What Soros causes did these Christian "mascots" directly or indirectly support? Some are mentioned in the paragraph above. But the letter called out others such as racial issues; the promotion of abnormal gender issues; advancement of euthanasia; drug legalization; abortion on demand; the legalization of the "sex worker" industry; advancement of climate change; promotion of anti-Israel projects; and the call for Muslims to have the rights of adopting sharia (Islamic law) in the United States.

The American Association of Evangelicals (AAE) published a video about Soros' infiltration of Christian America, the very same issue addressed by the letter from the 630 Christian leaders. That video revealed that at the time (2018) "Democrat minister Rev. Jim Wallis and allies are now touring many states on 'Vote Common Good' buses to…split the evangelical vote before the [2018] mid-term elections. The AAE video features the newly released voice recording of [Jim] Wallis of Sojourners as he publicly denied that he was a recipient of Soros funding."[539]

"Americans hate manipulation," said AAE spokesperson Kelly Monroe Kullberg in a statement. "Anti-American globalists like Soros are funding a growth industry of paid anarchists and political activists to divide and weaken America, including the Church."[540]

Soros is clearly one of Satan's proxies. He targets both the lost and Christians, and his billions are making a difference in the public arena, albeit an evil difference.

"Honorable" Mentions on Satan's Proxy List

"Honorable" mention for the title of "Satan's most effective human proxies" goes to others such as Senator Bernie Sanders, billionaire Michael Bloomberg, and Speaker Nancy Pelosi, as well as to an assortment of other foreign leaders, dictators, media personalities, and wealthy people. Space doesn't permit an exhaustive review, however. Consider three "honorable" mentions.

Senator Bernie Sanders, US Senator from Vermont and 2020 Democrat Party presidential candidate: Senator Sanders is a true radical who attracts considerable attention from the progressives, socialists, and the anti-Christian crowd. He fits the criteria to be an "honorable" mention as one of Satan's best proxies.

He is a communist by virtue of his statements, associations, and actions. I know for a fact that he would never pass a US government security investigation simply because of his past associations with foreign dictators, his associations with known communists and many anti-American organizations, and not the least, his questionable allegiance to the United States.

Sanders' radical actions began while attending the University of Chicago, where he joined the Young People's Socialist League, the youth wing of the Socialist Party USA. He also organized the United Packinghouse Workers Union, a communist front.[541]

Later, Sanders helped found the Liberty Union Party, which called for nationalizing all American banks and the public takeover of all private utility companies.

At home in Vermont, Sanders headed the American People's History Society, an organ for Marxist propaganda, and even produced a documentary on the life of Eugene Debs, who was jailed for espionage and hailed by the Soviet Bolsheviks as "America's greatest Marxist." Sanders still hangs a portrait of Debs in his US Senate office.[542]

In 1981, Sanders was elected mayor of Burlington, Vermont, where he quickly demonstrated his ideological views. He restricted property rights for landlords, set price controls, and raised property taxes to pay for land trusts. He became known as the mayor who "does not believe in free enterprise."[543]

His personal travels reveal a bent toward communist dictators. He made several "goodwill" trips to the Soviet Union, Cuba, and Nicaragua. His trip to Nicaragua in 1985 was used to celebrate the accession of the Marxist-Leninist Sandinista government, which he called a "heroic revolution." Sanders adopted Managua, Nicaragua, as a sister city and invited Sandinista leader Daniel Ortega to visit the United States, referring to the dictator as "an impressive guy."[544]

Sanders honeymooned with his second wife in the Soviet Union and even put a Soviet flag in his Vermont office.[545]

In 1989, Sanders addressed the national conference of the US Peace Council—a front for the Communist Party USA—a group that swore an oath to "the triumph of Soviet power in the US."[546]

Sanders embraces the entire landscape of radical, socialist policy proposals: Medicare for All (costing $32.6 trillion in new taxes over ten years and abolishing the private employer-based healthcare plans for 180 million people) that will put insurance and drug companies totally out of business. He favors the so-called Green New Deal with absurd ideas, such as abolishing airplanes and cows, which is a government-planning, industrial-policy nightmare. He also favors breaking up big banks, giving free college tuition to everyone, and guaranteeing homeownership for all. He said that, under a Sanders administration, everyone gets a job no matter their circumstances, and there would be a massive wealth redistribution.

Sanders even believes in giving hardened criminals—and yes, terrorists—the right to vote in this country. He publicly stated that he would give the Boston Marathon terror bomber the right to vote and would extend that right to all others incarcerated for any crime.[547]

Earlier in this book, I profiled Sanders' alarming anti-Christian views. This should be expected of a communist, an ideology that is radically anti-religion. You will recall that Senator Sanders, in a blatant violation of Article VI of the US Constitution, applied a religious test for a Trump administration nominee. He doesn't believe that Christians are fit to serve in government because they are religious bigots, and basic Christian theology, according to the Vermont senator, "is indefensible, it is hateful, it is Islamophobic, and it is an insult to over a billion Muslims throughout the world."[548]

Senator Sanders' 2020 presidential bid demonstrated his radical social agenda as well. Specifically, he stands for promoting everything outlined among Satan's most prominent proxies: pro-abortion, pro-homosexuality in all aspects of life, anti-Christian, and much more. He richly deserves the title of one of Satan's best proxies.

Billionaire Michael Bloomberg, former New York City mayor: Mike Bloomberg uses his deep pockets to promote social issues that offend many Christians and fit the criteria for him to be one of Satan's proxies.

In the 2018 midterm elections, Bloomberg gave $110 million to support House Democrat progressive candidates. Predictably, House

Speaker Nancy Pelosi lauded Bloomberg's generosity to Democrats: "In 2018, Mayor Bloomberg was a critical ally in helping House Democrats regain the majority." Of course, the House Democrats used that majority to advance many anti-Christian issues, so indirectly Bloomberg's significant contribution is partly responsible for many of the radical issues pushed by the Democrat Party beginning in 2019.[549]

In 2020, Mr. Bloomberg, a self-identified Jew, also spent in excess of $450 million in his campaign to unseat President Trump. The former mayor lines up on the social issues with the other radical progressives in the Democrat Party. He supports abortion on demand, having said, "Reproductive choice is a fundamental human right, and we can never take it for granted."[550]

He also backs homosexual marriage[551] and even "strongly defended a proposal to build an Islamic community center near ground zero."[552]

He richly deserves the title of one of Satan's best proxies.

Nancy Pelosi, Speaker of the House: Nancy Pelosi (D-CA) oversees the Democrats in the House of Representatives who promote rank evil and anti-Christian issues. As speaker of the House of Representatives, she wields great power and uses that power to promote an anti-Christian agenda.

Ms. Pelosi says she is a faithful Catholic. How then can she be a zealot for abortion? After all, so-called Catholic Pelosi invited as her guest the president of Planned Parenthood, Leana Wen, to President Trump's 2019 State of the Union address in Washington. She also invited a transgender service member and a variety of other like-minded supporters.[553]

Just how radical is Ms. Pelosi? During the crisis over the coronavirus pandemic, she tried to sneak across the finish line a way to fund all abortions. Specifically, she attempted to secure a funding stream of up to $1 billion for reimbursing laboratory claims that would establish a precedent under which health claims for all procedures, including abortion, could be reimbursed with federal funds, according to White House officials who spoke with the *Daily Caller*. That would render the Hyde Amendment, which blocks taxpayer funding for abortion clinics, obsolete.[554]

Nebraska's US Senator Ben Sasse slammed Pelosi for trying to ensure federal funding for abortion as part of the March 2020 coronavirus economic stimulus plan. "While schools are closing and hospitals are gearing up, Speaker Pelosi is waging unnecessary culture wars," Sasse said. "Speaker Pelosi should be fighting the coronavirus pandemic not politicizing emergency funding by fighting against the bipartisan Hyde Amendment."

Sasse continued, "We need to be ramping up our diagnostic testing, not waging culture wars at the behest of Planned Parenthood. Good grief."[555]

Prior to Mr. Trump's election, Mrs. Pelosi, at the time the House minority leader, said in an interview with PBS *Newshour* that "non-college-educated white males" vote Republican. Then she explained that outcome was, in her view, "because of guns, because of gays, and because of God. The three 'Gs,' God being the woman's right to choose." It must be that Pelosi, in spite of Catholic teaching, believes that God is pro-abortion and evidently endorses homosexual behavior such as so-called gay marriage.[556]

All this does matter, because it helps Satan's goals. After all, the speaker is a very powerful person who sets the agenda for the House of Representatives. Earlier, I profiled the radical so-called Equality Act, which Nancy Pelosi's majority passed in 2019, 236-173. That bill, which is very anti-Christian, would "enshrine an ideology of gender that destroys women's rights, forces supporters of traditional sexuality to violate their consciences, and forces health care providers to perform abortions."[557]

Clearly Ms. Pelosi's legislative power is significant and plays right into Satan's agenda.

There are many others among the world's most influential people who advance Satan's two goals—keeping the lost in spiritual darkness and the saved marginalized. Certainly, there are good people in the mix of the world's "rich and famous" who use their influence for righteous causes. Perhaps you ought to study that list and judge for yourself. Consider one such list assembled by CEO World, which in 2019 identified the one hundred most influential people in the world.[558]

Conclusion

Some high-profile people, like those identified above, are doing Satan's work. That was the topic of a 2019 interview on Salem Radio Network with the Reverend Franklin Graham. Here is what Peter Wehner, an adviser to Republican presidents on matters moral and spiritual, wrote about the Graham interview for the *Atlantic*:

> During his November 21 [2019] interview with [Franklin] Graham, [Eric] Metaxas, a Salem Radio Network talk-show host, asked the son of the late evangelist Billy Graham, "What do you think of what is happening now? I mean, it's a very bizarre situation to be living in a country where some people seem to exist to undermine the president of the United States. It's just a bizarre time for most Americans."[559]
>
> Franklin Graham, president and CEO of the Billy Graham Evangelical Association, responded, "Well, I believe it's almost a demonic power that is trying—"[560]
>
> At which point Metaxas interjected, "I would disagree. It's not almost demonic. You know and I know, at the heart, it's a spiritual battle."[561]

Indeed, we are engaged in a spiritual battle and there are some individuals as well as groups and media personalities who advance Satan's anti-Christian designs for this world.

They all deserve the title of "one of Satan's best proxies."

Section IV

A NEW BEGINNING FOR AMERICA
The Reemergence of "Christian Nationalism" and Making America Christian Again

America was founded by Christian nationalists, an ideology that faded in influence over the past two-plus centuries. However, in the wake of today's cultural divide, there is a new spirit emerging—a redo of Christian nationalism—that seeks to make America Christian again by turning back the radical gains made by Satan and his proxies, the progressives.

Those progressives are the antichrists introduced in the third section of this book. They seized control and reshaped America, pushing this nation down a dangerous course to a moral tipping point—which, if not quickly reversed, could doom this once-great country, straining out every last vestige of Christianity sewn into her fabric.

This final section of *Collision Course* offers a road map to make American Christian again—a total rejection of the gains of Satan's proxies—and provides a breath of hope and a bright future for our children and grandchildren. But this effort won't be easy or fast, and there will be great opposition.

It is understandable that Satan's proxies demonize the term "nationalism," as if patriotism and love of country are evil. Progressives don't believe America is or ever was an exceptional nation and eschew the interchangeable term "patriotism" as a misguided ideal. Rather, they promote a globalist agenda and would eliminate national borders to collapse all sovereign countries into one giant country ruled by their radical, godless ideology under a one-world government, a perfect scenario for ushering in the prophetic end times.

We already explained that progressives hate Christians almost as much as they do patriots, nationalists. For starters, they reject the view that this nation was built on a Christian foundation. Further the joining of the words "Christian" and "nationalism" creates an ideology that is anathema to progressives who are driven to oppose it at all costs.

The progressives' at-all-cost agenda and the growing cultural divide evident in this country today are documented by numerous national public-opinion polls. That divide gave us the spark that reignited many Christian and patriotic Americans to revive the Christian nationalism phenomenon. These people came to realize that our country has gone way off course from where it began, and there must be a counter revolution to bring America back closer to the formula that made it great. That's the genesis of the renewed rise of Christian nationalism.[562]

"Christian nationalism" isn't a dirty term except to progressives. It is associated with American patriots who believe this country's founding Christian principles and values are a big part of the reason this nation enjoyed great success from her early years. They want to recover those Christian principles and values within our key institutions.

Past efforts to revive our early Christian roots did enjoy brief periods of success. There were times of spiritual revivals over the past two centuries, and most recently, there was a surge in Christian nationalism thanks to a number of people such as Dr. Jerry Falwell's Moral Majority campaign in the 1980s that helped bring President Ronald Reagan into office. However, even that movement quickly faded, and progressivism regained momentum, bringing us to the Obama era, arguably the most radical progressive eight years in the history of this nation—perhaps with the exception of the Franklin D. Roosevelt presidency.

Thankfully, Christian nationalism did reemerge in 2016 to elect Donald Trump. Admittedly, Mr. Trump is an imperfect man, but he understood the mood in the country at the time. Once elected, he harnessed the national enthusiasm for a course correction and to fulfill his campaign promises to "Make America Great Again." For many Christian nationalists, Mr. Trump's campaign slogan translated to something quite different than intended. It meant for them to "make America godly again," and for secular conservatives, it meant something entirely different as well: to "make America prosperous again." Fortunately, the president's administration made progress on both fronts.

Meanwhile, and predictably, Mr. Trump's 2016 election caused an explosion of angst among progressives. Initially they went into a state of total denial. Once the reality of his election sank in, they set a course to resist any efforts Mr. Trump might try to reverse past progressive accomplishments and unseat him.

That resistance is now infamous for its disruption of government and the soiling of our national consciousness. We saw the Democrat Party (the primary home of American progressivism) go on a feeding frenzy over the so-called Russian-collusion, special-counsel investigation that accomplished nothing positive for the country, ended up exonerating Mr. Trump, and yet consumed the nation's attention for almost two years—and it cost many millions in taxpayer dollars. Meanwhile, we saw the so-called deep state, those embedded government progressives—many Obama leftovers—try to short-circuit the Trump administration's every effort to fulfill campaign promises via leaks and bureaucratic resistance. Then we saw the Ukraine-related impeachment campaign (2019–2020) led by progressives in the House of Representatives to upend the 2016 election, hoping to pave the way for a progressive (Democrat) victory in the 2020 presidential election.

Progressive-led resistance to Mr. Trump's Make America Great Again campaign, especially his first term in office, included the progressive cabal's recruitment of mainstream media to constantly bombard his administration with negative reports—no let-up. They also recruited a host of scholars to document the so-called causes for Hillary Clinton's 2016 loss, an effort that really aimed at demonizing Mr. Trump and his supporters and sought a way ahead for returning a progressive to the White House.

Predictably, those progressive scholars found a host of excuses for Clinton's election failure. For example, they ascertained from voter polling that Mr. Trump won because he attracted a rather undesirable cohort of voters: the economic disadvantaged, sexists, racists, islamophobics, and xenophobes.

One of those studies identified "Christian nationalists" as a significant contributing cohort to Mr. Trump's 2016 victory. That 2018 monograph in *Sociology of Religion*, "Make America Christian Again: Christian Nationalism and Voting for Donald Trump in the 2016 Presidential Election," defined Christian nationalism as a decisive ingredient in Mr. Trump's 2016 election. That analysis defined the term "Christian nationalism" as an "independent ideology that influences political actions by calling forth a defense of mythological narratives about America's distinctively Christian heritage and future."[563]

Put aside the authors' obvious anti-Christian historical bias— "mythological narratives"—to understand what they found and why the Christian nationalism ideology has resurfaced in America.

Mr. Trump apparently understood the grass-roots power behind this re-emergent movement—Christian nationalism—and tapped into it to win in 2016, and likely will do the same in 2020. He came to understand the Christian principles and values that made America an exceptional nation at its founding. Then, after entering office, he used his administration to recapture lost ground attributed to the radicalism of progressives and the influence of antichrists through the past century-plus.

That groundswell of Christian nationalist support swept the nation in 2016 and appears in a significant part of America today…and could help Make America Christian Again.

This final section of *Collision Course* will address Christian nationalism and how to Make America (more) Christian Again in three chapters. It doesn't assume that Mr. Trump is the answer to the most pressing question: How do we Make America (more) Christian again? However, he is one tool in a process that requires considerable prayer and great commitment if, in fact, making America more Christian again is even possible—or if this nation is doomed to historic obscurity for the end-times prophecy.

Collision Course concludes with three chapters.

Chapter 12 defines Christian nationalism, examines how it is distorted by the left, and assesses what it means for America's future. The current surge in Christian nationalism could well fade, and America could quickly return to its collision course toward the moral tipping point—especially if progressives regain the reins to this country. Or, is there an alternative to Christian nationalism that might help America recapture the lost Christian influence across our culture?

Chapter 13 defines what it might mean for America to abandon its present course to return to its founding Christian principles and values. What in today's modern world would a renewed, Christian-oriented America look like?

Chapter 14 is a comprehensive campaign plan to renew Christian America. Christians must clean their house first before tackling the broader culture and then redefine its key institutions. What are some of the steps/goals that must be taken/accomplished to bring about this modern miracle of transformation to redirect this nation from its present collision course aimed squarely at a moral tipping point?

CHAPTER TWELVE

What You Get When Mixing Christianity, Politics, Patriotism, and Nationalism: "Good Neighbors" and "PACs"

WHAT IS THE role of a Christian and patriot in today's American culture? Should that Christian engage in politics or focus his/her every waking hour outside of work and home life advancing the gospel of Christ and leaving politics to the secular world? Perhaps being an American patriot who loves this country and believes the culture needs more Christian influence is ample justification for believers to dive into the political realm to help prevent this country from going over the moral tipping point.

The challenge for Christians is discerning whether they should mix the two motivations—Christianity and patriotism/nationalism— to morph into what has become known as "Christian nationalism." That ideology has many critics, but the combination doesn't necessarily have to be bad news for the individual, the country, or Christianity. Of course, many of those critics lambast fundamentalist Christians anyway, and they denigrate others who self-identify as patriots and/or nationalists. But the worst of those characterizations goes to the self-identified "Christian nationalist" who supported President Trump in the 2016 election.

This chapter addresses those terms—"patriotism" and "nationalism"—and the mixing of them with Christianity, as well as participating in the political process and the effects that might follow. I answer six key questions in this chapter: Should the Christian participate in the American political process? What is the difference between patriotism and nationalism? What do Christian nationalists believe about the important issues? What does Christian nationalism mean for American Christians? Is there a middle ground for those who are uncomfortable with the starkness associated with the label "Christian nationalist"? Finally, what are some common criticisms of Christian nationalists and the considered responses?

Is Christian nationalism the elixir to keep this nation from slipping over the moral tipping point pushed by Satan's army of demons and the compliant proxies? You decide for yourself.

Should Christians participate in the American political process?
Christians have long debated among themselves whether believers ought to be involved in politics. After all, as some Christians contend, "faith and politics do not mix." This section of the chapter advances the proposition that Christians concerned with obeying the Scriptures have no choice but to be involved in the American political process.

There are clear scriptural reasons for Christians to do so, especially in the United States.

God's Word is intended for all aspects of our lives, not for just sharing the Scriptures with the lost. A properly grounded Christian worldview provides the believer with an appropriate perspective about this lost world and the believer's role, which is why avoiding politics is never a Bible-based alternative.

A Christian worldview includes a political theology that puts every aspect of our lives into the business of doing good works for the benefit of mankind. Keep in mind that believers are citizens of "the city of God," wisdom found in Augustine of Hippo's fifth-century AD book,

The City of God. That book responds to allegations that Christianity brought about the decline of Rome.[564]

Christians, according to Augustine's book, are to be good citizens wherever they are planted, even in hostile places like first-century Rome. Paul said as much in the Bible's Book of Acts (16:37), and it applies here in the US today as well. We Americans are particularly blessed with a Constitution focused on the rights and privileges of "We the people." Our founding documents make the citizenry sovereign over government, which means we possess the real power to elect and replace our representatives. That's why some form of participation in the political process, if nothing more than voting, is a necessity for American Christian citizens.

There is reason to caution fellow Christians who engage in the political fray even though participating is expected. Whether they seek an elected office or simply write letters to the editor entering the political arena presents real risks that the believer could compromise his faith for political expediency even though few Christians go into politics planning to undermine their faith. However, the reality is that what too often happens is politics changes you and compromises your Christian principles, thus your witness for Christ.

That is a valid concern for believers, which is why making the decision whether to enter politics as a candidate or even to become involved in a political campaign must be done so prayerfully and with godly counsel. However, there is an unselfish consideration for enlisting in the political fight that all believers must factor into their decision process—your neighbor.

The United States and her population need Christian involvement in the political process; otherwise, the nation's future is left in the hands of wicked and immoral secular man. Abandoning politics to the secular compromises the biblical teaching: "Thou shalt love thy neighbor as thyself" (Mark 12:31, KJV).

This prescription is familiar to Christians. Christ taught that the greatest commandment (Matthew 22:37) was to love God with our heart, soul, and mind, and the second greatest commandment is "Thou shalt love thy neighbor as thyself" (Matthew 22:39, KJV).

God's command to love "thy neighbor" as we love ourselves is mandatory, and that means also getting involved in the affairs of our community and nation (politics), so as to demonstrate that love. After all, Christ's command to love "thy neighbor" is a call to protect others' rights, freedoms, liberty, equality, and physical well-being.

Yes, we are our brother's keepers. I remind you of the parable of the good Samaritan (Luke 10:25–37, NIV), which illustrates the commandment. That Scripture passage reads:

> On one occasion an expert in the law stood up to test Jesus. "Teacher," he asked, "what must I do to inherit eternal life?"
>
> "What is written in the Law?" he replied. "How do you read it?"
>
> He answered, "'Love the Lord your God with all your heart and with all your soul and with all your strength and with all your mind'; and, 'Love your neighbor as yourself.'"
>
> "You have answered correctly," Jesus replied. "Do this and you will live."
>
> But he wanted to justify himself, so he asked Jesus, "And who is my neighbor?"
>
> In reply Jesus said: "A man was going down from Jerusalem to Jericho, when he was attacked by robbers. They stripped him of his clothes, beat him and went away, leaving him half dead. A priest happened to be going down the same road, and when he saw the man, he passed by on the other side. So too, a Levite, when he came to the place and saw him, passed by on the other side. But a Samaritan, as he traveled, came where the man was; and when he saw him, he took pity on him. He went to him and bandaged his wounds, pouring on oil and wine. Then he put the man on his own donkey, brought him to an inn and took care of

him. The next day he took out two denarii and gave them to the innkeeper. 'Look after him,' he said, 'and when I return, I will reimburse you for any extra expense you may have.'

"Which of these three do you think was a neighbor to the man who fell into the hands of robbers?"

The expert in the law replied, "The one who had mercy on him." Jesus told the lawyer, "Go and do likewise."

Note in the parable that the "expert in the law" asked Jesus, "And who is my neighbor?" Jesus responded to the lawyer's question by citing the parable of the man who was attacked by robbers. Then Jesus asked: "Which of these three [the priest, Levite or Samaritan] do you think was a 'neighbor' to the man who fell into the hands of robbers?"

The lawyer responded: "The one who had mercy on him." Jesus told him, "Go and do likewise."

Jesus used this parable to demonstrate that our "neighbor" is everyone in society without regard to race, ethnicity, background, religion, or social status.

You see, politics is a means for caring for our neighbors. It is the arena that arguably has the most profound impact on our basic rights and freedoms. In fact, we fulfill the biblical mandate to love "thy neighbor" and care for the "least of these" by embracing a holistic approach to meeting fellow citizens' needs—physical, social, and spiritual. After all, proper government plays a significant role in our physical and mental well-being, as well as our opportunities and freedoms.

The lesson from the good Samaritan for Christians is that we are called to care for our fellow man—the downtrodden, the poor, the oppressed, the defenseless, the widows, and orphans (Isaiah 1:17; Jeremiah 22:3). Unfortunately, America has all these problems today, and thus Christians are called to address these challenges for the benefit of our neighbors, using their God-given means and talents to influence government and the principles and values embedded in our Christian worldview.

That is why, in America, helping "our neighbors" involves participating in the democratic republican government (political) process to help make policy sympathetic to the condition of "our neighbors."

Dr. R. Albert Mohler, president of Southern Baptist Theological Seminary, agrees. He said that loving our neighbors requires Christians to participate "in the culture and in the political process." After all, we are designed by God—spiritually reborn—to participate "in the culture and in the political process" because in Christ we are "righteous" and thus can understand the rights of the less advantaged (Proverbs 29:7).[565]

Critics of this view argue that our Savior, Jesus Christ, wasn't a political person, and neither should be Christians. However, Jesus was concerned for more than just souls, as evidenced in the Gospels. He healed many, exorcised demons, and filled many stomachs. His ministry was holistic; He was political in the broad sense of the term.

It must be understood—and this is important—that, in Jesus' time on earth, Israel was ruled by Rome, an empire under Emperor Tiberius (AD 14–37). Jews at that time were an occupied people who had no say over the affairs of government. However, Jesus did engage in Jewish politics. Remember, Christ chastised Jewish authorities like the Pharisees and teachers of the law for their hypocrisy (Matthew 23).

Jesus showed His temper against the Jewish establishment—a political statement of sorts—in John 2:13–16 (NIV):

When it was almost time for the Jewish Passover, Jesus went up to Jerusalem. In the temple courts he found people selling cattle, sheep and doves, and others sitting at tables exchanging money. So he made a whip out of cords, and drove all from the temple courts, both sheep and cattle; he scattered the coins of the money changers and overturned their tables. To those who sold doves he said, "Get these out of here! Stop turning my Father's house into a market!"

Even the Apostle Paul encouraged Christians to be involved in their communities and politics. He called on Christians to do good to everyone (Galatians 6:10), as well as do good works "which God prepared in advance for us to do" (Ephesians 2:10, NIV). Doing "good" was not limited to fellow believers, but was more broadly extended to all mankind (neighbors).

Keep in mind that America today is a democratic republic whereby government authority is vested with the citizens—you and me. When Christians fail to exercise their constitutional rights and responsibilities, they remove Christ's intended influence on the political process, and our "neighbors" are disadvantaged as a direct result.

Carl Henry (1913–2003), an American evangelical Christian theologian, said as much. He explained that Christians should "work through civil authority for the advancement of justice and human good" in order to advance "critical illumination, personal example, and vocational leadership." This view is interpreted to mean that Christians' government involvement results in the promotion of good and the restraint of evil.[566]

There are numerous scriptural examples of God's people participating in the political process for the benefit of their "neighbors." Joseph was the second most powerful man in Egypt (Genesis 41:40), and Daniel (Daniel 2:48) was a top adviser to the king of Babylon. Esther was a queen in Persia (Esther 8), and David (Acts 13:22) was the king of Israel, a man after God's heart. These people exercised great political power in secular settings, and did so in the name of God.

Advocating for the defenseless is the trademark of the Christian. Who else is going to protect the unborn and strengthen marriages and families? When society goes against God's teaching, how can Christians turn a blind eye to the crying need for change?

The third section of this book identified the antichrists of this world, many progressives. They are radically anti-Christian and promote evils that God condemns. That's why Paul urges Christians "first of all, that petitions, prayers, intercession and thanksgiving be made for all people—

for kings and all those in authority, that we may live peaceful and quiet lives in all godliness and holiness" (1 Timothy 2:1–2, NIV). Prayer is only one way for Christians to participate in government, and responding within the political process to promote righteous government is an appropriate role for believers.

Good government promotes peace and stability. It guards against illegitimate use of state agencies and punishes offenders. Christians provide a conscience to help make government good by asserting their influence to restrain evil.

When Christians fail to participate in the public square, that creates a moral vacuum that makes society susceptible to influences that move government outside God's designs. After all, politics affects government and helps to shape culture.

Keep in mind that throughout the past two thousand years, Christians have positively influenced government to embrace policies that reject horrendous, morally wrong policies. The life story of William Wilberforce, a British member of Parliament and a devout Christian, reflects the power of one Christian man. He successfully led the effort to abolish slavery in England. There are many other examples in history whereby Christians were used by God to advance moral issues that affected government and culture—to protect "our neighbors."

The fact is that Christians have an opportunity, a scriptural mandate to be involved in "politics." When they participate in the political processes, they are vessels of God to provide a righteous influence on public policy rather than leaving the fate of future generations in the hands of the wicked and immoral. Being involved is what Christ intended when, in the story of the good Samaritan, He said "You go, and do likewise."

The absence of Christians in the government opens the door wider for Satan's attacks. Christians in government infuse the Holy Spirit into government, which greatly mitigates Satan's influence. Look at the Book of Revelation, which is a detailed description of the chaos, horrors, and wars that follow the Rapture when all Christians and the Holy Spirit have departed instantly from the planet. The void is quickly filled by

Satan, because at that time there will be no Christians on the planet and it goes to Hell—literally.

Should Christians just be patriots, or maybe nationalists?

The terms "patriotism" and "nationalism" were often used as synonyms in the eighteenth century, but since that time, they have come to have very different connotations. They have taken on special interest, especially since President Trump declared himself a "nationalist."

At an October 2018 rally in Houston, Texas, just before the midterm congressional elections, Mr. Trump staked his position on the topic of "nationalism" with the following statement. He introduced his view on the issue by juxtaposing it with another, globalism, which is defined as "the attitude or policy of placing the interests of the entire world above those of individual nations."[567]

Mr. Trump said at the Houston rally, "A globalist is a person that wants the globe to do well, frankly, not caring about our country so much. And you know what? We can't have that."[568]

(The argument for globalism takes on a new meaning in light of the 2020 coronavirus pandemic. All reports indicate that the virus originated in China and quickly spread across the world because of the easy flow of people. Further, globalization also means that manufacturing and commerce make nations more dependent on others, such as in the case of pharmaceuticals including virus-fighting drugs. We have become very dependent on China for many of our critical drugs. The pandemic illustrates why globalization can become a national security issue, when the US depends almost exclusively on another nation like China for critical products such as antibiotics. I recommend reading my 2018 book, *The Deeper State*, to better understand globalism.)

Then the president explained, "You know, they have a word—it's sort of became old-fashioned—it's called a nationalist. And I say, really, we're not supposed to use that word. You know what I am? I'm a nationalist, okay? I'm a nationalist. Nationalist. Nothing wrong. Use that word. Use that word."[569]

The next day, Mr. Trump was asked by a reporter whether he understood that "nationalism" is a "dog whistle" to some Americans for embracing a racist ideology. Mr. Trump said he was unaware that the term was considered racist, then explained: "I love our country, and our country has taken second fiddle." He argued that "we're giving all of our money, all of our wealth to other countries and then they don't treat us properly."[570]

Shortly after Mr. Trump's "nationalism" declaration, French President Emmanuel Macron on November 11, 2018, at the 100th Armistice Anniversary ceremony in Paris, made the question of patriotism and nationalism a conspicuous political issue. Macron expressed concern with the increase of nationalism in the US and in European countries.[571]

Mr. Macron reflected in his Armistice Anniversary speech that the post-World War I era, which was marked by humiliation, the spirit of revenge, economic crises, and, more recently (2016), the mass immigration from the Middle East fueled the rise of nationalism across Europe. Those concerns were on the French leader's mind, but his remarks about nationalism were mostly focused on Donald Trump's Houston speech.

Patriotism is the opposite of nationalism, said Macron. He defined nationalism as "putting our nation first, and not caring about the others." He continued, saying that nationalism is about not caring for other countries. "We erase what a nation holds dearest, what gives it life, what makes it great and what is essential, its moral values," the Frenchman explained.[572]

The Houston rally wasn't the first time President Trump used the term "nationalism" to refer to himself. Shortly after becoming President, Mr. Trump told the White House press corps that he is a nationalist "in a true sense." For him, nationalism is central to his political identity, and his 2016 campaign slogan, "Make America Great Again," was based on the term.

Predictably, that self-embraced label drew criticism from people like foreign-policy expert and author Max Boot, a "never Trumper" (elites who want Trump to fail), who said the "word 'nationalism' is not inherently toxic." However, he continued:

> In the 20th century, nationalism has come to be associated with far-right politics, with fascism, with leaders like Mussolini, Hitler, Pinochet, Franco and others. And that is perhaps part of the reason why previous American presidents did not describe themselves as nationalists. They called themselves patriots.[573]

Step back and consider both terms, "patriotism" and "nationalism," their roots, and the related positive and negative effects.

Author George Orwell wrote an essay, "Notes on Nationalism," whereby he identified the term "as the habit of identifying oneself with a single nation or unit, placing it beyond good and evil and recognizing no other duty than that of advancing its interests." He contrasted nationalism with patriotism, which he defined as "devotion to a particular place and way of life which one believed to be the best in the world, but has no wish to force on other people."[574]

Of course, Orwell was writing in his essay about two very divisive personalities, Adolf Hitler and Benito Mussolini. But not all nationalists are divisive like those men. Some can be uniters, such as Narendra Modi of India and Shinzo Abe in Japan.

Consider the root of both terms and a brief history.

"Patriotism" is from the Latin word *patriota*, which means "fellow citizen," and the suffix "ism" means a "system" or "doctrine." Today, "patriotism" is commonly defined as the "love, affection, feeling of pride, devotion, and attachment for one's country," and is said to be based on the belief in the "inherent goodness of the system of government in a county, and the goodness of its people."[575]

There are many examples of patriotism, such as standing for the national anthem and reciting the Pledge of Allegiance. Others include participating in elections, volunteering for community service, teaching our children about civics, serving on juries, obeying all laws, and understanding our civic responsibilities in the constitution.

Patriotism is important for countries. A love for one's country brings people together, especially in challenging times. It fostered unity during colonial America and led to our independence from Great Britain. It was important for helping us overcome the Great Depression and rallying the nation to be victorious in World War II.

Yes, there can also be a downside to out-of-control patriotism. It can be a tool to turn one group against another, such as it did after World War I, when fears of communism led to the Palmer Raids, a series of US government raids (November 1919 to January 1920) during the Red Scare under President Woodrow Wilson. The intent was to capture and arrest suspect leftists, mostly Eastern Europeans and especially anarchists and communists, who were then deported.[576]

Another example of misguided patriotism created a hysteria after the Japanese air raid on Pearl Harbor, December 7, 1941, which compelled President Franklin Roosevelt to order 127,000 American citizens of Japanese ancestry to be interned.[577]

By contrast, "nationalism" comes from the Latin word *nationem*, which means "origin" or "tribe." It is most often defined as the "love and affection for one's country," but is culturally rooted in the belief that one's country is superior to all others. That view "carries the connotation of disapproval of other nations or a rivalry with other nations."[578]

The contemporary differences in the terms is widely understood. "Patriotism" and "nationalism," according to the Merriam-Webster dictionary, do share part of a definition: "loyalty and devotion to a nation." However, nationalism includes "exalting one nation above all others and placing primary emphasis on promotion of its culture and interests as opposed to those of other nations or supranational groups."[579]

Modifiers are especially important when distinguishing between the terms, according to Merriam-Webster. Patriotism is "more often used in a general sense, often in conjunction with such words as bravery, valor, duty, and devotion. Nationalism, however, tends to find itself modified by specific movements, most frequently of a political bent."[580]

Perhaps that's why nationalism means different things to different people. John Breuilly, a professor of nationalism at the London School of Economics, defines the term in his book, *Nationalism and the State*. There are three parts to the term, according to Breuilly:[581]

1. There exists a nation with an explicit and peculiar character.
2. The interests and values of this nation take priority over all other interests and values.
3. The nation must be as independent as possible. This usually requires at least the attainment of political sovereignty.

Like patriotism, the effects of nationalism can be both positive and negative. The Zionist movement that led to the creation of modern Israel in 1948 was a positive effect, contrasted with the German Nazi party's nationalism that contributed to the Holocaust, which claimed six million Jewish lives and led to World War II.

To some observers, the Breuilly definition of nationalism fits Mr. Trump's political philosophy. Professor Breuilly said, "Now there is no question that on such criteria [above], Trump is a nationalist." He continued:

However, so is Gandhi, Nehru, Sukarno, F. D. Roosevelt. Most polls in most states today show that most people are proud of their nation and wish to protect and promote its interests. In that sense, most people in the world could be regarded as nationalists.[582]

That definition doesn't work for some people when they think of President Trump, however. "Nowadays we often find terms like 'ethno-nationalist' or 'far-right nationalist' or 'populist nationalist' or 'illiberal nationalist' used for people like Trump," said Breuilly.

Steve Bannon, Mr. Trumps' former White House adviser, helped the president craft his campaign and said Trump has long embraced "nationalism" and rejected "globalism."

Others weren't so charitable after the president identified himself as a nationalist. Those critics say Mr. Trump's embrace of the label signaled he favors racism and xenophobia associated with America's nationalist movements.

Michael McFaul, President Obama's former ambassador to Russia, tweeted: "Does Trump know the historical baggage associated with this word, or is he ignorant? Honest question."[583]

Carl Reiner, a film director and liberal activist, associated Mr. Trump's nationalist claim with Adolf Hitler. Reiner tweeted, "Just heard Trump declare that he is a nationalist. In 1938 wasn't there a German guy, who was a really big nationalist?"[584]

Other presidents used the term "nationalism" and did so in a way that was deemed positive. Former President Obama invoked Theodore Roosevelt's 1910 call for a "new nationalism." Obama said:

> We still believe that this should be a place where you can make it if you try. And we still believe, in the words of the man who called for a New Nationalism all those years ago, "The fundamental rule of our national life," he said, "The rule which underlies all others—is that, on the whole, and in the long run, we shall go up or down together."[585]

Some observers said Mr. Trump's use of the term was aimed at firing up his base just prior to the 2018 midterm elections. "The president's not really a nationalist," former White House communications director Anthony Scarmucci said. "He's an antagonist, he's not a nationalist."[586]

Scarmucci continued:

> He's doing it because he wanted to antagonize people. He understands that he's a great wrecking ball for that establishment. And he knows when that ball hits into the establishment, it galvanizes

his base and he instinctively knows it will turn out more voters for him come the midterm elections.[587]

Patriotism and nationalism mean different things to different people. That leads us to the ideology known as "Christian nationalism," a combination of the terms "Christianity" and "nationalism" and what that means for America and our future.

What are the contrary views about Christian nationalism?
There are many views about Christian nationalism. Here are two polar opposite positions to consider.

Author Michelle Goldberg claims to have created the term "Christian nationalism," the topic of her book, *Kingdom Coming: The Rise of Christian Nationalism*. Ms. Goldberg, an ideological progressive who writes for numerous leftist media outlets, says Christian nationalism differs from Christian fundamentalism, a very conservative interpretation of Christianity, as opposed to Christian nationalism, which she defines as "a political ideology that posits a Christian right to rule." She explains that the Christian nationalist believes in a "revisionist history which holds that the founders were devout Christians who never intended to create a secular republic; separation of church and state, according to this history, is a fraud perpetrated by god-hating subversives."[588]

To support her allegation, Ms. Goldberg quotes from a book by Presbyterian Church of America Pastor George Grant, *The Changing of the Guard*, which reads, "Christians have an obligation, a mandate, a commission, a holy responsibility to reclaim the land for Jesus Christ— to have dominion in civil structures, just as in every other aspect of life and godliness."[589]

She makes Christian nationalists sound like intolerant Islamists. Specifically, she states that "in the Christian nationalist vision of America, non-believers would be free to worship as they choose, as long as they know their place," arguably that's similar to the second-class citizenship (*kafir*-like) status for non-Muslims, as commanded in the Koran and reviewed in an earlier chapter.

Ms. Goldberg concludes a *Huffington Post* article, "What is Christian Nationalism?" by describing Christian nationalism as promoting images that "smacks of fascist agitprop [political propaganda]." Then she posits:

> It's important, I think, to separate their faith from the authoritarian impulses of the Christian nationalist movement. Christianity is a religion. Christian nationalism is a political program, and there is nothing sacred about it.[590]

That's a harsh view of Christians who happen to be nationalists, and it is certainly a very different assessment from that offered by the Christian Nationalist Alliance (CNA), which claims to "publicize opinions about current events through the lens of Christian ethics and from the political perspective of nationalism." Although CNA has a website, there is no evidence that it remains active as of 2020—but that doesn't mean the views expressed on the site are not representative of Christian nationalists.[591]

In 2017, CNA identified ten positions to identify the principles and values of Christian nationalists. Those are:[592]

1. Jesus Christ is the Son of God and Savior of man.
2. All life, from conception until death, is sacred and the right to life is paramount.
3. The United States of America were founded by Christian men upon Christian tenets. Freedom of religion is not an excuse to divorce the American culture from its origins. We will defend our rights as Christians in all aspects of American life.
4. Marriage is an institution sanctioned by God between one man and one woman.

5. There are two genders, and all attempts to claim otherwise are an attempt to further pervert the glory of the creation.
6. The family is the cornerstone of Western civilization and should be protected from government intrusion and manipulation.
7. Every American has the right to practical self-defense, and the right to bear arms is as important as any of our other liberties.
8. Capitalism is the best system for social development and Christian charity the world has ever known. It must be preserved and promoted as the solution to the social and economic problems caused by communism.
9. Strong borders are a necessity for a safe and prosperous society.
10. Islam is a heretical perversion of the Judeo-Christian doctrine and must be recognized and treated as a threat to America and Western civilization as a whole.

CNA claims that Christian nationalists embrace a political platform that advances the reliance on Christian principles in government. Although they support the constitutional design of separation of church and state, that doesn't mean government should suppress Christian values. Rather, Christian nationalists advocate our rights to live in a society that reflects God's biblical design—representative democracy, limited government, states' rights, Christian charity, and the Bible as a blueprint for a lawful society.[593]

A Christian nationalist, according to CNA, adheres to Christian principles in government and law. However, he or she does not believe that separation of church and state means that values are suppressed simply due to their biblical origin. Therefore, the Christian nationalist reasserts our rights to live in a society that reflects the will of God, albeit a representative democracy, with limited government, states' rights, Christian charity, the three "C's," and the Holy Bible.

The three C's are Christianity, culture, and capitalism. CNA "believes that America can only be made great again by adhering to these virtues."

The organization's website asserts that "our nation's culture is built upon Christian values and the attempt to separate God from American life only serves the destructive element that has derailed America from its original intent." It views capitalism as the economic engine that created and nurtures the American middle class that as a result has the resources for producing charity. Attacks on capitalism are similar to the assaults on Christianity, which are the dual pillars of Western civilization.

What is Christian nationalism to American Christians?

There is obviously a very different understanding of Christian nationalism when you juxtapose the progressive view with that of the CNA website. Who should we believe—Goldberg or CNA? Perhaps we should seek the counsel of others who represent considerable respect across American Christians.

Keep in mind that the options, given the nature of the anti-Christian movement, are pretty stark. Christians can either join the political process with the intent of righting the lost cultural influence but not necessarily the ranks of the Christian nationalists, or abandon the country to atheists who advance anti-Christian policies. Of course, the latter is what progressives and Satan want: a Christian-free political environment to promote their radical agenda.

I don't see a middle ground. I believe our founders expected our culture and government to be influenced by religion, especially Christianity. As illustrated in the first section of this book, Christian principles and values were embedded in our founding documents and throughout our critical institutions primarily because most of the colonists were Christian or at least abided by Christian precepts. That doesn't mean our founders intended to create a theocracy, but it does mean they expected us to be tolerant of everyone's beliefs (even non-Christians) vis-à-vis the First Amendment of the Constitution. They understood as well that religion, at that time primarily Christianity in this country, was the oxygen of society; it was the essential ingredient for this democratic republic.

It also meant that people of faith don't have to leave their principles and values at the door when they become elected officials or government servants, nor is there a biblical mandate to do so. God places believers in key positions not to create a theocracy but to influence government policy for the benefit of all of "our neighbors."

Christians aren't called to participate in a secular masquerade whereby we compromise God's truth in order to serve in godless government or please our critics. Rather, we are called to be salt and light in the workplace (Matthew 5:13–16), which includes participating in government without compromising our faith. In a broader sense, we must refuse to surrender our country to the forces of evil, Satan and his proxies.

After all, whose values and principles do we wish government to embrace? For me, I'd rather see Christian values and principles guiding government. We've already seen the scorched-earth, anti-Christian approach progressives like former President Obama took, which resulted in a variety of unpleasant outcomes for most Christians.

That brings us back to the ideology of Christian nationalism as an alternative for American Christians concerned about the country's direction. No doubt some people like Ms. Goldberg portray Christian nationalism ideology as divisive, because it presumably promotes laws and government that reflect Christianity and embraces the view that America is an exceptional nation, blessed by God. What's the alternative? Pushing progressive values that are anti-Christian and discarding national sovereignty to embrace globalist views?

Really?

Christians considering whether to self-identify as nationalists must also consider the cultural war raging in America today that really went into overdrive with the 2016 election. At that time, Mr. Trump wisely aligned himself with so-called Christian nationalists who were terribly dissatisfied with the results of the impact of anti-Christlike, progressive politics. Progressive policy proposals were evil, and Mr. Trump saw the threat, which explains why he proposed reversing their horrid policies.

At that time, Mr. Trump saw what many Christian nationalists understood as the significant hazards to our way of life and our traditional

Christian values. For example, our economic prosperity was endangered by failed progressive policies that Mr. Trump promised to reverse, which he did.

Before Mr. Trump arrived in the Oval Office, his predecessor, President Obama, implemented policies that threatened America's market economy and her future prosperity. Progressives like Obama reject the very essence of America's past economic success, the Protestant work ethic, and the economic engine of capitalism. Rather, they seek to replace our current economic model with big government subsidies and socialism, a bankrupt formula evidenced time and again across the last century in countries like the Soviet Union and present-day Venezuela.

Mr. Trump's social agenda was also attractive to Christian nationalists. For example, over many years, progressives used the levers of big government to redefine gender to promote what God condemns and at the same time redefine what God blessed, the institution of marriage and family, and they sought to snuff out the truth that life begins at conception. Mr. Trump succeeded in turning the ship of state around on many of these issues in his first term, but more remains to be done.

Numerous other issues contributed to the winning coalition of Christian nationalists and conservatives that became Mr. Trump's base of support in 2016. One such matter is the progressive effort to grow government social programs that encourage government dependency. Mr. Trump responded to that failed policy by creating a strong economy that grew millions of new jobs and put respectability back into many less-advantaged American lives by helping them leave government welfare programs for good-paying jobs.

The progressive left also promotes open borders and welcomes illegal immigration, which they hope will bolster their election chances. Nationalists reject that sovereignty-robbing and border-free globalist proposal that energized many Trump supporters among the Christian nationalists.

One aspect of Mr. Trump's immigration-policy response to the progressive open-border approach was to put in place a permanent barrier on our southern border. He promised during the 2016 campaign to close that gap in our defenses and then followed through, in spite of significant resistance from the Democrat-controlled House of Representatives with support from progressive jurists on the federal bench. He also put in place a host of new immigration policies that favor America's interests and reverse former President Obama's biased, pro-Muslim immigration policy. Of course, progressives quickly challenged those changes in the courts, which they labeled as Islamophobic. Those policies aren't anti-Muslim, however. The fact is Mr. Trump's immigration policy aims to stop radical Islamists from coming to this country to kill us and many who seek to change our culture to embrace Sharia law. Finally, and importantly, Mr. Trump established a balanced immigration policy that welcomes Christians who are subjected to genocidal conditions in many Islamic countries.

These and other policy differences with progressives energized Mr. Trump's base, and that includes Christian nationalists. That support didn't go unnoticed, which is why progressives and their allies, many journalists and academics alike, used their powerful platforms to target their new bogeyman, the Christian nationalists and other Trump supporters.

Earlier, in section III of this book, we identified journalists as part of the phalanx of antichrists ripping at the vestiges of Christian influence in this culture. However, progressives also enlisted a host of academics to study Mr. Trump's voter base with the intent of besmirching them as Hillary Clinton did during her campaign. She called Trump supporters "a basket of deplorables."[594]

One such study found that Mr. Trump's 2016 election success was in fact attributable—you guessed it—to Christian nationalists. The study's authors insisted that Christian nationalists supported Mr. Trump not so much because of their Christian faith, but because they really wanted power. That view feeds the prejudice evident in much of the mainstream media about Christian nationalists. Those academics also cited other studies that asserted that many Trump supporters harbored concerns about economic uncertainty, racism, sexism, and unfettered immigration from countries known for anti-Western terrorism.

Specifically, the 2018 study led by Clemson University sociologist Andrew Whitehead argues that Trump spoke to that dissatisfaction through his no-apologies, populist appeal, as compared to Democrat presidential candidate Hillary Clinton's perceived liberal, progressive elitism.

Another study found that anti-black prejudice was a predictor of Trump voters. Specifically, it suggested that blaming African Americans for white Christian nationalists' societal disadvantages or feeling that blacks have too much influence in society were strong predictors of Trump support. Do you sense a bit of bias here?

Yet another study considered widespread concerns among Trump supporters about the threat from the Islamic culture and terrorism, especially in the decades since 9/11. Complementary studies found that Trump supporters were especially fearful of refugees from Muslim countries because of the association with Islamic "terrorism," which has become code for "Muslims," according to those academics.

The Whitehead study made a distinction between American "civil religion" and "Christian nationalism." For those researchers, the concepts are evidently connected, but other studies suggest there are important differences.

Civil religion refers to "America's conventional relationship with a divine creator who promises blessings for the nation for fulfilling its responsibility to defend liberty and justice." This concept is traceable to our Christian founding and reflects the vision shared by some of our founders.

The study found that "civil religion" is different from "Christian nationalism," which draws from its roots in the "Old Testament" and thus finds parallels between America and Israel. It is true those roots are evangelical, believing (much the same as our early Puritan, Quaker, and Presbyterian founders) that America was a special place and an exceptional nation blessed by God.

As we saw in the first section of this book, some scholars—particularly those behind many of these recent anti-Trump studies—argue that America was never a Christian nation, a myth they say functions as a "symbolic boundary uniting both personally religious and irreligious members of conservative groups." They try to make the case that Trump's base of support is defined mostly by Christians and groups with a race bias.

Those same scholars argue that Mr. Trump tapped into the energy behind that group by repeating the refrain that the US is abdicating its Christian heritage, an issue totally lost on the progressive media. Rather, the leftist media wagged their collective fingers at Christians who dared to support Mr. Trump, a non-pious candidate, about which the *Washington Post* complained "despite porn stars and playboy models, white evangelicals aren't rejecting Trump."[595]

Those progressives are almost apoplectic when wondering out loud why Christians of any stripe favor Mr. Trump, given his spotty moral background. And they grasp at straws to criticize him for almost any mistake, such as his *faux pas* at Liberty University on January 18, 2016.

Remember when Mr. Trump spoke to a Liberty University student convocation and quoted from the Bible, identifying the Scripture used as "two Corinthians" rather than the customary familiar reference as "second Corinthians"? That *faux pas* set off alarm bells for some critics that the then-presidential candidate displayed a lack of knowledge about the Bible, which they presumed would hurt his candidacy with conservative Christians.

Trump's mistake in citing that reference failed to have the anticipated effect, however, because it was quickly followed by a strong statement that appealed to the evangelical Christian audience. Specifically, Mr. Trump said:

> But we are going to protect Christianity. And if you look what's going on throughout the world, you look at Syria where they're, if you're Christian, they're chopping off heads. You look at the

different places, and Christianity, it's under siege. I'm a Protestant. I'm very proud of it. Presbyterian to be exact. But I'm very proud of it, very, very proud of it. And we've gotta protect, because bad things are happening, very bad things are happening, and we don't—I don't know what it is—we don't band together, maybe. Other religions, frankly, they're banding together and they're using it. And here we have, if you look at this country, it's gotta be 70 percent, 75 percent, some people say even more, the power we have, somehow we have to unify. We have to band together.... Our country has to do that around Christianity.[596]

Mr. Trump said much the same later that summer in Florida. At that time, he told evangelical pastors:

You know that Christianity and everything we're talking about today has had a very, very tough time. Very tough, time.... We're going to bring [Christianity] back because it's a good thing. It's a good thing. They treated you like it was a bad thing, but it's a great thing.[597]

The president's commitment to defend Christianity and the values we hold dear earned him support. Who else were Christians going to support? Hillary Clinton staked out a godless, pro-progressive agenda that offended most Christians. This was a no brainer, especially for evangelicals.

Eric Metaxas, a Christian media personality with Salem Radio Network, claimed at that time "God will not hold us guiltless" if Clinton were elected instead of Trump. Other evangelicals agreed with Mr. Metaxas.[598]

James Dobson, the Focus on the Family founder, wrote that "if Christians stay home because he [Trump] isn't a better candidate, Hillary will run the world for perhaps eight years. The very thought of that haunts my nights and days."[599]

Dr. Dobson also called out what was at stake in the 2016 election by highlighting the importance of the Supreme Court vacancy and how "unelected, unaccountable, and imperialistic judges have a history of imposing horrendous decisions on the nation. One decision that still plagues us is *Roe v. Wade* [the 1973 abortion judgment]."[600]

Mr. Trump's anti-Christian critics even cited the eschatological implications of his presidency. They critically pontificated that Christians like Dobson and Metaxas were worried about the future, given, as they said, how rapidly America disintegrated under the leadership of Barack Obama. After all, Mr. Trump promised to restore America to its past glory, to defend Christianity, to restore respect to America—a reflection of his campaign slogan, "Make America Great Again."

Trump supporter and former Alaska governor and vice-presidential candidate Sarah Palin told an Oral Roberts University audience as much:

> In this great awakening [a double entendre], you all who realize that, man, our country is going to hell in a handbasket under this tragic fundamental transformation of America that Obama had promised us, know what we need now is a fundamental restoration of America.[601]

Other Christians echoed that view as well. Pat Robertson with Christian Broadcasting Network said, "If we don't win this election, you'll never see another Republican and you'll have a whole different church structure…a whole different Supreme Court structure."[602]

I agree with the scholars at least on this one point. "Christian nationalism operates as a set of beliefs and ideals that seek the national preservation of a supposedly unique Christian identity." That is why, according to those same scholars, that "voting for Donald Trump was for many Americans a Christian nationalist response to perceived threats to that identity."[603]

It's no wonder that progressives marvel at the Christian nationalists' support for Trump. After all, the president demonstrated a long history of "anti-Christian" behavior, to include bragging about sexually assaulting women, endorsing physical violence against his enemies, mocking the disabled, and questioning whether he has any need to apologize to God would, in most circumstances, be actions despised by many self-identified Christians in the United States.[604]

Let's be frank here. Most Christian nationalists look past the president's foibles and focus on him as a "tool"—a tool used by God at this moment in history. They argue that supporting Mr. Trump is not about his religious bona fides, which are very suspect, but about an expressive outlet for the perceived religious backsliding in the United States.

Today's Christian nationalists love their Lord and their country. Most don't fit the description the progressives portray. Rather, they are much as Gerald I. K. Smith, an American clergyman and leader of the Share Our Wealth Movement, described them:

> The Christian nationalist crusade is a nationwide political movement dedicated to the mobilization of citizens who respect American tradition and whose idealism is founded on Christian principle. General Douglas MacArthur in one of his great public pronouncements said: "The two greatest symbols in this civilization are the Cross and the Flag."[605]

That view is simple and should satisfy even the skeptics. The Christian nationalist's motive is belief that the destiny of America in relationship to its governing authority must be in the hands of our own people. Our founders would endorse that view, and so should all but today's progressives/globalists.

We must never be governed by non-Americans, which includes strict control over our economy and our own blood. We must be true to the Declaration of Independence that gave us our freedom, and we must be skeptical of contrary voices. General MacArthur appropriately reminded us:

> Listen not to these voices that are raised against our (American tradition), be they from the one political party or from the other; be they from the high and the mighty, or the lowly and the forgotten. Heed them not. Visit upon them a righteous scorn born of the past sacrifices of your fighting sons and daughters. Repudiate them in the market place, on the platform, from the pulpit. Those who are our friends will understand. Those who are not we can pass by. Be proud to be called patriots or nationalists or what you will, if it means that you love your country above all else, and will place your life if need be at the service of our Flag.[606]

Is there a middle ground for those who are uncomfortable with being labeled a "Christian nationalist"?
Perhaps you want to be faithful to the scriptural mandate to help your neighbor, you are patriotic, and yet you don't want to be identified with the label "Christian nationalist." There is an alternative view for the sincere Christian patriot.

I found a reasoned analysis that charts the space between Goldberg's progressive portrayal of Christian nationalists and CNA's sympathetic presentation. That analysis came from the hand of Ralph Drollinger, an American clergyman and retired professional basketball player, who now leads the White House Bible study group, a gathering sponsored by cabinet members that meets weekly. Mr. Drollinger tackled the issue of Christian nationalism in a 2019 article, "Better Understanding the Fallacy of Christian Nationalism."[607]

Mr. Drollinger accuses secular journalists like Goldberg of recklessly painting well-meaning Christians who serve in public positions with the title "Christian nationalist" to marginalize their influence.

He unpacks the term "Christian nationalism" in his article (Bible

study) to persuade readers not to be Christian nationalists. He explains
in the introduction that portraying public servants who trust Christ for
their salvation as "Christian nationalists" is done to instill fear in the
public. Then he explains why it is not a biblically based precept.

Goldberg and others, according to Drollinger, use the term "Christian nationalist" to label Christian public servants and others as dominionists, reconstructionists, and theonomists. He argues that these terms
need to be understood, but are very much related.

Christian nationalists are not the same as dominionists, who believe
Christians need to take dominion over civil government. That view is
rooted in a misinterpretation of Genesis 1:28[608] and the Great Commission (Matthew 28:19–20).

Christian nationalism is not necessarily the same as Christian reconstructionism, which believes that all our founding fathers were Christians and, as a result, the US is a Christian nation. However, they claim
that, over time, secularists revised our history, and now the reconstructionists feel obligated to restore that truth.

Christian theonomists believe that in "taking dominion and in
reconstructing America as a Christian nation, it follows that all of America's laws should be based on" Old Testament law, wrote Drollinger. He
then explained that to satisfy theonomists, Old Testament law must be
imported and become the basis for all America's civil law.

All three terms—dominionism, reconstructionism, and theono-
mism—are closely related and are "necessary ingredients to the idea of
establishing a theocratic nation."

He argues that those who throw about such a label ("Christian
nationalism") are "attempting to strike fear in the hearts of society by
falsely postulating that believers in office desire to turn American into a
theocracy—a church-controlled state." He goes on to dispute this view.

The left's accusation is fallacious on its face. Drollinger explains:

[If a Christian nationalist is] "someone who desires to create a Christian theocracy, then it stands to reason that such a person desires to

champion a cleric-controlled state. That could take the form of a Christian dictatorship, Christian republic, or perhaps a Christian oligarchy. Whatever the form of governance, such Christian individuals would have to hold absolute power and control over the state in order for that state to qualify as a bona fide theocracy.

The logic of the above follows that anything less than the above standard is not a theocracy. Further, the public servant, to be a Christian nationalist, would by necessity have to favor replacing our current form of government with something whereby Christians hold all power. Even the CNA doesn't call for that outcome.

What we have in America today among Christians who are patriotic and serving in government are believers "who are pursuing the objective of maturing in Christ so as to better represent Christ and his teachings in the existing government structure." Set aside labels and let's be Christians who happen to love our country, nothing more or less.

How should Christians respond to critics of Christian nationalism?
Whether you embrace Christian nationalism or Drollinger's model for Christian patriots, it's useful to consider some typical criticisms of Christian nationalists and how to respond.

First, Christian nationalists are expected to be politically neutral. That means we are to have no voice in public debate, even regarding moral issues. However, for the Spirit-filled Christian and even one who is a nationalist, our commission is to share the gospel of Jesus Christ, and that means where God has placed us—at home, in a factory, or in a government building.

Critics of Christians need to understand that other faiths like Islam reject church and state separation. They totally reject the notion of Islam being neutral. The idea of the *ummah* (the Islamic faithful) requires a united religious community that transcends tribe and rejects secularism—and, by the way, is mostly intolerant of other beliefs such as Christianity and Judaism. Rather, Muhammad required the establishment of

Sharia, Islamic law, to which all (nonbelievers as well) must submit, a distinction between *Dar al Islam* and *Dar al Harb* (the House of Islam and the House of War).

Second, ideological globalists reject the Christian nationalist's promotion of America as an exceptional nation. They call for a false piety for American Christian churches, insisting that they must be diverse (representing many nationalities), a wrongheaded view. Their real objective is to advance the false analogy that Christ calls on America and by association American churches to be blind to borders and welcome anyone, no matter their nationality or immigration status. They insist we are to be one big happy world (globalist) family with no borders.

America does accept many immigrants every year from countries across the world, but we insist they come in the right way, by obeying our laws. Once here, those who are Christian are welcome to join the church of their choice, such as my home church, which is very diverse in terms of race, ethnicity, and nation of origin.

Third, some critics of Christian nationalism confuse the roles of church and state. I don't see that confusion in CNA's principles and values statement, however. It is clear that religion (Christianity among all faiths) is charged with making disciples, while our civil government is to keep the peace. Both outcomes are God-ordained. For the Christian, Matthew 28 calls the church to make disciples, and Romans 13 calls on civil authorities to keep the peace.[609]

Fourth, some critics argue that Christian nationalists intend to use the state to harvest converts. Nonsense. Christian nationalists want to make government better. They do not want Christianity to manage civil affairs. Rather, the church should feed the consciences of those who manage civil affairs and be more faithful to those for whom it is responsible.

Finally, some critics believe that Christian nationalists seek to merge Christianity and the American identity. Their allegation is that Christianity enjoys a privileged position with the state, which implies that to be a good American, one must be Christian. Others really go overboard and claim that concept is associated with white supremacy and racial subjugation.

That's an unsubstantiated smear against Christians in general and Christian nationalists specifically. Christians are followers of Jesus Christ, not of a particular nation. Further, in the US, patriotism does not require citizens to align themselves with a particular faith, nor does government prefer one faith over another. The fact is that America's historic commitment to religious pluralism enables faith communities to live in civic harmony. Otherwise, the idea of conflating religious authority with politics is idolatrous and dangerous for any nation.[610]

Conclusion

This chapter establishes that Christians must engage in America's political processes. That's a scriptural mandate. We examined the distinctions between patriotism and nationalism, and then considered the criticisms, rationale, and drawbacks for Christians presenting themselves as so-called Christian nationalists. We also presented an alternative to that label.

"Christian nationalism" is not a dirty term, but progressives intend it to be. It has many redeeming qualities that depend on whose definition one uses, and some of the definitions offered by progressives are patently misinformation. However, I prefer to embrace a broad definition for the patriotic Christian's role in America's public life. Specifically, like Mr. Drollinger said, it's wrong to portray public servants and others engaged in the political life of our country who trust Christ for their salvation as simply "Christian nationalists." Rather, I prefer to call them what Christ might call them: "good neighbors," or perhaps catchier, "PACs" for "patriotic American Christians."

CHAPTER THIRTEEN

Choice:
Crash Across the Moral Tipping
Point or Christian Renewal

THERE IS A war raging in America on a number of fronts. At stake is the future of America, and the war is both in the seen and unseen realms, a spiritual one waged by Satan and his proxies for the souls of mankind. We either turn the tide of the war with God's help and His grace, or we continue our present course and crash across the moral tipping point.

Chapter 12 demonstrated that the war is quite real and serious. However, there is a spark of hope at the present time—not because Christians favor making America great again, which many do, or that President Trump is some kind of human savior. No, there is hope that God will intervene, perhaps for the last time, through His saints to pull America—and, by association, the Christian world—back from the moral abyss, that is, crossing the moral tipping point.

This chapter begins by musing about our Christian roots that made America an exceptional nation and suggests that recovering that foundation might yet be possible. After all, our founders wisely sewed into this country's fabric Christian principles and values, and remnants of that work are still quite evident within our institutions, but time to recover is short; evil forces seek to strain out the last of our embedded goodness.

I soberly accept that many indicators are lighting up our spiritual skies that suggest America might be lost. Yes, America just might be toast, too far gone morally to recover her past Christian roots, and the end times are rushing at us.

I'm determined to be hopeful and resilient, however. I agree that the hour is late and America has lost much of her original Christian fervor; and so has much of the Christian church. Yet there still remains a solid remnant of committed Christians—the "espresso cup" types—across this land who haven't given up. Many still see the real possibility for spiritual renewal.

This chapter provides a future hopeful view of that America, a country that returns to her Christian roots. How does that happen? Chapter 14, the final chapter in this book, provides a strategy, our marching orders that aim at making America more Christian, a plan built with the wise counsel of fine contemporary Christian leaders.

Can America Be Godly Again?

America is still a great country with a very productive population, great quality of life, and a mostly optimistic people. We are for the most part cohesive and have a remnant of moral people. Further, for many years after our founding, we were much more a godly nation than today, and this was the linchpin to our greatness and God's obvious blessings. We are a great nation today, but the future is questionable as we examine how far America has digressed morally.

America's greatness is correlated with her godliness, a quality that is in steep decline in these amoral times. That doesn't mean we were previously a theocracy or a godly nation without reservations. No, we had a spotty moral history—wars, slavery, political corruption, and other blemishes. However, our culture and the critical institutions for much of our history were unquestionably a reflection of Christian principles and values.

Our founders, as demonstrated earlier in this book, spoke of the importance of a morally grounded populace that seeded our institutions. Specifically, I quoted in the first section numerous founders who made the point that virtue and the Christian faith and teachings were important to our survival and prosperity as a nation. One such founder was Samuel Adams, a man born to a Puritan family who helped draft the Articles of Confederation and the Declaration of Independence, warned about losing that virtue. He said:

> A general dissolution of principles and manners will more surely overthrow the liberties of America than the whole force of the common enemy. While the people are virtuous, they cannot be subdued; but when once they lose their virtue, they will be ready to surrender their liberties to the first external or internal invader.[611]

Benjamin Rush, a signer of the Declaration of Independence and a ratifier of the US Constitution, echoed Adams' sentiment about the importance of virtue by calling out the critical role played by Christianity. He said, "The only means of establishing and perpetuating our republican forms of government is the universal education of our youth in the principles of Christianity by means of the Bible."[612]

Daniel Webster, a noted early American statesman, congressman, senator, and secretary of state, echoed Rush's view about the role of Christianity's influence on the young nation: "Whatever makes men good Christians makes them good citizens."[613] Further, Rush juxtaposed Christianity and civil society in an 1844 speech: "The Christian religion—its general principles—must ever be regarded among us as the foundation of civil society."[614]

The fathers of this nation weren't the only people who saw that America was great and Christianity was the ingredient that made her special. For example, the noted French statesman and philosopher Alexis de Tocqueville saw America as a unique civilization when visiting here in the 1830s. He wrote:

I sought for the key to the greatness and genius of America in her harbors...; in her fertile fields and boundless forests; in her rich mines and vast world commerce; in her public-school system and institutions of learning. I sought for it in her democratic Congress and in her matchless Constitution.[615]

De Tocqueville continued:

Upon my arrival in the United States the religious aspect of the country was the first thing that struck my attention; and the longer I stayed there, the more I perceived the great political consequences resulting from this new state of things.[616]

His most telling observation was:

Not until I went into the churches of America and heard her pulpits flame with righteousness did I understand the secret of her genius and power.[617]

Evidently, in the minds of these early observers, America was great—primarily because she embraced Christianity. But contemporary American society fails to understand our Christian history. Gary Bauer, the president of American Values and the former domestic policy adviser for President Ronald Reagan, said:

Contemporary Americans if they heard a founder speaking about being virtuous they would think him an extremist...

[because]…moral relativism has gained momentum [and as a result] every aspect of public and private life is corrupt.[618]

Our corruption has displaced greatness, and Christianity's influence is draining from America. Can Christianity's impact on America be recovered?

Dr. Michael Brown, a nationally syndicated radio host and founder and president of FIRE School of Ministry in Concord, North Carolina, observed:

> The undeniable reality is that America cannot be great again unless America is good again. And America cannot be good again without being godly—or, in short, without God's help, through the gospel.[619]

Dr. Brown acknowledged that America will "never be a perfectly Christian nation. No nation will, until Jesus returns." However, he concludes that to "the extent we can get back to our godly roots, not by imposing them on others but by living them out, to that extent we can be great—again."[620]

Other Christian leaders believe America has moral challenges as well, but they remain hopeful. My pastor, Victor Stanley, of Calvary Baptist Church in Woodbridge, Virginia, believes that in spite of our slide away from moral absolutes, America still has a significant measure of moral conviction. He explained, "We still have a moral compass, however the magnetic pull of relativism in America is causing the arrow of the compass to fail to give an accurate reading." He argues that "any remnant of moral rightness in America must, in part, be attributed to the intent of some of its founding fathers to establish a country with Christian values, as defined in the scriptures."[621]

Christian leaders such as those above hold out hope for renewal, but others believe America is toast. Those skeptics point out that America is absent from end-times biblical prophecy and, at present, all indicators are that she is just about to slip over the moral tipping point.

Reason to Be Concerned about Our Future

Admittedly, there is compelling evidence to believe that America is on a collision course toward a moral tipping point, and there might not be any turning back. Consider some of the bad news that points toward that moral tipping point.

The American Christian church is shrinking. Earlier in this book, I wrote that, in 2019, the Pew Research Center reported the number of Americans who self-identify as Christian is down 12 percentage points over the past decade. The same report found a rise in the religiously unaffiliated, now at 26 percent up from 17 percent in 2009.[622]

Pew also reports that a growing number of Americans are turning their backs on the conservative Christian faith and embracing milk-toast therapeutic deism. For example, sociologist Christian Smith, a professor at the University of Notre Dame, said America is moving to a civil religion that is more pluralistic for this diversified country. He identifies the following characteristics of that growing "civic" faith:[623]

1. "A God exists who created and ordered the world and watches over human life on earth."
2. "God wants people to be good, nice, and fair to each other, as taught in the Bible and by most world religions."
3. "The central goal of life is to be happy and to feel good about oneself."
4. "God does not need to be particularly involved in one's life except when God is needed to resolve a problem."
5. "Good people go to heaven when they die."

Professor Smith's description of an emergent civil religion is likely the product of ramped-up pluralism and the Christian church's abandonment of its scriptural obligations. It is certainly not what the founders endorsed and won't lead to a renewed Christian America. And these five points of a growing "civic" faith are a false doctrine that can lead millions of Americans away from true salvation.

Some notable Christian leaders are distressed by the church's lackluster attention to its scriptural obligations. R. Albert Mohler Jr., president of Southern Baptist Theological Seminary and someone described as "one of America's most influential evangelicals," reacted to news that the number of Americans who claim no religious affiliation has almost doubled since 1990:[624]

> A remarkable culture-shift has taken place around us. The most basic contours of American culture have been radically altered. The so-called Judeo-Christian consensus of the last millennium has given way to a post-modern, post-Christian, post-Western cultural crisis which threatens the very heart of our culture.[625]

It isn't surprising to some leaders that the demographic changes to the American Christian church are accompanied by prophetic indicators of the end times. Keep in mind that a third of the Bible is steeped in prophecy, which means it addresses "things to come."

Jan Markell, a radio talk show hostess and founder and president of Olive Tree Ministries, encourages everyone to be like the sons of Issachar in 1 Chronicles 12, who understood the times in which they lived. She would have us be aware of the events lighting up the spiritual skies today.[626]

Modern America is a nation and people who are living in a time that manifests significant signs of the prophetic end times, according to Markell. She calls attention to scriptural evidence that we are approaching those times. For example, she cites Matthew 24:34 to demonstrate that Israel's rebirth, when Israel became a nation again in 1948, as a reminder that God keeps His promises.

Ms. Markell calls attention to "birth pangs," unprecedented disasters that are a foretaste of what will happen in the Tribulation or the "time of Jacob's trouble." Certainly, the floods, storms, global spread of viruses (like the novel coronavirus [COVID-19]), diseases, and more are evidence of a growing sense of disaster engulfing this world.

Moral depravity is growing in America, another indication of the coming end times. Ms. Markell notes the widespread depraved mentality (Romans 1); evidence of self-love (2 Timothy 3); and godlessness, immorality, and lawlessness abounding, such as in the times of Noah and Lot. Examples of the depravity of mankind are obvious to any observer of our culture; note examples such as widespread voter fraud, a growing evidence of occultism, and clerical compromise on what God calls abomination.

Satan and his demons are enjoying more success with their spread of evil as well. In fact, the Bible warns that in the last days, "evildoers and impostors will go from bad to worse" (2 Timothy 3:13, NIV). Ms. Markell calls our attention to the fact that most Americans embrace some kind of "new age" beliefs. Specifically, she points out the popularization of sorceries and a growing love of evil (Isaiah 5:20).

The "woke" (socially aware) contemporary Christian church is caving to apostasy and social-justice agendas in an effort to refashion Christianity to appeal to more people. Meanwhile, Bible prophecy is seldom spoken of from contemporary pulpits, suggesting that God never warned about these bankrupt times.

Little wonder, given the above, that Ms. Markell is very pessimistic about America. "Everything about America is tainted by leftist antics. They are determined to make us a godless country," she explained. "America is a Titanic [a rhetorical reference to the British passenger liner that sank in the North Atlantic Ocean on April 15, 1912] two-thirds under water…I don't see how it can be turned around."[627]

She does see the present as a temporary reprieve from the inevitable falling off the moral cliff, however. "God for some reason gave us four years, eight years [perhaps] with Mr. Trump," said Ms. Markell. However, she cautions that when the left inevitably returns to power "they will so completely finish Obama's job."[628]

William "Bill" Federer is an American author of twenty books, including his best-selling *America's God and Country: Encyclopedia of Quotations*. He agrees with Markell's assessment that America could soon be "toast." "America departed from its founding and unless it has a course correction it will probably not survive as we've known it," Federer said.[629]

That view is echoed by Monsignor Charles Pope, the pastor of Holy Comforter-St. Cyrian, a Catholic parish in Washington, DC. The monsignor said:

> For those of us who love our country and our culture, the pain is real. It appears that we are at the end of an era. We are in a tailspin we don't seem to be able to pull ourselves out of. Greed, aversion to sacrifice, secularism, divorce, promiscuity, and the destruction of the most basic unit of civilization (the family), do not make for a healthy culture. There seems to be no basis for true reform and the deepening darkness suggests that we are moving into the last stages of a disease. This is painful but not unprecedented.[630]

Both Federer and Pope call out the fact that cultures and civilizations go through cycles. Although that's no comfort, it does appear their observation very much applies to America today but not necessarily to the church. However, both men agree the Christian church requires reform to a true biblical culture, which is necessary for renewal.

A Renewal after So Much Corruption Would Be a Historic First for Mankind (with One Biblical Exception)

I have to be realistic about America's future. Our only hope for renewal, given her present condition, is to make her Christian again, at least much more Christian than she is today. However, remaking a corrupt and morally backslidden nation is unheard of in the secular history of mankind, which reminds me of something founder John Adams wrote to Thomas Jefferson in 1819:

> Have you ever found in history one single example of a nation thoroughly corrupted that was afterwards restored to virtue?... And without virtue, there can be no political liberty.... Will you tell me how to prevent luxury from producing effeminacy, intoxication, extravagance, vice and folly?... No effort in favor of virtue is lost.[631]

Adams' view is supported by a raft of modern sociology; national rebirth has never happened once a country crosses the moral tipping point, however.

There are a variety of explanations about the rise and fall of the world's great civilizations. Below I summarize two explanations.

One view about the rise and fall of civilizations is attributed to Scottish philosopher Alexander Tyler of the University of Edinburg. He postulates there are eight stages civilizations pass through from rise to fall. Those are identified in Ted Flynn's book, *The Great Transformation*, and explained below in Monsignor Pope's words.[632]

> 1. From bondage to spiritual growth—Great civilizations are formed in the crucible. The Ancient Jews were in bondage for 400 years in Egypt. The Christian faith and the Church came out of 300 years of persecution. Western Christendom emerged from the chaotic conflicts during the decline of the Roman Empire and the movements of often fierce "barbarian" tribes. American culture was formed by the injustices that grew in colonial times. Sufferings and injustices cause—even force—spiritual growth. Suffering brings wisdom and demands a spiritual discipline that seeks justice and solutions.
>
> 2. From spiritual growth to great courage—Having been steeled in the crucible of suffering, courage and the ability to

endure great sacrifice come forth. Anointed leaders emerge and people are summoned to courage and sacrifice (including loss of life) in order to create a better, more just world for succeeding generations. People who *have* little or nothing, also have little or nothing to *lose* and are often more willing to live for something more important than themselves and their own pleasure. A battle is begun, a battle requiring courage, discipline, and other virtues.

3. From courage to liberty—As a result of the courageous fight, the foe is vanquished and liberty and greater justice emerges. At this point a civilization comes forth, rooted in its greatest ideals. Many who led the battle are still alive, and the legacy of those who are not is still fresh. Heroism and the virtues that brought about liberty are still esteemed. The ideals that were struggled for during the years in the crucible are still largely agreed upon.

4. From liberty to abundance—Liberty ushers in greater prosperity, because a civilization is still functioning with the virtues of sacrifice and hard work. But then comes the first danger: abundance. Things that are in too great an abundance tend to weigh us down and take on a life of their own. At the same time, the struggles that engender wisdom and steel the soul to proper discipline and priorities move to the background. Jesus said that man's life does not consist in his possessions. But just try to tell that to people in a culture that starts to experience abundance. Such a culture is living on the fumes of earlier sacrifices; its people become less and less willing to make such sacrifices. Ideals diminish in importance and abundance weighs down the souls of the citizens. The sacrifices, discipline, and virtues responsible for the thriving of the civilization are increasingly remote from the collective conscience; the enjoyment of their fruits becomes the focus.

5. From abundance to complacency—To be complacent means to be self-satisfied and increasingly unaware of serious

trends that undermine health and the ability to thrive. Everything *looks* fine, so it must *be* fine. Yet foundations, resources, infrastructures, and necessary virtues are all crumbling. As virtues, disciplines, and ideals become ever more remote, those who raise alarms are labeled by the complacent as "killjoys" and considered extreme, harsh, or judgmental.

6. From complacency to apathy—The word apathy comes from the Greek and refers to a lack of interest in, or passion for, the things that once animated and inspired. Due to the complacency of the previous stage, the growing lack of attention to disturbing trends advances to outright dismissal. Many seldom think or care about the sacrifices of previous generations and lose a sense that they must work for and contribute to the common good. "Civilization" suffers the serious blow of being replaced by personalization and privatization in growing degrees. Working and sacrificing for others becomes more remote. Growing numbers becoming increasingly willing to live on the carcass of previous sacrifices. They park on someone else's dime, but will not fill the parking meter themselves. Hard work and self-discipline continue to erode.

7. From apathy to dependence—Increasing numbers of people lack the virtues and zeal necessary to work and contribute. The suffering and the sacrifices that built the culture are now a distant memory. As discipline and work increasingly seem "too hard," dependence grows. The collective culture now tips in the direction of dependence. Suffering of any sort seems intolerable. But virtue is not seen as the solution. Having lived on the sacrifices of others for years, the civilization now insists that "others" must solve their woes. This ushers in growing demands for governmental, collective solutions. This in turns deepens dependence, as solutions move from personal virtue and local, family-based sacrifices to centralized ones.

8. From dependence back to bondage—As dependence increases, so does centralized power. Dependent people tend to become increasingly dysfunctional and desperate. Seeking a savior, they look to strong central leadership. But centralized power corrupts, and tends to usher in increasing intrusion by centralized power. Injustice and intrusion multiply. But those in bondage know of no other solutions. Family and personal virtue (essential ingredients for any civilization) are now effectively replaced by an increasingly dark and despotic centralized control, hungry for more and more power. In this way, the civilization is gradually ended, because people in bondage no longer have the virtues necessary to fight.

Author Bill Federer called my attention to an alternative view that explains the rise and fall of civilizations. Specifically, he said the "cycle of men and women and sex drive" explains the civilizational phenomenon. "Men want what women have and if women command a covenant then men will make a commitment and bring back support for their wives." Ultimately across society, this man-woman relationship leads to stable homes and brings stability to entire cultures.[633]

Federer's view about the importance of societal control of male sex drives is backed by plenty of science.

Joseph Daniel Unwin, a twentieth-century English ethnologist and social anthropologist at Oxford University, is the author of the definitive work on the rise and fall of civilizations, *Sex and Culture*. Unwin studied eighty-six civilizations and found that a society's destiny is linked to the limits it imposes on sexual expression, which not surprisingly correlates directly to the civilization's theological sophistication and religious commitment.[634]

Those societies with greater restrictions on sexual expression achieved greater social development. In fact, populations that enforced "absolute monogamy" produced the "most vigorous, economically productive, artistically creative, scientifically innovative, and geographically expansive societies on earth."

"Absolute monogamy," what the Bible calls marriage between a man and a woman, is key. Societies succeed that embrace "absolute monogamy," which holds that sex can occur only within one-man/one-woman marriage and premarital and extramarital sex are prohibited. And of course, as history reveals that practice, "absolute monogamy" only occurs in societies that take their faith—religion—very seriously, such as much of early America.

"In other words," Unwin found "that the survival of a civilization or society depends on keeping sexual energy focused on supporting family life and not allowing individuals access to sex in ways that do not support family life."[635]

British historian Arnold Toynbee, an Unwin contemporary, also charted the rise and fall of civilizations. In his twelve-volume *Study of History*, he echoes Unwin's view about the importance of religion: "The course of human history consists of a series of encounters...in which each man or woman or child...is challenged by God to make the free choice between doing God's will and refusing to do it."[636]

Sociologists consistently find that "absolute monogamy" is key to keeping civilizations stable. It fosters growth, which famed anthropologist Margaret Mead called the "central problem of every society," the roles of men.[637]

Conservative religious-based monogamous civilizations, like much of colonial America, required their men to choose either lifelong celibacy or the responsibilities of a husband: fidelity, breadwinning, and fatherhood. In such societies, the practice is for men to choose to marry "to their good fortune, because married men tend to be healthier, happier, and more productive than bachelors."[638]

Married and committed husbands create stable marriages, which then foster the best opportunity for raising healthy, productive children to keep society strong. That outcome also makes the best economic sense for a society.

Economist Joseph Schumpeter claims the success of capitalism works in a stable society because men love their families. Schumpeter explains that the "central pillar of any healthy civilization is the self-sacrificing married man who doesn't spend his income on his pleasures, but prefers 'to work and save primarily for his wife and children.'"[639]

Not surprising to many readers might be the conclusion that when society has strong families, it is most productive. Harvard historian Carle Zimmerman, author of *Family and Civilization*, concludes that "the creative periods in civilization have been based upon" the strongest form of family. He continues: "The domestic family affords a comparatively stable social structure and yet frees the individual sufficiently from family influence to perform the creative work necessary for a great civilization."[640]

Strong marriages and families are the critical ingredient to cultural success. What then leads to civilizational decline?

The answer should be obvious. Zimmerman says decline comes during "periods of family decay in which civilization is suffering internally from the lack of basic belief in the forces which make it work." For contemporary America, that means if people lose their faith in God, Christianity's influence fades, the population loses its motivation to abide by a strict moral code, and then the civilization begins to disintegrate.[641]

Sociologist Robert Nesbit wrote in *This Present Age* that "what sociologists are prone to call social disintegration is really nothing more than the spectacle of a rising number of individuals playing fast and loose with other individuals in relationships of trust and responsibility." The simple explanation is that societal moral standards erode when the people reject "absolute monogamy" and give in to their personal impulses while ignoring the consequences of their sin.[642]

America reflects this perspective, having become less godly and more amoral, which results in a hedonistic society. Trust is thrown away and relationships are broken at will, and there are no repercussions or social stigma for abandoning committed marriage relations. Children pay a high price and society picks up the bill.

Pitirim Sorokin, the founder of Harvard's sociology department, warns in *The American Sex Revolution* (1956) that if selfishness and self-seeking are not checked by society, it will lapse into "sexual anarchy," and as a result, the culture becomes "sexually obsessed." He continues:

> Both man and society are degraded as a culture becomes sexually obsessed. The members of such a society are habituated to look at the opposite sex as a mere instrument for pleasure…. To these individuals, talk of human dignity, religions, and moral commandments, and rules of decency is just bosh. The society degrades the values of womanhood and manhood, of motherhood and fatherhood and venerable age, of marriage and family, and even of love itself.[643]

Most likely, anthropologist Unwin would agree with the others cited above. After all, in his research, he found:

> A society would begin with high standards limiting sex to one partner in marriage for life. This produced great social strength, and that society or culture would flourish. Then a new generation would arise demanding sex on easier terms and would lower moral standards. But when that happened the society would lose vitality, grow weak, and then die.

Contemporary America's sexual mores demonstrate that it is at a moral tipping point. Today our men have abandoned their women and children. Women less often than ever before demand marriage before sex, and promiscuity and homosexual sex are celebrated. Meanwhile, too often Christians complain about the amoral culture only within the confines of their homes and churches, as if what happens in the broader culture is of no consequence for them.

A Christian Makeover of America

Progressives like to remind the world that history does not move backwards. In other words, progressives don't believe the old America, with its well-embedded Christian principles and values, will spontaneously regenerate.

Progressives may be right and America might just be finished, perhaps not because the Rapture is moments away, but because we are at the end stage of civilization and drifting into history as did those who came before us. It is true historically that renewal after great corruption as seen in the last few decades is unheard of, and contemporary America appears to be imploding morally because it abandoned biblical principles and values.

Those are hard words to write. America has abandoned the Christianity of our founders, making our past almost incomprehensible to many contemporaries. Today, many of us look at our Christian ancestors as aliens, a minority cult, certainly strangers to these modern times. We arrogantly look down our modern relativistic noses at those primitive, biblical believers.

In our haughty, modern, sophisticated way of thinking, we've lost sight of what is truly noble and worthy. Contemporary America has abandoned what made her once good, as de Tocqueville correctly said almost two hundred years ago.

To save America from progressives and their sponsor, Satan and his demonic army, the Christian core of America—the "espresso cup" Christians—must refocus on making this nation good, godly— "Christian"—again. Admittedly, this is a very steep if not impossible challenge, but we have a big God, and I am optimistic in spite of all the moral challenges.

I will address a renewal process, the battle plan, to make America more Christian again in the final chapter. However, to set the stage for that plan, I will present here a vision of a future more Christian America.

Dr. Frank Drowota, the founding pastor of Woodmont Christian

Church, said he dreamed of a time the church would "interpret truth in terms of the times, but challenge times in terms of the truth." That's my dream for the future America and especially the Christian church.[644]

My dream, vision, for the future Christian America is that it will stand for the truth as informed by the Word of God. It will awaken from its apathy and immorality to revive the Christian principles and values within our key institutions. Specifically, I'm praying for what happened to the Assyrian Empire in the eighth century before Christ to happen to America. Contrary to the sociologists' studies above, there is an example of a civilization turning around morally—but that transformation required the direct intervention of God.

The history of that turn-around is found in the biblical Book of Jonah. God told the prophet Jonah, "Go to the great city of Nineveh and preach against it, because its wickedness has come up before me" (Jonah 1:2, NIV).

Jonah fled from the presence of the Lord instead (Jonah 1:10). He ended up in Joppa, a coastal city where he boarded a ship bound for Tarshish, a city in present-day Spain, just the opposite direction from where God called him to go.

Jonah evidently refused God's missionary call because the Assyrians were an idolatrous, proud, and ruthless nation. Jonah knew they deserved God's judgment, and he didn't want to be the vessel God used to extend mercy to his enemies.

Jonah soon discovered that no man can run from God: "'Can a man hide himself in secret places so that I cannot see him,' declares the Lord." Jonah's plan to escape God's call landed him in the belly of a whale for three days, just enough time for Jonah to reconsider his disobedience and reach out to God in desperate prayer.

The whale expelled Jonah onto dry land with a second chance to obey God's call. Not surprisingly, this time Jonah went directly to Nineveh and proclaimed God's judgment. Here is what the Scripture states when Jonah delivered God's message to the people at Nineveh (Jonah 3:6–10, NKJV):

Then the word came to the king of Nineveh; and he arose from his throne, laid aside his robe, covered himself in sackcloth and sat in ashes. And he caused it to be proclaimed and published throughout Nineveh, by the decree of the king and his nobles saying, let neither man nor beast, herd or flock taste anything; do not let them eat or drink water, and cry mightily to God, yes, and let everyone turn from his evil way and from the violence that is in his hands. Who can tell if God will turn and relent and turn away His fierce anger, so that we may not perish?

Then God saw their works; that they turned from their evil way; and God relented from the disaster that He said He would bring upon them; and He did not do it.

This biblical account of national repentance gives me hope. It illustrates that even a pagan and ruthless king and a totally lost people can be rescued from their sin.

The Assyrian king was the lynchpin here. He heard Jonah's word and responded in humility. He came to realize his spiritual condition and repented. Then the king sent word to his people to fast and cry out for God's mercy that He would spare them from destruction.

The Lord responded and turned back from His judgment. The Assyrians were spared, and according to history books, peace reigned over that land for eighty years following the time of Jonah.

It is my prayer that, like the Assyrians, America will repent and God will be merciful and spare this nation. Specifically, the outcome of God's mercy is evidenced in my vision for a Christian remake of America's five key institutions.

A Vision for a New Christianized America

Section II of this book includes five chapters, each profiling a key institution. I explained how each of those institutions at America's birth reflected Christian principles and values. Then I outlined how each lost much of its original Christian influence over the centuries, especially in the last few decades.

Below is my vision of what each of those key institutions might become if the plan in section IV of this book succeeds in making America more Christian again.

What does a remade Christian America mean for the institution of government? In section I of this book we established that our founders built our republic upon biblical principles. That divine guidance included the proper role of government as outlined in 1 Timothy 2:1–2 (NIV): We are to pray "for kings and all those in authority, that we may live peaceful and quiet lives in all godliness and holiness."

Timothy writes that government's primary function is to provide a peaceful and quiet environment, which means it must protect the citizens at home and from foreign threats. That's consistent with America's Constitution.

Our Constitution is consistent with biblical principles and values. It limits and protects the citizens' rights identified by our founders in the Bill of Rights, the first 10 Amendments to our Constitution. The founding document necessarily limits government's interference in the citizens' personal affairs and restricts its expenditures, creating a three-part base—judicial, legislative, and executive.

Unfortunately, today, more than two centuries after our founding, our government is giant, intrusive, and often corrupt. It spends far more than it should. It regulates almost every aspect of our lives, an outcome far different than our founders ever intended. A future remade government discards the progressives' intent to make government god and replaces it with less-intrusive government that promotes the cornerstone of civilization, biblical marriage and family. Our judiciary interprets the Constitution; it doesn't make new laws. Our executive reduces regulation and offers a leaner bureaucracy closer to the founders' original intent.

What does a remade Christian America mean for the institution of religion? It respects religious pluralism and grants all citizens freedom of religion. For the Christian church, it means the majority Christian population insists that all aspects of our lives reflect biblical principles and values. It means that we fight for the truth in the public square.

America will be known as a Christian nation, mostly because the majority (65 percent) of our citizens self-identify as Christian. The same view applies to other countries, such as Middle East nations, which are properly known as Islamic nations, and predominantly Buddhist and Hindu nations in Asia are known for their majority faith. The difference in America, as our founders intended, is that people of all faiths are welcome and free to practice their religion. However, America is a Christian nation and other faith groups should expect the culture to reflect that foundation. They should not come here, as do some Muslims who intend to change our laws to reflect Sharia (Islamic) law.[645]

Founder John Adams said as much: "Our constitution was made for a moral and religious people. It is wholly inadequate to the government of any other."[646] Our Constitution and the government it spawned relies on a moral and religious people, and for our founders that meant Christianity.

It also means that in America, the people, the citizens, are "king." That's our form of republican government. When the majority of "We the people" are Christian, then it must be understood and expected that Christian principles and values are the guides for every aspect of our collective public lives.

What does a remade Christian America mean for the institution of education? It means both public and private education systems are receptive to Christian values. They reject progressive, anti-Christian dogma and focus on academic excellence.

It also means parents have education choices as to where to send their children. Empowering parents to take responsibility for their children's education is a necessary and Christian principle.

Former US Secretary of Education Rod Paige agrees. He said:

All things equal, I would prefer to have a child in a school that has a strong appreciation for the values of the Christian community, where a child is taught to have a strong faith.

Our children's education isn't just the business of parents and teachers and schools—educating our children is everyone's business. I encourage pastors and the church community to work closely with parents and students.[647]

Quality education should be modeled on religious values, Page said:

Religious values are wonderful values that we should embrace in our daily lives. I think it's even more important that we embrace those values in our homes. We would have a much calmer, compassionate society.[648]

Our future educational system makes certain our youth have a solid education to prepare them for a bright future. They are limited only by their natural talent. A proper education also includes instruction in civics, to make certain our offspring understand their responsibilities as citizens in this constitutional republic.

What does a remade Christian America mean for the institution of the family? It means biblical marriage is celebrated and encouraged. It also means that parents, especially fathers, take care of their children by making them a priority.

A Christian view of marriage, as demonstrated in the previous chapter, is the antidote to a stable, prosperous civilization. A Christian America rewards absolute monogamy within marriage and sanctions divorce, living together outside of marriage, and same-sex "marriage."

A Christian America holds parents accountable for their children and demands children obey their parents and honors them (Ephesians 6:1–3).

When families are lifted up, societies tend to be stable and prosperous.

What does a remade Christian America mean for the institution of the economy? It means businesses and corporations reflect Christian ethical principles in dealing with their customers. It means our economy is fueled by the Protestant work ethic and capitalism, two concepts that explain America's past prosperity that have a Christian foundation.

John Chamberlain, a noted twentieth-century British theologian, explained why adherence to Christian principles is responsible for our prosperity now and will be in the future as long as we reject the siren call of socialism. He wrote:

> "Thou shalt not steal" means that the Bible countenances private property—for if a thing is owned in the first place it can scarcely be stolen. "Thou shalt not covet" means that it is sinful to even contemplate the seizure of another man's goods—which is something Socialists, whether Christian or otherwise, have never managed to explain away. Furthermore, the prohibitions against false witness and adultery mean that contracts should be honored and double-dealing eschewed. As for the Commandment to "honor thy father and thy mother that thy days may be long," this implies that the family, not the State, is the basic continuing unit and constitutive element of society.[649]

In other words, Chamberlain is saying Christian character is the very foundation for fortune, and that's what it means to return to a principled Christian economy.

Conclusion

Is America about to stumble over the moral tipping point or might she step back from the cliff? This chapter offers some tough insights about that pregnant question.

I'm optimistic, hopeful that America can in fact become godly again.

It won't be easy, because at present, American civilization is at risk of following the footsteps of past failed civilizations.

I ended this chapter with an optimistic vision of what might be a renewed, Christian America in terms of the five critical national institutions.

The next and final chapter provides a battle plan (strategy) to change course and turn America away from the moral tipping point. Yes, that would be a historic first—but our alternatives are unacceptably bleak.

Of course, should the present moral turmoil tearing at the fabric of America really be a precursor of the rapidly coming end times, then any effort to revive America will be to no good end. However, for me and mine, I will pray that God isn't finished with America as yet, and this country will rise up in obedience to renew this land. I feel a mandate from God to work to that end, and so do millions of American "espresso cup" Christians.

CHAPTER FOURTEEN

Change Course to Avoid the Moral Tipping Point: A Plan to Renew Christian America

AMERICA IS LOSING its reliance on God and following the collision course of other past failed civilizations. Prosperity has blinded the United States to God's blessings and design. Now a committed Christian remnant faces a real choice: either renew their influence on America or watch as this country crosses the moral tipping point, never to return to its former greatness, and then fades into history to become absent at the prophetic end times.

Let's review the *Collision Course* journey to this juncture before considering a renewal plan.

The first section of *Collision Course* demonstrated that America was founded on Christian principles and values. Although our founders never intended to make these United States a theocracy, they did intend that she be influenced by a mostly godly people and no other.

The second section demonstrates that America's five defining institutions—government, family, education, religion, and economy—lost much of their original Christian influence over the history of this nation. Today, as a result, America is almost unrecognizable in terms of her original Christian persona. She is rapidly shedding any of the last vestiges of her former association with God, and our culture is becoming undeniably post-Christian, preparing for an un-ceremonial final rush toward the moral precipice.

Earlier, I profiled many of our moral failures as a post-Christian nation. A refresher is appropriate here before we consider a plan to reverse course.

America today promotes what our founders and God condemn: homosexual behavior and so-called gay marriage; the haggling over the price of preborn baby parts; an education system that endangers our children's minds and character with contempt for our faith and founders; a culture that promotes socialism—the forced redistribution of wealth robbing every one of the incentive to work; divides us by race, ethnicity, and religion; and we have become a self-centered, amoral people prophesied in the apocalyptic Scriptures.

I don't believe God ever intended for this formerly Christian nation to surrender to satanic, nihilistic forces of evil that sponsor the amoral behavior outlined above. Yet that's exactly what happened, and daily we see across our culture evidence of further moral compromise. For example, our cultural "arts" community displays perhaps the most obvious evidence of a public moral implosion.

Historically, a civilization's art reflects cultural health and is intended to "elevate," but many of today's American artists celebrate despicable portrayals of humanity that reflect crass evil, not promise. For example, and outrageously, the Orange County Museum of Art in Los Angeles, California, placed a huge sculpture of a dog outside, where periodically the creature urinates a yellow fluid on the facility's wall. That "art" is the product of a sick mind and sanctioned by an equally evil progressive political class.

Satan's evil influence is also evident in terms of what's acceptable speech. The same depraved "leaders" who support rancid "art" support the twisting of what's acceptable speech especially on our publicly funded university campuses. Too often our college students, some from Christian homes, come to reject true free speech, which their leftist, progressive professors promote as "hate speech." They reject the whole point of free speech as allowing opposing views, especially Christian views.

Many of those same leftists, Satan's proxies, poison race and ethnic relations as well. Even though America today is the least racist multiracial society in the world, progressive leaders divide us by poisoning the social well with hate-filled diatribes against whites, "white privilege, systemic racism," lies about race-based intentions and relations. There is also an uptick in anti-Semitic actions across the culture, which reflects a similar amoral trend and an indication of intolerance for people of faith.

Obviously, our culture is becoming a poisoned well, which mostly rejects the Christian wholesomeness our founders embedded in our governing documents and our defining institutions.

The third section of *Collision Course* identified the antichrist forces that strain much of the original Christian influence out of the fabric of this nation. These antichrists and their sick, progressive ideas are remaking America into a land that rejects virtually all Christian principles and values.

Consider what they did to the Boy Scouts of America. This outcome illustrates their morally bankrupt strategic aims as well as how Christian-influenced leaders surrendered the moral high ground.

The Boy Scouts of America once hosted the future moon walkers and presidents, America's best and brightest. That organization invested virtues and value of leadership into young lives, and then it changed course; it fell off the moral tipping point. Why? It turned its moral compass to chase the approval of amoral critics and quickly found it could never win.

In February 2020, the Boy Scouts filed for bankruptcy, a place many former Eagle Scouts like me long ago warned was the likely outcome of their compromising decisions. Moral decisions have consequences, and the Scouts compromised away goodness for evil.

The Scouts' demise has been slow and painful. For much of its 110-year history, the Scouts were a pillar of Christian principle. However, over the past few years, the organization battled waves of homosexual activists who pressured the group until 2013 it gave in to the lie that compromise would be their salvation. That's never the case when deep-seated moral issues are at stake.

What happened to the Scouts could easily happen to other mostly Christian-based institutions and organizations, even churches and church schools. The Scouts are a case study in moral compromise, a story whereby truth was surrendered for cowardly conformism. The leaders dropped their moral mandate to accommodate what they had long rejected, and inclusion became betrayal.

Leaders of other moral institutions such as Christian colleges and businesses face similar threats. Caving to amoral pressure to compromise is at their doorsteps as well. They either stand by the Bible's truth or compromise away the very spiritual soul of their charges. Every Christian organization in America needs to take to heart what the Apostle Paul wrote to the Galatian church (Galatians 1:6–7 and 10, NIV):

> I am astonished that you are so quickly deserting the one who called you to live in the grace of Christ and are turning to a different gospel—which is really no gospel at all. Evidently, some people are throwing you into confusion and are trying to pervert the gospel of Christ…am I now trying to win the approval of human beings or of God? … If I were still trying to please people, I would not be a servant of Christ.

Family Research Council president Tony Perkins opined about the Scout's moral collapse, which reflects the apostle's warning:

> The Boy Scouts wandered so far away from who they are that by the end of 2016, they even dropped their most defining characteristic: boys. In the end, it ruined them. That's the destiny of any Christian who takes the naïve view that the world can be placated. It can't. True love, 1 Corinthians 13:6 tells us, is truth.

It's being salt and light in a draining, hostile, unforgiving culture. "Come out from them and be separate," Paul urged, because he understands that in the end, it's not our sameness with the world that transforms people. It's our distinction of standing on truth in their midst. That may not be easy—but, as the Boy Scouts are finding out, it's a whole lot better than the alternative.[650]

I fear much of our culture is following the amoral footsteps left by the Scouts. America's culture is at grave risk, and time is running out before every institution collides headway over the moral tipping point.

The fourth and final section (chapters 12–14) of *Collision Course* identifies an emergent opposition movement to the radical direction Satan and his proxies are taking America. Perhaps, as some argue, we are enjoying a brief respite, thanks to the election of Donald Trump. He is the vessel that has stopped some of the moral hemorrhaging—and, in fact, many Christians now rally to the view that hope is back and America has a bright future.

Chapter 12 outlined the movement that marshalled forces to elect the Cyrus-like President Trump. But the question remains: Is America too far gone morally and thus can't recover its Christian heritage? (Cyrus the Great, 576–530 BC, was the patron and deliverer of the Jews. He is mentioned twenty-three times in the Bible. Cyrus, the King of Persia, ended the Babylonian captivity and was prompted by God to decree that the temple in Jerusalem be rebuilt and that Jews return to their land.)[651]

Chapter 13 explained that past civilizations rose and fell for many of the same challenges facing America today. Sociologists confirm from historical studies that, once empires are corrupted by prosperity and unfettered sexual behavior, they quickly weaken and then expire. They become lost causes, failures. But there is at least one exception to the historic record found in the biblical prophet Jonah's missionary work to Nineveh. God commissioned Jonah to warn the Assyrians to repent or face destruction. The Assyrians wisely heard God's prophet, humbled themselves, and repented—and God spared them. Might God spare America as well?

This final chapter in *Collision Course* offers a Jonah-like, last-minute plan to make America more Christian again. Otherwise, as established earlier, America could soon become irrelevant. It is rushing headlong into the bliss of self-destruction and likely the prophetic end times.

Against the Odds, Planning for a Christian Renewal of America

What follows is a lifesaver-like pathway (a renewal plan), washed in prayer and consistent with God's Word, a plan informed by the wise recommendations of multiple contemporary Christian leaders.

I hope by now you agree with me that America is in serious moral trouble. We need a radical change, a veering away from the current collision course before we collapse over the moral tipping point. We need God's grace, a plan, and godly leaders to pull off a Nineveh-like outcome for our contemporary amoral America.

A plan of such magnitude must begin with God. We should never try to plan something as significant as a national moral course-correction, which will be vigorously opposed by Satan and his proxies, without first bathing it in much prayer and making certain we are aligned with God's scriptural intentions. Of course, there is no guarantee at this late date that God will favor America as He did Nineveh and renew her before the growing momentum pushes her across the moral tipping point.

That said, we must begin by charting the path to renew America by heeding God's Word. We see in Psalm 37:5 (NKJV) an exhortation: "Commit your way to the Lord, trust also in him, and he shall bring it to pass." No doubt some of our founders understood that prescription and they embraced the promise and moved ahead in faith. They succeeded in establishing a new nation by trusting God; His blessing was the result.

Early twentieth-century Scottish Christian writer Oswald Chambers warns against making plans without God. He wrote:

God seems to have a delightful way of upsetting the plans we have made, when we have not taken him into account. We get ourselves into circumstances that were not chosen by God, and suddenly we realize that we have been making our plans without him—that we have not even considered him to be a vital, living factor in the planning of our lives [much less our nation]. And yet the only thing that will keep us from even the possibility of worrying is to bring God in as the greatest factor in all of our planning.[652]

Our national renewal planning begins with a commitment to a season of prayer, seeking God's direction for a plan to reverse the slide of amoral America. We must also remind ourselves what God has already communicated in his Word, the Bible.

Below are some of the Lord's Scriptures to inform our planning.

We are to carefully plan by counting the cost before beginning. Luke 14:28–33 (ESV) states:

For which of you, desiring to build a tower, does not first sit down and count the cost, whether he has enough to complete it? Otherwise, when he has laid a foundation and is not able to finish, all who see it begin to mock him, saying, "This man began to build and was not able to finish." Or what king, going out to encounter another king in war, will not sit down first and deliberate whether he is able with ten thousand to meet him who comes against him with twenty thousand?

What might be the cost of renewing an amoral America? Certainly, those with the most to lose—Satan and his proxies—will vigorously oppose any such plan. The cost for believers could be dear. We must understand that our comfort and resources are at risk should we move forward. Being heavenly minded and committed to following God's direction here on earth is critical in the difficult times ahead.

Leave the outcome of plans up to God. Proverbs 16:9 (ESV) states:

> The heart of man plans his way, but the Lord establishes his
> steps.

We will make our plans, informed by prayer and God's Word, but
the outcome must be trusted to God. That's no different than what
America's early Pilgrims and Puritans faced when they came to America
to find freedom of religion. Trusting God means obedience to Him,
waiting on His timing, and prayer.

Trust in the Lord and He will direct our paths. Proverbs 3:5–6
(ESV) states:

> Trust in the Lord with all your heart, and do not lean on your
> own understanding. In all your ways acknowledge him, and he
> will make straight your paths.

Likely we will come to the point in the execution of the plan when
doubt creeps into our minds. At that point we are not to lean on our
"own understanding." God's ways may not make sense. At that point,
when doubt clouds our thinking, we must "acknowledge him" and trust
that He will make our paths straight.

Be diligent in our planning. Proverbs 21:5 (ESV) states:

> The plans of the diligent lead surely to abundance, but everyone
> who is hasty comes only to poverty.

Diligence means to be steady, earnest, and energetic. We are to be
like Nehemiah, who rebuilt the walls of Jerusalem after returning from
the Babylonian exile. He refused to be distracted by his critics and diligently pressed forward against all odds. God provided, and Nehemiah
was successful (Nehemiah 1–7).[653]

Partnering with God means to count the cost, allow Him to direct the process, leave the outcome of the plan to Him, and be diligent, steadfast with all our effort bathed in prayer. Even that scriptural formula might not be God's ultimate intention, but that's what we are called to do.

MACA Strategy 101

When God is our planning partner, anything is possible. We seek His guidance through prayer and apply His Word as outlined above. Now that we are rightly partnered with God, we need to build the plan.

I know how the military plans big events (campaigns), which is a template for making America more Christian again. First, let's begin with a brief lesson on writing such a strategy. I'll call it the Make American Christian Again (MACA) Strategy 101.

My day job is writing military policy, doctrine, and strategy for the Pentagon, so forgive my obvious military-style of structuring a plan. However, I know the approach works (most of the time), therefore my proclivity is to apply that approach on a grand scale to provide direction on renewing America.

Working with God as our planning partner doesn't mean we sit idly on the sidelines, however. We must use the brains God gave us to work through the challenges of putting together a way ahead, a renewal plan that might work.

I'm reminded of what former British Prime Minister Winston Churchill said about the subject: "He who fails to plan is planning to fail."[654] Churchill's contemporary, former five-star general and US President Dwight D. Eisenhower, said on many occasions that "planning is useless…but the process itself is indispensable."[655]

Even though our initial plans will likely be flawed and "useless," the process of planning is "indispensable," whether in making war or in renewing a country. We learn much from the planning process, and as we execute that plan, we adjust our efforts to overcome the inevitable, often unanticipated, obstacles.

Keep in mind that strategic planning is a deliberate process that balances the ways, means, and risks to achieve the goals and ultimately attains the desired end state. The process is both an art and science of interpreting direction and guidance and translating that into executable activities to achieve the end state.

There are common elements to most strategic plans. Most have what the military calls the commander's intent or vision. It describes the way the leader envisions the effort. It communicates that vision to the team, and in our case, the committed Christian remnant, in an inspirational manner.

A possible vision for a renewed America was outlined in chapter 13 as it related to each of the five critical institutions. That vision is a view of what each institution ought to look like if America were made Christian again. That's where our plan is designed to take America.

Every plan has a mission statement that tends to be a short paragraph describing the organization's (nation's) essential tasks, purpose, and action containing the elements of who, what, when, where, and why.

For the purpose of this MACA Strategy 101, the mission statement might be:

> The United States re-Christianizes the five key institutions—government, religion, family, economy, and education—to renew them to reflect God's principles and values, an effort undertaken by the remnant of American Christians, led by her pastors, beginning immediately and bathed in constant prayer, beginning with the Christian church and expanding outward throughout the culture in order to renew this country before it falls off the moral tipping point.

Now that we've established the vision and the mission for MACA, we need to operationalize the strategy.

A MACA Strategy 101 uses both art and science under God's guidance that describes what we seek (the ends—re-Christianize the key institutions), we need to determine the operational approach (the ways), and how we intend to make America Christian again. We need to identify the resources such as time and people, and the means necessary to reach the end state (the MACA vision for the five institutions) while dealing with the risks (the inevitable resistance from Satan and his proxies.)

Our strategy requires goals that help drill down below the vision and mission to describe how we plan to achieve them. They can be thought of as milestones that are often sequenced over time and lead ultimately to the satisfaction of parts that build ultimately to realize the vision.

Finally, there is an action plan to tackle each goal. Against each goal, resources are committed, to include time. The plan is executed and constantly monitored for progress and adjusted as circumstances warrant.

The Warriors and the Goals That Lead to MACA

I'm reminded as noted earlier that American statesman Daniel Webster said: "Whatever makes men good Christians makes them good citizens." That's an important guide when writing our MACA Strategy 101 to help realize the vision in chapter 13.[656]

It is pretty clear to me that Christian America's first priority must be to correct the wayward church—make good Christians, who then become good citizens. We must begin with renewal as individual Christians (repentance as did the Ninevites); then our pastors need to understand and begin to fulfill their critical role; and finally, more broadly, "We the people," need to reassert our influence on America's key institutions.

For this effort, I consulted some mature, godly men—leaders of America's Christian remnant. It doesn't take a lot of people for the fight ahead, just a dedicated core to begin renewal. I'll call this core a modern version of Gideon's army.

Therefore, before exploring the specifics of the MACA Strategy 101, please recall the biblical account of how God called a literal handful of dedicated—totally committed—men from among tens of thousands to renew the fallen nation of Israel. The parallels with contemporary America are stark and should be encouraging when we consider that partnering with God can bring renewal to the country.

The story of Gideon in Judges 6–7 shows the power of God to turn the nation of Israel from doing evil. After coming to the Promised Land, the nation of Israel did evil in the sight of the Lord by worshiping Baal. As a result, the Lord left them to suffer at the hands of the Midianites. In time, the Lord called Gideon, a simple man, to "save Israel out of Midian's hand" (Judges 6:14, NIV).

Gideon's first task was to free the Israelites from their service to Baal and Asherah, the two idols most frequently worshiped. Obediently, Gideon and ten other men tore down the image of Baal, cut in pieces the wooden image of Asherah, and destroyed the altar, then set the rubble on fire.

Once the house of Israel was cleansed of the evil, God called on Gideon to destroy the Midianites. Yet, Gideon doubted God's call, so he tested the Lord's command using the well-known fleece of wool. Once convinced of God's direction, Gideon marshalled the vast Israeli army. But:

> The Lord said to Gideon, "You have too many men. I cannot deliver Midian into their hands, or Israel would boast against me, 'My own strength has saved me.' Now announce to the army, 'Anyone who trembles with fear may turn back and leave Mount Gilead.'" So, twenty-two thousand men left, while ten thousand remained. (Judges 7:2–3, NIV)

The final winnowing of the Gideon's army came at the water's edge. God said, "Separate those who lap the water with their tongues as a dog laps from those who kneel down to drink" (Judges 7:5, NIV). That left only three hundred from among tens of thousands.

Gideon's plan did not require a large army, however. It only needed a few careful, bold men who would perform exactly as ordered—the remnant.

Not surprisingly, Gideon's plan made no earthly sense. He issued his "army" strange weapons: a lamp, a pitcher, and a trumpet. Gideon formed the men into three companies, which he quietly led through the darkness to positions surrounding the sleeping camp of the Midianites.

In the predawn darkness, Gideon shouted: "The sword of the Lord and of Gideon." At that command, Gideon's three hundred each broke their pitchers, exposing the light from within in every direction. They shouted and blew their trumpets. The noise and light surrounding the camp roused the Midianites, who were filled with sudden terror. They trampled each other to death, fleeing before the Israelites.

The Israelites (God) soundly defeated the Midianites, who never again warred on the tribes of Israel. After that victory, the Israelites wanted to make Gideon king. But Gideon said: "I will not rule over you, nor will my son rule over you. The LORD will rule over you" (Judges 8:22, NIV).

The illustration should be clear. God called Gideon to lead Israel away from their sin of worshiping idols. Then God gave Israel victory, albeit in a bizarre fashion, over their enemies through a handful of faithful warriors. That's the essence of the MACA Strategy 101 that follows.

Begin with Renewal of the Church

God's people must be obedient and conform to His direction before they are useful in MACA, much like God used Gideon to turn Israel away from doing evil, worshiping idols. Unfortunately, the contemporary Christian church is much like ancient Israel, having bowed to evil (modern idols). It has lost much of its saltiness and has abandoned God.

Mr. David Barton is the founder of the previously mentioned

WallBuilders, a Texas-based organization dedicated to presenting America's forgotten history with an emphasis on the moral, religious, and constitutional foundation on which America was built. He reminded me of an unfortunate fact about the contemporary American Christian church. "There is no difference between Christians and non-Christians today in terms of behavior," Mr. Barton said. Evidently, Christians have lost their saltiness. "In fact," Mr. Barton explained, "some of the highest divorce rates are among Christians and the lowest among atheists, and concerning abortions and Christians, statistics show that each year 65 percent of abortions are performed on professing Christians, two hundred thousand abortions each year are performed on born-again Christians, and 76 percent of Protestants do not want to see abortion on demand ended."[657]

Mr. Barton's statement reminded me of the Scripture attributed to Jesus. Here the Lord said to believers, "You are the salt of the earth. But if the salt loses its saltiness, how can it be made salty again?" (Matthew 5:13, NIV).

Renewal—regaining the saltiness—is in order for America's Christianity, and it must begin with the wayward church!

Renewal begins by going back to the basics. Dr. Stu Weber, a best-selling author and pastor for forty years, told me that genuine renewal requires a "return to the *fundamentals* of scripture and our Constitution." He illustrated that perspective with a football story.[658]

In July 1961, the Green Bay Packers football team was assembled for the first day of training camp. The prior season was disappointing; it ended with a last-second loss for the National Football League championship to the Philadelphia Eagles.

The Green Bay players had the entire off-season to think about that loss, and now, the first day of training camp was a fresh start. They were eager to move on and to win a championship.

Coach Vince Lombardi had a different idea, however. Lombardi walked into the locker room that summer morning in 1961. He held in the air above his head a pigskin and announced: "Gentlemen, this is a football."

The coach took nothing for granted. He began a Packer tradition of starting from scratch each season. He assumed his players were blank slates and forgot everything they ever knew about football. What followed was Lombardi's methodical coverage of the fundamentals—back to the basics. The formula worked. Six months later, the Packers beat the New York Giants 37-0 to win the NFL Championship.

America's Christian church needs to go back to the basics as well. It is pretty obvious that a vast swath of the church has forgotten the fundamentals of the faith. They desperately need a journey back to righteousness.

Getting back to the basics also means we as American citizens need to dust off the Declaration of Independence, the Constitution, and our other founding documents. We need to understand our obligation as citizens as well and begin to act accordingly.

My pastor, Victor Stanley, provided a great starting point for our back-to-the-basics Christian retraining strategy. He reminded me of 2 Chronicles 7:14 (NIV), God's Word that called the nation Israel (read "America") back to righteousness, a call for renewal.

If my people, who are called by my name, will humble themselves and pray and seek my face and turn from their wicked ways, then I will hear from heaven, and I will forgive their sin and will heal their land.

This prescription for calling Israel back to righteousness is a template for calling America's Christian remnant to the same outcome: godliness and obedience. Consider seven goals that could well become the back-to-the-basics, decisive steps toward renewal of the church and making America more Christian again.

Goal #1: My people will become water-walkers instead of wave-gazers.

Let me explain. This idea was inspired by Pastor Carl Gallops' sermon delivered at his church, Hickory Hammock Baptist Church, in Milton, Florida, on January 26, 2020.

Pastor Gallops used Matthew 14:22–33 (NIV) for his sermon Scripture. You will recall that passage finds the disciples aboard a ship sailing at night across the Sea of Galilee when, suddenly, a storm comes up and they fear for their lives. As the swell grows, they see the Lord walking on water toward the ship. Jesus calls out to His disciples not to be afraid.

The impetuous Peter responds to the Lord's words: "Lord, if it's you, tell me to come to you on the water." The Lord responds, "Come." Then Peter steps out onto the open sea and begins walking on the water toward Jesus. However, "when he [Peter] saw the wind, he was afraid and, beginning to sink, cried out, 'Lord, save me!" Why is he sinking? He has taken his eyes off the Lord. "Immediately Jesus reached out his hand and caught him. 'You of little faith,' he said, 'Why did you doubt?'"

Christians today are like Peter. They tend to focus on the waves and the darkness, not on the Lord. We are too ready to take our eyes off Jesus and look at our troubles, challenges. Then we wonder why things have gone so wrong.

Pastor Gallops reminded me that the account of Peter's water-walking challenge is captured in one of my favorite contemporary Christian songs, "Oceans," by Hillsong United.[659] Read a few excerpts of that song below and reflect on your personal obedience to the Lord. It should remind us to fix our eyes on Christ when we face the storms of life.

> You call me out upon the waters
> The great unknown where feet may fail
> And there I find You in the mystery
> In oceans deep my faith will stand
> And I will call upon Your Name

And keep my eyes above the waves
When oceans rise
My soul will rest in Your embrace
For I am Yours and You are mine.

"Oceans" then repeats a stanza six times beginning with "Spirit lead me where my trust is without borders." The song concludes:

I will call upon Your Name
Keep my eyes above the waves
My soul will rest in Your embrace
I am Yours and You are mine."

That's reassuring to the Christian. The message is clear. We must learn to walk on the water of life's challenges with our eyes firmly fixed on the Savior. This goal is about our faith centered on Christ, an important step to renewing us individually and as the Body of Christ.

Mr. Barton offered similar advice that is key to renewal: Ingest God's Word. He said that only 14 percent of Christians read the Bible on a daily basis. "We can't live out our faith unless we know it and the Bible instructs Christians in their faith."[660]

Part of living for Christ is committing His Word in our hearts as well. Mr. Barton said, "Christians need to ingest the content of the word of God by memorizing scriptures." He continued, "We must become active in our faith by sharing it with others. That makes our faith strong."

This formula—making God's Word a priority in our lives and resting in his embrace—is how to become a water-walker for Jesus.

Goal #2: My people, especially Christian men, will focus on their families; then America will begin to heal morally.
Lieutenant General William Gerald "Jerry" Boykin, US Army retired, and executive vice president for the Family Research Council, said that "Men are the key to the restoration of America." They are key because

when men act responsibly regarding their wives and children, their God-given roles, they "restore the families and ultimately the family is the foundation of society."[661]

Restoring the family is critical to the restoration of the nation, Boykin said. Science long ago found that when men are distracted, their families suffer. The general called out the result of the absence of the father and husband in the African-American family: 70 percent of black families don't have the biological father in the home, which results in sad outcomes for children, such as very high out-of-wedlock births, more crime, poor academic performance, and more often than not living in poverty.

Men, especially those who claim Christ, must return to their families both physically and mentally. Those who abandoned their children ought to renew those bonds. Perhaps worse, many men who are with their families physically are too often distracted by the world. Many are hooked on pornography, and others spend their free time on computer games. Yet still others engage in time-consuming, outside-of-the-home activities, you name it. Meanwhile, wives and children suffer when fathers and husbands are absent, which leads to a wide assortment of problems for the children, who are starved for their father's attention, and for the wives, who are tempted to wander from their marriage vows.

Pastor Weber also called out the "importance of reinvesting in father accountability." He told me about the "unique place for male leadership in the home." He reminded me that "when God starts anything, he starts with a man." Thus, restoring the American family must start with men.[662]

Back in the 1980s, Pastor Weber delivered a series of messages to his congregation about the family. His first message in the series was about the man, husband, and father. "There was a holy hush, a palpable spiritual impact, at the end of that message," the pastor explained. So, he gave a second message on manhood the following Sunday. Again, a palpable impact occurred that suggested more was needed. So, near the conclusion of that second message, he spontaneously announced that the following Saturday morning he would be happy to meet with any who had questions about biblical masculinity. That Saturday morning, a time when most men in Oregon intensely avoid meetings at any cost and much prefer "doing their own thing," well over two hundred men showed up, full of questions! Ever since then, for several decades now, that church has hosted a weekly ministry to men intended to provide mutual encouragement and biblical instruction in how to be better men, better husbands, and better fathers. You see, explained Pastor Weber, "When men get it right, everyone wins, especially women and children." Biblical manhood is essential to cultural renewal.

Once American Christian men give their wives and children the right type of attention they deserve, then America will begin to heal morally—a critical part of renewal.

Goal #3: My people will focus on their neighbor more than themselves; then they will become right with God and move America in a godly direction.

When we focus on others more than ourselves, much like our founders did, then there is hope for the future of America.

Earlier in *Collision Course*, I reminded you of the two greatest commandments:

> Jesus said, "Love the Lord your God with all your heart, with all your soul, and with all your mind. This is the greatest and most important commandment. The second is like it: Love your neighbor as yourself. All the Law and the Prophets depend on these two commandments." (Matthew 22: 37–40, NIV)

Our character is exposed by the focal point of our attention. Typically, Americans are self-absorbed, which is not consistent with the second commandment, to "love your neighbor as yourself." Thus, the goal for renewing requires believers to think more about God and others and less about themselves.

That reminds me of the ancient Hebrew King Hezekiah, who acted much like many contemporary Christian Americans. He was so self-absorbed that he ultimately cost the Jewish nation of Judah its total destruction and exile.

Hezekiah was a faithful king who knew of God's past acts and His involvement in the lives of the Hebrew people. The Bible describes the king as one who did "what was good and right and faithful before the Lord his God" (2 Chronicles 31:2, NIV).

Then Hezekiah acted out of character when he showed his adversary, the Babylonians, the wealth of Judah and its arsenal. The prophet Isaiah rebuked Hezekiah for this act and prophesied that all the king had shown the Babylonians would be taken to Babylon—and that included Hezekiah's own descendants. The Book of Daniel is evidence of the fulfillment of that prophecy.

Evidently, Hezekiah's good-natured exhibition of Judah's wealth and arms to the ambassadors of the Babylonian king was a serious error in judgment. He was duped by the ambassadors' flattery. One Bible commentary addressed the implications of the king's failed judgment: "Even political sharp-sightedness might have foreseen that some such disastrous consequences would follow Hezekiah's imprudent course."[663]

Hezekiah's conduct was the result of mixed motives. He was prideful with the display; as a result, surrendered to the flattery of the Babylonians. He also demonstrated a sense of self-sufficiency, which made him set a higher value on himself and his earthly wealth than on the God who blessed him.

Fortunately for early America, our founders were not prideful like King Hezekiah. Those early American leaders sacrificed all—their wealth, freedom, and lives—to give "We the people" our freedoms by waging a campaign to win freedom from the tyrannical British monarch. They evidently thought of their children and grandchildren when making those early, critical decisions rather than only of their personal comfort.

That's a lesson, a goal for us today. Christians need to think more about their legacy and their offspring than about their own well-being and comfort. What are we leaving for our children? Are we leaving them with an impossible debt? Are we leaving them with an anti-Christian government educational system, amorally redefined marriage, and "families" that are totally alienated from the Bible?

We must become our brothers' keepers and quit being so self-absorbed like Hezekiah.

Goal #4: My people will understand the times; then they will fearlessly confront the evil within our culture.

We must be fearless in this antichrist culture, a mandate from the Lord, and then we must confront pervasive evil to protect the innocent.

Pastor Weber said, "If repetition is any indicator of importance, then right up there with the greatest commandment and the second like it, the third most common command to Christians from Jesus' lips is one form or another of 'Don't fear! …quit worrying! …Don't be anxious!'" In other words, fear God and nothing or no one else.[664]

Jesus deals with the topic of fear, as recorded in the Gospels. For example, in Luke 12 (ESV), Jesus reassured and encouraged His followers. "I tell you, my friends, do not fear those who kill the body, and after that can do nothing more" (verse 4). "Therefore, I tell you, not to worry about your life" (verse 22). Finally, He lovingly said, "Do not be afraid, little flock, for it is your father's good pleasure to give you the kingdom" (verse 32).

Fear is not becoming of the Christian. Discard fear, become fearless, and confront the evil within our culture, remembering that we are accountable to God for our actions, yet our most precious possession—our children—are in many instances thrown to the wolves—our evil culture.

Our godless culture puts a guilt trip on we Christians and our children by accusing us of being intolerant. The so-called cultural elite push a radical, anti-Christian sexual agenda and claim that even Jesus loves sexually perverse people. Of course, Jesus loves the sinner, but not the sin.

When we compromise on clear biblical principles and values just to satisfy our spiritual adversaries, we stiff-arm God and compromise the world we will leave to our next generation.

Don't be a fool. Jesus said in the beginning that mankind was made up of only male and female. Satan and his proxies tell us that if we are really Christians, then we would embrace alternative sexual behavior—homosexuality, transgender identity, and more. They claim Jesus would do the same. Not true.

God's Word is clear about sexual behavior. He is also clear about our obligation to train children in the way they ought to go, and we must protect our young from the perverted teachings of our lost culture.

That reminds me of something Jesus said about protecting the children:

> If anyone causes one of these little ones—those who believe in me—to stumble, it would be better for them to have a large millstone hung around their neck and to be drowned in the depths of the sea. (Matthew 18:6, NIV)[665]

I understand this to apply to all those with authority over children. Jesus will not tolerate abuse of children, and that includes psychological and moral abuse by knowingly placing them into situations that challenge their souls with evil influences beyond their ability to resist. Many secular government schools expose them to evil media and put them under the charge of inscrutable people.

Righteous people will confront the evil culture by taking special care of the next generation. That's something Mr. David Barton is doing through a program that helps eighteen- to twenty-five-year-olds "to discover the truth about our nation, our past, and how to lead it into the future."[666]

WallBuilders works with Mercury One, a humanitarian and educational institution, to host a two-week summer program of "nonstop projects, research, lectures, and outings for people who want to know the truth about America's history, how to identify the philosophies and ideologies that shaped our laws and original documents, and methods of effective leadership in today's culture."

Mr. Barton said this program empowers young adults to face the evil world. Equipping the next generation with a Christian worldview is our first obligation as parents, and programs such as what Mr. Barton offers ideally helps young adults to prepare to face the evil world.

Evidently, according to a Barna study, the American Worldview Inventory 2020, very few (21 percent) of those attending evangelical Protestant churches have a biblical worldview, as compared to one-sixth of those attending charismatic or Pentecostals churches (16 percent). Sadly, the number of American adults holding a biblical worldview has declined by 50 percent over the past quarter century, according to Barna, and regarding the next generation, a mere 2 percent of those eighteen to twenty-nine years old possess a biblical worldview today.[667]

Christians must fearlessly confront evil. We must protect the innocent and at the same time prepare the next generation to stand in the gap.

Goal #5: My people will raise up Christian leaders who are Nathanlike to call the "king" to account and teach him a righteous path; then the nation will move toward righteousness.

America was founded not as a monarchy, which was the practice of mankind across the world until the time of America's founding. Our Constitution is unique because it grants the citizens the obligation to have the final say through their vote as to what and how government functions. So, "We the people" are ultimately in charge in these United States, even though at present many have abandoned that responsibility.

"We the people" are essentially "king," as our Constitution established. Unfortunately, the "king" continues to make some pretty bad decisions, especially over the past couple of decades. The "king" has stepped back and allowed radical-thinking, evil people (Satan's proxies) to guide this country waywardly, down an amoral path. This is especially distressing, given that the "king" remains three-fourths (76 percent) Christian among all North Americans, according to the Pew Research Center.[668]

There is a scriptural parallel to our present situation. Many readers will recall the biblical account of King David and his prophet counselor, Nathan. Even though God said David was a man "after His own heart" (1 Samuel 13:14), still, the young king made some horrendous errors in judgment. On a number of occasions, the prophet came to the king to set him straight. Nathan confronted King David with his sin and called on him to repent and to make it right.

The best-known encounter is in 2 Samuel 12:5–9 (NIV), the account of David's adulterous relationship with Bathsheba. Nathan illustrates David's sin with a story about a rich man taking a poor man's lone lamb. King David, according to the Scripture:

> …burned with anger against the man and said to Nathan, "As surely as the Lord lives, the man who did this must die!" Nathan responds, "You are that man! This is what the Lord, the God of Israel, says: 'I anointed you king over Israel, and I delivered you from the hand of Saul'…. Why did you despise the word of the Lord by doing what is evil in his eyes?… You struck down Uriah the Hittite with the sword and took his wife [Bathsheba] to be your own."

David realized his guilt and said to Nathan, "I have sinned against the Lord" (2 Samuel 12:13, NIV).

Today, as America has slipped deeply into sin and farther away from her Christian roots, it is well past time for the Nathans of this country to confront the "king" by calling out his sin, insist upon repentance, and make things right with God.

The Nathans of today are Christian pastors who too frequently fail to call out sin committed by the "king." Keep in mind the "king" sits in the pastors' pews every Sunday, and too few of our pastors use that

God-given opportunity to confront us with our sin. More often than not, they call out personal infractions if at all, and most ignore the moral blight across our nation—government's amoral behavior.

The "king" has for a long time permitted rank sin to permeate this formerly Christian nation. The Nathans of this land have allowed Satan and his proxies to usurp the "king" to redefine the family and marriage; call killing babies a "woman's choice"; pretend that God embraces homosexuality and condones the redistribution of wealth; pretends removing prayer from schools is okay; and much more. The "king" fails our founders and our God. America's Nathans consistently fail the "king."

There is a precedent for Nathan-like pastor leaders in America's history.

General Jerry Boykin called my attention to the Black Robed Regiment of pastors who played a critical role in our colonial march to independence. He said, "Pastors are supposed to be spiritual warriors and that includes within the culture. And that hasn't changed since the creation of this nation."[669] Boykin continued:

> It was the Black Robed Regiment that preached the message of biblical separation from the British crown. We would still be a British colony if not for the Black Robed pastors who encouraged separation from the crown. Today's pastors need to follow in the tradition established by the Black Robed Regiment...to be bold enough to preach unpopular messages. The people in the pews must hear the biblical truth.

The Black Robed Regiment was a courageous and patriotic group of colonial-era clergy whom the British blamed for American independence. Those clergymen spoke boldly concerning the issues of the day, wearing their black clerical robes while in the pulpit; they preached the Word of God without fear or favor. They told the "king" what and whom they should elect, because they understood that to have a good government, the people must first be good citizens.

That assessment is borne out by our history.

Author Alice Baldwin wrote in *The New England Clergy and the American Revolution*, "There is not a right asserted in the Declaration of Independence which had not been discussed by the New England clergy before 1763."[670]

Our founders agreed with the British authorities and Ms. Baldwin that the American pulpit was largely responsible for American independence and government. John Adams said that "the pulpits have thundered,"[671] and he identified several ministers as being among the "characters the most conspicuous, the most ardent, and influential" that awakened "a revival of American principles and feelings" that led to American independence.[672]

Founder John Adams also warned about the critical role the Christian clergy must play in the new American republic where the people are "king." Specifically, Adams wrote:

> It is the duty of the clergy to accommodate their discourses to the times, to preach against such sins as are most prevalent, and recommend such virtues as are most wanted.... If exorbitant ambition and venality are predominant, ought they not to warn their hearers against those vices? If public spirit is much wanted, should they not inculcate this great virtue? If the rights and duties of Christian magistrates and subjects are disputed, should they not explain them, show their nature, ends, limitations, and restrictions, how much soever it may move the gall of Massachusetts.[673]

Many publications over the history of this nation confirm the Christian pastors' influence on early America.[674] Consider:

- The 1833 *American Quarterly Register* wrote: "As a body of men, the clergy were pre-eminent in their attachment to liberty. The pulpits of the land rang with the notes of freedom."[675]

- The 1856 British periodical, *Bibliotheca Sacra*, stated: "If Christian ministers had not preached and prayed, there might have been no revolution as yet—or had it broken out, it might have been crushed."[676]
- American historian B. F. Morris wrote in 1864: "The ministers of the Revolution were, like their Puritan predecessors, bold and fearless in the cause of their country. No class of men contributed more to carry forward the Revolution and to achieve our independence than did the ministers.... [B]y their prayers, patriotic sermons, and services [they] rendered the highest assistance to the civil government, the army, and the country."[677]
- American historian Clinton Rossiter wrote in 1953: "Had ministers been the only spokesman of the rebellion—had Jefferson, the Adamses, and [James] Otis never appeared in print—the political thought of the Revolution would have followed almost exactly the same line.... In the sermons of the patriot ministers...we find expressed every possibly refinement of the reigning political faith."[678]

What's clear from these citations is that colonial American clergy were faithful exponents of the fullness of God's Word to the "king" in the pews and weren't bowed by the offending British Crown. They led the charge to proclaim liberty and oppose tyranny, and stood firm against any encroachments on God-given rights and freedoms.

Today's pastors need to follow in the tradition set by the Black Robe Regiment, said General Boykin. "They must be bold enough to preach unpopular messages [because]...the people in the pews [the "king"] must hear the biblical truth."

Pastor Weber agrees with General Boykin. He believes the men "behind the pulpit must understand the power." They need to know "the book [Bible] and know it well." Then he said today is the "time to stand up with courage and conviction.... They need to preach the *full* counsel of God" [which means what Christ commanded to be taught, not what pleases the "king's" ears].[679]

Another lesson from our rich history is that moral issues that involve the political arena are also the domain of the church. Unfortunately, too many contemporary pastors say it is wrong to call out government policy from the pulpit because mixing politics and religion is wrong. But when moral issues are at stake, that's a necessity—even if it means loss of so-called tax-exempt status or jail for protesters, such as during the 1960s when Dr. Martin Luther King called for peaceful protests to focus attention on the travesty of segregation.

President Abraham Lincoln dealt with the same hypocrisy when dealing with the sinful scourge of slavery. First, he spoke to political crowds where he mentioned the moral scourge of slavery, but those audiences complained that he shouldn't mix politics and religion. Then Lincoln spoke in churches, and the "king" in the pews complained that he was mixing Christianity with politics.

Stop! Any government policy that has moral implications is the domain of the Christian pastor. It is past time pastors take their heads out of the sand, understand they are Nathans, put on their Black Robes, call out the "king's" sin, and insist he do the righteous thing for God and this country.

Goal #6: My people will learn to distinguish between their Christian convictions and their political affiliation; instead, they will focus on the moral issues.

Victor Stanley, my pastor, observed that the 2016 election seemed to prove that evangelicals still have significant influence in America. However, he said, "I am disturbed by the current state of evangelicalism." He indicates that "evangelicalism" has been redefined. "Evangelical" used to mean an adherence to Christian orthodoxy, a belief in the Bible as the infallible Word of God. However, as Pastor Stanley observed, "Now evangelicalism seems to have been redefined as a social stance, over creedal adherence." He continued, "It is defined more as a political persuasion, over Christian practice."[680]

I agree with my pastor. I've been a conservative in my political beliefs most of my adult life. Most recently I've self-identified as a Republican because that party tends to support pro-life and pro-family policies. Further, I wrestle with the question: How can a Bible-believing Christian support a political candidate or party that clearly embraces what God calls evil?

I've now considered my political affiliation and decided to allow my Christian convictions to influence my moral decisions rather than my conservative political views. That means when my political affiliation clashes with my biblical convictions, my Christianity will trump all others.

The entire issue of politics and church was an issue extensively explored by Christian pollster George Barna. In 2015, Barna evaluated the potential role of the Christian church in the 2016 election. He surveyed "spiritually active Christians who are politically conservative or moderate." Specifically, he sought to understand "what role Christian churches have played in recent elections, what issues pastors are most likely to consider important in the 2016 election, and what kind of issue-related teaching Christians want from their churches."[681]

Barna's findings are shocking. Only one in ten "spiritually active Christians" surveyed said their church has been "very involved in the election process in the last two voting cycles," even with critical moral issues at stake. Further, just one in five "spiritually active Christians" said their church "has provided a lot of information about what the Bible teaches related to current issues during recent election cycles." Finally, Christian conservatives are hungry for direction. They "want their church to get in the game: six out of ten (58 percent) said they want their church to be more involved in the election process."[682]

The Barna study said a majority of survey respondents stated it is "extremely important" for their pastor to preach or teach about the following issues: abortion (71 percent), religious persecution (61 percent), sexual identity (56 percent), Israel (54 percent), poverty (54 percent), and cultural restoration (53 percent).[683]

I believe that's a tough goal for some Christian conservatives, especially those I call PACs (Patriotic American Christians). However, if we are to truly renew America, make her Christian again, our faith in Christ must always take first place in our decisions individually and for this nation.

Goal #7: My people will default to Jesus rather than to Washington.
Dr. Michael Heiser, an Old Testament scholar, Christian author, and executive director of the School of Ministry at Celebration Church in Jacksonville, Florida, told me: "Christians must stop depending on the state and become part of the Great Commission and live a life like Jesus." That's the way to renew the American Christian church.[684]

Dr. Heiser explained that we can legislate behavior through punishment, but people will tend "to improvise ways to defy, disobey or undermine the law." He continued:

> We really need to change hearts. People have hard hearts and want autonomy. It's more effective if we convince people of the rightness of behavior by telling them how self-destructive their behavior is.

However, he admitted, "People need to learn the hard way."[685]

He used the scriptural story of Jesus meeting the woman at the well to illustrate his point. The story found in John 4:1–40 illustrates Jesus' character and sets an example for us to follow. Specifically, it demonstrates that Jesus is a loving and accepting God, no matter the circumstances. We need to be like Jesus.

The story begins as Jesus and His disciples travel through Samaria on their way to Galilee. Jesus stops by Jacob's well while His disciples go to a nearby village to buy food. At noon, the hottest part of the day, a Samaritan woman comes to draw water at the well.

Jesus speaks with the woman, an act that breaks Jewish custom because she is a woman, a Samaritan, and He asks her for water served from a jar that is ceremonially unclean. Jesus doesn't mention these issues, but shocks the woman by offering her "living water" to quench her thirst forever.

Then Jesus reveals that He knows her sin: she's had five husbands and is living with a man who is not her husband. That statement catches her attention and demonstrates, according to Dr. Heiser, that Jesus cares for her in spite of her sin.

The lesson from the Scripture is we need to look past the sin to the sinner, a lost soul who needs a Savior, the "living water." Jesus speaks the truth about her sin but demonstrates compassion.

The application for the believer today should be obvious. Rather than push "our neighbor"—the sinner—into the arms of the "state" to deal with his or her problem, we need to be like Jesus by speaking the truth in compassion and simply being there. Our aim is to "break people to resistance to the gospel," Dr. Heiser said.

The math demonstrates that being Jesus-like will go a long way toward renewing America. Dr. Heiser explained that Jesus followers need each year to become a friend to a lost soul who has problems. "Be in their corner...be a constant reminder that this 'nutty' Christian cares for them," Heiser said. Then he explained, "The spirit of God will use that relationship to break people to resistance to the gospel." Should we do this, the current remnant of up to 70 million American Christian evangelicals can quickly grow to become the vast majority in a few short years. Spiritual multiplication is what the Great Commission is all about and the only way to renew America, explained Heiser.

As we make progress regarding these seven goals, then and only then will America's Christian remnant be prepared to take on the task of renewing the rest of the nation—the five key institutions.

Making America's Institutions Christian Again

Earlier, I quoted James Adams as stating that our form of government is only suited for a moral and religious people. That is why the first step of renewal demands that the Christian "king" put his house in order. Only then can the "king" do the necessary renovation of the institutions that define this country.

Let me be clear at the outset of this section, which is focused on how to make America's key institutions Christian again. I do not favor establishing a theocracy. Rather, I favor what our founders gave us: a form of government that works well when fair-minded people are elected to office and strict constitutionalists are appointed to the judiciary. More broadly, I seek a culture that is accepting, confirming to Christians and their biblical principles and values.

What follows are recommendations the "king" can insist his government embrace to make it more welcoming to Christians.

Goal #8: Make America's government more Christian-favoring again. The "king" must place faithful, obedient Christians into positions of government. Those same persons will advance and put into law policies that are consistent with Christian principles and values. That's the bottom line.

Dr. Heiser called on Christians to "help government do what it is supposed to do…[which is] to protect citizens from evil and get out of the way by not impeding Christians from doing good." Christians in government must advance individual liberty, fairness, and justice, the "first principles," explained Heiser.

America's government is in a precarious state, according to Gary Bauer, the president of American Values, a nonprofit organization. Mr. Bauer warns that "America's reservoir of goodness is running low" and when it "runs dry people will get a real jolt." At that point, there "will be no restraint on the radical left." Before America reaches that place, we must place godly people in positions of authority. The "king" has the authority and responsibility to do so, and must act quickly.

Who are those good, Christian people? They are you and me, all of us. Put aside your preferences and seek God's direction on whether He wants to enlist you to a responsible government position. Only if smart, dedicated Christian men and women willingly heed the call to join the political fray for Christ's sake will government change.

Mr. Bauer called my attention to the second paragraph in our Declaration of Independence. That series of sentences is a sobering reminder of where our founders were psychologically leading up to our Revolution. It should be a reminder that, should in the future we face similar situations, then we, the "king," must act once again. What was their situation?

The Declaration states "governments are instituted among men, deriving their just powers from the consent of the governed [the "king"], that whenever any form of government becomes destructive of these ends, it is the right of the people to alter or to abolish it, and to institute new government." That plainly means we the "king" may abolish government when it becomes destructive.

The Declaration continues to caution us to be prudent about taking such a step. We must not change our government "for light and transient causes." However, there may come a time "when a long train of abuses and usurpations, pursuing invariably the same object evinces a design to reduce them under absolute despotism, it is their right, it is their duty, to throw off such government, and to provide new guards for their future security."

Yes, I'm calling for a revolution, starting with Christian voters, to replace Satan's proxies with men and women of integrity, Christian principles, and values to "throw off such [a corrupted] government." We must prayerfully consider whether we've reached that point and do so peacefully. I'm not advocating violence or a civil war, but renewal by replacing the evil in government with God's righteous representatives.

That view is similar to what Dr. Stu Weber said: "I will obey human government so long as government does not forbid what God commands or commands what God forbids." He continued, "If I'm reading the Bible correctly, both Scripture and Jesus Himself explicitly command Christian believers to actively participate in the politics and policies of a constitutional republic such as ours."

Pastor Weber explained by referring to multiple Scriptures. Follow his logic here.

1. In Revelation 21:23–26 (ASV), **God expresses an eternal interest in nations.** In fact, He goes so far as to state that He will see to it that earthly leaders will *"bring the glory and honor of the nations into"* the eternal holy city, the heavenly Jerusalem.

2. In Acts 17:26 (ASV), **God, who sanctioned human government in the first place,** "made of one every nation of men to dwell on all the face of the earth, having determined their appointed seasons, and the bounds of their habitation." God, in His sheer sovereignty, determined the times and places we should live, and by that sovereignty, He placed us here and now, in this nation [these United States] in this day.

3. In Jeremiah 29:7 (NASB), **God commanded His people to actively seek the nation's good where He had placed them.** "Seek the welfare of the city [nation-state] where I have sent you into exile, and pray to the LORD on its behalf; for in its welfare you will have welfare." "Seek" is a very strong verb here. Sometimes referring to the most earnest of human activity—worship itself, as in "seek the Lord."

4. In Matthew 22:21 (ASV), **Jesus commanded our participation in human governance (politics) very dramatically and unforgettably:** *"Render to Caesar the things that are Caesar's."* When the Herodians tried to entrap Him, Jesus requested a coin used for the poll tax, and asked whose inscription was on it. The answer, of course, was *"Caesar's."* Jesus ended the argument with a clear directive: *"Render therefore unto Caesar the things that are Caesar's; and unto God the things that are God's."*

"Render" is another strong imperative here. It's a deliberate act of submission.

Jesus' message is clear. We have two obligations, first to God in Heaven and then to our earthly Caesar. Fortunately for us here in America, we serve no single human as Caesar. Our nation is a constitutional republic ("if you can keep it," said Benjamin Franklin, a student of human behavior). America's Caesar is the US Constitution. As citizens of a constitutional republic, "We the people" are fully obligated to actively exercise our citizenship by participating (rendering) thoughtfully and intelligently in our constitutional political process. The most obvious and fundamental such participation is that of voting. In fact, Pastor Weber indicated that it may be said, "If you are a Christian, and choose not to vote, you are disobeying your Lord Jesus Christ." Unfortunately, on recent national elections, tens of thousands of Christians have failed to vote (render). You are the salt. What good is it if the salt has lost its flavor?

Unfortunately, Pastor Weber's clear viewpoint is too often blunted by progressive lies that persuade many Americans, including Christians, who have come to believe that this country's government power-brokers are the end-all. That was never intended to be the case. For years now, we've seen how the deep state and their sponsors hoodwink the "king" to believe in their lie. That must stop!

I'm not the first to call America to wake up and return to God. None other than President Eisenhower said as much in a February 20, 1955, speech:

> The founding fathers...recognizing God as the author of individual rights, declared that the purpose of Government is to secure those rights.... But in many lands the State claims to be the author of human rights.... If the State gives rights, it can—and inevitably will—take away those rights. Without

God, there could be no American form of Government, nor an American way of life. Recognition of the Supreme Being is the first—the most basic—expression of Americanism. Thus, the Founding Fathers saw it, and thus, with God's help, it will continue to be.... Veterans realize, perhaps more clearly than others, the prior place that Almighty God holds in our national life.[686]

So, Christians today must answer the call to renew government. After all, they are following a long list of fellow believers, veterans who sacrificed for the good of the nation. Those same valiant men not only gave birth to our republic by participating in the Constitutional Convention, but they also greatly contributed to the Christian faith in their communities.

The Constitutional Convention included many godly men who publicly practiced their Christian faith. Charles Pinckney and John Langdon founded the American Bible Society. James McHenry founded the Baltimore Bible Society, and Rufus King helped establish a Bible society for Anglicans. Abraham Baldwin was a chaplain in the army during the Revolutionary War. James Wilson and William Paterson prayed over juries as Supreme Court justices. Roger Sherman, William Samuel Johnson, John Dickinson, and Jacob Broom were Christian authors.[687]

What must Christians who join government remember? Like our founders, they must insist that the government reflects Christian principles and values. Specifically, Congress will pass policies that clearly embrace Christian ideals, such as protecting innocent life, advancing the family, and promoting liberty and equality for all. They also advance judicial candidates who are strictly constitutionalists, who don't legislate from the bench.

The executive branch will minimize regulation, the size of the federal workforce, and never weaponize the federal government against its political opponents.

All three branches of the government must recognize the rights outlined in the Constitution's Bill of Rights by being truly accountable to the "king."

Goal #9: Make the American family reflect Christian values again.

That goal means that the federal government embraces biblical marriage and protects the family, the cornerstone of civilization. It does everything possible to keep fathers in the homes and provides ample tax incentives to encourage marriage and child-rearing.

Of course, these actions require a judiciary that interprets the Constitution as prohibiting what homosexual activists demanded in 2013, a redefined "marriage" and, for that matter, a socially reconstructed family.

The Family Research Council published twenty-five pro-family policy goals for the nation. That list of goals can't be improved upon with the exception of the reversal of the so-called high court's decision on homosexual marriage, mentioned above.

Some of the outcomes FRC called for include pro-family initiatives to address bioethics, culture and media; protecting children and the public from pornography and media indecency; implementing family-friendly tax cuts; eliminating marriage penalties; enacting health reform that helps families; providing opportunity for parental choice in education; strengthening marriage laws, and much more.[688]

I'd recommend a Christian summit focused on building family-friendly legislation. FRC's list of pro-family public policies is a good starting point.

Goal #10: Make the American economy Christian-friendly again.

State and federal governments must pressure businesses to get out of politics. Make it a condition of operating those entities that they must focus on the bottom line, not on the political fray. They also must shutter anti-Christian workplace policies that include eschewing the demonstration of one's faith such as praying, hosting Bible studies during lunch time, and putting a Bible on their desk. Hostility to Christians in the workforce will not be a corporate value!

Recall the situation Vice President (then former governor) Mike Pence experienced in Indiana when his legislature passed a religious liberty bill. Businesses and even professional sports teams threatened the state with consequences. Gary Bauer explained those corporations threatened to pull jobs from Indiana. That shouldn't be. The politicians in a state represent the state's people and they, not a bunch of businesses or sports franchises, ought to dictate social policy.

States and the federal government must make it clear that decisions about family and life are local affairs. Businesses that can't abide by what the local people and their representatives want can take their plants to states and countries that allow such cultural interference.

Goal #11: Make American religious institutions Christian-friendly again.

The majority of Americans self-identify as Christian. That means, by association, the United States should represent the majority's religious values. It also means that Christians from all sectors of society must engage in the policy life of the country, because the political fray is about the future morality of the country.

Pastor Victor Stanley quoted A. W. Tozer to me: "What we think of God is the most important thing about us."[689] Our view of God has a lot to do with how we think about the culture in which we live. Believing that our God is right about the condition of man and the fountain of truth, then we ought to promote that view widely across the culture.

Yes, we should embrace pluralism in the marketplace of ideas. However, that doesn't mean Christianity takes a backseat in any situation compared to other faiths. Unfortunately, over the past few years, Christianity and Christians in particular have experienced significant discrimination while other faiths and their followers are given a free pass. That will end.

There will be no tolerance for anti-Christian actions. Progressives who dislike our bias to Christianity can leave for places where their faith and choice enjoys higher degrees of tolerance, if such places really exist.

Goal #12: Make the American education establishment Christian-friendly again.

American public education has become a progressive cesspool of anti-Christian secularism. To correct that, we must provide parents with more education choice. We will also insist that taxpayer-funded education teaches civics and subjects that will make young American adults competitive again.

We will also hold government-paid educators to a high standard of academic performance. Eliminate the politically correct, anti-Christian pabulum being forced down the throats of our children.

Universities and other educational institutions that accept public funds must be severely sanctioned for advancing anti-free-speech agendas and rhetoric that is anti-Christian. Government schools must stop advocating what the taxpaying majority Christian population hates—amoral values. Rather, truth must be promoted.

The "king" ought to insist that a Christian worldview is taught in American classrooms.

Earlier in *Collision Course*, I addressed the influence of media across our culture. Although I haven't previously identified media as an "institution," it, too, desperately needs attention because much of our mainstream media are tools of Satan.

Goal #13: Make the media Christian-friendly again.

One aspect of culture that ought to be closely watched and adjusted is the mass media. It plays a significant anti-Christian role in America, which must change.

While we Americans respect our First Amendment, we also respect religious freedom. Much of today's media is incredibly anti-Christian, which means the "king" must seek to turn the tide.

As a minimum, the government can deny special status and especially taxpayer funds going to outlets that demonstrate an anti-Christian bias.

Christians must also boycott media outlets that demonstrate a clear bias while supporting those that advance biblical principles and values. They must also make it clear to commercial sponsors that there will be an economic price to pay for advancing anti-Christian programming.

Hollywood is a special, mostly evil, challenge. Much of what Hollywood produces today is anti-Christian. The "king" needs to make certain that government upholds moral standards in our media, and Christians must stop catering and fawning over those so-called celebrities who attack the values we hold dear.

One Final Thought and Recommendation

Who is going to bring America together to address the above thirteen goals? I recommend a consortium of pastors and national leaders be formed to band together under the banner of "Make America Christian Again." That organization would tackle the goals outlined above and flesh out a comprehensive strategy going forward. Short of coming together, these goals will fall to the wayside, much like other calls for action amidst so many global crises.

Conclusion

This chapter calls for a national course correction, a renewal, and provides a MACA Strategy 101 that begins that process. It starts with the individual Christian, then our pastors, and eventually involves the broader Christian community. Once America's Christian church writ large is spiritually renewed, they need to then focus on revamping our cultural institutions by making them reflect Christian principles and values, not all that different from where we started in 1778 with the newborn nation of the United States.

Admittedly, the MACA Strategy is incomplete. Like President Eisenhower said, plans are worthless, but planning is invaluable. Christians across America can seize this starter-kit of national renewal and expand upon it to regrow the Christian influence in their personal lives, their family, the local church, communities, states, and eventually our nation. That's the mandate, and I firmly believe it's possible—and yes, it's what our God should expect as we approach the prophetic end times.

MACA or Bust—End Times Coming!

SOBERLY, PASTOR WEBER told me:

We as a nation are on the brink, at a tipping point. Never in my lifetime had I imagined a day like ours. Over a lifetime of ministry, I have studiously avoided any sensationalism when it comes to biblical prophecy. But I must admit, it seems to me that the elements are in place for the onset of the end times— significant disorder, worldwide, at every level—marriage and family, socially, politically, financially, our health; even the environment is getting in on the act at a remarkable scale— earthquakes, hurricanes, floods, tsunamis, and pestilence as the Bible describes fatal disease. Is this the real end, or merely a rehearsal? Either way, it's time to sit up and take notice.

We are told the twentieth century was by far the most brutal and deadly century in human history. It appears the twenty-first century, if there is one, may fall over the edge.

How did we get here so quickly when the end of World War II seemed to have brought such worldwide peace? We became a society of materialists and forgot the spiritual realities. We decayed from the inside out.

However! Pastor Weber does believe we can turn around the downhill slide to avoid the cliff's brink. "There is, you know, the God Factor.... So long as we look to the Word of God, there is hope," he said.

He continued, and *"with God all things are possible"* (Matthew 19:26, NASB).

Dr. Heiser agrees with Pastor Weber, but with a caveat: Christians may well only begin to renew the church and the country when they suffer real persecution. He pointed out that the current persecution of the Christian church in places like Africa, Europe, and Asia demonstrates what happens when Satan effectively manipulates his proxies like Islamists. In those circumstances, the real Christian believers rise to the occasion and the lost seek answers to life's meaning in strange places.[690]

American Christians will soon face real persecution, warns Dr. Heiser. He believes this will begin to happen especially when President Trump is gone and unless genuine Christian renewal starts and soon. Today, Christians in America enjoy a brief respite from Satan and his proxies because Mr. Trump is fearless against the left. He stands up against evil not because he's some great Christian leader. Rather, he represents much that we Christians consider right about America—the Bill of Rights, which grants religious freedom and promise, opportunity, and hope. However, when Mr. Trump inevitably leaves office, the left will doubledown on their effort to continue radically transforming America. Their hatred for Trump will be redirected toward those who supported him, which especially includes conservative, evangelical Christians.

The left will then embrace even more tyrannical tactics, and Katie bar the door. They hate conservative, Trump-supporting Christians, and will harness every key institution (especially the alphabet government agencies) to target their opponents. I'm not exaggerating that an emboldened, progressive radical left (Satan and his proxies) will use government to do to Trump-supporting Christians what the Nazi regime's *Sturmabteilung* (paramilitary) did to the Jews on *Kristallnacht* ("Crystal Night"), November 9–10, 1938.

On those days, Jewish homes, hospitals, and schools were ransacked by paramilitary thugs. Hitler's true hatred for Jews became clear to the whole world. Hundreds of synagogues were destroyed, and thousands of Jewish businesses were damaged. Tens of thousands of Jewish men were arrested and sent to concentration camps to a certain death.

For German Jews, "Crystal Night" was terrifying, and so will be the last days for Christians. The Apostle Paul describes that future situation in 2 Timothy 3:1–4, NKJV:

> But know this, that in the last days perilous times will come: For men will be lovers of themselves, lovers of money, boasters, proud, blasphemers, disobedient to parents, unthankful, unholy, unloving, unforgiving, slanderers, without self-control, brutal, despisers of good, traitors, headstrong, haughty, lovers of pleasure rather than lovers of God.

Don't think that's possible? Wrong. The progressives already showed their intentions. The words "perilous times" in the Scripture above can also be translated "raging insanity." That's what we are seeing daily, especially from the progressives. Evidently, Dr. Heiser agrees. He told me that the left has "a maniacal [I'm willing to say 'satanic'] lust for moral autonomy and are living in their utopian, fascist fantasy land." We've already had a taste of the future.

Under President Obama, the left weaponized the FBI, the IRS, the intelligence agencies, and the courts. They impeached President Trump for opposing them, and they are prepared to do much worse because of their lust for absolute power.

These Christian-haters use thugs like ANTIFA (anti-fascists), and their mainstream-media allies to attack their political opponents. Look what the leftist deep state and the Democrat-controlled House did to the Trump administration—total resistance and attacking people of faith and patriots. They are "anti" much of what our founders put into place at the birth of this nation.

Therefore, NOW is the time to change course, avoid the coming collision by renewing the Christian church using the MACA Strategy 101, and only should we succeed can we effectively turn America's key institutions around—away from the moral tipping point—to embrace the Christian principles and values that made America once great.

That's America's hope, that's the Christians' firewall, and a legacy we desperately owe our children and their children. However, it is past time to fight to reclaim our moral compass before it is too late!

May God bless America with a Nineveh-like repentance and rescue her from the grips of Satan and his proxies by Making America Christian Again!

NOTES

1. Evan Andrews, "8 Reasons Why Rome Fell," History, January 29, 2019, https://www.history.com/news/8-reasons-why-rome-fellUPDATED.
2. "Early Settlements," American History, accessed February 25, 2020, http://www.let.rug.nl/usa/outlines/history-1994/early-america/early-settlements.php.
3. H. F. M. Prescott, Mary Tudor 299, 381 (1953), as cited in Marci A. Hamilton and Rachel Steamert, "The Religious Origins of Disestablishment," *Notre Dame Law Review*, Vol. 81, Issue 5, June 1, 2006, https://scholarship.law.nd.edu/cgi/viewcontent.cgi?article=1357&=&context=ndlr&=&sei-redir=1&referer=https%253A%252F%252Fwww.bing.com%252Fsearch%253Fq%253Ddisestablishment%252Bprinciples%2526src%253DIE-SearchBox%2526FORM%253DIESR4S#search=%22disestablishment%20principles%22.
4. Carl H. Esbeck, *The Establishment Clause as a Structural Restraint on Governmental Power*, 84 Iowa L. Rev. 1 (1998); see also Richard W. Garnett, *Christian Witness, Moral Anthropology, and the Death Penalty*, 17 Notre Dame J.L. Ethics * Pub. Pol'y, 541, 550 (2003), as cited in Marci A. Hamilton and Rachel Steamert, "The Religious Origins of Disestablishment," *Notre Dame Law Review*, Vol. 81, Issue 5, June 1, 2006, https://scholarship.law.nd.edu/cgi/viewcontent.cgi?article=1357&=&context=ndlr&=&sei-redir=1&referer=https%253A%252F%252Fwww.bing.com%252Fsearch%253Fq%253Ddisestablishment%252Bprinciples%2526src%253DIE-SearchBox%2526FORM%253DIESR4S#search=%22disestablishment%20principles%22

5. Edmund S. Morgan, *The Puritan Dilemma: The Story of John Winthrop* 7 (1958); see also Frank Lambert, *The Founding Fathers and the Place of Religion in America* 41 (2003), as cited in Marci A. Hamilton and Rachel Steamert, "The Religious Origins of Disestablishment," *Notre Dame Law Review*, Vol. 81, Issue 5, June 1, 2006, https://scholarship.law.nd.edu/cgi/viewcontent.cgi?article=1357&=&context=ndlr&=&sei-redir=1&referer=https%253A%252F%252Fwww.bing.com%252Fsearch%253Fq%253Ddisestablishment%252Bprinciples%2526src%253DIE-SearchBox%2526FORM%253DIESR4S#search=%22disestablishment%20principles%22.

6. Morgan, supra note 21, at 28 as cited in Marci A. Hamilton and Rachel Steamert, "The Religious Origins of Disestablishment," *Notre Dame Law Review*, Vol. 81, Issue 5, June 1, 2006, https://scholarship.law.nd.edu/cgi/viewcontent.cgi?article=1357&=&context=ndlr&=&sei-redir=1&referer=https%253A%252F%252Fwww.bing.com%252Fsearch%253Fq%253Ddisestablishment%252Bprinciples%2526src%253DIE-SearchBox%2526FORM%253DIESR4S#search=%22disestablishment%20principles%22

7. John Calvin, Wikipedia, accessed February 25, 2020, https://en.wikipedia.org/wiki/John_Calvin.

8. Morgan, supra note 21, at 46–47 as cited in Marci A. Hamilton and Rachel Steamert, "The Religious Origins of Disestablishment," *Notre Dame Law Review*, Vol. 81, Issue 5, June 1, 2006, https://scholarship.law.nd.edu/cgi/viewcontent.cgi?article=1357&=&context=ndlr&=&sei-redir=1&referer=https%253A%252F%252Fwww.bing.com%252Fsearch%253Fq%253Ddisestablishment%252Bprinciples%2526src%253DIE-SearchBox%2526FORM%253DIESR4S#search=%22disestablishment%20principles%22.

9. Id. at 46 as cited in Marci A. Hamilton and Rachel Steamert, "The Religious Origins of Disestablishment," *Notre Dame Law Review*, Vol. 81, Issue 5, June 1, 2006, https://scholarship.law.nd.edu/cgi/viewcontent.cgi?article=1357&=&context=ndlr&=&sei-redir=1&referer=https%253A%252F%252Fwww.bing.com%252Fsearch%253Fq%253Ddisestablishment%252Bprinciples%2526src%253DIE-SearchBox%2526FORM%253DIESR4S#search=%22disestablishment%20principles%22.

10. Oscar Zeichner, "Massachusetts Bay Company," scholastic.com, accessed February 25, 2020, https://www.scholastic.com/teachers/articles/teaching-content/massachusetts-bay-company/.

11. "History of the Puritans in North America," Wikipedia,

accessed February 25, 2020, https://en.wikipedia.org/wiki/
History_of_the_Puritans_in_North_America.

12. Frank Lambert, *The Founding Fathers and the Place of Religion in America*
41 (2003) ("[Puritans] wanted to 'purify' the church of everything not
explicitly sanctioned by Scripture."), supra note 21, at 44–45, as cited
in Marci A. Hamilton and Rachel Steamert, "The Religious Origins of
Disestablishment," *Notre Dame Law Review*, Vol. 81, Issue 5, June 1, 2006,
https://scholarship.law.nd.edu/cgi/viewcontent.cgi?article=1357&=&contex
t=ndlr&=&sei-redir=1&referer=https%253A%252F%252Fwww.bing.com
%252Fsearch%253Fq%253Ddisestablishment%252Bprinciples%2526src
%253DIE-SearchBox%2526FORM%253DIESR4S#search=%22disestabli
shment%20principles%22.

13. Zeichner, Op cit.

14. Timothy L. Hall, Roger Williams, and the Foundations of Religious Liberty,
71 B.U. L. Rev. 455, 466 (1991), as cited in Marci A. Hamilton and Rachel
Steamert, "The Religious Origins of Disestablishment," *Notre Dame Law
Review*, Vol. 81, Issue 5, June 1, 2006, https://scholarship.law.nd.edu/cgi/
viewcontent.cgi?article=1357&=&context=ndlr&=&sei-redir=1&referer=ht
tps%253A%252F%252Fwww.bing.com%252Fsearch%253Fq%253Ddise
stablishment%252Bprinciples%2526src%253DIE-SearchBox%2526FOR
M%253DIESR4S#search=%22disestablishment%20principles%22.

15. Id. at 467–68 as cited in Marci A. Hamilton and Rachel Steamert, "The
Religious Origins of Disestablishment," *Notre Dame Law Review*, Vol. 81,
Issue 5, June 1, 2006, https://scholarship.law.nd.edu/cgi/viewcontent.cgi?ar
ticle=1357&=&context=ndlr&=&sei-redir=1&referer=https%253A%252F
%252Fwww.bing.com%252Fsearch%253Fq%253Ddisestablishment%252
Bprinciples%2526src%253DIE-SearchBox%2526FORM%253DIESR4S#
search=%22disestablishment%20principles%22.

16. Jack Zavada, "Quakers History," Learn Religions, March 28, 2019, https://
www.learnreligions.com/quakers-history-4590178.

17. Ibid.

18. Margaret H. Bacon, *The Quiet Rebels: The Story of Quakers in America* 38
(1969), pp. 30–31, as cited in Marci A. Hamilton and Rachel Steamert,
"The Religious Origins of Disestablishment," *Notre Dame Law Review*, Vol.
81, Issue 5, June 1, 2006, https://scholarship.law.nd.edu/cgi/viewcontent.cgi

?article=1357&=&context=ndlr&=&sei-redir=1&referer=https%253A%25
2F%252Fwww.bing.com%252Fsearch%253Fq%253Ddisestablishment%2
52Bprinciples%2526src%253DIE-SearchBox%2526FORM%253DIESR4
S#search=%22disestablishment%20principles%22.

19. Id. at 31 as cited in Marci A. Hamilton and Rachel Steamert, "The
    Religious Origins of Disestablishment," *Notre Dame Law Review*, Vol. 81,
    Issue 5, June 1, 2006, https://scholarship.law.nd.edu/cgi/viewcontent.cgi?ar
    ticle=1357&=&context=ndlr&=&sei-redir=1&referer=https%253A%252F
    %252Fwww.bing.com%252Fsearch%253Fq%253Ddisestablishment%252
    Bprinciples%2526src%253DIE-SearchBox%2526FORM%253DIESR4S#
    search=%22disestablishment%20principles%22.

20. Lambert, supra note 21, at 46, as cited in Marci A. Hamilton and Rachel
    Steamert, "The Religious Origins of Disestablishment," *Notre Dame Law
    Review*, Vol. 81, Issue 5, June 1, 2006, https://scholarship.law.nd.edu/cgi/
    viewcontent.cgi?article=1357&=&context=ndlr&=&sei-redir=1&referer=ht
    tps%253A%252F%252Fwww.bing.com%252Fsearch%253Fq%253Ddise
    stablishment%252Bprinciples%2526src%253DIE-SearchBox%2526FOR
    M%253DIESR4S#search=%22disestablishment%20principles%22.

21. "History of Jamestown, Virginia," Wikipedia, accessed
    February 25, 2020, https://en.wikipedia.org/wiki/
    History_of_Jamestown,_Virginia_(1607%E2%80%931699).

22. Lambert at 50, as cited in Marci A. Hamilton and Rachel Steamert, "The
    Religious Origins of Disestablishment," *Notre Dame Law Review*, Vol. 81,
    Issue 5, June 1, 2006, https://scholarship.law.nd.edu/cgi/viewcontent.cgi?ar
    ticle=1357&=&context=ndlr&=&sei-redir=1&referer=https%253A%252F
    %252Fwww.bing.com%252Fsearch%253Fq%253Ddisestablishment%252
    Bprinciples%2526src%253DIE-SearchBox%2526FORM%253DIESR4S#
    search=%22disestablishment%20principles%22.

23. Id. at 51, as cited in Marci A. Hamilton and Rachel Steamert, "The
    Religious Origins of Disestablishment," *Notre Dame Law Review*, Vol. 81,
    Issue 5, June 1, 2006, https://scholarship.law.nd.edu/cgi/viewcontent.cgi?ar
    ticle=1357&=&context=ndlr&=&sei-redir=1&referer=https%253A%252F
    %252Fwww.bing.com%252Fsearch%253Fq%253Ddisestablishment%252
    Bprinciples%2526src%253DIE-SearchBox%2526FORM%253DIESR4S#
    search=%22disestablishment%20principles%22.

24. Lambert, supra note 21, at 67 (quoting 1 *Colony Laws of Virginia* 180 (John D. Cushing ed., 1978)), as cited in Marci A. Hamilton and Rachel Steamert, "The Religious Origins of Disestablishment," *Notre Dame Law Review*, Vol. 81, Issue 5, June 1, 2006, https://scholarship.law.nd.edu/cgi/ viewcontent.cgi?article=1357&=&context=ndlr&=&sei-redir=1&referer=ht tps%253A%252F%252Fwww.bing.com%252Fsearch%253Fq%253Ddise stablishment%252Bprinciples%2526src%253DIE-SearchBox%2526FOR M%253DIESR4S#search=%22disestablishment%20principles%22.

25. See id. at 68–72 as cited in Marci A. Hamilton and Rachel Steamert, "The Religious Origins of Disestablishment," *Notre Dame Law Review*, Vol. 81, Issue 5, June 1, 2006, https://scholarship.law.nd.edu/cgi/viewcontent.cgi?ar ticle=1357&=&context=ndlr&=&sei-redir=1&referer=https%253A%252F %252Fwww.bing.com%252Fsearch%253Fq%253Ddisestablishment%252 Bprinciples%2526src%253DIE-SearchBox%2526FORM%253DIESR4S# search=%22disestablishment%20principles%22.

26. Leonard Levy, *The Establishment Clause* 5 (2d ed. 1994), as cited in Marci A. Hamilton and Rachel Steamert, "The Religious Origins of Disestablishment," *Notre Dame Law Review*, Vol. 81, Issue 5, June 1, 2006, https://scholarship.law.nd.edu/cgi/viewcontent.cgi?article=1357&=&contex t=ndlr&=&sei-redir=1&referer=https%253A%252F%252Fwww.bing.com %252Fsearch%253Fq%253Ddisestablishment%252Bprinciples%2526src %253DIE-SearchBox%2526FORM%253DIESR4S#search=%22disestabli shment%20principles%22.

27. Frederick Mark Gedicks, *A Two-Track Theory of the Establishment Clause*, 43 B.C. L. Rev. 1071, 1092–93 (2002) (citing A.G. Rober, *Faithful Magistrates and Republican Lawyers: Creators of Virginia Legal Culture*, 1680-1810, at 141–42 (1981)), as cited in Marci A. Hamilton and Rachel Steamert, "The Religious Origins of Disestablishment," *Notre Dame Law Review*, Vol. 81, Issue 5, June 1, 2006, https://scholarship.law.nd.edu/cgi/viewcontent.cgi?ar ticle=1357&=&context=ndlr&=&sei-redir=1&referer=https%253A%252F %252Fwww.bing.com%252Fsearch%253Fq%253Ddisestablishment%252 Bprinciples%2526src%253DIE-SearchBox%2526FORM%253DIESR4S# search=%22disestablishment%20principles%22.

28. Leonard Levy, *The Establishment Clause* 5 (2d ed. 1994), supra note 43, at 17, as cited in Marci A. Hamilton and Rachel Steamert, "The Religious

Origins of Disestablishment," *Notre Dame Law Review*, Vol. 81, Issue 5, June 1, 2006, https://scholarship.law.nd.edu/cgi/viewcontent.cgi?article=13 57&=&context=ndlr&=&sei-redir=1&referer=https%253A%252F%252F www.bing.com%252Fsearch%253Fq%253Ddisestablishment%252Bprinci ples%2526src%253DIE-SearchBox%2526FORM%253DIESR4S#search= %22disestablishment%20principles%22.

29. Id. at 61, as cited in Marci A. Hamilton and Rachel Steamert, "The Religious Origins of Disestablishment," *Notre Dame Law Review*, Vol. 81, Issue 5, June 1, 2006, https://scholarship.law.nd.edu/cgi/viewcontent.cgi?ar ticle=1357&=&context=ndlr&=&sei-redir=1&referer=https%253A%252F %252Fwww.bing.com%252Fsearch%253Fq%253Ddisestablishment%252 Bprinciples%2526src%253DIE-SearchBox%2526FORM%253DIESR4S# search=%22disestablishment%20principles%22.

30. Timothy L. Hall, Roger Williams, and the Foundations of Religious Liberty, 71 B.U. L. Rev. 455, 466 (1991), supra note 45, at 463, as cited in Marci A. Hamilton and Rachel Steamert, "The Religious Origins of Disestablishment," *Notre Dame Law Review*, Vol. 81, Issue 5, June 1, 2006, https://scholarship.law.nd.edu/cgi/viewcontent.cgi?article=1357&=&contex t=ndlr&=&sei-redir=1&referer=https%253A%252F%252Fwww.bing.com %252Fsearch%253Fq%253Ddisestablishment%252Bprinciples%2526src %253DIE-SearchBox%2526FORM%253DIESR4S#search=%22disestabli shment%20principles%22.

31. John Witte, Jr., *How To Govern a City on a Hill: The Early Puritan Contribution to American Constitutionalism*, 39 Emory L. J. 41, 44 (1990), as cited in Marci A. Hamilton and Rachel Steamert, "The Religious Origins of Disestablishment," *Notre Dame Law Review*, Vol. 81, Issue 5, June 1, 2006, https://scholarship.law.nd.edu/cgi/viewcontent.cgi?article=1357&= &context=ndlr&=&sei-redir=1&referer=https%253A%252F%252Fwww. bing.com%252Fsearch%253Fq%253Ddisestablishment%252Bprinciples %2526src%253DIE-SearchBox%2526FORM%253DIESR4S#search=%2 2disestablishment%20principles%22.

32. Peter Whitney, *The Transgression of a Land Punished by a Multitude of Rulers* 21 (1774), as cited in Marci A. Hamilton and Rachel Steamert, "The Religious Origins of Disestablishment," *Notre Dame Law Review*, Vol. 81, Issue 5, June 1, 2006, https://scholarship.law.nd.edu/cgi/viewcontent.cgi?ar

ticle=1357&=&context=ndlr&=&sei-redir=1&referer=https%253A%252F
%252Fwww.bing.com%252Fsearch%253Fq%253Ddisestablishment%252
Bprinciples%2526src%253DIE-SearchBox%2526FORM%253DIESR4S#
search=%22disestablishment%20principles%22.

33. Hall, supra note 45, at 463 (quoting 1 McLoughlin, supra note 71, at 12),
as cited in Marci A. Hamilton and Rachel Steamert, "The Religious Origins
of Disestablishment," *Notre Dame Law Review*, Vol. 81, Issue 5, June 1,
2006, https://scholarship.law.nd.edu/cgi/viewcontent.cgi?article=1357&=
&context=ndlr&=&sei-redir=1&referer=https%253A%252F%252Fwww.
bing.com%252Fsearch%253Fq%253Ddisestablishment%252Bprinciples
%2526src%253DIE-SearchBox%2526FORM%253DIESR4S#search=%2
2disestablishment%20principles%22.

34. Id. at 464, as cited in Marci A. Hamilton and Rachel Steamert, "The
Religious Origins of Disestablishment," *Notre Dame Law Review*, Vol. 81,
Issue 5, June 1, 2006, https://scholarship.law.nd.edu/cgi/viewcontent.cgi?ar
ticle=1357&=&context=ndlr&=&sei-redir=1&referer=https%253A%252F
%252Fwww.bing.com%252Fsearch%253Fq%253Ddisestablishment%252
Bprinciples%2526src%253DIE-SearchBox%2526FORM%253DIESR4S#
search=%22disestablishment%20principles%22.

35. William Tennent, *Speech on the Dissenting Petition* (Charlestown, S.C., Peter
Timothy 1778) (delivered in the House of Assembly, Charlestown, S.C. on
Jan. 11, 1777), as cited in Marci A. Hamilton and Rachel Steamert, "The
Religious Origins of Disestablishment," *Notre Dame Law Review*, Vol. 81,
Issue 5, June 1, 2006, https://scholarship.law.nd.edu/cgi/viewcontent.cgi?ar
ticle=1357&=&context=ndlr&=&sei-redir=1&referer=https%253A%252F
%252Fwww.bing.com%252Fsearch%253Fq%253Ddisestablishment%252
Bprinciples%2526src%253DIE-SearchBox%2526FORM%253DIESR4S#
search=%22disestablishment%20principles%22.

36. Levy, supra note 43, at 5–6, as cited in Marci A. Hamilton and Rachel
Steamert, "The Religious Origins of Disestablishment," *Notre Dame Law
Review*, Vol. 81, Issue 5, June 1, 2006, https://scholarship.law.nd.edu/cgi/
viewcontent.cgi?article=1357&=&context=ndlr&=&sei-redir=1&referer=ht
tps%253A%252F%252Fwww.bing.com%252Fsearch%253Fq%253Ddise
stablishment%252Bprinciples%2526src%253DIE-SearchBox%2526FOR
M%253DIESR4S#search=%22disestablishment%20principles%22.

37. Letter from James Madison to James Monroe (Apr. 12, 1785), as cited in Marci A. Hamilton and Rachel Steamert, "The Religious Origins of Disestablishment," *Notre Dame Law Review*, Vol. 81, Issue 5, June 1, 2006, https://scholarship.law.nd.edu/cgi/viewcontent.cgi?article=1357&=&context=ndlr&=&sei-redir=1&referer=https%253A%252F%252Fwww.bing.com%252Fsearch%253Fq%253Ddisestablishment%252Bprinciples%2526src%253DIE-SearchBox%2526FORM%253DIESR4S#search=%22disestablishment%20principles%22.

38. Thomas J. Curry, *The First Freedoms: Church and State in America to the Passage of the First Amendment* 145 (1986). As Professor Douglas Laycock points out in his article for this *Symposium Issue*, Presbyterians also eventually rejected state aid to religion altogether, supporting the no-aid principle. Douglas Laycock, *Regulatory Exemptions of Religious Behavior and the Original Understanding of the Establishment Clause*, 81 *Notre Dame Law Review*, 1793, 1831–32. (2006), as cited in Marci A. Hamilton and Rachel Steamert, "The Religious Origins of Disestablishment," *Notre Dame Law Review*, Vol. 81, Issue 5, June 1, 2006, https://scholarship.law.nd.edu/cgi/viewcontent.cgi?article=1357&=&context=ndlr&=&sei-redir=1&referer=https%253A%252F%252Fwww.bing.com%252Fsearch%253Fq%253Ddisestablishment%252Bprinciples%2526src%253DIE-SearchBox%2526FORM%253DIESR4S#search=%22disestablishment%20principles%22.

39. Bernard Bailyn, *The Ideological Origins of the American Revolution* 263–64 (1967) (quoting "Letter from Andrew Eliot to Thomas Hollis" (Jan. 29, 1771)), 261–267, as cited in Marci A. Hamilton and Rachel Steamert, "The Religious Origins of Disestablishment," he *Notre Dame Law Review*, Vol. 81, Issue 5, June 1, 2006, https://scholarship.law.nd.edu/cgi/viewcontent.cgi?article=1357&=&context=ndlr&=&sei-redir=1&referer=https%253A%2525 2F%252Fwww.bing.com%252Fsearch%253Fq%253Ddisestablishment%2 52Bprinciples%2526src%253DIE-SearchBox%2526FORM%253DIESR4 S#search=%22disestablishment%20principles%22.

40. John Witte, Jr., *How To Govern a City on a Hill: The Early Puritan Contribution to American Constitutionalism*, 39 Emory L. J. 41, 44 (1990), supra note 42, at 29, as cited in Marci A. Hamilton and Rachel Steamert, "The Religious Origins of Disestablishment," *Notre Dame Law Review*, Vol. 81, Issue 5, June 1, 2006, https://scholarship.law.nd.edu/cgi/viewcontent.cgi

?article=1357&=&context=ndlr&=&sei-redir=1&referer=https%253A%25
2F%252Fwww.bing.com%252Fsearch%253Fq%253Ddisestablishment%2
52Bprinciples%2526src%253DIE-SearchBox%2526FORM%253DIESR4
S#search=%22disestablishment%20principles%22.

41. Bernard Bailyn, *The Ideological Origins of the American Revolution* 263–64
(1967) supra note 87, at 262-63, as cited in Marci A. Hamilton and Rachel
Steamert, "The Religious Origins of Disestablishment," *Notre Dame Law
Review,* Vol. 81, Issue 5, June 1, 2006, https://scholarship.law.nd.edu/cgi/
viewcontent.cgi?article=1357&=&context=ndlr&=&sei-redir=1&referer=ht
tps%253A%252F%252Fwww.bing.com%252Fsearch%253Fq%253Ddise
stablishment%252Bprinciples%2526src%253DIE-SearchBox%2526FOR
M%253DIESR4S#search=%22disestablishment%20principles%22.

42. Isaac Backus, *An Appeal to the Public for Religious Liberty* (1773), reprinted
in *Pamphlets,* supra note 92, at 313, as cited in Marci A. Hamilton and
Rachel Steamert, "The Religious Origins of Disestablishment," *Notre Dame
Law Review,* Vol. 81, Issue 5, June 1, 2006, https://scholarship.law.nd.edu/
cgi/viewcontent.cgi?article=1357&=&context=ndlr&=&sei-redir=1&referer
=https%253A%252F%252Fwww.bing.com%252Fsearch%253Fq%253D
disestablishment%252Bprinciples%2526src%253DIE-SearchBox%2526F
ORM%253DIESR4S#search=%22disestablishment%20principles%22.

43. William G. McLoughlin, Introduction to *Pamphlets,* supra note 92, at
47 (quoting Isaac Backus, *Draft for a Bill of Rights for the Massachusetts
Constitution, 1779*)., as cited in Marci A. Hamilton and Rachel Steamert,
"The Religious Origins of Disestablishment," *Notre Dame Law Review,* Vol.
81, Issue 5, June 1, 2006, https://scholarship.law.nd.edu/cgi/viewcontent.cgi
?article=1357&=&context=ndlr&=&sei-redir=1&referer=https%253A%25
2F%252Fwww.bing.com%252Fsearch%253Fq%253Ddisestablishment%2
52Bprinciples%2526src%253DIE-SearchBox%2526FORM%253DIESR4
S#search=%22disestablishment%20principles%22.

44. Levy, supra note 43, at 136, as cited in Marci A. Hamilton and Rachel
Steamert, "The Religious Origins of Disestablishment," *Notre Dame Law
Review,* Vol. 81, Issue 5, June 1, 2006, https://scholarship.law.nd.edu/cgi/
viewcontent.cgi?article=1357&=&context=ndlr&=&sei-redir=1&referer=ht
tps%253A%252F%252Fwww.bing.com%252Fsearch%253Fq%253Ddise
stablishment%252Bprinciples%2526src%253DIE-SearchBox%2526FOR
M%253DIESR4S#search=%22disestablishment%20principles%22.

45. Thomas D. Hamm, *The Quakers in America* 18 (2003), supra note 34, at
    13-16, as cited in Marci A. Hamilton and Rachel Steamert, "The Religious
    Origins of Disestablishment," *Notre Dame Law Review*, Vol. 81, Issue 5,
    June 1, 2006, https://scholarship.law.nd.edu/cgi/viewcontent.cgi?article=13
    57&=&context=ndlr&=&sei-redir=1&referer=https%253A%252F%252F
    www.bing.com%252Fsearch%253Fq%253Ddisestablishment%252Bprinci
    ples%2526src%253DIE-SearchBox%2526FORM%253DIESR4S#search=
    %22disestablishment%20principles%22.

46. Id. at 21, as cited in Marci A. Hamilton and Rachel Steamert, "The
    Religious Origins of Disestablishment," *Notre Dame Law Review*, Vol. 81,
    Issue 5, June 1, 2006, https://scholarship.law.nd.edu/cgi/viewcontent.cgi?ar
    ticle=1357&=&context=ndlr&=&sei-redir=1&referer=https%253A%252F
    %252Fwww.bing.com%252Fsearch%253Fq%253Ddisestablishment%252
    Bprinciples%2526src%253DIE-SearchBox%2526FORM%253DIESR4S#
    search=%22disestablishment%20principles%22.

47. Id. at 15. as cited in Marci A. Hamilton and Rachel Steamert, "The
    Religious Origins of Disestablishment," *Notre Dame Law Review*, Vol. 81,
    Issue 5, June 1, 2006, https://scholarship.law.nd.edu/cgi/viewcontent.cgi?ar
    ticle=1357&=&context=ndlr&=&sei-redir=1&referer=https%253A%252F
    %252Fwww.bing.com%252Fsearch%253Fq%253Ddisestablishment%252
    Bprinciples%2526src%253DIE-SearchBox%2526FORM%253DIESR4S#
    search=%22disestablishment%20principles%22.

48. Margaret H. Bacon, *The Quiet Rebels: The Story of Quakers in America* 38
    (1969), supra note 55, at 47, as cited in Marci A. Hamilton and Rachel
    Steamert, "The Religious Origins of Disestablishment," *Notre Dame Law
    Review*, Vol. 81, Issue 5, June 1, 2006, https://scholarship.law.nd.edu/cgi/
    viewcontent.cgi?article=1357&=&context=ndlr&=&sei-redir=1&referer=ht
    tps%253A%252F%252Fwww.bing.com%252Fsearch%253Fq%253Ddise
    stablishment%252Bprinciples%2526src%253DIE-SearchBox%2526FOR
    M%253DIESR4S#search=%22disestablishment%20principles%22.

49. Id. at 22, as cited in Marci A. Hamilton and Rachel Steamert, "The
    Religious Origins of Disestablishment," *Notre Dame Law Review*, Vol. 81,
    Issue 5, June 1, 2006, https://scholarship.law.nd.edu/cgi/viewcontent.cgi?ar
    ticle=1357&=&context=ndlr&=&sei-redir=1&referer=https%253A%252F
    %252Fwww.bing.com%252Fsearch%253Fq%253Ddisestablishment%252

Bprinciples%2526src%253DIE-SearchBox%2526FORM%253DIESR4S#
search=%22disestablishment%20principles%22.

50. William S. Holdsworth, *A History of English Law* 591–92 (A. L. Goodhart & H. G. Hanbury eds., 7th ed. 1956), as cited in Marci A. Hamilton and Rachel Steamert, "The Religious Origins of Disestablishment," *Notre Dame Law Review*, Vol. 81, Issue 5, June 1, 2006, https://scholarship.law.nd.edu/cgi/viewcontent.cgi?article=1357&=&context=ndlr&=&sei-redir=1&referer=https%253A%252F%252Fwww.bing.com%252Fsearch%253Fq%253Ddisestablishment%252Bprinciples%2526src%253DIE-SearchBox%2526FORM%253DIESR4S#search=%22disestablishment%20principles%22.

51. "William Penn," Wikipedia, accessed February 25, 2020, https://en.wikipedia.org/wiki/William_Penn.

52. Holdsworth, supra note 13, at 591–92, as cited in Marci A. Hamilton and Rachel Steamert, "The Religious Origins of Disestablishment," *Notre Dame Law Review*, Vol. 81, Issue 5, June 1, 2006, https://scholarship.law.nd.edu/cgi/viewcontent.cgi?article=1357&=&context=ndlr&=&sei-redir=1&referer=https%253A%252F%252Fwww.bing.com%252Fsearch%253Fq%253Ddisestablishment%252Bprinciples%2526src%253DIE-SearchBox%2526FORM%253DIESR4S#search=%22disestablishment%20principles%22.

53. James W. Torke, *The English Religious Establishment*, 12 J. L. & Religion 399, 412 (1995–96); see also Arlin M. Adams & Charles Emmerich, A Nation Dedicated to Religious Liberty 53-54 (1990) (stating that the monarchs of England "exercise control of 'Lords Spiritual and Temporal'"), as cited in Marci A. Hamilton and Rachel Steamert, "The Religious Origins of Disestablishment," *Notre Dame Law Review*, Vol. 81, Issue 5, June 1, 2006, https://scholarship.law.nd.edu/cgi/viewcontent.cgi?article=1357&=&context=ndlr&=&sei-redir=1&referer=https%253A%252F%252Fwww.bing.com%252Fsearch%253Fq%253Ddisestablishment%252Bprinciples%2526src%253DIE-SearchBox%2526FORM%253DIESR4S#search=%22disestablishment%20principles%22.

54. Marci A. Hamilton and Rachel Steamert, "The Religious Origins of Disestablishment," *Notre Dame Law Review*, Vol. 81, Issue 5, June 1, 2006, p. 1779, https://scholarship.law.nd.edu/cgi/viewcontent.cgi?article=1357&=&context=ndlr&=&sei-redir=1&referer=https%253A%252F%252Fwww.bing.com%252Fsearch%253Fq%253Ddisestablishment%252Bprinciples

%2526src%253DIE-SearchBox%2526FORM%253DIESR4S#search=%2
2disestablishment%20principles%22.

55. "University of Pennsylvania," Ben Franklin Historical Society, accessed
February 25, 2020, http://www.benjamin-franklin-history.org/
university-of-pennsylvania/.

56. Lambert, supra note 21, at 43; Morgan, supra note 21, at 27–28, as cited
in Marci A. Hamilton and Rachel Steamert, "The Religious Origins of
Disestablishment," *Notre Dame Law Review*, Vol. 81, Issue 5, June 1, 2006,
https://scholarship.law.nd.edu/cgi/viewcontent.cgi?article=1357&=&contex
t=ndlr&=&sei-redir=1&referer=https%253A%252F%252Fwww.bing.com
%252Fsearch%253Fq%253Ddisestablishment%252Bprinciples%2526src
%253DIE-SearchBox%2526FORM%253DIESR4S#search=%22disestabli
shment%20principles%22.

57. Arlin M. Adams & Charles Emmerich, A Nation Dedicated to Religious
Liberty 53–54 (1990), supra note 19, at 7, as cited in Marci A. Hamilton
and Rachel Steamert, "The Religious Origins of Disestablishment," *Notre
Dame Law Review*, Vol. 81, Issue 5, June 1, 2006, https://scholarship.law.
nd.edu/cgi/viewcontent.cgi?article=1357&=&context=ndlr&=&sei-redir
=1&referer=https%253A%252F%252Fwww.bing.com%252Fsearch%2
53Fq%253Ddisestablishment%252Bprinciples%2526src%253DIE-Sear
chBox%2526FORM%253DIESR4S#search=%22disestablishment%20
principles%22.

58. Marci A. Hamilton and Rachel Steamert, "The Religious Origins of
Disestablishment," *Notre Dame Law Review*, Vol. 81, Issue 5, June 1, 2006,
note 126, https://scholarship.law.nd.edu/cgi/viewcontent.cgi?article=1357&
=&context=ndlr&=&sei-redir=1&referer=https%253A%252F%252Fwww.
bing.com%252Fsearch%253Fq%253Ddisestablishment%252Bprinciples
%2526src%253DIE-SearchBox%2526FORM%253DIESR4S#search=%2
2disestablishment%20principles%22.

59. Marci A. Hamilton and Rachel Steamert, "The Religious Origins of
Disestablishment," *Notre Dame Law Review*, Vol. 81, Issue 5, June 1, 2006,
see note 131, https://scholarship.law.nd.edu/cgi/viewcontent.cgi?article=13
57&=&context=ndlr&=&sei-redir=1&referer=https%253A%252F%252F
www.bing.com%252Fsearch%253Fq%253Ddisestablishment%252Bprinci

ples%2526src%253DIE-SearchBox%2526FORM%253DIESR4S#search=
%22disestablishment%20principles%22.

60. Marci A. Hamilton and Rachel Steamert, "The Religious Origins of
Disestablishment," *Notre Dame Law Review,* Vol. 81, Issue 5, June 1, 2006,
see note 133, https://scholarship.law.nd.edu/cgi/viewcontent.cgi?article=13
57&=&context=ndlr&=&sei-redir=1&referer=https%253A%252F%252F
www.bing.com%252Fsearch%253Fq%253Ddisestablishment%252Bprinci
ples%2526src%253DIE-SearchBox%2526FORM%253DIESR4S#search=
%22disestablishment%20principles%22.

61. Maryland Act Concerning Religion, in 5 *The Founders' Constitution,* Supra
note 117, at 49, 50, as cited in Marci A. Hamilton and Rachel Steamert,
"The Religious Origins of Disestablishment," *Notre Dame Law Review,* Vol.
81, Issue 5, June 1, 2006, https://scholarship.law.nd.edu/cgi/viewcontent.cgi
?article=1357&=&context=ndlr&=&sei-redir=1&referer=https%253A%25
2F%252Fwww.bing.com%252Fsearch%253Fq%253Ddisestablishment%2
52Bprinciples%2526src%253DIE-SearchBox%2526FORM%253DIESR4
S#search=%22disestablishment%20principles%22.

62. "Jesuit," Encyclopedia Britannica, accessed March 1, 2020, https://www.
britannica.com/topic/Jesuits. " Jesuit, member of the Society of Jesus (S.J.),
a Roman Catholic order of religious men founded by St. Ignatius of Loyola,
noted for its educational, missionary, and charitable works. The order has
been regarded by many as the principal agent of the Counter-Reformation
and was later a leading force in modernizing the church."

63. Jay P. Dolan, *The American Catholic Experience: A History from Colonial
Times to the Present* 75 (1985), at 96, as cited in Marci A. Hamilton and
Rachel Steamert, "The Religious Origins of Disestablishment," *Notre
Dame Law Review,* Vol. 81, Issue 5, June 1, 2006, https://scholarship.law.
nd.edu/cgi/viewcontent.cgi?article=1357&=&context=ndlr&=&sei-redir
=1&referer=https%253A%252F%252Fwww.bing.com%252Fsearch%2
53Fq%253Ddisestablishment%252Bprinciples%2526src%253DIE-Sear
chBox%2526FORM%253DIESR4S#search=%22disestablishment%20
principles%22.

64. "Jefferson's Religious Beliefs," The Jefferson Monticello, accessed February
25, 2020, https://www.monticello.org/site/research-and-collections/
jeffersons-religious-beliefs.

65. Matthew Wills, "Who Wrote the Declaration of Independence?" JSTOR Daily, July 2, 2016, https://daily.jstor.org/who-wrote-the-declaration-independence/.

66. James R. Stoner, Jr., "Declaration of Independence," Natural Law, Natural Rights and American Constitutionalism, accessed February 25, 2020, http://www.nlnrac.org/american/declaration-of-independence.

67. "Natural Law and Sir William Blackstone," All About Philosophy, accessed February 25, 2020, https://www.allaboutphilosophy.org/natural-law-and-sir-william-blackstone-faq.htm.

68. Joseph Mattera, "The Christian Influence Behind the Declaration of Independence, charismanews.com, July 4, 2013, https://www.charismanews.com/us/40100-the-christian-influence-behind-the-declaration-of-independence.

69. Romans 13:1–2 and 1 Peter 2:13–14.

70. "Huguenots," Wikipedia, accessed March 1, 2020, https://en.wikipedia.org/wiki/Huguenots.

71. Cited in "Where does the concept of a 'God-shaped hole' originate?," Christianity, accessed February 25, 2020, https://christianity.stackexchange.com/questions/2746/where-does-the-concept-of-a-god-shaped-hole-originate.

72. James Madison, "Federalist paper #10: The Union as a Safeguard Against Domestic Faction and Insurrection," The New York Packet, November 23, 1787, as published in Openstax.org, https://openstax.org/books/american-government-2e/pages/c-federalist-papers-10-and-51.

73. Alex Swayer, "Federal Court Upholds Prayer in Congress," *Washington Times*, October 11, 2017, https://www.washingtontimes.com/news/2017/oct/11/federal-court-upholds-prayer-congress/.

74. Thomas Kidd, "Why Ben Franklin Called for Prayer at the Constitutional Convention," thegospelcoalition.org, September 17, 2017, https://www.thegospelcoalition.org/blogs/evangelical-history/why-ben-franklin-called-for-prayer-at-the-constitutional-convention/.

75. Tamara Christine Van Hooser, "How Did the Bible Influence the U.S. Constitution?, theclassroom.com, May 10, 2019, https://www.theclassroom.com/did-bible-influence-us-constitution-11384841.html.

76. Mark Weldon Whitten, "Manufactured Myth: America Isn't a 'Christian

Nation' as the Religious Right Claims and the Constitutional Convention Proves It," Church & State, Vol. 62, Issue 2, February 1, 2009 https://link.gale.com/apps/doc/A194193378/AONE?u=wash92852&sid=AONE&xid=f284fb20.

77. Mark Weldon Whitten, "Manufactured Myth: America Isn't a 'Christian Nation' as the Religious Right Claims, and the Constitutional Convention Proves It," Church & State, Vol. 62, Issue 2, February 1, 2009 https://link.gale.com/apps/doc/A194193378/AONE?u=wash92852&sid=AONE&xid=f284fb20.

78. Mark Weldon Whitten, "Manufactured Myth: America Isn't a 'Christian Nation' as the Religious Right Claims and the Constitutional Convention Proves It," Church & State Vol. 62, Issue 2, February 1, 2009 https://link.gale.com/apps/doc/A194193378/AONE?u=wash92852&sid=AONE&xid=f284fb20.

79. Rob Natelson, "The Relationship Between the Declaration of Independence and the Constitution," Independenceinstitute.org, March 21, 2017, https://i2i.org/the-relationship-between-the-declaration-of-independence-and-the-constitution/.

80. Ibid.

81. Ibid. Admittedly, for most Christians, the founders' moral failure to address slavery in the Constitution was a major shortfall and reflected poorly on the young nation. However, Christian leaders were at the forefront to abolish slavery. Specifically, in the late seventeenth century, Quakers and some evangelical denominations condemned slavery as un-Christian. Then, by the turn of the century (1804), all Northern states, beginning with An Act for the Gradual Abolition of Slavery from Pennsylvania in 1780, outlawed slavery, as did Massachusetts, which declared all men equal in the state's constitution. Finally, in 1808, the US federal government criminalized the international slave trade and made slavery unconstitutional, which contributed to the American Civil War (1861–1865).

82. Ralph Benko, "A Huge Victory for Free Speech In Boston," Forbes, August 20, 2017, https://www.forbes.com/sites/ralphbenko/2017/08/20/a-huge-victory-for-free-speech-in-boston/#24e510c71e40.

83. "George Washington, Brainy Quote, accessed March 1, 2020, https://www.brainyquote.com/quotes/george_washington_146829.

84. "Social Institutions," Stanford Encyclopedia of Philosophy, January 4, 2007; revised April 9, 2019, https://plato.stanford.edu/entries/social-institutions/.

85. Dave Meyer, "Defining a Christian Nation," America, accessed February 25, 2020, https://joycemeyer.org/america/articles/defining-a-christian-nation.

86. Eddie Hyatt, "5 Founding Principles That Made America Great," charimanews.com, July 4, 2018, https://www.charismanews.com/politics/opinion/71951-5-founding-principles-that-made-america-great.

87. "James Madison," Ponding Principles, accessed March 1, 2020, https://ponderingprinciples.com/quotes/madison/.

88. "James Madison," AZ Quotes, accessed March 1, 2020, https://www.azquotes.com/quote/610753.

89. George Washington, "George Washington's Thanksgiving Proclamation, 1789: 'Duty of All Nations to Acknowledge God'," LifeNews.com, accessed March 1, 2020, https://www.lifenews.com/2012/11/22/george-washingtons-thanksgiving-proclamation-1789/.

90. "This event was recorded by the French sociologist, Alexis de Tocqueville, and occurred during his visit to America in 1831. Tocqueville said the incident was merely noted in the newspaper without further comment." https://www.charismanews.com/politics/opinion/71951-5-founding-principles-that-made-america-great.

91. *Journals of the American Congress from 1774–1788: In Four Volumes, Journals of Congress 1782*, Way and Gideon, Harvard University, 1823, p. 76.

92. "President's Quotes on the Bible," Presidents Quotes on the Bible, accessed February 25, 2020, http://allianceforreligiousfreedom.com/educate-yourself/quotes/presidents-quotes-on-the-bible/.

93. Eddie Hyatt, "5 Founding Principles That Made America Great," ChristmaNews, July 4, 2018, https://www.charismanews.com/politics/opinion/71951-5-founding-principles-that-made-america-great.

94. Robert Higgs, "If Men Were Angels," MisesInstitute, October 15, 2010, https://mises.org/library/if-men-were-angels.

95. "The Phrase Finder," accessed February 25, 2020, https://www.phrases.org.uk/meanings/absolute-power-corrupts-absolutely.html.

96. Washington's Farewell Address 1796, The Avalon Project, Yale University, accessed February 25, 2020, https://avalon.law.yale.edu/18th_century/washing.asp.

97. "George Washington's Farewell Address," The Library of Congress, accessed February 25, 2020, https://www.loc.gov/rr/program/bib/ourdocs/farewell.html.

98. Charles B. Sanford, *The Religious Life of Thomas Jefferson*, University of Virginia Press, 1984, p. 124.

99. "From John Adams to Massachusetts Militia, 11 October 1798," Founders Online, accessed February 25, 2020, https://founders.archives.gov/documents/Adams/99-02-02-3102.

100. "Jefferson's 'Wall of Separation between Church & State,'" Jamestown Settlement & American Revolution Museum at Yorktown, accessed February 25, 2020, https://www.historyisfun.org/blog/wall-of-separation/.

101. Dinesh D'Souza, "What's So Great About Christianity," Goodreads, accessed February 25, 2020, https://www.goodreads.com/quotes/323466-christianity-enhanced-the-notion-of-political-and-social-accountability-by.

102. John Adams, "A Dissertation on the Canon and Feudal Law," The Federalist Papers Project, accessed March 1, 2020, www.thefederalistpapers.org.

103. Samuel Adams cited in "Rule of Law," Patriot Week Foundation, accessed March 1, 2020, https://www.patriotweek.org/copy-of-revolution.

104. "Thomas Jefferson," Founders' Quotes, accessed March 1, 2020, https://foundersquotes.com/founding-fathers-quote/a-free-people-claim-their-rights-as-derived-from-the-laws-of-nature-and-not-as-the-gift-of-their-chief-magistrate/.

105. "Alexander Hamilton," goodreads.com, accessed March 1, 2020, https://www.goodreads.com/quotes/159813-the-sacred-rights-of-mankind-are-not-to-be-rummaged.

106. "Founders' Quotes," accessed February 25, 2020, https://billofrightsinstitute.org/founding-documents/founders-quotes/.

107. "The Analysis of Thomas Hobbes And the Government Philosophy Essay," UK Essays, May 12, 2016, https://www.ukessays.com/essays/philosophy/the-analysis-of-thomas-hobbes-and-the-government-philosophy-essay.php.

108. Scott J. Hammond, Kevin R. Hardwick, Howard Leslie, *Classics of American Political and Constitutional Thought: Origins through the Civil War*, Hackett Publishing, 2007, p. 538.

109. Michael Warren, "The Limited Government," America's Survival Guide, accessed March 1, 2020, http://www.americassurvivalguide.com/limited-government.php.

110. Myron Magnet, "Tom Paine's Two Radicalisms, And their consequences—for his era and ours, *City Journal*, Autumn 2013, https://www.city-journal.org/html/tom-paine%E2%80%99s-two-radicalisms-13611.html.

111. Martin Carnoy, *The State and Political Theory*, Princeton University Press, July 14, 2014, p.18.

112. "Core Values," Bible Fellowship Church, accessed February 25, 2020, https://www.bfc.org/who-we-are/core-values/.

113. Ning Kang, *Puritanism and Its Impact upon American Values*, School of Foreign Languages, Qingdao University of Science and Technology, 69 Songling Lu, Qingdao 266061, China.

114. "Great Benjamin Franklin Quotes, Quotes for Ever," accessed February 25, 2020, https://quotes4ever.com/benjamin-franklin-quotes/.

115. Alan Burrow, "The Foremost Reading for Everybody Should Be Holy Scripture," FaithWorking, August 25, 2010, http://www.faithworking.com/2010/08/25/the-foremost-reading-for-everybody-should-be-holy-scripture/.

116. "Harvard Divinity School," Wikipedia, accessed February 25, 2020, https://en.wikipedia.org/wiki/Harvard_Divinity_School.

117. "Alexis de Tocqueville," Wikiquote, accessed February 25, 2020, https://en.wikiquote.org/wiki/Alexis_de_Tocqueville.

118. "Thomas Jefferson," Deo Vindice, May 15, 2012 https://sesquicentenary.wordpress.com/2012/05/15/i-consider-the-foundation-of-the-constitution-as-laid-on-this-ground-that-all-powers-not-delegated-to-the-united-states-by-the-constitution-nor-prohibited-by-it-to-the-states-are-reserve/.

119. Ralph Ketcham, *James Madison: A Biography*, University of Virginia Press, 1990, p. 320.

120. "Religion in Early America," shmoop.com, accessed February 25, 2020, https://www.shmoop.com/church-and-state/religion-early-america.html.

121. Elizabeth Youmans, "The Role of the Bible in Early American Education," darrowmillerandfriends.com, June 22, 2017, http://darrowmillerandfriends.com/2017/06/22/bible-role-early-american-education/.

122. Ibid.

123. Ibid.

124. John Calvin, "Institutes of the Christian Religion," Christian Classics Ethereal Library, accessed February 25, 2020, https://www.ccel.org/ccel/calvin/institutes.html.

125. Ron Gleason, "John Calvin and Civil Government," Christian Library, accessed February 25, 2020, https://www.christianstudylibrary.org/article/john-calvin-and-civil-government.

126. Sam Blumenfeld, "Religion in Early American Education," *New American*, October 18, 2012, https://www.thenewamerican.com/reviews/opinion/item/13262-religion-in-early-american-education.

127. Ibid.

128. Ibid.

129. "Boston Latin School," Wikipedia, accessed February 25, 2020, https://en.wikipedia.org/wiki/Boston_Latin_School.

130. Blumenfeld, Op cit.

131. Youmans, Op cit.

132. *U.S. History I: United States History 1607–1865* Text for History 121.

133. "Colonial Life: Faith, Family, Work," sageamericanhistory.net, accessed February 25, 2020, http://sageamericanhistory.net/colonial/topics/coloniallife.html.

134. "Families in Colonial America," Digital History, Topic ID 75, 2019, http://www.digitalhistory.uh.edu/topic_display.cfm?tcid=75.

135. Ibid.

136. Ibid.

137. Michele Meleen, "Family Life in the 1920s," Lovetoknow, accessed February 25, 2020, https://family.lovetoknow.com/about-family-values/family-life-1920s.

138. "Colonial Life: Faith, Family, Work," Op cit.

139. Ibid.

140. Henry J. Sage, *U.S. History I: United States History 1607-1865*, Third Edition Revised and Updated, June 2010, Academic American History, http://elibrary.bsu.az/books_400/N_377.pdf.

141. Sarah Pruitt, , "How Henry VIII's Divorce Led to Reformation," History, January 6, 2020, https://www.history.com/news/henry-viii-divorce-reformation-catholic-church.

142. Ibid.

143. Ibid.

144. Ibid.

145. C. N. Trueman, "The Reformation, "History Learning Site, March 17, 2017, https://www.historylearningsite.co.uk/tudor-england/the-reformation/.

146. "Religion and the Founding of the American Republic: Religion in Eighteenth-Century America," Library of Congress, accessed February 25, 2020, https://www.loc.gov/exhibits/religion/rel02.html.

147. Ibid.

148. Ibid.

149. Ibid.

150. Ibid.

151. Ibid.

152. Jonathan Edwards, "Sinners in the Hands of an Angry God," Sermon VI delivered on July 8, 1741, in Enfield, Massachusetts (now Connecticut), reproduced at https://www.monergism.com/thethreshold/sdg/pdf/edwards_angry.pdf.

153. "George Mason and Religious Liberty," George Washington Institute for Religious Freedom, accessed February 25, 2020, https://www.gwirf.org/george-mason-and-religious-liberty/.

154. "Colonial Life: Faith, Family, Work," Op cit.

155. "The American Economy Prior to the Revolutionary War," History Central, accessed February 25, 2020, https://www.historycentral.com/Revolt/Americans/prioreconomic.html

156. Ibid.

157. Michael Slattery, "The Catholic Origins of Capitalism: Max Weber Clarified ," *Crisis Magazine*, April 1, 1988, https://www.crisismagazine.com/1988/the-catholic-origins-of-capitalism-max-weber-clarified.

158. Michael Novak, "How Christianity Created Capitalism," Acton Institute, July 20, 2010, https://acton.org/pub/religion-liberty/volume-10-number-3/how-christianity-created-capitalism.

159. Daniel Luzer, "The Protestant Work Ethic is Real," *Pacific Standard*, June 14, 2017, https://psmag.com/economics/protestant-worth-ethic-real-65544.

160. Ibid.

161. Ibid.

162. Becky Little, "Why Lincoln's 'House Divided' Speech Was So Important," History, November 26, 2019, https://www.history.com/news/ abraham-lincoln-house-divided-speech.

163. Nicholas Kristof, "We're Less and Less a Christian Nation, and I Blame Some Blowhards," *New York Times*, October 26, 2019, https://www. nytimes.com/2019/10/26/opinion/sunday/christianity-united-states.html.

164. "Transcript of Federalist Papers, No. 10 & No. 51," www.ourdocuments. gov, accessed February 25, 2020, https://www.ourdocuments.gov/print_ friendly.php?flash=false&page=transcript&doc=10&title=Transcript+of+Fe deralist+Papers%2C+No.+10+%26amp%3B+No.+51+.

165. "Thomas Jefferson," Op. cit.

166. Ketcham, Op cit.

167. William P. Barr, *Remarks to the Law School and the de Nicola Center for Ethics and Culture*, University of Notre Dame, South Bend, IN, October 11, 2019.

168. Ibid.

169. Ibid.

170. Carlo Invernizzi-Accetti, "The Unholy Alliance of the Religious Right and Trumpism Is Deeply anti-Christian," *Guardian*, October 24, 2019, https://www.theguardian.com/commentisfree/2019/oct/24/ trump-william-barr-christianity-church-state.

171. Joe Carter, "Two U.S. Senators Apply an Anti-Christian Religious Test for Government Officials," thegospelcoalition.org, June 8, 2017, https://www. thegospelcoalition.org/article/two-u-s-senators-apply-an-anti-christian- religious-test-for-government-officials/.

172. Invernizzi-Accetti, Op cit.

173. Ibid.

174. Ibid.

175. Ibid.

176. David French, "Anti-Christian Ideology Is an Emerging Aspect of White Progressive Populism," *National Review*, January 21, 2019, https://www. nationalreview.com/2019/01/anti-christian-ideology-is-an-emerging- aspect-of-white-progressive-populism/.

177. Ibid.

178. Trevor Thomas, "Today's Democrats: Anti-Christian, Anti-Israel, Anti-God," *American Thinker*, January 17, 2019, https://www.americanthinker.com/articles/2019/01/todays_democrats_antichristian_antiisrael_antigod.html#ixzz68O1KwkYB.

179. Jack Jenkins, "5 Faith Facts about Mike Pompeo: A Divisive Devotion," religionnews.com, April 19, 2018, https://religionnews.com/2018/04/19/5-faith-facts-about-mike-pompeo-a-divisive-devotion/.

180. Samuel Smith, "Pompeo Faces Criticism for Giving Speech on Being a 'Christian leader,'" christianpost.com, October 15, 2019, https://www.christianpost.com/news/pompeo-faces-criticism-for-giving-speech-being-christian-leader.html.

181. Ibid.

182. Thomas, Op. Cit.

183. Ibid.

184. Ibid.

185. Morgan Marietta, "Christianity at the Supreme Court: From majority power to minority rights," The Conversation, September 24, 2019, https://theconversation.com/christianity-at-the-supreme-court-from-majority-power-to-minority-rights-119718.

186. Ibid.

187. Ibid.

188. John Hawkins, "7 Examples of Discrimination against Christians in America," townhall.com, September 17, 2013, https://townhall.com/columnists/johnhawkins/2013/09/17/7-examples-of-discrimination-against-christians-in-america-n1701966.

189. Ibid.

190. Marietta, Op. cit.

191. Ibid.

192. Mike Less, "Obama Told Us 'Elections Have Consequences.' Here's One Way to Reverse His Liberal Legacy," *Daily Signal*, January 17, 2017, https://www.dailysignal.com/2017/01/17/elections-have-consequences-for-housing-policy/.

193. Sami K. Martin, "Franklin Graham Says the US Government Has an 'Anti-Christian' Bias," christianpost.com, March 12, 2015, https://www.

christianpost.com/news/franklin-graham-says-the-american-government-has-an-anti-christian-bias.html.

194. Ibid.

195. Hawkins, Op. cit.

196. Ibid.

197. Ibid.

198. Todd Starns, "Government Hostility to Religion Spiked under Obama, New Report Finds," Fox News, June 29, 2017, https://www.foxnews.com/opinion/government-hostility-to-religion-spiked-under-obama-new-report-finds.

199. Ibid.

200. Ibid.

201. Ibid.

202. "Wallbuilders," accessed February 25, 2020, https://wallbuilders.com/about-us/#partner.

203. "America's Most Biblically-Hostile U.S. President," Wallbuilders, accessed February 25, 2020, https://wallbuilders.com/americas-biblically-hostile-u-s-president/.

204. "The Westminster Shorter Catechism," The Westminster Presbyterian, accessed February 25, 2020, http://www.westminsterconfession.org/confessional-standards/the-westminster-shorter-catechism.php.

205. "Harvard GSAS Christian Community," Harvard, accessed February 25, 2020, http://www.hcs.harvard.edu/~gsascf/shield-and-veritas-history/.

206. John Milton, Quotable Quotes, accessed February 25, 2020, https://www.goodreads.com/quotes/464705-the-end-then-of-learning-is-to-repair-the-ruins.

207. Youmans, Op. cit.

208. "Boston Latin School," Wikipedia, accessed February 25, 2020, https://en.wikipedia.org/wiki/Boston_Latin_School.

209. Elliot Hannon, "New Test Scores Show U.S. Students Continue to Trail Global Peers in Reading and Math," Slate, December 3, 2019, https://slate.com/news-and-politics/2019/12/global-test-scores-us-american-students-performance-trail-reading-math-science.html.

210. Nadia Pflaum, "Trump: U.S. Spends More Than 'almost any other major country' on Education," politifact.com, September 21, 2016, https://

www.politifact.com/ohio/statements/2016/sep/21/donald-trump/
trump-us-spends-more-almost-any-other-major-countr/.

211. "A Nation at Risk," Department of Education, April 1983, https://www2.
ed.gov/pubs/NatAtRisk/risk.html.

212. "Church Dropouts Have Risen to 64%—But What About Those Who
Stay?" Barna, September 4, 2019, https://www.barna.com/research/
resilient-disciples/.

213. Ken Ham and Brett Beemer, *Already Gone: Why Your Kids Will Quit
Church and What You Can Do to Stop it* (Green Forest, AR: Master Books,
2009), 24,179.

214. Alex Newman, "Christians Urged to Pull Children
from Public Schools," *New American*, March 23, 2017,
https://www.thenewamerican.com/culture/education/
item/25675-christians-urged-to-pull-children-from-public-schools.

215. Robert Stroud, "Christians and Contemporary Culture," Mere
Inkling, December 4, 2019, https://mereinkling.net/2019/12/04/
christians-and-contemporary-culture/.

216. As cited in *Save the Children: Good K–12 Formal Education Is Necessarily
Christian,* by Bruce H Smith, a thesis presented to the faculty in partial
fulfillment of the requirements for the degree Master of Arts (Religion) at
Reformed Theological Seminary.

217. R. J. Rushdoony, *The Messianic Character of American Education*
(Philadelphia: Presbyterian and Reformed Publishing Company, 1963),
160.

218. Blair Adams, *Who Owns the Children: Public Compulsion, Private
Responsibility and the Dilemma of UltimateAuthority*, Book Five, "Education
as Religious War" (Waco, TX: Truth Forum, 1991), 9.

219. Murray N. Rothbard, *The Progressive Era*, Ludwig von Mises Institute,
2017.

220. Merriam-Webster, accessed February 25, 2020, https://www.merriam-
webster.com/dictionary/brainwashing.

221. Merriam-Webster, accessed February 25, 2020, https://www.merriam-
webster.com/dictionary/Weltanschauung.

222. Matt Walsh, "Christian Parents, Your Kids Aren't Equipped to Be Public
School Missionaries," The Blaze, April 3, 2017, www.theblaze.com/

contributions/matt-walsh-christian-parents-your-kids-arent-equipped-to-be-public-school-missionaries/.

223. Ibid.

224. Al Benson Jr., "Government Schools Really Are Anti-Christian," Gospel Herald Ministries, November 19, 2003, https://www.gospelherald.com/article/education/19166/government-schools-really-are-anti-christian.htm.

225. Ibid.

226. Ibid.

227. Ibid.

228. Walsh, Op. cit.

229. Ibid.

230. Ibid.

231. Ibid.

232. "What is the Family?," Blessings, accessed February 26, 2020, https://www.blessings-us.com/what-is-the-family/.

233. "Blackstone: Introduction to the Laws of England," Online Library of Liberty, accessed February 26, 2020, https://oll.libertyfund.org/pages/blackstone-introduction-to-the-laws-of-england.

234. Courtney G. Joslin, "The Evolution of the American Family," American Bar Association, July 1, 2009, https://www.americanbar.org/groups/crsj/publications/human_rights_magazine_home/human_rights_vol36_2009/summer2009/the_evolution_of_the_american_family/.

235. Ibid.

236. Matt Ridley, *The Rational Optimist: How Prosperity Evolves*, HarperCollins, New York, 2010, p. 13.

237. "The Foundation of National Morality—John Adams (1735–1826)," First Baptist Church of Perryville, January 25, 2014, http://www.perryville.org/2014/01/the-foundation-of-national-morality%E2%80%94john-adams-1735-%E2%80%93-1826/.

238. "Lawrence Stone," AZQuotes, accessed February 26, 2020, https://www.azquotes.com/quote/680154.

239. Hillel Halkin, The Rabbinic Imagination," Commentary, March 1993, https://www.commentarymagazine.com/articles/the-rabbinic-imagination/.

240. "More Weddings, But Trend Won't Last," *USA Today*, June 17, 2013, https://www.usatoday.com/story/news/nation/2013/06/17/marriage-trends-demographics/2424641/.

241. "Parenting in America," Pew Social Trends, Pew Research Institute, December 17, 2015, https://www.pewsocialtrends.org/2015/12/17/parenting-in-american-acknowledgments/.

242. "Premarital Sex: Almost Everyone's Doing It," CBS News, December 19, 2006, https://www.cbsnews.com/news/premarital-sex-almost-everyones-doing-it/.

243. Michael Snyder, "Culture Upside Down: There Has Been a Colossal Shift in America's Values Since 2001," InfoWars, June 4, 2014, https://www.infowars.com/culture-upside-down-there-has-been-a-colossal-shift-in-americas-values-since-2001/.

244. "Adolescents and Young Adults," Center for Disease Control and Prevention, accessed February 26, 2020, https://www.cdc.gov/std/life-stages-populations/adolescents-youngadults.htm.

245. John Amis, "1 in 4 Teen Girls Have STD," USA Today, March 11, 2008, https://usatoday30.usatoday.com/news/health/2008-03-11-std_n.htm.

246. William J. Bennett, The Broken Hearth: Reversing the Moral Collapse of the American Family, Doubleday, 2001, https://www.worldcat.org/wcpa/servlet/DCARead?standardNo=0385499159&standardNoType=1&excerpt=true.

247. Michael Snyder, "100 Facts About The Moral Collapse Of America That Are Almost Too Crazy To Believe," The Truth, June 4, 2016, http://thetruthwins.com/archives/100-facts-about-the-moral-collapse-of-america-that-are-almost-too-crazy-to-believe.

248. Bennett, Op. cit.

249. "Parenting in America," Op. cit.

250. Bennett Op. cit.

251. Merriam-Webster, accessed February 25, 2020, https://www.merriam-webster.com/dictionary/pornography .

252. Synder, Op. cit.

253. Penny Starr, "George Washington Drummed Out Soldier for 'Infamous Crime' of Attempted 'Sodomy'," CNS News, January 3, 2011, https://www.cnsnews.com/news/article/george-washington-drummed-out-soldier-infamous-crime-attempted-sodomy.

254. William Bennett, "Stronger Families Stronger Societies," New York Times, April 24, 2012, https://www.nytimes.com/roomfordebate/2012/04/24/are-family-values-outdated/stronger-families-stronger-societies.

255. "Parenting in America," Op. cit.

256. "The Consequences of Fatherlessness," fathers.com, accessed February 25, 2020, http://fathers.com/statistics-and-research/the-consequences-of-fatherlessness/

257. "Parenting in America," Op. cit.

258. Snyder, Op. cit.

259. Jenny Kutner, "This Is What the Modern American Family Will Look Like by 2050," MIC.com, August 14, 2015, https://www.mic.com/articles/123908/this-is-what-the-modern-american-family-will-look-like-by-2050.

260. Joanna L. Grossman, "California Allows Children to Have More Than Two Legal Parents," Verdict, 15 October 2013, https://verdict.justia.com/2013/10/15/california-allows-children-two-legal-parents.

261. Kutner, Op. cit. and Erin Duffin, "Average number of people per family in the United States from 1960 to 2019," Statista, November 28, 2019, https://www.statista.com/statistics/183657/average-size-of-a-family-in-the-us/.

262. Megan Brenan, "Americans Say U.S. Moral Values Not Good and Getting Worse," Gallup, May 31, 2019, https://news.gallup.com/poll/257954/americans-say-moral-values-not-good-getting-worse.aspx.

263. "Mayflower Compact," National Constitution Center, accessed February 26, 2020, https://constitutioncenter.org/learn/educational-resources/historical-documents/mayflower-compact.

264. Glenn T. Stanton, "New Harvard Research Says U.S. Christianity Is Not Shrinking, But Growing Stronger," Federalist, January 22, 2018, https://thefederalist.com/2018/01/22/new-harvard-research-says-u-s-christianity-not-shrinking-growing-stronger/.

265. Claude Fischer, "AG Barr Says Attacks on Religion Are Loosening the Hounds of Hell. Are They?," Made in America, February 6, 2020, http://madeinamericathebook.wordpress.com/.

266. "In U.S., Decline of Christianity Continues at Rapid Pace," Pew Research Center, October 17, 2019, https://www.pewforum.org/2019/10/17/in-u-s-decline-of-christianity-continues-at-rapid-pace/.

267. Ibid.

268. Ibid.

269. Ibid.

270. Stanton, Op. cit.

271. Ibid.

272. Ibid.

273. Ibid.

274. As cited in Stanton, Op. cit.

275. J. Warner Wallace, "Is Christianity Shrinking in America? 'Yes' and 'No'," Cold-Case Christianity, February 19, 2018, https://coldcasechristianity. com/writings/is-christianity-shrinking-in-america-yes-and-no/.

276. Ibid.

277. David Millard Haskell, "Why Conservative Churches Grow and Liberal Churches Shrink," *Dallas Morning News*, December 15, 2016, https://www.dallasnews.com/opinion/commentary/2016/12/15/ why-conservative-churches-grow-and-liberal-churches-shrink/.

278. Ibid.

279. Steven Waldman, "Religious Freedom Is America's Greatest Export—and It's Under Attack," *Newsweek*, May 9, 2019, https://www.newsweek. com/2019/05/17/religious-freedom-americas-greatest-export-under-attack-1418121.html.

280. "Competing Worldviews Influence Today's Christians," Barna, May 9, 2017, https://www.barna.com/research/ competing-worldviews-influence-todays-christians/.

281. Ibid.

282. Ibid.

283. Ibid.

284. Ibid.

285. Ibid.

286. Jerry Falwell Jr., "Liberals Proved Pence Right about Anti-Christian Discrimination," RealClear Politics, May 15, 2019, https://www. realclearpolitics.com/articles/2019/05/15/liberals_proved_pence_right_ about_anti-christian_discrimination_140338.html.

287. Ibid.

288. Ibid.

289. Kate Shellnutt, "Study: Anti-Christian Bias Hasn't Grown. It's Just Gotten Richer," *Christianity Today*, October 10, 2017, https://www. christianitytoday.com/news/2017/october/anti-christian-bias-richer-evangelicals-persecution-complex.html.

290. Ibid.

291. George Yancey, "What Christianophobia Looks Like in America," *Christianity Today*, March 27, 2015, https://www.christianitytoday.com/ct/2015/march-web-only/what-christianophobia-looks-like-in-america.html.

292. Ibid.

293. Gunnar Gundersen, "Post-Christian America?," *Catholic Thing*, November 16, 2019, https://www.thecatholicthing.org/2019/11/16/post-christian-america-2/.

294. Ibid.

295. "Alexis de Tocqueville," Quotefancy.com, accessed February 26, 2020, https://quotefancy.com/quote/1444945/Alexis-de-Tocqueville-There-is-no-country-in-the-world-where-the-Christian-religion.

296. "Benjamin Franklin," AZ Quotes, accessed February 26, 2020, https://www.azquotes.com/quote/650863.

297. "John Adams Quotes1811–1816," Revolutionary War and Beyond, accessed February 26, 2020, https://www.revolutionary-war-and-beyond.com/john-adams-quotations-2.html.

298. "The U.S. Economy: A Brief History," accessed February 26, 2020, http://countrystudies.us/united-states/economy-3.htm.

299. "John Locke: Natural Rights to Life, Liberty, and Property," Foundation for Economic Education, August 1, 1996, https://fee.org/articles/john-locke-natural-rights-to-life-liberty-and-property/.

300. Novak, Op. cit.

301. Dante Alighieri, *Love that Moves the Sun and Other Stars*, Penguin Books, March 3, 2016, https://www.goodreads.com/book/show/29456649-love-that-moves-the-sun-and-other-stars.

302. Novak, Op. cit.

303. Christopher Clark, "A Wealth of Notions: Interpreting Economy and Morality in Early America," Early American Studies, Vol. 8, No. 3, University of Pennsylvania Press, Fall 2010, pp. 672–683.

304. Cited by Clark, "Capitalism and the Origins of the Humanitarian Sensibility," first published in the *American Historical Review* in 1985, is collected, together with responses by David Brion Davis and John Ashworth and askell's reply, in Thomas Bender, ed., *The Antislavery Debate:*

Capitalism and Abo litionism as a Problem in Historical Interpretation (Berkeley: University of California Press, 1992).

305. Cited by Clark, Jack D. Marietta, *The Reformation of American Quakerism, 1748–1783* (1984; reprint edition, Philadelphia: University of Pennsylvania Press, 2007), 24–5, noted that while indebtedness did not always lead to disownment, it did so in over 51.4 percent of the 613 cases he examined (p. 7, Table 1).

306. "Benjamin Franklin," AZ Quotes, accessed February 26, 2020, https://www.azquotes.com/quote/394939.

307. Norman S. Ream, "Morality in America," Foundation for Economic Education, July 1, 1993, https://fee.org/articles/morality-in-america/.

308. Justin McCarthy, "About Half of Americans Say U.S. Moral Values Are 'Poor,'" Gallup, June 1, 2018, https://news.gallup.com/poll/235211/half-americans-say-moral-values-poor.aspx.

309. Richard Ebeling, "Business Ethics and Morality of the Marketplace," American Institute for Economic Research, November 19, 2019, https://www.aier.org/article/business-ethics-and-morality-of-the-marketplace/.

310. Walter Williams, "Morality of Free Markets," OA Online, December 15, 2019, https://www.oaoa.com/editorial/columns/opinion_columnist/article_e402f10c-1d26-11ea-8689-e747a5c1f55d.htm.

311. Ibid.

312. Ibid.

313. Mohamed Younis, "Four in 10 Americans Embrace Some Form of Socialism," Gallup, May 20, 2019, https://news.gallup.com/poll/257639/four-americans-embrace-form-socialism.aspx.

314. "What Is Cultural Marxism?" Got Questions, accessed February 26, 2020, https://www.gotquestions.org/cultural-Marxism.html.

315. "Secular Humanism," Got Questions, accessed February 26, 2020, https://www.gotquestions.org/secular-humanism.html.

316. Soeren Kern, "Europe: Anti-Christian Attacks Reach All-Time High in 2019," Gatestone Institute, January 1, 2020, https://www.gatestoneinstitute.org/15366/europe-anti-christian-attacks#.

317. Ibid.

318. Ibid.

319. Ibid.

320. Cheryl Wetzstein, "200 'Openly Bigoted' Anti-Christian Groups Tagged as Intolerant," *Washington Times*, February 24, 2015, https://www.washingtontimes.com/news/2015/feb/24/200-openly-bigoted-anti-christian-groups-identifie/.

321. Ibid.

322. Ibid.

323. Ted Pike, "Anti-bias Laws Persecuting Christian Businesses," Political Cesspool, March 3, 2014, http://truthtellers.org/alerts/Anti-Bias-Laws-Persecuting-Christian-Businesses.html.

324. Jonathon Van Maren, "No Christian Persecution in the US? Try Telling That to These Christians," Lifesite News, November 21, 2016, https://www.lifesitenews.com/blogs/if-you-think-christians-arent-being-persecuted-in-the-u.s.-its-because-your.

325. Ibid.

326. Dom DiFurio, "Chick-fil-A Will End Donations to Christian Organizations with Anti-LGBT Values in 2020," *Dallas Morning News*, November 18, 2019, https://www.dallasnews.com/business/philanthropy/2019/11/18/chick-fil-a-will-end-donations-to-organizations-with-anti-lgbt-values/.

327. Ibid.

328. Ibid.

329. Ibid.

330. "A Victory for Americans Who Seek to Live by Faith," Hobby Lobby, June 30, 2014, http://hobbylobbycase.com/.

331. Faith Equality Index Debuts, Seven Brands Rise to the Top, MarketWatch, November 2, 2015, https://www.marketwatch.com/press-release/faith-equality-index-debuts-seven-brands-rise-to-the-top-2015-11-02.

332. Grace E. Cutler, "Not Everyone Thinks Starbucks' New Holiday Cups Are So Great," November 6, 2015, https://www.foxnews.com/food-drink/not-everyone-thinks-starbucks-new-holiday-cups-are-so-great.

333. Bradford Richardson, "Persecution of Christians Is on the Rise, Americans Say," *Washington Times*, April 5, 2016, https://www.washingtontimes.com/news/2016/apr/5/christians-facing-increased-persecution-america-po/.

334. Ibid.

335. "American Views on Intolerance and Religious Liberty in America,"

LifeWay Research, http://lifewayresearch.com/wp-content/uploads/2016/03/American-Views-on-Intolerance-and-Religious-Liberty-Sept-2015.pdf.

336. "Christian Persecution: The Persecution of Christians Is on the Rise Worldwide," Aid to the Church in Need, accessed February 26, 2020, https://www.churchinneed.org/christian-persecution/.

337. Ibid.

338. Ibid.

339. "Persecution of Christians Is 'Set to Rise' in 2019," *Christianity Today*, January 3, 2019, https://www.christiantoday.com/article/persecution-of-christians-is-set-to-rise-in-2019/131375.htm.

340. Sun Tzu, *The Art of War*, goodreads.com, accessed February 26, 2020, https://www.goodreads.com/quotes/17976-if-you-know-the-enemy-and-know-yourself-you-need.

341. "How Does Satan Wage War?," The Spiritual War, accessed February 26, 2020, https://truthnet.org/Spiritual-warfare/4Satanswar/Satans-war.htm.

342. Ibid.

343. "Psychological Warfare," Fandom, accessed February 26, 2020, https://mind-control.fandom.com/en/wiki/Psychological_warfare.

344. 2 Corinthians 4:4, Biblehub, accessed February 26, 2020, https://biblehub.com/lexicon/2_corinthians/4-4.htm.

345. "How Does Satan Wage War," Op. cit.

346. Shari Abbott, "How Does Satan Attack Christians? What Are the Big Three Schemes of the Devil?," Reason for Hope, October 15, 2018, https://reasonsforhopejesus.com/satan-attack-christians-devil-three-schemes/.

347. "Christianity," C. S. Lewis Quotes, accessed February 26, 2020, http://lewisquotes.com/quotations/christianity/.

348. "The Bishop of Truro's Independent Review for the Foreign Secretary of FCO Support for Persecuted Christians," Press Release, *Anglican Ink*, July 10, 2019, http://anglican.ink/2019/07/10/the-bishop-of-truros-independent-review-for-the-foreign-secretary-of-fco-support-for-persecuted-christians./.

349. Homer, *The Odyssey*, goodreads.com, accessed March 4, 2020, https://www.goodreads.com/quotes/432804-out-of-sight-out-of-mind.

350. "Why Does the Mainstream Media Purposely Ignore Mass Killings of Christians Across the Globe?, From the Trenches Worldreport.com, March 19, 2019, https://fromthetrenchesworldreport.com/why-does-the-mainstream-media-purposely-ignore-mass-killings-of-christians-across-the-globe/243528.

351. Ibid.

352. Arthur Chrenkoff, "Ignoring the War on Christians— Media Bias or Merely News as Usual?," Daily Chrenk, March 21, 2019, http://thedailychrenk.com/2019/03/21/ignoring-war-christians-media-bias-merely-news-usual/.

353. Ibid.

354. Ibid.

355. Matthew Miller, "Chinese President Warns of Foreign Infiltration through Religion," Christian Examiner, April 24, 2016, https://www.christianexaminer.com/article/chinese-president-warns-of-foreign-infiltration-through-religion/50637.htm.

356. "Persecuted and Forgotten?" Aid to the Church in Need, Brooklyn, NY, accessed February 26, 2020, https://www.churchinneed.org/wp-content/uploads/2017/10/persecution-1-1.pdf.

357. Remarks by Vice President Pence at the 2nd Annual Religious Freedom Ministerial, U.S. State Department, July 18, 2019, https://www.whitehouse.gov/briefings-statements/remarks-vice-president-pence-2nd-annual-religious-freedom-ministerial/

358. Ibid.

359. Ibid.

360. Ibid.

361. Ibid.

362. John Pontifex, "The Unprecedented Scale of Anti-Christian Persecution in Asia," Catholic Herald, October 24, 2019, https://catholicherald.co.uk/magazine/the-unprecedented-scale-of-anti-christian-persecution-in-asia/.

363. Ibid.

364. Ibid.

365. Ibid.

366. Ibid.

367. "Persecuted and Forgotten?" Op. cit.

368. Marta Dhanis, Sasha Savitsky, and Tyler McCarthy, "Harvey Weinstein Sentenced to 23 Years in Prison on Rape, Criminal Sex Act Convictions," Fox News, March 12, 2020, https://www.foxnews.com/entertainment/harvey-weinstein-sentenced-rape-criminal-sex-acts-convictions.

369. Samantha Chang, "Nick Sandmann's Attorney Warns More Lawsuits Are Coming Over 'Reprehensible' Media Conduct," BPR Business & Politics, February 21, 2019, https://www.bizpacreview.com/2019/02/21/nick-sandmanns-attorney-warns-more-lawsuits-pending-over-reprehensible-media-conduct-725941.

370. Jack Crowe, "CNN Settles Lawsuit Brought by Covington Catholic Student Nicholas Sandmann," *National Review*, January 7, 2020, https://news.yahoo.com/cnn-settles-lawsuit-brought-covington-201206829.html.

371. Brooke Sopelsa, "Mike Pence Calls Criticism of Wife's Job at Anti-LGBTQ School 'Deeply offensive'," NBC News, January 17, 2019, https://www.nbcnews.com/feature/nbc-out/mike-pence-calls-criticism-wife-s-job-anti-lgbtq-school-n960091.

372. Ibid.

373. Warner Todd Huston, "Atheist Group Calls Kanye West Prison Worship Service 'Egregious' Violation of Constitution," Breitbart, November 22, 2019, https://www.breitbart.com/entertainment/2019/11/22/atheist-group-calls-kanye-west-prison-worship-service-egregious-violation-of-constitution/.

374. Ibid.

375. Jeannie Law, "Kanye West Reveals Record Labels Have Contracts Prohibiting Artists from Talking about Jesus," *Christian Post*, February 4, 2020, https://www.christianpost.com/news/kanye-west-reveals-record-labels-have-contracts-prohibiting-artists-from-talking-about-jesus.html?fbclid=IwAR0wZZ9gkdkhtkNj_722kzAnIYh30W4fJDkWCvN23KETxdiVupJIbeurz0s.

376. Ibid.

377. Jay Maxson, "Anti-Christian Media Slam Brees for Appearance in 'Anti-LGBT' Focus on the Family Video," Newsbusters, September 9, 2019, https://www.newsbusters.org/blogs/culture/jay-maxson/2019/09/06/drew-brees-rapped-association-focus-family-video.

378. Ibid.

379. Kelsey Bolar, "MSNBC Rolls Out Sexist, Anti-Christian Smears Against Female Trump Employees," *Federalist*, December 21, 2018, https://thefederalist.com/2018/12/21/msnbc-rolls-sexist-anti-christian-smears-female-trump-employees/.

380. Ibid.

381. Ibid.

382. Brian Flood, "Pressure Grows for 'The View' Star Joy Behar to Apologize over anti-Christian Comments, but ABC Is Silent," Fox News, March 12, 2018, https://www.foxnews.com/entertainment/pressure-grows-for-the-view-star-joy-behar-to-apologize-over-anti-christian-comments-but-abc-is-silent.

383. Ibid.

384. Ibid.

385. David Roach, "Sri Lanka Christian Massacre 'Shocking in Its Cruelty'," Baptist Press, April 22, 2019, http://www.bpnews.net/52772/sri-lanka-christian-massacre-shocking-in-its-cruelty.

386. L. Brent Bozell III and Tim Graham, "Bozell & Graham: Christian Persecution Is Real. *New York Times* and Other Media Could Care Less," Fox News, January 1, 2020, https://www.foxnews.com/opinion/christian-persecution-new-york-times-media-bozell-graham.

387. Bernard-Henri Lévy, "The New War Against Africa's Christians," *Wall Street Journal,* December 20, 2019, https://www.wsj.com/articles/the-new-war-against-africas-christians-11576880200.

388. Ibid.

389. Tyler O'Neil, "CNN's LGBT Town Hall Will Put Dems' Anti-Christian Bigotry on Full Display," PJ Media, September 6, 2019, https://pjmedia.com/faith/cnns-lgbt-town-hall-will-put-dems-anti-christian-bigotry-on-display/.

390. Ken Webster and Sandra Peterson, "Media Silence Over Colorado Shooters' Anti-Christian & Anti-Trump Positions," KPRC, May 5, 2009, https://kprcradio.iheart.com/featured/the-pursuit-of-happiness/content/2019-05-09-media-silence-over-colorado-shooters-anti-christian-anti-trump-positions/.

391. Emily Jones, ""They Will Not Tolerate Christianity in Any Forum': Lady Gaga's Attack on Pence and Christian Schools Reveals Next Phase of

Culture War," CBN News, January 22, 2019, https://www1.cbn.com/
cbnnews/entertainment/2019/january/they-will-not-tolerate-christianity-
in-any-forum-lady-gagas-attack-on-pence-and-christian-schools-reveals-
next-phase-of-culture-war.

392. Ibid.

393. Katherine Dempsey, "Christians Continue to Be Undermined by
Mainstream Media," *Christian Post*, September 3, 2013, https://www.
christianpost.com/news/christians-continue-to-be-undermined-by-
mainstream-media.html.

394. Ibid.

395. Hadas Gold, "Survey: 7 Percent of Reporters Identify as Republican,"
Politico, May 6 2014, https://www.politico.com/blogs/media/2014/05/
survey-7-percent-of-reporters-identify-as-republican-188053.

396. Jack Shafer and Tucker Doherty, "The Media Bubble Is Worse Than You
Think," *Politico*, May/June 2017, https://www.politico.com/magazine/
story/2017/04/25/media-bubble-real-journalism-jobs-east-coast-215048.

397. James Ostrowski, "Why Progressives Make Bad Journalists," LewRockwell.
com, December 30, 2015, https://www.lewrockwell.com/2015/12/
james-ostrowski/never-trust-progressive-journalist/.

398. Ibid.

399. Ibid.

400. Stella Morabito, "How Journalism Turns Into Propaganda," *Federalist*,
November 21, 2016, https://thefederalist.com/2016/11/21/
journalism-turns-propaganda/.

401. Ibid.

402. Ibid.

403. Ibid.

404. Ibid.

405. Brent Baker, "By Overwhelming 10-1, Public Thinks Media
Want Clinton to Win," Newsbusters, October 29, 2016, https://
www.newsbusters.org/blogs/nb/brent-baker/2016/10/29/
overwhelming-10-1-public-thinks-media-want-clinton-win.

406. "SUPRC National Polling," Suffolk University, Boston, accessed February
25, 2020, https://www.suffolk.edu/academics/research-at-suffolk/
political-research-center/polls/national.

407. Morabito, Op. cit.

408. "2889. Kosmos," Bible Hub, accessed February 26, 2020, https://biblehub.com/greek/2889.htm.

409. "Anti-Christian Extremist Groups," Christian Civil Rights Watch, accessed February 26, 2020, https://truecivilrights.org/anti-christian-extremist-groups/.

410. American Atheists, accessed March 15, 2020, https://www.atheists.org/.

411. Ken Ham, "American Atheists Jump on FFRF's Anti-Christian Bandwagon," Answers in Genesis, January 11, 2019, https://answersingenesis.org/blogs/ken-ham/2019/01/11/american-atheists-jump-on-ffrf-bandwagon/.

412. Ibid.

413. Ibid.

414. Lee Morgan, "American Atheists Launch Anti-religion Billboard Campaign in Bible Belt, Urge People to Skip Church," *New York Daily News*, December 12, 2014, https://www.nydailynews.com/news/national/atheists-launch-anti-religion-billboards-bible-belt-article-1.2042909.

415. Ibid.

416. Ham, Op. cit.

417. Diane Dew, "Revealing FACTS on the ACLU," accessed February 26, 2020, http://dianedew.com/aclu.htm.

418. Robert L. Waggoner, "Organized Humanism Produces a Growing Anti-Christian Society," The Bible Net, February 26, 2020, http://www.thebible.net/biblicaltheism/organhuman.htm#_ftn5.

419. Dave Kinney, "The Christmas Confrontation, Pt. 1," Sermon Central, December 3, 2005, https://www.sermoncentral.com/sermons/the-christmas-confrontation-pt-1-dave-kinney-sermon-on-christmas-85851.

420. "Is the ACLU Anti-Christian?," PROCON.ORG, October 5, 2007, https://aclu.procon.org/questions/is-the-aclu-anti-christian/.

421. "ACLU in Court in Case Over Taxpayer-Funded Religious Training," States News Service, June 24, 2019.

422. Ibid.

423. Laura Meckler, "A Christian Ministry Won't Change its Christians-Only Criteria for Foster-Care Parents. Is That Okay with Trump?" *Washington Post*, January 7, 2019.

424. Ibid.

425. Miracle Hill Ministries, accessed March 15, 2020, https://miraclehill.org/who-we-are/history/.

426. "ACLU Attorneys Blame Christians for Muslim's Orlando Massacre," States News Service, June 14, 2016.

427. Ibid.

428. Ibid.

429. Ibid.

430. "ACLU and Americans United Demand Connecticut School District Stop Holding Graduation at Christian Church," States News Service, November 18, 2009.

431. Nathan Black, "Graduations at Conn. Church Ruled Unconstitutional," Christian Post, June 1, 2010, https://www.christianpost.com/news/judge-graduations-at-church-is-unconstitutional.html.

432. Enfield High School Graduation Class of 2019, accessed March 15, 2020, https://enfieldhigh.sharpschool.com/activities/graduation.

433. Julie Zauzmer, "A Conservative Christian Group Is Pushing Bible Classes in Public Schools Nationwide—and It's Working," Washington Post, May 8, 2019.

434. Jenna Browder, "'Hate-Filled, Anti-Christian, Anti-Conservative Organization': Why the SPLC Has Been Given an 'F' by Charity Watch," CBN News, April 4, 2019, https://www1.cbn.com/cbnnews/politics/2019/april/hate-filled-anti-christian-anti-conservative-organization-why-the-splc-has-been-given-an-f-by-charity-watch.

435. Laurie Higgins, "The SPLC: An Anti-Christian Hate Group," Illinois Family Institute, August 19, 2017, https://illinoisfamily.org/politics/splc-anti-christian-hate-group/.

436. Ibid.

437. Ibid.

438. Browder, Op. cit.

439. Brian Kelly, "SPLC's Offshore Bank Accounts and Huge Salaries for Its Executives," Catholicism.org, August 31, 2017, https://catholicism.org/splcs-offshore-bank-accounts-huge-salaries-executives.html.

440. Browder, Op. cit.

441. "About American Humanist Association," American Humanist

Association, accessed March 15, 2020, https://americanhumanist.org/about/.

442. As cited in Robert L. Waggoner, "Organized Humanism Produces a Growing Anti-Christian Society," accessed March 15, 2020, http://www.thebible.net/biblicaltheism/Organized_Humanism.pdf.

443. "What Is Unitarianism?" dividedbytruth.org, accessed February 27, 2020, http://dividedbytruth.org/FR/wiu.htm.

444. "Robert G. Ingersoll," AZ Quotes, accessed March 15, 2020, https://www.azquotes.com/author/7171-Robert_Green_Ingersoll/tag/partnership.

445. "Birth Control Organizations, World Population Emergency Campaign," Margaret Sanger Papers Project, New York University, accessed February 27, 2020, https://www.nyu.edu/projects/sanger/aboutms/organization_wpec.php.

446. Jim Sedlak, "Shutting Down Planned Parenthood and Its Anti-Christian Agenda," *Celebrate Life Magazine*, September–October 2006, https://clmagazine.org/topic/enemies-of-life/shutting-down-planned-parenthood-and-its-anti-christian-agenda/.

447. Ibid.

448. Ibid.

449. Ibid.

450. "The Big List of Anti-Religious/Un-Christian Businesses, Celebrities, and Geographic Locations in the U.S.," The Bible Blender, April 23, 2016, https://www.bibleblender.com/2016/christian-news/list-anti-religious-un-christian-businesses-organizations-people-celebrities-locations.

451. Scott Smith, "Top 5 Most Anti-Christian & Anti-Life Insurance and Financial Companies," thescottsmithblog.com, November 12, 2018, https://www.thescottsmithblog.com/2018/11/top-5-most-anti-christian-anti-life.html.

452. Ibid.

453. Ibid.

454. Alex Newman, "Equality Act," *New American*, May 6, 2019, p. 19f.

455. Ibid.

456. Ibid.

457. Ibid.

458. "Equality Act Reaches 100 Corporate Cosponsors," Human

Rights Campaign, September 15, 2017, https://www.hrc.org/blog/equality-act-reaches-more-than-100-corporate-cosponsors.

459. Ibid.

460. Ibid.

461. Tom Wallace, "Islam the Anti-Christ Religion," Fortress of Faith, accessed February 27, 2020, https://fortressoffaith.com/islam-the-anti-christ-religion/.

462. Bernard Lewis, "Islam and the West: A Conversation with Bernard Lewis," Catholic Education Resource Center, *The Pew Forum on Religion & Public Life*, April 27, 2006. Hay-Adams Hotel Washington, DC), https://www.catholiceducation.org/en/culture/catholic-contributions/islam-and-the-west-a-conversation-with-bernard-lewis.html.

463. Koran 40:35(as cited in Warner, *The Islamic Trilogy*, Vol. 2, *The Political Traditions of Mohammed, The Hadith for the Unbelievers*).

464. Sahih Bukhari, Vol. 5, book 58, No. 148 (as cited in Warner, *The Islamic Trilogy*, Vol, 2, *The Political Traditions of Mohammed, The Hadith for the Unbelievers*).

465. Ishaq, 125 (as quoted in Warner, *The Islamic Doctrine of Christians and Jews*).

466. Koran 47:4 (as cited in Warner, *The Islamic Trilogy*, Vol, 2, The Political Traditions of Mohammed, The Hadith for the Unbelievers).

467. Koran 6:25 (as cited in Warner, *The Islamic Trilogy*, Vol. 2, *The Political Traditions of Mohammed, The Hadith for the Unbelievers*).

468. Koran 86:15 (as cited in Warner, *The Islamic Trilogy*, Vol. 2, *The Political Traditions of Mohammed, The Hadith for the Unbelievers*).

469. Koran 8:12 (as cited in Warner, *The Islamic Trilogy*, Vol. 2, *The Political Traditions of Mohammed, The Hadith for the Unbelievers*).

470. Koran 9:29 (as cited in Warner, *The Islamic Trilogy*, Vol. 2, *The Political Traditions of Mohammed, The Hadith for the Unbelievers*).

471. Koran 3:28 (as cited in Warner, *The Islamic Trilogy*, Vol. 2, *The Political Traditions of Mohammed, The Hadith for the Unbelievers*).

472. Bill Warner, editor, "The Political Traditions of Mohammed," *The Islamic Trilogy*, Vol. 2 (The Center for the Study of Political Islam, 2006) p. 4.

473. Ibid., p. 72.

474. Ibid, p. 51.

475. Ibid, p. 53.

476. Ibid.

477. "Christian Persecution," Open Doors USA, accessed February 27, 2020, https://www.opendoorsusa.org/christian-persecution/

478. Ibid.

479. "Islamic Terror on Christians," What Makes Islam so Different?," accessed February 27, 2020, https://www.thereligionofpeace.com/attacks/christian-attacks.aspx

480. Ibid.

481. "What Makes Islam So Different?" accessed March 15, 2020, https://www.thereligionofpeace.com/pages/quran/violence.aspx.

482. Answers, Yahoo.com, accessed March 15, 2020, https://answers.yahoo.com/question/index?qid=20100418194241AA9QLHM.

483. Quran 8:12. as cited by Discover the Truth, accessed March 15, 2020, https://discover-the-truth.com/2014/09/29/quran-812-i-will-cast-terror-into-the-hearts-of-those-who-disbelieve-therefore-strike-off-their-heads/.

484. Ibid.

485. Answers, Op. cit.

486. "Jesus and Muhammad, Islam and Christianity: A Side-by-Side Comparison, What Makes Islam so Different?," accessed February 27, 2020, https://www.thereligionofpeace.com/pages/articles/jesus-muhammad.aspx.

487. Robert Maginnis, *Never Submit: Will the Extermination of Christians Get Worse before It Gets Better?*" Defender, 2014, p. 279.

488. Ibid.

489. Frank Wolf telephonic interview, March 31, 2015.

490. William Boykin telephonic interview, April 14, 2015.

491. David Curry telephonic interview, April 9, 2015.

492. "Muslim Colonization of America: The Hijra and the Hijacking Of America's Refugee Resettlement Program," Religious Freedom Coalition, April 22, 2015, http://www.religiousfreedomcoalition.org/2015/04/22/muslim-colonization-of-america-the-hijra-and-the-hijacking-of-americas-refugee-resettlement-program/.

493. Sam Solomon and E Al Maqdisi, *Modern Day Trojan Horse: The Islamic Doctrine of Immigration* (Charlottesville, VA: ANM Publishers), 10.

494. As cited in "Refugee Resettlement and the Hijra to America," published by the Center for Security Policy Press, http://www.centerforsecuritypolicy.org/wp-content/uploads/2015/04/Refugee_Resettlement_Hijra.pdf.

495. Tom Doyle interview via telephone, March 25, 2015.

496. "Special Report: The Council on American Islamic Relations," Clarion Project, http://www.clarionproject.org/sites/default/files/CAIR-Council-on-American-Islamic-Relations-factsheet.pdf.

497. "The Muslim Brotherhood," *The Investigative Project on Terrorism,* http://www.investigativeproject.org/profile/173.

498. Leslie Stahl, "Homeland Security," *60 Minutes,* April 5, 2015, http://www.cbsnews.com/news/homeland-security-jeh-johnson-60-minutes-lesley-stahl/.

499. Greg Hannah, Lindsay Clutterbuck, Jennifer Rubin, "Radicalization or Rehabilitation," RAND Corporation Technical Report, 2008, http://www.rand.org/content/dam/rand/pubs/technical_reports/2008/RAND_TR571.pdf , p.x.

500. Ibid., p.x.

501. Akarsh Mehrotra, "15 Of the Most Evil Men the World Has Ever Seen," Scoopwhoomp.com, June 5, 2015, https://www.scoopwhoop.com/world/most-evil-people/.

502. Ibid.

503. Ibid.

504. "Persecution of Christians," Wikipedia, accessed February 27, 2020, https://en.wikipedia.org/wiki/Persecution_of_Christians.

505. "Allah as Moon-god," Wikipedia, http://en.wikipedia.org/wiki/Allah_as_Moon-god.

506. Raphael Moore, "In Memory of the 50 Million Victims of the Orthodox Christian Holocaust," serfes.org, accessed February 27, 2020, http://www.serfes.org/orthodox/memoryof.htm.

507. Albert Speer, *Inside the Third Reich* (New York: Avon), 1971, p. 734.

508. "Nazi Persecution of the Catholic Church in Germany," Wikipedia, accessed February 27, 2020, https://en.wikipedia.org/wiki/Nazi_persecution_of_the_Catholic_Church_in_Germany.

509. "Demon Possession," GotQuestions.org, accessed February 27, 2020, https://www.gotquestions.org/demon-possession.html.

510. Ibid.

511. Hollie McKay, "North Korea: How Christians Survive in the World's most anti-Christian Nation," Fox News, September 25, 2017, https://www.foxnews.com/world/north-korea-how-christians-survive-in-the-worlds-most-anti-christian-nation.

512. Ibid.

513. Ibid.

514. Ibid.

515. Ibid.

516. Wesley Rahn, "In Xi We Trust—Is China Cracking Down on Christianity?" DW.com, January 19, 2018, https://www.dw.com/en/in-xi-we-trust-is-china-cracking-down-on-christianity/a-42224752.

517. Stoyan Zaimo, "Chinese President Xi Jinping to Communist Members: You Must Be 'Unyielding Marxist Atheists'," Christian Post, April 25, 2016, https://www.christianpost.com/news/chinese-president-xi-jinping-communist-christian-house-church-atheists.html.

518. Ibid.

519. Ibid.

520. Ibid.

521. Ibid.

522. Ibid.

523. Rahn, Op. cit.

524. William Z. Nardi, "Xi Jinping Ramps Up Religious Persecution," National Review, July 29, 2019, https://www.nationalreview.com/2019/07/religious-persecution-china-xi-jinping/.

525. Ibid.

526. Ibid.

527. Ibid.

528. Ibid.

529. Ibid.

530. "America's Most Biblically-Hostile U. S. President," Wallbuilders, accessed February 27, 2020, https://wallbuilders.com/americas-biblically-hostile-u-s-president/.

531. Gregory Korte, "White House Turns to Rainbow after Gay Marriage Ruling," USA Today, June 26, 2015, https://www.usatoday.com/story/theoval/2015/06/26/white-house-rainbow-gay-marriage/29374471/.

532. "The Life of George Soros," georgesoros.com, accessed February 27, 2020, https://www.georgesoros.com/the-life-of-george-soros/.

533. Alex Newman, "In Abortion Push, Soros Exposed Trying to Corrupt Christianity," *New American*, August 30, 2016, https://www.thenewamerican.com/culture/faith-and-morals/item/23962-in-abortion-push-soros-exposed-trying-to-corrupt-christianity.

534. Alex Newman, "Soros Co-opting Churches to Push New World Order," *New American*, April 4, 2016, https://www.thenewamerican.com/world-news/europe/item/22916-soros-co-opting-churches-to-push-new-world-order.

535. Ibid.

536. Alex Newman, "In Abortion Push, Soros Exposed Trying to Corrupt Christianity," Op. cit.

537. "Christian Leaders Warn of Soros-Funded "Hijack" of Christian Left," Stream, October 4, 2016, https://stream.org/christian-leaders-warn-of-progressive-attempt-to-hijack-the-gospel/.

538. Ibid.

539. Cheryl K. Chumley, "George Soros and His 'Rented Evangelicals' Outed by Christian Leaders," *Washington Times*, October 22, 2018, https://www.washingtontimes.com/news/2018/oct/22/george-soros-and-his-rented-evangelicals-outed-chr/.

540. Ibid.

541. Paul Sperry, "Don't Be Fooled by Bernie Sanders— He's a Diehard Communist," *New York Post*, January 16, 2016, https://nypost.com/2016/01/16/dont-be-fooled-by-bernie-sanders-hes-a-diehard-communist/.

542. Ibid.

543. Ibid.

544. Ibid.

545. Ibid.

546. Ibid.

547. Dov Fisher, "Basically, Bernie Sanders Is a Communist," *American Spectator*, June 18, 2019, https://spectator.org/basically-bernie-sanders-is-a-communist/.

548. Carter, Op. cit.

549. Sasha Pezenik, "Bloomberg to Donate $10 Million to House

Democrats Targeted by GOP," ABC News, December 11, 2019, https://abcnews.go.com/Politics/bloomberg-donate-10-million-house-democrats-targeted-gop/story?id=67657394.

550. Evie Fordham, "Here's How Much Bloomberg Spent on the 2020 Race," Fox News, March 4, 2020, https://www.foxbusiness.com/money/bloomberg-campaign-spending.

551. "Mike Bloomberg Civil Rights," On the Issues, accessed February 27, 2020, https://www.ontheissues.org/2020/Mike_Bloomberg_Civil_Rights.htm.

552. John Fea, "Can Any of the Democratic Candidates Appeal to Evangelicals?" Religion News Service, January 30, 2020, https://religionnews.com/2020/01/30/can-any-of-the-democratic-candidates-appeal-to-evangelicals/.

553. Cristina Laila, "HOW AWFUL! 'Catholic' Speaker Pelosi Invited Planned Parenthood President as her Guest to SOTU Address," Gateway Pundit, February 5, 2019, https://www.thegatewaypundit.com/2019/02/heres-a-list-of-radical-leftists-speaker-pelosi-is-bringing-to-the-state-of-the-union/.

554. Tobias Hoonhout, "Sasse Rips Pelosi for Trying to Smuggle Hyde Amendment Loophole into Coronavirus Package," *National Review*, March 13, 2020, https://news.yahoo.com/sasse-rips-pelosi-trying-smuggle-133653616.html.

555. Ibid.

556. Jerry Newcombe, "Nancy Pelosi Accidentally Speaks Truth About God and Abortion," *Christian Post*, August 8, 2016, https://www.christianpost.com/news/nancy-pelosi-accidentally-speaks-truth-about-god-and-abortion.html.

557. Tyler O'Neil, "House Passes Bigoted, Anti-Christian 'Equality Act' with 8 GOP Votes," PJ Media, May 17, 2019, https://pjmedia.com/trending/house-passes-intolerant-anti-woman-pro-abortion-equality-act-with-8-republican-votes/.

558. Amardendra Bhushan Dhiraj, "Revealed: The 100 Most Influential People in the World 2019," CEOWorld Magazine, April 19, 2019, https://ceoworld.biz/2019/04/19/revealed-the-100-most-influential-people-in-the-world-2019/.

559. Ed Kilgore, "Christian Right Leaders Suggest Trump Critics Are Possessed by Demons," *New Yorker*, November 26, 2019, http://nymag.com/

intelligencer/2019/11/christian-right-leaders-trump-critics-possessed-by-demons.html.

560. Ibid.

561. Ibid.

562. Andrew L. Whitehead, Samuel L. Perry, and Joseph O. Baker, "Make America Christian Again: Christian Nationalism and Voting for Donald Trump in the 2016 Presidential Election," *Sociology of Religion: A Quarterly Review* 2018, 79:2. https://academic.oup.com/socrel/article-abstract/79/2/147/4825283 by guest on 21 January 2020.

563. Ibid.

564. "The City of God," Wikipedia, accessed February 27, 2020, https://en.wikipedia.org/wiki/The_City_of_God.

565. Jesse Rojo, "Should Christians Be Involved In Politics," *Christian Post*, April 22, 2015, https://www.christianpost.com/news/should-christians-be-involved-in-politics.html.

566. David Closson, "4 Reasons Christians Should Care about Politics," Ethics and Religious Liberty Commission, August 4, 2015, https://erlc.com/resource-library/articles/4-reasons-christians-should-care-about-politics.

567. "Globalism," Dictionary.com, accessed February 27, 2020, https://www.dictionary.com/browse/globalism.

568. William Cummings, "'I Am a Nationalist': Trump's Embrace of Controversial Label Sparks Uproar," *USA Today*, October 24, 2018, https://www.usatoday.com/story/news/politics/2018/10/24/trump-says-hes-nationalist-what-means-why-its-controversial/1748521002/.

569. Ibid.

570. Ibid.

571. Michael Curtis, "Patriotism vs. Nationalism," *American Thinker*, November 15, 2018, https://www.americanthinker.com/articles/2018/11/patriotism_vs_nationalism.html.

572. Ibid.

573. Ibid.

574. George Orwell, "Notes on Nationalism," *Polemic*, London, May 1945, https://www.orwell.ru/library/essays/nationalism/english/e_nat.

575. "Patriotism vs. Nationalism," *Grammarist*, accessed February 27, 2020, https://grammarist.com/usage/patriotism-vs-nationalism/.

576. "Palmer Raids," Wikipedia, accessed February 27, 2020, https://en.wikipedia.org/wiki/Palmer_Raids.

577. Curtis, Op. cit.

578. "Patriotism vs. Nationalism," *Grammarist*, Op. cit.

579. "Patriotism vs. Nationalism," Merriam-Webster, accessed February 27, 2020, https://www.merriam-webster.com/words-at-play/patriotism-vs-nationalism.

580. Ibid.

581. Cummings, Op. cit.

582. Ibid.

583. Michael McFaul (@McFaul) October 23, 2018.

584. Carl Reiner (@carlreiner) October 23, 2018.

585. Cummings, Op. cit.

586. Ibid.

587. Ibid.

588. Michelle Goldberg, "What Is Christian Nationalism?," *Huffington Post*, May 25, 2011, https://www.huffpost.com/entry/what-is-christian-nationa_b_20989.

589. Ibid.

590. Ibid.

591. "About Christian Nationalism," christiannationalism.com, accessed February 27, 2020, https://www.christiannationalism.com/about-christian-nationalism/.

592. Ibid.

593. "Christian Nationalist FAQ," christiannationationalm.com, accessed February 27, 2020, https://www.christiannationalism.com/christian-nationalist-faq/.

594. Katie Reilly, "Read Hillary Clinton's 'Basket of Deplorables' Remarks About Donald Trump Supporters," *Time*, September 10, 2016, https://time.com/4486502/hillary-clinton-basket-of-deplorables-transcript/.

595. Andrew L. Whitehead, Joseph O. Baker, and Samuel L. Perry, "Despite Porn Stars and Playboy Models, White Evangelicals Aren't Rejecting Trump. This Is Why," *Washington Post*, March 26, 2018, https://www.washingtonpost.com/news/monkey-cage/wp/2018/03/26/despite-porn-stars-and-playboy-models-white-evangelicals-arent-rejecting-trump-this-is-why/.

596. "Presidential Candidate Donald Trump at Liberty University." Video Posted by C-Span, January 18, https://www.c-span.org/video/?403331-1/donald-trump-remarksliberty-university..

597. "Donald Trump Remarks in Orlando, Florida." Video Posted by C-Span. August 11, https://www.c-span.org/video/?413877-1/donald-trump-addresses-evangelicalleaders-orlando-florida.

598. Cited in Whitehead, Op. cit.

599. Ibid.

600. Ibid.

601. Ibid.

602. Ibid.

603. Ibid.

604. Ibid.

605. Gerald L. K. Smith, "The Cross and the Flag," accessed March 6, 2020 http://thecrossandflag.com/articles/christian_nationalism.html.

606. Gerald L. K. Smith, "This Is Christian Nationalism," The Cross and the Flag, accessed February 27, 2020, http://thecrossandflag.com/articles/christian_nationalism.html

607. Ralph Drollinger, "Better Understanding the Fallacy of Christian Nationalism," Capitol Ministries, May 14, 2019, https://capmin.org/better-understanding-fallacy-christian-nationalism-ralph-drollinger/.

608. "Be fruitful and multiply, and replenish the earth, and subdue it; and have dominion over the fish of the sea, and over the fowl of the air, and over every living thing that moveth upon the earth" (Genesis 1:28, NIV).

609. Matthew Cochran, "Their Problem Is with Nations, Not Nationalism," Matthewcochran.net, September 26, 2019, http://matthewcochran.net/blog/?p=1470.

610. "Christians Against Christian Nationalism," accessed February 27, 2020, https://www.christiansagainstchristiannationalism.org/statement.

611. "Samuel Adams," Patriot Post, accessed February 27, 2020, https://patriotpost.us/fqd/64812-founders-quote-daily.

612. "Benjamin Rush," Quote Master, accessed February 27, 2020, https://www.quotemaster.org/qcb53b148b8ffa495af6c88ef7503147b.

613. "Daniel Webster," Brainy Quote, accessed February 27, 2020, https://www.brainyquote.com/quotes/daniel_webster_399876.

614. Daniel Webster, "Mr. Webster's Speech in Defence of the Christian Ministry and in Favor of the Religious Instruction of the Young." Delivered in the Supreme Court of the United States, February 10, 1844, in the Case of Stephen Girard's Will (Washington: Printed by Gales and Seaton, 1844), p. 41.

615. "Alexis de Tocqueville," Bartleby.com, accessed February 27, 2020, https://www.bartleby.com/73/829.html.

616. "Alexis de Tocqueville," AZ Quotes, accessed February 27, 2020, https://www.azquotes.com/quote/1404713.

617. "Alexis de Tocqueville," Bartleby.com, accessed February 27, 2020, https://www.bartleby.com/73/829.html.

618. Interview with Gary Bauer, February 14, 2020.

619. Michael Brown, "MAGA: Make America Godly Again," *Christian Post*, February 2, 2019, https://www.christianpost.com/voice/maga-make-america-godly-again.html.

620. Ibid.

621. Victor Stanley interview. February 11, 2020.

622. "In U.S., Decline of Christianity Continues at Rapid Pace," Pew Research Institute, October 17, 2019, https://www.pewforum.org/2019/10/17/in-u-s-decline-of-christianity-continues-at-rapid-pace/.

623. Damon Linker, "The Future of Christian America," *New Republic*, April 7, 2019, https://newrepublic.com/article/48917/the-future-christian-america.

624. Jon Meacham, "Meacham: The End of Christian America," *Newsweek*, April 3, 2009, https://www.newsweek.com/meacham-end-christian-america-77125.

625. Ibid.

626. Jan Markell, "Falling Into Place: The Top 10 Bible Prophecy-Related Stories of 2018," Olive Tree Ministries, December 31, 2018, .https://myemail.constantcontact.com/Falling-Into-Place—Top-10-Prophecy-Stories-2018.html?soid=1101818841456&aid=9PrfcRBw-XM

627. Interview with Jan Markell, February 12, 2020.

628. Ibid.

629. Interview with William Federer, February 13, 2020.

630. Charles Pope, "The Eight Stages of the Rise and Fall of Civilizations," Community in Mission, October 12, 2016, http://blog.adw.org/2016/10/eight-stages-rise-fall-civilizations/.

631. Bill Federer, "John Adams: Wise, Amazing, Incorruptible," WorldNetDaily, October 29, 2018, https://www.wnd.com/2018/10/john-adams-wise-amazing-incorruptible/.

632. Pope, Op. cit.

633. Interview with William Federer, Op. cit.

634. Brian Fitzpatrick, "The Rise and Fall of Civilization," theroadtoemmaus.org, accessed February 27, 2020, http://www.theroadtoemmaus.org/RdLb/21PbAr/CltWr/RiseFallCvlzation.htm.

635. Excerpt from Daniel R. Heimbach, *True Sexual Morality: Recovering Biblical Standards for a Culture in Crisis* (Wheaton: Crossway Books, 2004), 345–348.

636. Fitzpatrick, Op. cit.

637. Ibid.

638. Ibid.

639. Ibid.

640. Ibid.

641. Ibid.

642. Ibid.

643. Roger Wheelock, "Sex and Society—The Weinstein Effect: A Warning to a Sexually Obsessed Nation," GTI Ministries, December 1, 2017, https://gtimin.com/blogs/worldview/sex-and-society-the-weinstein-effect-a-warning-to-a-sexually-obsessed-nation.

644. Clay Stauffer, "What Will the Future of Christianity in America Look Like?," *Tennessean*, August 20, 2015, https://www.tennessean.com/story/news/religion/2015/08/20/what-future-christianity-america-look-like/32073681/.

645. "In U.S., Decline of Christianity Continues at Rapid Pace," Op cit.

646. John Adams, Brainy Quote, accessed March 6, 2020, https://www.brainyquote.com/quotes/john_adams_391045.

647. "Religion should play a role in public education," Christian Post, April 8, 2003, https://www.christianpost.com/news/religion-should-play-a-role-in-public-education.html

648. Ibid.

649. Mark Creech, "America's Christian Roots and Its impact on the Economy," *Christian Post*, June 2, 2014, https://www.christianpost.com/news/americas-christian-roots-and-its-impact-on-the-economy.html.

650. Tony Perkins, "A Badge of Disgrace: The Fall of the Boy Scouts," Family Research Council, February 18, 2020, https://www.frc.org/updatearticle/20200218/badge-disgrace.

651. "Cyrus the Great in the Bible," Wikipedia, accessed February, 27, 2020, https://en.wikipedia.org/wiki/Cyrus_the_Great_in_the_Bible.

652. Oswald Chambers, "Don't Plan Without God," My Upmost for His Highest, accessed February 27, 2020, https://utmost.org/don't-plan-without-god/.

653. "The first chapter of the Book of Nehemiah introduces the book bearing his name as a resident of Susa, the capital of the Persian Empire. When Nehemiah heard that the walls of Jerusalem were still broken down more than a half century after the completion of the rebuilding of the temple, he "sat down and wept," fasting and praying before God (Neh. 1:4). Implicitly, he was formulating a plan to remedy the situation in Jerusalem." https://www.theologyofwork.org/old-testament/ezra-nehemiah-esther/nehemiah/restoration-of-the-wall-of-jerusalem-nehemiah-11-773.

654. "Winston Churchill," AZ Quotes, accessed February 27, 2020, https://www.azquotes.com/quote/855229.

655. "Dwight D. Eisenhower," AZ Quotes, accessed February 27, 2020, https://www.azquotes.com/quote/1464987.

656. "Daniel Webster," AZ Quotes, accessed March 17, 2020, https://www.azquotes.com/quote/309551.

657. Telephonic interview with David Barton, March 9, 2020.

658. Telephonic interview with Stu Weber, March 16, 2020.

659. Hillsong United, "Oceans," accessed February 27, 2020, https://www.bing.com/search?q=oceans+lyrics&form=EDNTHT&mkt=en-us&httpsmsn=1&msnews=1&plvar=0&refig=0fca52ccb71e4c6bcadaff4f544447579&PC=DCTS&sp=1&qs=LS&pq=oceans+&sk=PRES1&sc=8-7&cvid=0fca52ccb71e4c6bcadaff4f544447579&cc=US&setlang=en-US.

660. Barton, Op. cit.

661. Interview with William Gerald Boykin, March 4, 2020.

662. Weber, Op. cit.

663. Keil & Delitzsch Commentary on the Old Testament Isaiah 2, studylight.org, accessed February 27, 2020, https://www.studylight.org/commentaries/kdo/isaiah-2.html.

664. Weber, Op. cit.

665. "A millstone is a stone used to grind grain. When grain is milled, two stones are actually used: the bed stone, or base, which remains stationary; and the runner stone, which turns on top of the base, grinding the grain." A millstone is a common item mentioned in the Bible (Deuteronomy 24:6, Job 41;24, Judges 9:53, 2 Samuel 11:21).

666. "Leadership Training Program," WallBuilders, accessed March 9, 2020, https://wallbuilders.com/leadershiptraining/.

667. Jason Jones, "Only 6% of Americans have biblical worldview," God Reports, March 27, 2020, https://godreports.com/2020/03/only-6-of-americans-have-biblical-worldview/.

668. Household patterns by religion, Pew Research Center, December 12, 2019, https://www.pewforum.org/2019/12/12/household-patterns-by-religion/.

669. Interview with William Boykin on March 4, 2020.

670. Alice M. Baldwin, *The New England Clergy and the American Revolution* (New York: Frederick Ungar, 1958), p. 170.

671. John Adams, *The Works of John Adams,* Charles Francis Adams, editor (Boston: Charles C. Little and James Brown, 1851), Vol. III, p. 476, "The Earl of Clarendon to William Pym," January 20, 1766.

672. John Adams, *The Works of John Adams*, Charles Francis Adams, editor (Boston: Little, Brown and Company, 1850), Vol. X, p. 284, to Hezekiah Niles, February 13, 1818. See also John Adams, The Works of John Adams, Charles Francis Adams, editor (Boston: Little, Brown, and Co., 1856), Vol. X, pp. 271-272, letter to William Wirt, January 5, 1818.

673. Bill Federer, "John Adams: Wise, Amazing, Incorruptible," Op. cit.

674. "History of the Black Robe Regiment," National Black Robe Regiment, accessed March 5, 2020, http://nationalblackroberegiment.com/history-of-the-black-robe-regiment/.

675. "History of Revivals of Religion, From the Settlement of the Country to the Present Time," *American Quarterly Register* (Boston: Perkins and Marvin, 1833) Vol. 5, p. 217. See also Benjamin Franklin Morris, *Christian Life and Character of the Civil Institutions of the United States* (Philadelphia: George W. Childs, 1864), pp. 334–335.

676. Alpheus Packard, "Nationality," *Bibliotheca Sacra and American Biblical Repository* (London: Andover: Warren F. Draper, 1856), Vol. XIII p.193, Article VI. See also Benjamin Franklin Morris, Christian Life and

Character of the Civil Institutions of the United States (Philadelphia: George W. Childs, 1864), pp. 334–335.

677. Benjamin Franklin Morris, *Christian Life and Character of the Civil Institutions of the United States* (Philadelphia: George W. Childs, 1864), pp. 334–335.

678. Clinton Rossiter, *Seedtime of the Republic* (New York: Harcourt, Brace and Co., 1953), pp. 328–329.

679. Weber, Op. cit.

680. Stanley, Op. cit.

681. George Barna, "What God's People Want to Know," WallBuilders, accessed March 9, 2020, https://wallbuilders.com/gods-people-want-know/.

682. Ibid.

683. Ibid.

684. Interview with Michael Heiser, February 27, 2020.

685. Ibid.

686. Bill Federer, "The 1 Thing That Will Take Away Rights of States," WND, August 16, 2015, https://www.wnd.com/2015/08/the-1-thing-that-will-take-away-rights-of-states/.

687. "Christianity in Government," Kneelingmedia.org, accessed February 27, 2020, http://www.kneelingmedia.org/one/christianityingovernment.htm.

688. "25 Pro-Life Policy Goals for the Nation," Family Research Council, Washington, D.C., August 2008, https://downloads.frc.org/EF/EF11D02.pdf.

689. Justin Taylor, "Tozer vs. Lewis: What's the Most Important Thing about Us?" the gospelcoalition.com, June 4, 2016, Tozer quotehttps://www.thegospelcoalition.org/blogs/justin-taylor/tozer-vs-lewis-whats-the-most-important-thing-about-us/.

690. Heiser, Op. cit.